D0745186
JUMP
NEW EDITION
AT HOME
GRADE
7

ALSO BY JOHN MIGHTON

The Myth of Ability

The End of Ignorance

JUMP MATH SERIES

JUMP at Home Grade 1

JUMP at Home Grade 2

JUMP at Home Grade 3

JUMP at Home Grade 4

JUMP at Home Grade 5

JUMP at Home Grade 6

JUMP at Home Grade 7

JUMP at Home Grade 8

Worksheets for the JUMP Math Program

JOHN MIGHTON

This edition published in 2010 by
House of Anansi Press Inc.
110 Spadina Avenue, Suite 801
Toronto, ON, M5V 2K4
Tel. 416-363-4343
Fax 416-363-1017
www.houseofanansi.com

Distributed in Canada by
HarperCollins Canada Ltd.
1995 Markham Road
Scarborough, ON, M1B 5M8
Toll free tel. 1-800-387-0117

Distributed in the United States by
Publishers Group West
1700 Fourth Street
Berkeley, CA 94710
Toll free tel. 1-800-788-3123

House of Anansi Press is committed to protecting our natural environment. As part of our efforts, the interior of this book is printed on Ancient Forest Friendly paper that contains 100% recycled fibres (40% post-consumer waste and 60% pre-consumer waste) and is processed chlorine-free.

Some of the material in this book has previously been published by JUMP Math.

Every reasonable effort has been made to contact the holders of copyright for materials reproduced in this work. The publishers will gladly receive information that will enable them to rectify any inadvertent errors or omissions in subsequent editions.

16 15 14 13 12   2 3 4 5 6

Library and Archives Canada Cataloguing in Publication

Cataloguing data available from Library and Archives Canada

Library of Congress Control Number: 2010924082

Acknowledgements
Writers: Dr. John Mighton, Dr. Sindi Sabourin, and Dr. Anna Klebanov
Text design: Pam Lostracco
Layout: Laura Brady, Rita Camacho, Lyubava Fartushenko, Nuria Gonzalez, Pam Lostracco, Ilyana Martinez, and Craig Wing-King

This book, like the JUMP program itself, is made possible by the efforts of the volunteers and staff of JUMP Math.

Canada Council for the Arts   Conseil des Arts du Canada

ONTARIO ARTS COUNCIL
CONSEIL DES ARTS DE L'ONTARIO

We acknowledge for their financial support of our publishing program the Canada Council for the Arts, the Ontario Arts Council, and the Government of Canada through the Canada Book Fund.

Printed and bound in Canada

Contents

Introduction

Introduction ix

Mental Math xiv

Fractions xxvii

Games, Activities, and Puzzles

Binary Code xxix

Always/Sometimes/Never True (Numbers) xli

Pattern Puzzles xlii

2-Dimensional Patterns xliii

Hundreds Charts xliv

Sudoku xlv

Models of Fractions lii

Models of Decimals lv

Magic Trick lvi

Models for Algebra lvii

Unit 1: Number Sense 1

NS7-1 Place Value 3

NS7-2 Order of Operations 5

NS7-3 Equations 8

NS7-4 Properties of Operations 10

NS7-5 Breaking Multiplication into Simpler Problems 14

NS7-6 Long Multiplication 15

Unit 2: Patterns and Algebra 1

PA7-1 Extending Patterns 21

PA7-2 Describing Patterns 22

PA7-3 T-tables 24

PA7-4 Constant Rates 27

PA7-5 Solving Equations — Guess and Check 31

PA7-6 Modelling Equations 33

PA7-7 Solving Equations — Preserving Equality 34

PA7-8 Solving Equations — Two Operations 36

PA7-9 Modelling Equations — Advanced 38
PA7-10 Solving Equations — Advanced 39

Unit 3: Number Sense 2

NS7-7 Factors and Multiples 43
NS7-8 Organized Search 45
NS7-9 LCMs and GCFs 47
NS7-10 Perfect Squares and Square Roots 50
NS7-11 Divisibility by 2, 5, and 10 53
NS7-12 Divisibility by 3, 6, and 9 55
NS7-13 Divisibility by 2, 4, and 8 58
NS7-14 Fractions 59
NS7-15 Mixed Numbers 61
NS7-16 Improper Fractions 62
NS7-17 Mixed Numbers and Improper Fractions 63
NS7-18 Fractions of Whole Numbers 66
NS7-19 Comparing Fractions — Introduction 68
NS7-20 Equivalent Fractions 70
NS7-21 Comparing Fractions Using Equivalent Fractions 71
NS7-22 Problems and Puzzles 73
NS7-23 Adding and Subtracting Fractions 74
NS7-24 Lowest Terms 77
NS7-25 Adding and Subtracting Mixed Numbers 78
NS7-26 Decimal Fractions 81
NS7-27 Place Value and Decimals 83
NS7-28 Fractions and Decimals 85
NS7-29 Decimals, Money, and Measurements 87
NS7-30 Decimals and Fractions Greater Than 1 88
NS7-31 Comparing and Ordering Tenths and Hundredths 90
NS7-32 Ordering Decimals and Fractions to Thousandths 92
NS7-33 Regrouping Decimals 95
NS7-34 Addition Strategies for Decimals 97
NS7-35 Adding and Subtracting Decimals 99
NS7-36 Multiplying Decimals by 10 101
NS7-37 Multiplying Decimals by 100 and 1000 102
NS7-38 Dividing Decimals by 100 and 1000 103

NS7-39 Multiplying and Dividing by Powers of 10 104
NS7-40 Multiplying Decimals by Whole Numbers 105
NS7-41 Multiplying Decimals Using Different Strategies 106
NS7-42 Dividing Decimals Using Different Strategies 107
NS7-43 Long Division 108
NS7-44 Dividing Decimals by Whole Numbers 112

Unit 4: Measurement 1

ME7-1 Changing Units 117
ME7-2 Changing Units to Divide Decimals 119
ME7-3 Equivalent Ratios 120
ME7-4 Solving Proportions 121
ME7-5 Word Problems 122
ME7-6 Rates 123

Unit 5: Number Sense 3

NS7-45 Relating Fractions and Decimals (Review) 127
NS7-46 Fraction and Decimal Patterns 128
NS7-47 Relating Fractions and Division 129
NS7-48 Repeating Decimals 130
NS7-49 Using Decimals to Compare Fractions 132
NS7-50 Is the Fraction a Terminating or Repeating Decimal? 133
NS7-51 Adding and Subtracting Repeating Decimals 134
NS7-52 Writing Repeating Decimals as Fractions 135
NS7-53 Writing Repeating Decimals as Fractions (Advanced) 136
NS7-54 Percents 137
NS7-55 Adding and Subtracting Percents 138
NS7-56 Tenths, Decimals, and Percents 139
NS7-57 Fractions and Percents 140
NS7-58 Visual Representations of Percents 141
NS7-59 Comparing Fractions, Decimals, and Percents 142
NS7-60 Finding Percents 143
NS7-61 Further Percents 145
NS7-62 Writing Equivalent Statements for Proportions 146
NS7-63 Using Proportions to Solve Percent Problems 148
NS7-64 Percent Problems 150

NS7-65 Relating Fractions, Ratios, and Percents	151
NS7-66 Using Linear Models to Solve Problems	153
NS7-67 Finding the Whole from the Part	154
NS7-68 Multiplying Fractions by Whole Numbers	155
NS7-69 Multiplying Fractions by Fractions	157
NS7-70 Dividing Whole Numbers by Fractions	159
NS7-71 Word Problems	161
NS7-72 Gains and Losses	162
NS7-73 Integers	164
NS7-74 Adding Integers	165
NS7-75 Adding Integers on a Number Line	167
NS7-76 Subtracting Integers on a Number Line	168
NS7-77 Subtraction Using a Thermometer	170
NS7-78 Subtraction Using Distance Apart	172
NS7-79 Subtraction Using Gains and Losses	173

Glossary	175
About the Authors	177

Introduction: About JUMP Math

There is a prevalent myth in our society that people are born with mathematical talent, and others simply do not have the ability to succeed. Recent discoveries in cognitive science are challenging this myth of ability. The brain is not hard-wired, but continues to change and develop throughout life. Steady, incremental learning can result in the emergence of new abilities.

The carefully designed mathematics in the JUMP Math program provide the necessary skills and knowledge to give your child the joy of success in mathematics. Through step-by-step learning, students celebrate success with every question, thereby increasing achievement and reducing math anxiety.

John Mighton: Founder of JUMP Math

> *"Nine years ago I was looking for a way to give something back to my local community. It occurred to me that I should try to help kids who needed help with math. Mathematicians don't always make the best teachers because mathematics has become obvious to them; they can have trouble seeing why their students are having trouble. But because I had struggled with math myself, I wasn't inclined to blame my students if they couldn't move forward."*
>
> — John Mighton, *The End of Ignorance*

JUMP Math, a national charity dedicated to improving mathematical literacy, was founded by John Mighton, a mathematician, bestselling author, and award-winning playwright. The organization grew out of John's work with a core group of volunteers in a "tutoring club"; their goal was to meet the needs of the most challenged students from local schools. Over the next three years John developed the early material — simple handouts for the tutors to use during their one-on-one teaching sessions with individual students. This period was one of experimentation in developing the JUMP Math method. Eventually, John began to work in local inner-city schools, by placing tutors in the classrooms. This led to the next period of innovation: using the JUMP Math method on small groups of students.

Teachers responded enthusiastically to the success they saw in their students and wanted to adapt the method for classroom use. In response, the needs of the teachers for curriculum-based resources were met by the development of workbooks. These started out as a series of three remedial books with limited accompanying teacher materials, released in fall 2003. The effectiveness of these workbooks led quickly to the development of grade-specific, curriculum-based workbooks. The grade-specific books were first released in 2004. Around that time, the power of teacher networks in creating learning communities was beginning to take shape.

Inspired by the work he has done with thousands of students over the past twenty years, John has systematically developed an approach to teaching mathematics that is based on fostering brain plasticity and emergent intelligence, and on the idea that children have more potential in mathematics than is generally believed. Linking new research in cognitive science to his extensive observations of students, John calls for a re-examination of the assumptions that underlie current methods of teaching mathematics.

JUMP Math, as a program and as an organization, developed in response to the needs of the students, teachers, schools, and communities where John and the volunteers were working. Recognizing the potential of all students to succeed in mathematics, and to succeed in school, was the motivation that John needed to dedicate more than ten years of his life developing a mathematics program that achieved his vision.

JUMP Math: An Innovative Approach

In only ten years, JUMP Math has gone from John's kitchen table to a thriving organization reaching more than 50,000 students with high-quality learning resources and training for 2,000 teachers. It continues to work with community organizations to reach struggling students through homework clubs and after-school programs. Through the generous support of our sponsors, JUMP Math donates resources to classrooms and homework clubs across Canada. The organization has also inspired thousands of community volunteers and teachers to donate their time as tutors, mentors, and trainers.

JUMP Math is unique; it builds on the belief that every child can be successful at mathematics by

- Promoting positive learning environments and building confidence through praise and encouragement;
- Maintaining a balanced approach to mathematics by concurrently addressing conceptual and procedural learning;
- Achieving understanding and mastery by breaking mathematics down into small sequential steps;
- Keeping all students engaged and attentive by "raising the bar" incrementally; and,
- Guiding students strategically to explore and discover the beauty of mathematics.

JUMP Math recognizes the importance of reducing math anxiety. Research in psychology has shown that our brains are extremely fallible: our working memories are poor, we are easily overwhelmed by too much new information, and we require a good deal of practice to consolidate skills and concepts. These mental challenges are compounded when we are anxious. The JUMP approach has been shown to reduce math anxiety significantly.

JUMP Math scaffolds mathematical concepts rigorously and completely. The materials were designed by a team of mathematicians and educators who have a deep understanding of and a love for mathematics. Concepts are introduced in rigorous steps, and prerequisite skills are included in the lesson. Breaking down concepts and skills into steps is often necessary even with the more able students. Math is a subject in which a gifted student can become a struggling student almost overnight, because mathematical knowledge is cumulative.

Consistent with emerging brain research, JUMP Math provides materials and methods that minimize differences between students, allowing teachers, tutors, and parents to more effectively improve student performance in mathematics. Today, parents have access to this unique innovation in mathematics learning with the revised JUMP at Home books.

JUMP Math at Home

JUMP at Home has been developed by mathematicians and educators to complement the mathematics curriculum that your child learns at school. Each grade covers core skills and knowledge to help your child succeed in mathematics. The program focuses on building number sense, pattern recognition, and foundations for algebra.

JUMP at Home is designed to boost every student's confidence, skills, and knowledge. Struggling students will benefit from practice in small steps, while good students will be provided with new ways to understand concepts that will help them enjoy mathematics even more and to exceed their own expectations.

JUMP Math in Schools

JUMP Math also publishes full curriculum-based resources — including student workbooks, teacher guides with daily lesson plans, and blackline masters — that cover all of the Ontario and the Western Canada mathematics curriculum. For more information, please visit the JUMP Math website, www.jumpmath.org, to find out how to order.

Evidence that JUMP Math Works

JUMP Math is a leader in promoting third-party research about its work. A recent study by researchers at the Ontario Institute for Studies in Education (OISE), the University of Toronto, and Simon Fraser University found that in JUMP Math classrooms conceptual understanding improved significantly for weaker students. In Lambeth, England, researchers reported that after using JUMP Math for one year, 69 percent of students who were two years behind were assessed at grade level.

Cognitive scientists from The Hospital for Sick Children in Toronto recently conducted a randomized-controlled study of the effectiveness of the JUMP math program. Studies of such scientific rigour remain relatively rare in mathematics education research in North America. The results showed that students who received JUMP instruction outperformed students who received the methods of instruction their teachers would normally use, on well-established measures of math achievement.

Using JUMP at Home

Helping your child discover the joy of mathematics can be fun and productive. You are not the teacher but the tutor. When having fun with mathematics, remember the JUMP Math T.U.T.O.R. principles:

Take responsibility for learning:
If your child doesn't understand a concept, it can always be clarified further or explained differently. As the adult, you are responsible for helping your child understand. If they don't get it, don't get frustrated — get creative!

Use positive reinforcement:
Children like to be rewarded when they succeed. Praise and encouragement build excitement and foster an appetite for learning. The more confidence a student has, the more likely they are to be engaged.

Take small steps:
In mathematics, it is always possible to make something easier. Always use the JUMP Math worksheets to break down the question into a series of small steps. Practice, practice, practice!

Only indicate correct answers:
Your child's confidence can be shaken by a lack of success. Place checkmarks for correct answers, then revisit questions that your child is having difficulty with. Never use Xs!

Raise the bar:
When your child has mastered a particular concept, challenge them by posing a question that is slightly more difficult. As your child meets these small challenges, you will see their focus and excitement increase.

And remember: if your child is falling behind, teach the number facts! It is a serious mistake to think that students who don't know their number facts can always get by in mathematics using a calculator or other aids. Students can certainly perform operations on a calculator, but they cannot begin to solve problems if they lack a sense of numbers. Students need to be able to see patterns in numbers, and to make estimates and predictions about numbers, in order to have any success in mathematics.

Introductory Unit on Fractions

"In the twenty years that I have been teaching mathematics to children, I have never met an educator who would say that students who lack confidence in their intellectual or academic abilities are likely to do well in school. Our introductory unit has been carefully designed and tested with thousands of students to boost confidence. It has proven to be an extremely effective tool for convincing even the most challenged student that they can do well in mathematics."

— John Mighton

Cognitive scientists have discovered that in order for the brain to be "ready to learn" it cannot be distracted by anxiety. If your child struggles with mathematics or has "math anxiety," be sure to start JUMP Math with the introductory unit on Fractions found on page xxvii.

In recent years, research has shown that students are more apt to do well in subjects when they believe they are capable of doing well. It seems obvious, then, that any math program that aims to harness the potential of every student must start with an exercise that builds the *confidence* of every student. The introductory unit on Fractions was designed for this purpose. It has proven to be an extremely effective tool for convincing even the most challenged students that they can do well in mathematics.

The method used in the introductory unit can be described as *guided discovery*. The individual steps that you will follow in teaching the unit are extremely small, so even the weakest student needn't be left behind. Throughout the unit, students are expected to

- Discover or extend patterns or rules on their own;
- See what changes and what stays the same in sequences of mathematical expressions; and
- Apply what they have learned to new situations.

Students become very excited at making these discoveries and meeting these challenges as they learn the material. For many, it is the first time they have ever been motivated to pay attention to mathematical rules and patterns or to try to extend their knowledge in new cases.

How Does the Introductory Unit Build Confidence?

The introductory unit on Fractions has been specifically designed to build confidence by

- **Requiring that students possess only a few very simple skills.** To achieve a perfect score on the final test in the unit, students need only possess three skills. These skills can be taught to the most challenged students in a very short amount of time. Students must be able to do these three things:
  1. Skip count on their fingers.
  2. Add one-digit numbers.
  3. Subtract one-digit numbers.
- **Eliminating heavy use of language.** Mathematics functions as its own symbolic language. Since the vast majority of children are able to perform the most basic operations (counting and grouping objects into sets) long before they become expert readers, mathematics is the lone subject in which the vast majority of kids are naturally equipped to excel at an early age. By removing language as a barrier, students can realize their full potential in mathematics.
- **Allowing you to continually provide feedback.** Moving on too quickly is both a hindrance to a student's confidence and an impediment to their eventual success. In the introductory unit, the mathematics are broken down into small steps so that you can quickly identify difficulties and help as soon as they arise.
- **Keeping the student engaged through the excitement of small victories.** Children respond more quickly to praise and success than to criticism and threats. If students are encouraged, they feel an incentive to learn. Students enjoy exercising their minds and showing off to a caring adult.

Since the introductory unit is about building confidence, work with your child to ensure that they are successful. Celebrate every correct answer. Take your time. Encourage your child. And, most importantly, have fun!

Work on Mental Math

Included in *JUMP at Home Grade 7* is a Mental Math unit, which will provide you with strategies and techniques for sharpening your child's math brain. Mental math is the foundation for all further study in mathematics. Students who cannot see number patterns often become frustrated and disillusioned with their work. Consistent practice in mental math allows students to become familiar with the way numbers interact, enabling them to make simple calculations quickly and effectively without always having to recall their number facts.

Mental math confronts people at every turn, making the ability to quickly calculate numbers an invaluable asset. Calculating how much change you are owed at a grocery store or deciding how much of a tip to leave at a restaurant are both real-world examples of mental math in action. For this reason, it may be the single most relevant strand of mathematics to everyday life.

How Can a Parent Best Use Math Time?

To keep your child engaged and attentive, consider breaking up your half-hour math time together into thirds:

- **First 10 Minutes:** Use this time to focus on Mental Math. This will sharpen your child's mental number skills, and they will find the remainder of the session much more enjoyable if they are not constantly struggling to remember their number facts.
- **Second 10 Minutes:** Use this time to work on grade-specific material. These worksheets have been designed by mathematicians and educators to fill gaps in learning, strengthen basic skills, and reinforce fundamental concepts.
- **Final 10 Minutes:** Save this portion of the session for math games, cards, or board games.

It is important to remember that mathematics can be fun! Liven up things by playing games and being as active as possible. If the opportunity to visually demonstrate a concept arises, JUMP at it! Have your child sort out change, look around them for geometric objects, or pace out a perimeter.

> "*Children will never fulfill their extraordinary potential until we remember how it felt to have so much potential ourselves. There was nothing we weren't inspired to look at or hold, or that we weren't determined to find out how to do. Open the door to the world of mathematics so your child can pass through.*"
>
> — John Mighton

Mental Math Skills: Addition and Subtraction

PARENT:
If your child doesn't know their addition and subtraction facts, teach them to add and subtract using their fingers by the methods taught below. You should also reinforce basic facts using drills, games, and flash cards. There are mental math strategies that make addition and subtraction easier. Some effective strategies are taught in the next section. (Until your child knows all their facts, allow them to add and subtract on their fingers when necessary.)

To **add** 4 + 8, Grace says the greater number (8) with her fist closed. She counts up from 8, raising one finger at a time. She stops when she has raised the number of fingers equal to the lesser number (4):

8 9 10 11 12

She said "12" when she raised her 4th finger, so: **4 + 8 = 12**

1. Add:

a) 5 + 2 = ______ b) 3 + 2 = ______ c) 6 + 2 = ______ d) 9 + 2 = ______

e) 2 + 4 = ______ f) 2 + 7 = ______ g) 5 + 3 = ______ h) 6 + 3 = ______

i) 11 + 4 = ______ j) 3 + 9 = ______ k) 7 + 3 = ______ l) 14 + 4 = ______

m) 21 + 5 = ______ n) 32 + 3 = ______ o) 4 + 56 = ______ p) 39 + 4 = ______

To **subtract** 9 – 5, Grace says the lesser number (5) with her fist closed. She counts up from 5 raising one finger at a time. She stops when she says the greater number (9):

5 6 7 8 9

She has raised 4 fingers when she stops, so: **9 – 5 = 4**

2. Subtract:

a) 7 – 5 = ______ b) 8 – 6 = ______ c) 5 – 3 = ______ d) 5 – 2 = ______

e) 9 – 6 = ______ f) 10 – 5 = ______ g) 11 – 7 = ______ h) 17 – 14 = ______

i) 33 – 31 = ______ j) 27 – 24 = ______ k) 43 – 39 = ______ l) 62 – 58 = ______

PARENT:
To prepare for the next section (Mental Math), teach your child to add 1 to any number mentally (by counting forward by 1 in their head) and to subtract 1 from any number (by counting backward by 1)

Mental Math Skills: **Addition and Subtraction** *(continued)*

PARENT: Children who don't know how to add, subtract, or estimate readily are at a great disadvantage in mathematics. Children who have trouble memorizing addition and subtraction facts can still learn to mentally add and subtract numbers in a short time if they are given daily practice in a few basic skills.

SKILL 1 – Adding 2 to an Even Number

This skill has been broken down into a number of sub-skills. After teaching each sub-skill, you should give your child a short diagnostic quiz to verify that they have learned the skill. I have included sample quizzes for Skills 1 to 4.

i) *Naming the next one-digit even number:*

Numbers that have ones digit 0, 2, 4, 6, or 8 are called *even numbers*. Using drills or games, teach your child to say the sequence of one-digit even numbers without hesitation. Ask them to imagine the sequence going on in a circle so that the next number after 8 is 0 (0, 2, 4, 6, 8, 0, 2, 4, 6, 8, . . .). Then play the following game: name a number in the sequence and ask your child to give the next number in the sequence. Don't move on until they have mastered the game.

ii) *Naming the next greatest two-digit even number:*

Case 1 – Numbers that end in 0, 2, 4, or 6

Write an even two-digit number that ends in 0, 2, 4, or 6 on a piece of paper. Ask your child to name the next greatest even number. They should recognize that if a number ends in 0, then the next even number ends in 2; if it ends in 2 then the next even number ends in 4, etc. For instance, the number 54 has ones digit 4, so the next greatest even number will have ones digit 6.

QUIZ

Name the next greatest even number:

a) 52 : ______ b) 64 : ______ c) 36 : ______ d) 22 : ______ e) 80 : ______

Case 2 – Numbers that end in 8

Write the number 58 on a piece of paper. Ask your child to name the next greatest even number. Remind them that even numbers must end in 0, 2, 4, 6, or 8. But 50, 52, 54, and 56 are all less than 58, so the next greatest even number is 60. Your child should see that an even number ending in 8 is always followed by an even number ending in 0 (with a tens digit that is one higher).

QUIZ

Name the next greatest even number:

a) 58 : ______ b) 68 : ______ c) 38 : ______ d) 48 : ______ e) 78 : ______

iii) *Adding 2 to an even number:*

Point out to your child that adding 2 to any even number is equivalent to finding the next even number: e.g., $46 + 2 = 48$, $48 + 2 = 50$, etc. Knowing this, your child can easily add 2 to any even number.

Mental Math Skills: **Addition and Subtraction** *(continued)*

QUIZ

Add:

a) 26 + 2 = ___ b) 82 + 2 = ___ c) 40 + 2 = ___ d) 58 + 2 = ___ e) 34 + 2 = ___

SKILL 2 – Subtracting 2 from an Even Number

i) *Finding the preceding one-digit even number:*

Name a one-digit even number and ask your child to give the preceding number in the sequence. For instance, the number that comes before 4 is 2, and the number that comes before 0 is 8. (Remember: the sequence is circular.)

ii) *Finding the preceding two-digit even number:*

Case 1 – Numbers that end in 2, 4, 6, or 8

Write a two-digit number that ends in 2, 4, 6, or 8 on a piece of paper. Ask your child to name the preceding even number. They should recognize that if a number ends in 2, then the preceding even number ends in 0; if it ends in 4, then the preceding even number ends in 2, etc. For instance, the number 78 has ones digit 8, so the preceding even number has ones digit 6.

QUIZ

Name the preceding even number:

a) 48 : ______ b) 26 : ______ c) 34 : ______ d) 62 : ______ e) 78 : ______

Case 2 – Numbers that end in 0

Write the number 80 on a piece of paper and ask your child to name the preceding even number. They should recognize that if an even number ends in 0, then the preceding even number ends in 8 (but the ones digit is one less). So the even number that comes before 80 is 78.

QUIZ

Name the preceding even number:

a) 40 : ______ b) 60 : ______ c) 80 : ______ d) 50 : ______ e) 30 : ______

ii) *Subtracting 2 from an even number:*

Point out to your child that subtracting 2 from any even number is equivalent to finding the preceding even number: e.g., 48 – 2 = 46, 46 – 2 = 44, etc.

QUIZ

Subtract:

a) 58 – 2 = ___ b) 24 – 2 = ___ c) 36 – 2 = ___ d) 42 – 2 = ___ e) 60 – 2 = ___

Mental Math Skills: Addition and Subtraction *(continued)*

SKILL 3 – Adding 2 to an Odd Number

i) *Naming the next one-digit odd number:*

Numbers that have ones digit 1, 3, 5, 7, or 9 are called *odd numbers*. Using drills or games, teach your child to say the sequence of one-digit odd numbers without hesitation. Ask them to imagine the sequence going on in a circle so that the next number after 9 is 1 (1, 3, 5, 7, 9, 1, 3, 5, 7, 9, . . .). Then play the following game: name a number in the sequence and ask your child to give the next number in the sequence. Don't move on until they have mastered the game.

ii) *Naming the next greatest two-digit odd number:*

Case 1 – Numbers that end in 1, 3, 5, or 7

Write an odd two-digit number that ends in 1, 3, 5, or 7 on a piece of paper. Ask your child to name the next greatest odd number. They should recognize that if a number ends in 1, then the next odd number ends in 3; if it ends in 3, then the next odd number ends in 5, etc. For instance, the number 35 has ones digit 5, so the next greatest odd number will have ones digit 7.

QUIZ

Name the next greatest odd number:

a) 51 : ______ b) 65 : ______ c) 37 : ______ d) 23 : ______ e) 87 : ______

Case 2 – Numbers that end in 9

Write the number 59 on a piece of paper. Ask your child to name the next greatest odd number. Remind them that odd numbers must end in 1, 3, 5, 7, or 9. But 51, 53, 55, and 57 are all less than 59. The next greatest odd number is 61. Your child should see that an odd number ending in 9 is always followed by an odd number ending in 1 (with a tens digit that is one higher).

QUIZ

Name the next greatest odd number:

a) 59 : ______ b) 69 : ______ c) 39 : ______ d) 49 : ______ e) 79 : ______

iii) *Adding 2 to an odd number:*

Point out to your child that adding 2 to any odd number is equivalent to finding the next odd number: e.g., 47 + 2 = 49, 49 + 2 = 51, etc. Knowing this, your child can easily add 2 to any odd number.

QUIZ

Add:

a) $27 + 2 =$ ___ b) $83 + 2 =$ ___ c) $41 + 2 =$ ___ d) $59 + 2 =$ ___ e) $35 + 2 =$ ___

Mental Math Skills: Addition and Subtraction *(continued)*

SKILL 4 – Subtracting 2 from an Odd Number

i) *Finding the preceding one-digit odd number:*

Name a one-digit odd number and ask your child to give the preceding number in the sequence. For instance, the number that comes before 3 is 1, and the number that comes before 1 is 9. (Remember: the sequence is circular.)

ii) *Finding the preceding two-digit odd number:*

Case 1 – Numbers that end in 3, 5, 7, or 9

Write a two-digit number that ends in 3, 5, 7, or 9 on a piece of paper. Ask your child to name the preceding odd number. They should recognize that if a number ends in 3, then the preceding odd number ends in 1; if it ends in 5, then the preceding odd number ends in 3, etc. For instance, the number 79 has ones digit 9, so the preceding odd number has ones digit 7.

QUIZ

Name the preceding odd number:

a) 49 : ______ b) 27 : ______ c) 35 : ______ d) 63 : ______ e) 79 : ______

Case 2 – Numbers that end in 1

Write the number 81 on a piece of paper and ask your child to name the preceding odd number. They should recognize that if an odd number ends in 1, then the preceding odd number ends in 9 (but the ones digit is one less). So the odd number that comes before 81 is 79.

QUIZ

Name the preceding odd number:

a) 41 : ______ b) 61 : ______ c) 81 : ______ d) 51 : ______ e) 31 : ______

iii) *Subtracting 2 from an odd number:*

Point out to your child that subtracting 2 from any odd number is equivalent to finding the preceding odd number: e.g., 49 – 2 = 47, 47 – 2 = 45, etc.

QUIZ

Subtract:

a) 59 – 2 = ___ b) 25 – 2 = ___ c) 37 – 2 = ___ d) 43 – 2 = ___ e) 61 – 2 = ___

SKILLS 5 and 6:

Once your child can add and subtract the numbers 1 and 2, then they can easily add and subtract the number 3: Add 3 to a number by first adding 2, then adding 1 (e.g., 35 + 3 = 35 + 2 + 1). Subtract 3 from a number by subtracting 2, then subtracting 1 (e.g., 35 – 3 = 35 – 2 – 1).

Mental Math Skills: Addition and Subtraction *(continued)*

PARENT: All of the addition and subtraction tricks you teach your child should be reinforced with drills, flashcards, and tests. Eventually they should memorize their addition and subtraction facts and shouldn't have to rely on the mental math tricks. One of the greatest gifts you can give your child is to teach them their number facts.

SKILLS 7 and 8

Add 4 to a number by adding 2 twice (e.g., $51 + 4 = 51 + 2 + 2$). Subtract 4 from a number by subtracting 2 twice (e.g., $51 - 4 = 51 - 2 - 2$).

SKILLS 9 and 10

Add 5 to a number by adding 4 then 1. Subtract 5 by subtracting 4 then 1.

SKILL 11

Your child can add pairs of identical numbers by doubling (e.g., $6 + 6 = 2 \times 6$). They should either memorize the 2 times table or they should double numbers by counting on their fingers by 2s.

Add a pair of numbers that differ by 1 by rewriting the larger number as 1 plus the smaller number, then use doubling to find the sum: e.g., $6 + 7 = 6 + 6 + 1 = 12 + 1 = 13$; $7 + 8 = 7 + 7 + 1 = 14 + 1 = 15$.

SKILLS 12, 13, and 14

Add a one-digit number to 10 by simply replacing the zero in 10 with the one-digit number: e.g., $10 + 7 = 17$.

Add 10 to any two-digit number by simply increasing the tens digit of the two-digit number by 1: e.g., $53 + 10 = 63$.

Add a pair of two-digit numbers (with no carrying) by adding the ones digits of the numbers and then adding the tens digits: e.g., $23 + 64 = 87$.

SKILLS 15 and 16

To add 9 to a one-digit number, subtract 1 from the number and then add 10: e.g., $9 + 6 = 10 + 5 = 15$; $9 + 7 = 10 + 6 = 16$. (Essentially, your child simply has to subtract 1 from the number and then stick a 1 in front of the result.)

To add 8 to a one-digit number, subtract 2 from the number and add 10: e.g., $8 + 6 = 10 + 4 = 14$; $8 + 7 = 10 + 5 = 15$.

SKILLS 17 and 18

To subtract a pair of multiples of ten, simply subtract the tens digits and add a zero for the ones digit: e.g., $70 - 50 = 20$.

To subtract a pair of two-digit numbers (without carrying or regrouping), subtract the ones digit from the ones digit and the tens digit from the tens digit: e.g., $57 - 34 = 23$.

Mental Math — Further Strategies

Further Mental Math Strategies

1. Your child should be able to explain how to use the strategies of "rounding the subtrahend (i.e., the number you are subtracting) up to the nearest multiple of ten."
Examples:

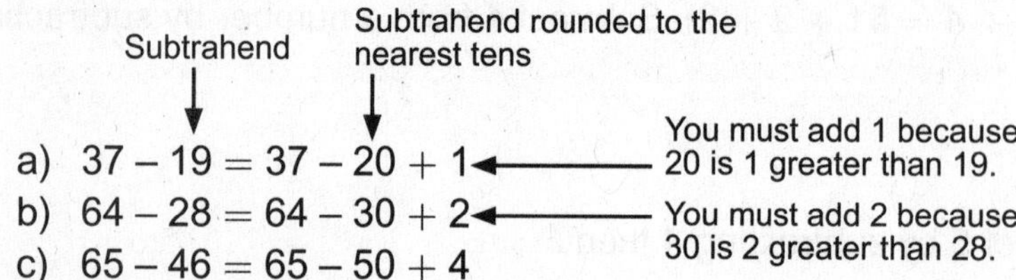

a) $37 - 19 = 37 - 20 + 1$
b) $64 - 28 = 64 - 30 + 2$
c) $65 - 46 = 65 - 50 + 4$

Practice Questions:

a) $27 - 17 = 27 -$ ____ + ____
b) $52 - 36 = 52 -$ ____ + ____
c) $76 - 49 = 76 -$ ____ + ____
d) $84 - 57 = 84 -$ ____ + ____
e) $61 - 29 = 61 -$ ____ + ____
f) $42 - 18 = 42 -$ ____ + ____

PARENT: This strategy works well with numbers that end in 6, 7, 8, or 9.

2. Your child should be able to explain how to subtract by thinking of adding.
Examples:

Count by ones from 45 to the nearest tens (50). Count from 50 until you reach the first number (62).

a) $62 - 45 = 5 + 12 = 17$ ← The sum of counting up to the nearest ten and the original number is the difference.
b) $46 - 23 = 3 + 20 = 23$
c) $73 - 17 = 6 + 50 = 56$
(b and c) ← What method did we use here?

Practice Questions:

a) $88 - 36 =$ ____ + ____ = ____
b) $58 - 21 =$ ____ + ____ = ____
c) $43 - 17 =$ ____ + ____ = ____
d) $74 - 28 =$ ____ + ____ = ____
e) $93 - 64 =$ ____ + ____ = ____
f) $82 - 71 =$ ____ + ____ = ____

3. Your child should be able to explain how to "use doubles."
Examples:

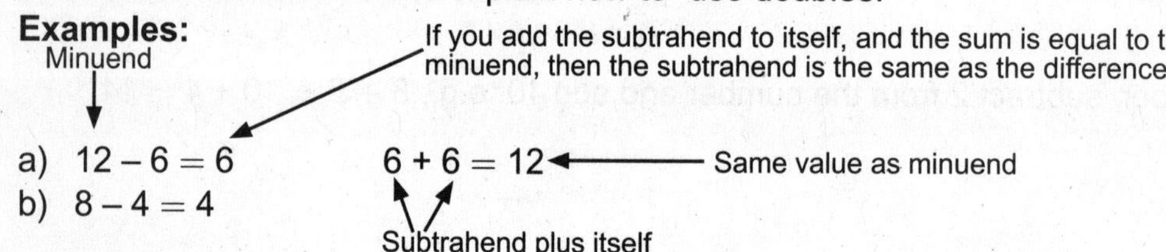

a) $12 - 6 = 6$ $6 + 6 = 12$
b) $8 - 4 = 4$

Practice Questions:

a) $6 - 3 =$ ____
b) $10 - 5 =$ ____
c) $14 - 7 =$ ____
d) $18 - 9 =$ ____
e) $16 - 8 =$ ____
f) $20 - 10 =$ ____

Mental Math Exercises

PARENT: Teaching the material on these Mental Math worksheets may take several lessons. Your child will need more practice than is provided on these pages. These pages are intended as a test to be given when you are certain your child has learned the materials fully.

PARENT: Teach skills 1, 2, 3, and 4 as outlined on pages xv-xviii before you allow your child to answer Questions 1 through 12:

1. Name the even number that comes after the number. Answer in the blank provided:

a) 32 ______ b) 46 ______ c) 14 ______ d) 92 ______ e) 56 ______

f) 30 ______ g) 84 ______ h) 60 ______ i) 72 ______ j) 24 ______

2. Name the even number that comes after the number:

a) 28 ______ b) 18 ______ c) 78 ______ d) 38 ______ e) 68 ______

3. Add:

REMEMBER: Adding 2 to an even number is the same as finding the next even number.

a) $42 + 2 =$ ______ b) $76 + 2 =$ ______ c) $28 + 2 =$ ______ d) $16 + 2 =$ ______

e) $68 + 2 =$ ______ f) $12 + 2 =$ ______ g) $36 + 2 =$ ______ h) $90 + 2 =$ ______

i) $70 + 2 =$ ______ j) $24 + 2 =$ ______ k) $66 + 2 =$ ______ l) $52 + 2 =$ ______

4. Name the even number that comes before the number:

a) **38** ______ b) **42** ______ c) **56** ______ d) **72** ______ e) **98** ______

f) **48** ______ g) **16** ______ h) **22** ______ i) **66** ______ j) **14** ______

5. Name the even number that comes before the number:

a) **30** ______ b) **70** ______ c) **60** ______ d) **10** ______ e) **80** ______

6. Subtract:

REMEMBER: Subtracting 2 from an even number is the same as finding the preceding even number.

a) $46 - 2 =$ ______ b) $86 - 2 =$ ______ c) $90 - 2 =$ ______ d) $14 - 2 =$ ______

e) $54 - 2 =$ ______ f) $72 - 2 =$ ______ g) $12 - 2 =$ ______ h) $56 - 2 =$ ______

i) $32 - 2 =$ ______ j) $40 - 2 =$ ______ k) $60 - 2 =$ ______ l) $26 - 2 =$ ______

7. Name the odd number that comes after the number:

a) 37 ______ b) 51 ______ c) 63 ______ d) 75 ______ e) 17 ______

f) 61 ______ g) 43 ______ h) 81 ______ i) 23 ______ j) 95 ______

8. Name the odd number that comes after the number:

a) 69 ______ b) 29 ______ c) 9 ______ d) 79 ______ e) 59 ______

Mental Math Exercises *(continued)*

9. Add:
REMEMBER: Adding 2 to an odd number is the same as finding the next odd number.

a) $25 + 2 =$ ______ b) $31 + 2 =$ ______ c) $47 + 2 =$ ______ d) $33 + 2 =$ ______

e) $39 + 2 =$ ______ f) $91 + 2 =$ ______ g) $5 + 2 =$ ______ h) $89 + 2 =$ ______

i) $11 + 2 =$ ______ j) $65 + 2 =$ ______ k) $29 + 2 =$ ______ l) $17 + 2 =$ ______

10. Name the <u>odd</u> number that comes <u>before</u> the number:
a) **39** ______ b) **43** ______ c) **57** ______ d) **17** ______ e) **99** ______

f) **13** ______ g) **85** ______ h) **79** ______ i) **65** ______ j) **77** ______

11. Name the <u>odd</u> number that comes <u>before</u> the number:
a) **21** ______ b) **41** ______ c) **11** ______ d) **91** ______ e) **51** ______

12. Subtract:
REMEMBER: Subtracting 2 from an odd number is the same as finding the preceding odd number.

a) $47 - 2 =$ ______ b) $85 - 2 =$ ______ c) $91 - 2 =$ ______ d) $15 - 2 =$ ______

e) $51 - 2 =$ ______ f) $73 - 2 =$ ______ g) $11 - 2 =$ ______ h) $59 - 2 =$ ______

i) $31 - 2 =$ ______ j) $43 - 2 =$ ______ k) $7 - 2 =$ ______ l) $25 - 2 =$ ______

PARENT: Teach skills 5 and 6 as outlined on page xviii before you allow your child to answer Questions 13 and 14.

13. Add 3 to the number by adding 2, then adding 1 (e.g., $35 + 3 = 35 + 2 + 1$):

a) $23 + 3 =$ ______ b) $36 + 3 =$ ______ c) $29 + 3 =$ ______ d) $16 + 3 =$ ______

e) $67 + 3 =$ ______ f) $12 + 3 =$ ______ g) $35 + 3 =$ ______ h) $90 + 3 =$ ______

i) $78 + 3 =$ ______ j) $24 + 3 =$ ______ k) $6 + 3 =$ ______ l) $59 + 3 =$ ______

14. Subtract 3 from the number by subtracting 2, then subtracting 1 (e.g., $35 - 3 = 35 - 2 - 1$):
a) $46 - 3 =$ ______ b) $87 - 3 =$ ______ c) $99 - 3 =$ ______ d) $14 - 3 =$ ______

e) $8 - 3 =$ ______ f) $72 - 3 =$ ______ g) $12 - 3 =$ ______ h) $57 - 3 =$ ______

i) $32 - 3 =$ ______ j) $40 - 3 =$ ______ k) $60 - 3 =$ ______ l) $28 - 3 =$ ______

15. Fred has 49 stamps. He gives 2 stamps away. How many stamps does he have left?

16. There are 25 minnows in a tank. Alice adds 3 more to the tank. How many minnows are now in the tank?

Mental Math Exercises *(continued)*

PARENT: Teach skills 7 and 8 as outlined on page xix.

17. Add 4 to the number by adding 2 twice (e.g., $51 + 4 = 51 + 2 + 2$):

a) $42 + 4 =$ _______ b) $76 + 4 =$ _______ c) $27 + 4 =$ _______ d) $17 + 4 =$ _______

e) $68 + 4 =$ _______ f) $11 + 4 =$ _______ g) $35 + 4 =$ _______ h) $8 + 4 =$ _______

i) $72 + 4 =$ _______ j) $23 + 4 =$ _______ k) $60 + 4 =$ _______ l) $59 + 4 =$ _______

18. Subtract 4 from the number by subtracting 2 twice (e.g., $26 - 4 = 26 - 2 - 2$):

a) $46 - 4 =$ _______ b) $86 - 4 =$ _______ c) $91 - 4 =$ _______ d) $15 - 4 =$ _______

e) $53 - 4 =$ _______ f) $9 - 4 =$ _______ g) $13 - 4 =$ _______ h) $57 - 4 =$ _______

i) $40 - 4 =$ _______ j) $88 - 4 =$ _______ k) $69 - 4 =$ _______ l) $31 - 4 =$ _______

PARENT: Teach skills 9 and 10 as outlined on page xix.

19. Add 5 to the number by adding 4, then adding 1 (or add 2 twice, then add 1):

a) $84 + 5 =$ _______ b) $27 + 5 =$ _______ c) $31 + 5 =$ _______ d) $44 + 5 =$ _______

e) $63 + 5 =$ _______ f) $92 + 5 =$ _______ g) $14 + 5 =$ _______ h) $16 + 5 =$ _______

i) $9 + 5 =$ _______ j) $81 + 5 =$ _______ k) $51 + 5 =$ _______ l) $28 + 5 =$ _______

20. Subtract 5 from the number by subtracting 4, then subtracting 1 (or subtract 2 twice, then subtract 1):

a) $48 - 5 =$ _______ b) $86 - 5 =$ _______ c) $55 - 5 =$ _______ d) $69 - 5 =$ _______

e) $30 - 5 =$ _______ f) $13 - 5 =$ _______ g) $92 - 5 =$ _______ h) $77 - 5 =$ _______

i) $45 - 5 =$ _______ j) $24 - 5 =$ _______ k) $91 - 5 =$ _______ l) $8 - 5 =$ _______

PARENT: Teach skill 11 as outlined on page xix.

21. Add:

a) $6 + 6 =$ _______ b) $7 + 7 =$ _______ c) $8 + 8 =$ _______

d) $5 + 5 =$ _______ e) $4 + 4 =$ _______ f) $9 + 9 =$ _______

22. Add by thinking of the larger number as a sum of two smaller numbers. The first one is done for you:

a) $6 + 7 = 6 + 6 + 1$ b) $7 + 8 =$ _______________ c) $6 + 8 =$ _______________

d) $4 + 5 =$ _______________ e) $5 + 7 =$ _______________ f) $8 + 9 =$ _______________

Mental Math Exercises *(continued)*

PARENT: Teach skills 12, 13, and 14 as outlined on page xix.

23. a) 10 + 3 = ______ b) 10 + 7 = ______ c) 5 + 10 = ______ d) 10 + 1 = ______
    e) 9 + 10 = ______ f) 10 + 4 = ______ g) 10 + 8 = ______ h) 10 + 2 = ______

24. a) 10 + 20 = ______ b) 40 + 10 = ______ c) 10 + 80 = ______ d) 10 + 50 = ______
    e) 30 + 10 = ______ f) 10 + 60 = ______ g) 10 + 10 = ______ h) 70 + 10 = ______

25. a) 10 + 25 = ______ b) 10 + 67 = ______ c) 10 + 31 = ______ d) 10 + 82 = ______
    e) 10 + 43 = ______ f) 10 + 51 = ______ g) 10 + 68 = ______ h) 10 + 21 = ______
    i) 10 + 11 = ______ j) 10 + 19 = ______ k) 10 + 44 = ______ l) 10 + 88 = ______

26. a) 20 + 30 = ______ b) 40 + 20 = ______ c) 30 + 30 = ______ d) 50 + 30 = ______
    e) 20 + 50 = ______ f) 40 + 40 = ______ g) 50 + 40 = ______ h) 40 + 30 = ______
    i) 60 + 30 = ______ j) 20 + 60 = ______ k) 20 + 70 = ______ l) 60 + 40 = ______

27. a) 20 + 23 = ______ b) 32 + 24 = ______ c) 51 + 12 = ______ d) 12 + 67 = ______
    e) 83 + 14 = ______ f) 65 + 24 = ______ g) 41 + 43 = ______ h) 70 + 27 = ______
    i) 31 + 61 = ______ j) 54 + 33 = ______ k) 28 + 31 = ______ l) 42 + 55 = ______

PARENT: Teach skills 15 and 16 as outlined on page xix.

28. a) 9 + 3 = ______ b) 9 + 7 = ______ c) 6 + 9 = ______ d) 4 + 9 = ______
    e) 9 + 9 = ______ f) 5 + 9 = ______ g) 9 + 2 = ______ h) 9 + 8 = ______

29. a) 8 + 2 = ______ b) 8 + 6 = ______ c) 8 + 7 = ______ d) 4 + 8 = ______
    e) 5 + 8 = ______ f) 8 + 3 = ______ g) 9 + 8 = ______ h) 8 + 8 = ______

PARENT: Teach skills 17 and 18 as outlined on page xix.

30. a) 40 − 10 = ______ b) 50 − 10 = ______ c) 70 − 10 = ______ d) 20 − 10 = ______
    e) 40 − 20 = ______ f) 60 − 30 = ______ g) 40 − 30 = ______ h) 60 − 50 = ______

31. a) 57 − 34 = ______ b) 43 − 12 = ______ c) 62 − 21 = ______ d) 59 − 36 = ______
    e) 87 − 63 = ______ f) 95 − 62 = ______ g) 35 − 10 = ______ h) 17 − 8 = ______

Mental Math (Advanced)

Multiples of Ten

NOTE: In the exercises below, you will learn several ways to use multiples of ten in mental addition or subtraction.

I

542 + 214 = 542 + 200 + 10 + 4 = 742 + 10 + 4 = 752 + 4 = 756

827 − 314 = 827 − 300 − 10 − 4 = 527 − 10 − 4 = 517 − 4 = 713

Sometimes you will need to carry:

545 + 172 = 545 + 100 + 70 + 2 = 645 + 70 + 2 = 715 + 2 = 717

1. Warm up:

a) 536 + 100 = b) 816 + 10 = c) 124 + 5 = d) 540 + 200 =

e) 234 + 30 = f) 345 + 300 = g) 236 − 30 = h) 442 − 20 =

i) 970 − 70 = j) 542 − 400 = k) 160 + 50 = l) 756 + 40 =

2. Write the second number in expanded form and add or subtract one digit at a time. The first one is done for you:

a) 564 + 215 = *564 + 200 + 10 + 5* = *779*

b) 445 + 343 = ________ = ____

c) 234 + 214 = ________ = ____

3. Add or subtract mentally (one digit at a time):

a) 547 + 312 = b) 578 − 314 = c) 845 − 454 =

II If one of the numbers you are adding or subtracting is close to a number that is a multiple of ten, add the multiple of ten and then add or subtract an adjustment factor:

645 + 99 = 645 + 100 − 1 = 745 − 1 = 744

856 + 42 = 856 + 40 + 2 = 896 + 2 = 898

III Sometimes in subtraction it helps to think of a multiple of ten as a sum of 1 and a number consisting entirely of 9s (e.g., 100 = 1 + 99; 1000 = 1 + 999). You never have to borrow or exchange when you are subtracting from a number consisting entirely of 9s.

100 − 43 = 1 + 99 − 43 = 1 + 56 = 57 ← *Do the subtraction, using 99 instead of 100, and then add 1 to your answer*

1000 − 543 = 1 + 999 − 543 = 1 + 456 = 457

4. Use the tricks you've just learned:

a) 845 + 91 = b) 456 + 298 = c) 100 − 84 = d) 1000 − 846 =

Mental Math Game: Modified Go Fish

PURPOSE:

If children know the pairs of one-digit numbers that add up to particular **target numbers**, they will be able to mentally break sums into easier sums.

EXAMPLE:

As it is easy to add any one-digit number to 10, you can add a sum more readily if you can decompose numbers in the sum into pairs that add to ten. For example:

$$7 + 5 = \underbrace{7 + 3}_{\text{These numbers add to 10.}} + 2 = 10 + 2 = 12$$

To help children remember pairs of numbers that add up to a given target number, I developed a variation of "Go Fish" that I have found very effective.

THE GAME:

Pick any target number and remove all the cards with value greater than or equal to the target number out of the deck. In what follows, I will assume that the target number is 10, so you would take all the tens and face cards out of the deck (aces count as one).

The dealer gives each player six cards. If a player has any pairs of cards that add to 10, they are allowed to place these pairs on the table before play begins.

Player 1 selects one of the cards in their hand and asks Player 2 for a card that adds to 10 with the chosen card. For instance, if Player 1's chosen card is a 3, they may ask Player 2 for a 7.

If Player 2 has the requested card, Player 1 takes it and lays it down along with the card from their hand. Player 1 may then ask for another card. If Player 2 does not have the requested card, they say, "Go fish," and Player 1 must pick up a card from the top of the deck. (If this card adds to 10 with a card in Player 1's hand, they may lay down the pair right away.) It is then Player 2's turn to ask for a card.

Play ends when one player lays down all of their cards. Players receive 4 points for laying down all of their cards first and 1 point for each pair they have laid down.

PARENT: If your child is having difficulty, I would recommend that you start with pairs of numbers that add to 5. Take all cards with value greater than 4 out of the deck. Each player should be dealt only four cards to start with.

I have worked with several children who have had a great deal of trouble sorting their cards and finding pairs that add to a target number. I have found that the following exercise helps:

Give your child only three cards, two of which add to the target number. Ask them to find the pair that adds to the target number. After your child has mastered this step with three cards, repeat the exercise with four cards, then five cards, and so on.

PARENT: You can also give your child a list of the pairs that add to the target number. As your child gets used to the game, gradually remove pairs from the list so that they learn the pairs by memory.

Fractions

1. Name the following fractions.

a) 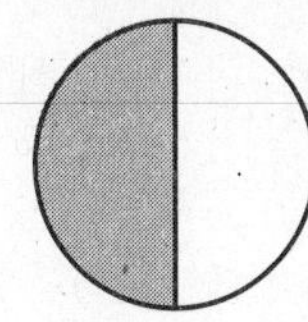

b) 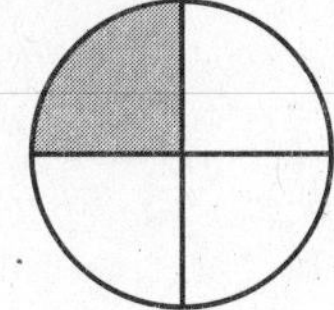

c) 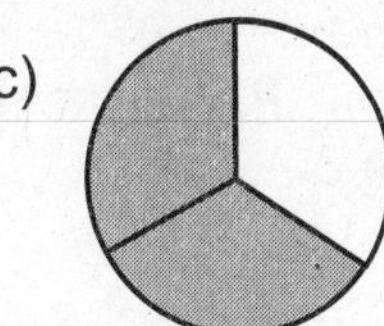

d) 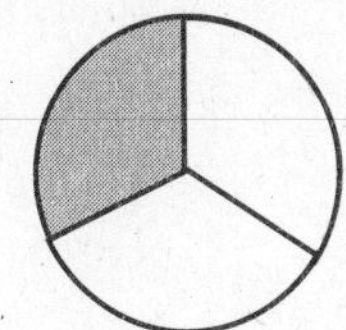

e) 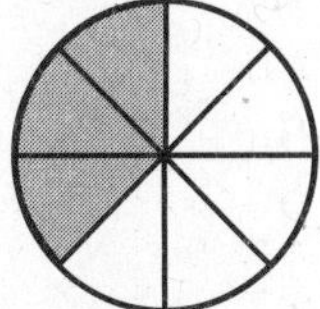

f) 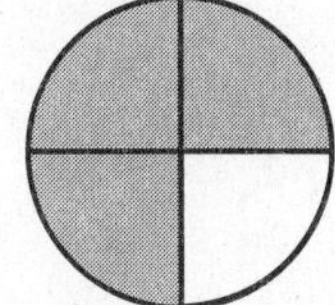

g) 

h) 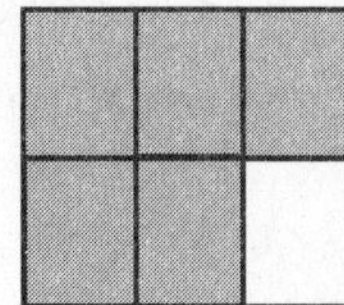

i) 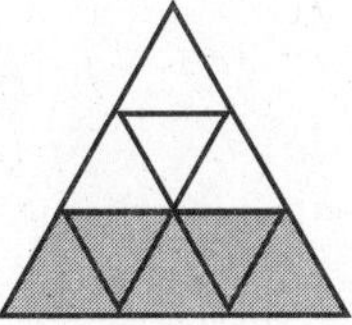

j) 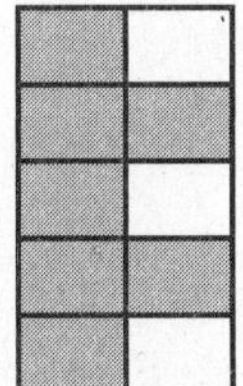

k) 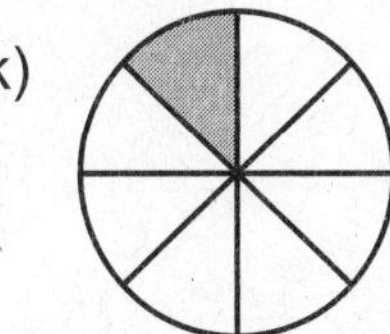

l) 

2. Shade the fractions named.

a) $\frac{1}{2}$ 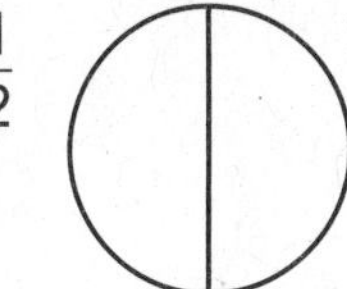

b) $\frac{1}{3}$ 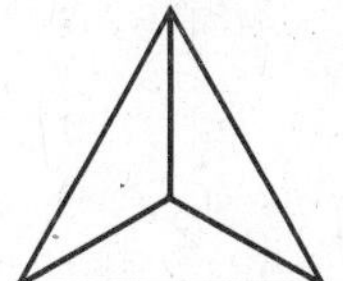

c) $\frac{3}{4}$ 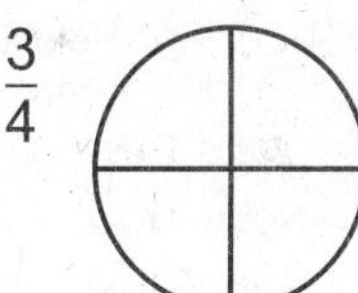

d) $\frac{3}{6}$ 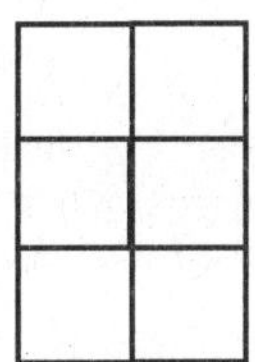

e) $\frac{2}{5}$ 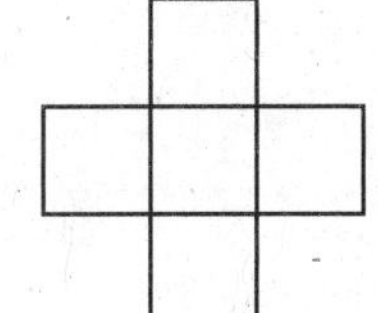

f) $\frac{5}{9}$ 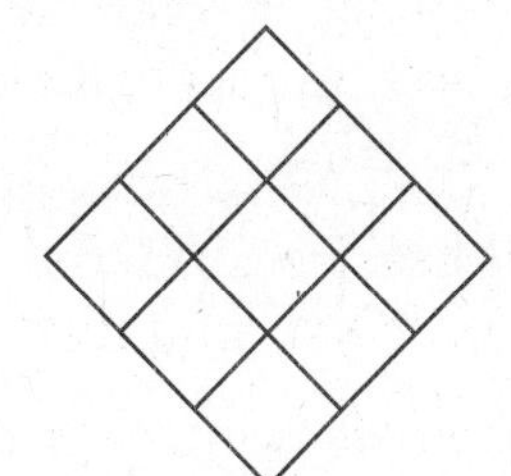

Fractions *(continued)*

3. Add.

a) $\frac{1}{3} + \frac{1}{3}$ b) $\frac{2}{7} + \frac{3}{7}$ c) $\frac{2}{11} + \frac{1}{11}$

d) $\frac{2}{5} + \frac{2}{5}$ e) $\frac{2}{11} + \frac{3}{11}$ f) $\frac{3}{8} + \frac{4}{8}$

g) $\frac{3}{17} + \frac{2}{17}$ h) $\frac{1}{21} + \frac{4}{21}$ i) $\frac{4}{9} + \frac{3}{9}$

4. Subtract.

a) $\frac{3}{5} - \frac{1}{5}$ b) $\frac{2}{7} - \frac{1}{7}$ c) $\frac{4}{11} - \frac{2}{11}$

d) $\frac{5}{8} - \frac{2}{8}$ e) $\frac{6}{17} - \frac{2}{17}$ f) $\frac{5}{9} - \frac{1}{9}$

5. **Advanced:** Add or Subtract.

a) $\frac{1}{7} + \frac{1}{7} + \frac{1}{7}$ b) $\frac{1}{7} + \frac{2}{7} + \frac{3}{7}$ c) $\frac{1}{15} + \frac{2}{15} + \frac{5}{15}$

BONUS:

d) $\frac{16}{21} - \frac{5}{21} - \frac{3}{21}$ e) $\frac{7}{9} - \frac{4}{9} + \frac{2}{9}$ f) $\frac{2}{11} + \frac{5}{11} - \frac{3}{11}$

Fractions *(continued)*

6. Write times signs beside the fractions.

Example: $\frac{1}{5} + \frac{1}{3} \longrightarrow \frac{\times\ 1}{\times\ 5} + \frac{1\ \times}{3\ \times}$

$\frac{1}{2} + \frac{1}{3}$	$\frac{1}{2} + \frac{1}{5}$	$\frac{1}{3} + \frac{1}{5}$

7. Switch the bottom numbers.

Example: $\frac{1}{5} + \frac{1}{3} \longrightarrow \frac{\mathbf{3} \times 1}{\mathbf{3} \times 5} + \frac{1 \times \mathbf{5}}{3 \times \mathbf{5}}$

$\frac{\times\ 1}{\times\ 2} + \frac{1\ \times}{3\ \times}$	$\frac{\times\ 1}{\times\ 2} + \frac{1\ \times}{5\ \times}$	$\frac{\times\ 1}{\times\ 3} + \frac{1\ \times}{5\ \times}$

8. Write times signs and switch the numbers.

Example: $\frac{1}{5} + \frac{1}{3} \longrightarrow \frac{\mathbf{3} \times 1}{\mathbf{3} \times 5} + \frac{1 \times \mathbf{5}}{3 \times \mathbf{5}}$

$\frac{1}{2} + \frac{1}{3}$	$\frac{1}{2} + \frac{1}{5}$	$\frac{1}{3} + \frac{1}{5}$
$\frac{2}{3} + \frac{1}{2}$	$\frac{2}{3} + \frac{1}{5}$	$\frac{2}{5} + \frac{1}{3}$

9. Perform the multiplications.

Example: $\frac{1}{5} + \frac{1}{3} \longrightarrow \frac{3 \times 1}{3 \times 5} + \frac{1 \times 5}{3 \times 5}$

$$= \frac{\mathbf{3}}{\mathbf{15}} + \frac{\mathbf{5}}{\mathbf{15}}$$

$\frac{3 \times 1}{3 \times 2} + \frac{1 \times 2}{3 \times 2}$ $= \frac{\quad}{\quad} + \frac{\quad}{\quad}$	$\frac{5 \times 1}{5 \times 2} + \frac{1 \times 2}{5 \times 2}$ $= \frac{\quad}{\quad} + \frac{\quad}{\quad}$	$\frac{5 \times 1}{5 \times 3} + \frac{1 \times 3}{5 \times 3}$ $= \frac{\quad}{\quad} + \frac{\quad}{\quad}$

Fractions *(continued)*

$\frac{2 \times 2}{2 \times 3} + \frac{1 \times 3}{2 \times 3}$ $= \text{—} + \text{—}$	$\frac{5 \times 2}{5 \times 3} + \frac{1 \times 3}{5 \times 3}$ $= \text{—} + \text{—}$	$\frac{3 \times 2}{3 \times 5} + \frac{1 \times 5}{3 \times 5}$ $= \text{—} + \text{—}$

10. Perform the additions.

Example: $\frac{1}{5} + \frac{1}{3} \longrightarrow \frac{3 \times 1}{3 \times 5} + \frac{1 \times 5}{3 \times 5}$

$$= \frac{3}{15} + \frac{5}{15} = \mathbf{\frac{8}{15}}$$

$\frac{3 \times 1}{3 \times 2} + \frac{1 \times 2}{3 \times 2}$ $= \frac{3}{6} + \frac{2}{6} = \_\_\_$	$\frac{5 \times 1}{5 \times 2} + \frac{1 \times 2}{5 \times 2}$ $= \frac{5}{10} + \frac{2}{10} = \_\_\_$	$\frac{5 \times 1}{5 \times 3} + \frac{1 \times 3}{5 \times 3}$ $= \frac{5}{15} + \frac{3}{15} = \_\_\_$
$\frac{2 \times 2}{2 \times 3} + \frac{1 \times 3}{2 \times 3}$ $= \frac{4}{6} + \frac{3}{6} = \_\_\_$	$\frac{5 \times 2}{5 \times 3} + \frac{1 \times 3}{5 \times 3}$ $= \frac{10}{15} + \frac{3}{15} = \_\_\_$	$\frac{3 \times 2}{3 \times 5} + \frac{1 \times 5}{3 \times 5}$ $= \frac{6}{15} + \frac{5}{15} = \_\_\_$

11. Perform the multiplications and the additions.

Example: $\frac{1}{5} + \frac{1}{3} \longrightarrow \frac{3 \times 1}{3 \times 5} + \frac{1 \times 5}{3 \times 5}$

$$= \mathbf{\frac{3}{15}} + \mathbf{\frac{5}{15}} = \mathbf{\frac{8}{15}}$$

$\frac{3 \times 1}{3 \times 2} + \frac{1 \times 2}{3 \times 2}$ $= \text{—} + \text{—} = \text{—}$	$\frac{5 \times 1}{5 \times 2} + \frac{1 \times 2}{5 \times 2}$ $= \text{—} + \text{—} = \text{—}$	$\frac{5 \times 1}{5 \times 3} + \frac{1 \times 3}{5 \times 3}$ $= \text{—} + \text{—} = \text{—}$
$\frac{2 \times 2}{2 \times 3} + \frac{1 \times 3}{2 \times 3}$ $= \text{—} + \text{—} = \text{—}$	$\frac{5 \times 2}{5 \times 3} + \frac{1 \times 3}{5 \times 3}$ $= \text{—} + \text{—} = \text{—}$	$\frac{3 \times 2}{3 \times 5} + \frac{1 \times 5}{3 \times 5}$ $= \text{—} + \text{—} = \text{—}$

Fractions *(continued)*

12. Add.

a) $\frac{1}{2} + \frac{1}{3}$ b) $\frac{1}{3} + \frac{1}{5}$ c) $\frac{1}{2} + \frac{1}{5}$

13. **Advanced:** Add or Subtract.

a) $\frac{2}{5} + \frac{1}{3}$ b) $\frac{3}{5} + \frac{1}{2}$ c) $\frac{2}{3} + \frac{1}{2}$

d) $\frac{1}{5} + \frac{2}{3}$ d) $\frac{4}{5} + \frac{1}{2}$ f) $\frac{2}{3} + \frac{2}{5}$

BONUS:

a) $\frac{1}{2} - \frac{1}{3}$ b) $\frac{2}{3} - \frac{1}{2}$ c) $\frac{3}{5} + \frac{1}{2}$

Fractions *(continued)*

14. Write how many times the lesser denominator goes into the greater denominator.

Example: $\frac{1}{2} + \frac{1}{10} \longrightarrow \frac{\mathbf{5} \times 1}{\mathbf{5} \times 2} + \frac{1}{10}$

$\frac{1}{2} + \frac{1}{10}$	$\frac{1}{5} + \frac{1}{10}$	$\frac{1}{2} + \frac{1}{8}$
$\frac{1}{3} + \frac{1}{6}$	$\frac{1}{5} + \frac{1}{20}$	$\frac{1}{2} + \frac{1}{6}$
$\frac{2}{5} + \frac{1}{25}$	$\frac{3}{5} + \frac{1}{15}$	$\frac{1}{2} + \frac{7}{8}$

15. Change the fraction with the lesser denominator and keep the other fraction the same.

Example: $\frac{1}{2} + \frac{1}{10} \longrightarrow \frac{\mathbf{5} \times 1}{\mathbf{5} \times 2} + \frac{1}{10}$

$$= \frac{\mathbf{5}}{\mathbf{10}} + \frac{\mathbf{1}}{\mathbf{10}}$$

$\frac{1}{2} + \frac{1}{10}$	$\frac{1}{5} + \frac{1}{10}$	$\frac{1}{2} + \frac{1}{8}$
$\frac{1}{3} + \frac{1}{6}$	$\frac{1}{5} + \frac{1}{20}$	$\frac{1}{2} + \frac{1}{6}$
$\frac{2}{5} + \frac{1}{25}$	$\frac{3}{5} + \frac{1}{15}$	$\frac{1}{2} + \frac{7}{8}$

Fractions *(continued)*

16. Add. (Remember to change only one denominator.)

a) $\frac{1}{2} + \frac{1}{10}$ b) $\frac{1}{5} + \frac{1}{10}$ c) $\frac{1}{2} + \frac{1}{8}$

d) $\frac{1}{3} + \frac{1}{6}$ e) $\frac{1}{5} + \frac{1}{20}$ f) $\frac{1}{2} + \frac{1}{6}$

17. **Advanced:** Add or Subtract.

a) $\frac{2}{3} + \frac{1}{15}$ b) $\frac{2}{5} + \frac{1}{10}$ c) $\frac{3}{5} + \frac{2}{15}$

d) $\frac{2}{3} + \frac{1}{12}$ e) $\frac{1}{4} + \frac{3}{8}$ f) $\frac{1}{4} + \frac{3}{12}$

g) $\frac{3}{4} + \frac{1}{2}$ h) $\frac{4}{25} + \frac{1}{5}$ i) $\frac{3}{15} + \frac{4}{5}$

BONUS:

j) $\frac{7}{20} - \frac{1}{5}$ k) $\frac{3}{8} - \frac{1}{4}$ l) $\frac{1}{2} - \frac{3}{10}$

Fractions *(continued)*

18. Write **yes** beside the number in bold if you say the number when counting by 2s. If you don't, write **no**.

a) **6** ________ b) **3** ________ c) **9** ________ d) **8** ________

e) **10** ________ f) **4** ________ g) **5** ________ h) **7** ________

19. Write **yes** beside the given number if you say the number when counting by 3s. If you don't, write **no**.

a) **9** ________ b) **4** ________ c) **12** ________ d) **13** ________

e) **6** ________ f) **5** ________ g) **8** ________ h) **14** ________

20. Write **yes** beside the given number if you say the number when counting by 5s. If you don't, write **no**.

a) **10** ________ b) **12** ________ c) **15** ________ d) **8** ________

e) **20** ________ f) **9** ________ g) **14** ________ h) **11** ________

21. Circle the smaller denominator. The first one has been done for you.

a) $\frac{1}{2} + \frac{1}{3}$ (2 circled) b) $\frac{1}{3} + \frac{1}{5}$ c) $\frac{2}{6} + \frac{1}{2}$

d) $\frac{1}{4} + \frac{1}{8}$ e) $\frac{3}{5} + \frac{1}{2}$ f) $\frac{1}{2} + \frac{1}{8}$

22. Count by the lesser denominator, and write **yes** if you say the greater denominator. Write **no** if you don't. The first one has been done for you.

a) *no* — $\frac{1}{2} + \frac{1}{3}$ (2 circled)

b) ________ — $\frac{1}{3} + \frac{1}{5}$ (3 circled)

c) ________ — $\frac{2}{6} + \frac{1}{2}$ (2 circled)

d) ________ — $\frac{1}{4} + \frac{1}{8}$

e) ________ — $\frac{3}{5} + \frac{1}{2}$

f) ________ — $\frac{1}{2} + \frac{1}{8}$

g) ________ — $\frac{1}{2} + \frac{1}{8}$

h) ________ — $\frac{3}{15} + \frac{1}{3}$

i) ________ — $\frac{1}{5} + \frac{1}{9}$

Fractions *(continued)*

23. Count by the lesser denominator until you reach the greater denominator. Write the number of fingers you have raised beside the times signs.

a) yes

$\times\frac{1}{2}\times + \frac{1}{6}$

b) yes

$\times\frac{1}{5}\times + \frac{1}{10}$

c) yes

$\times\frac{1}{3}\times + \frac{1}{9}$

24. Complete the first step of addition by multiplying each fraction by the opposite denominator.

a) no

$\times\frac{1}{2}\times + \frac{1}{6}\times\times$

b) no

$\times\frac{1}{5}\times + \frac{1}{10}\times\times$

c) no

$\times\frac{1}{3}\times + \frac{1}{9}\times\times$

25. Write **yes** or **no** above the following fractions. If you wrote **yes**, then complete the first step of addition as in Question 23 above. If you wrote **no**, complete the first step as in Question 24.

a) ______ $\frac{1}{3} + \frac{1}{5}$

b) ______ $\frac{3}{5} + \frac{1}{10}$

c) ______ $\frac{1}{2} + \frac{1}{4}$

d) ______ $\frac{1}{3} + \frac{1}{4}$

BONUS:

e) ______ $\frac{3}{15} + \frac{1}{5}$

f) ______ $\frac{1}{10} + \frac{1}{5}$

26. Add or Subtract. Change *one* denominator or change *both*. (For each question you have to decide what to do. Start by writing **yes** or **no** above the fraction.)

a) ______ $\frac{1}{4} + \frac{1}{5}$

b) ______ $\frac{2}{3} + \frac{1}{5}$

c) ______ $\frac{2}{5} + \frac{1}{20}$

BONUS:

d) ______ $\frac{3}{20} + \frac{4}{5}$

e) ______ $\frac{2}{15} + \frac{3}{5}$

f) ______ $\frac{1}{16} + \frac{1}{4}$

Fractions *(continued)*

27. **Advanced:** Add or Subtract. (Change *one* denominator or change *both*.)

a) $\frac{1}{3} + \frac{1}{9}$ b) $\frac{2}{3} + \frac{1}{5}$ c) $\frac{1}{5} + \frac{1}{20}$

d) $\frac{1}{2} + \frac{1}{3}$ e) $\frac{1}{4} + \frac{1}{5}$ f) $\frac{1}{4} + \frac{5}{16}$

g) $\frac{1}{2} - \frac{1}{10}$ h) $\frac{3}{4} - \frac{1}{3}$ i) $\frac{7}{20} - \frac{1}{4}$

28. If the denominators are the same, write **same**. Otherwise change *one* denominator or change *both*. Then complete all the questions.

a) $\frac{1}{3} + \frac{1}{12}$ b) $\frac{1}{4} + \frac{3}{5}$ c) $\frac{1}{7} + \frac{1}{7}$

d) $\frac{2}{3} + \frac{1}{2}$ e) $\frac{10}{11} - \frac{6}{11}$ f) $\frac{4}{5} - \frac{3}{20}$

Fractions *(continued)*

29. Write times signs and numbers where necessary.

Example: $\frac{1}{2} + \frac{1}{3} + \frac{1}{6} \longrightarrow \frac{\mathbf{3} \times 1}{\mathbf{3} \times 2} + \frac{\mathbf{2} \times 1}{\mathbf{2} \times 3} + \frac{1}{6}$

$\frac{1}{2} + \frac{1}{3} + \frac{1}{6}$	$\frac{1}{3} + \frac{1}{6} + \frac{1}{15}$
$\frac{1}{2} + \frac{1}{4} + \frac{3}{8}$	$\frac{1}{4} + \frac{1}{5} + \frac{1}{20}$
$\frac{2}{3} + \frac{1}{4} + \frac{1}{12}$	$\frac{1}{5} + \frac{3}{10} + \frac{2}{20}$

30. Write times signs and numbers, and carry out multiplication as needed.

Example: $\frac{1}{2} + \frac{1}{3} + \frac{1}{6} \longrightarrow \frac{\mathbf{3} \times 1}{\mathbf{3} \times 2} + \frac{\mathbf{2} \times 1}{\mathbf{2} \times 3} + \frac{1}{6}$

$$= \frac{\mathbf{3}}{\mathbf{6}} + \frac{\mathbf{2}}{\mathbf{6}} + \frac{\mathbf{1}}{\mathbf{6}}$$

$\frac{1}{2} + \frac{1}{3} + \frac{1}{6}$	$\frac{1}{3} + \frac{1}{6} + \frac{1}{15}$
$\frac{1}{2} + \frac{1}{4} + \frac{3}{8}$	$\frac{1}{4} + \frac{1}{5} + \frac{1}{20}$
$\frac{2}{3} + \frac{1}{4} + \frac{1}{12}$	$\frac{1}{5} + \frac{3}{10} + \frac{2}{20}$

Fractions *(continued)*

31. Solve completely.

a) $\frac{1}{2} + \frac{1}{3} + \frac{3}{6}$

b) $\frac{1}{3} + \frac{1}{5} + \frac{1}{15}$

c) $\frac{1}{2} + \frac{1}{4} + \frac{3}{8}$

d) $\frac{1}{4} + \frac{1}{5} + \frac{5}{20}$

e) $\frac{2}{3} + \frac{1}{4} + \frac{1}{12}$

f) $\frac{1}{5} + \frac{3}{10} + \frac{2}{20}$

BONUS:

g) $\frac{17}{20} - \frac{1}{4} - \frac{1}{5}$

h) $\frac{3}{4} - \frac{1}{8} - \frac{1}{2}$

i) $\frac{1}{2} - \frac{1}{6} + \frac{1}{3}$

j) $\frac{2}{3} + \frac{1}{4} - \frac{5}{12}$

Binary Code

Step 1 – Warm-up

a) Review single digit addition (Basic Number Sense)

i.e., $8 + 2 =$

$8 + 4 + 2 =$

Write down a few questions. Check your child's work.

b) Review Place Value (2 7 3)

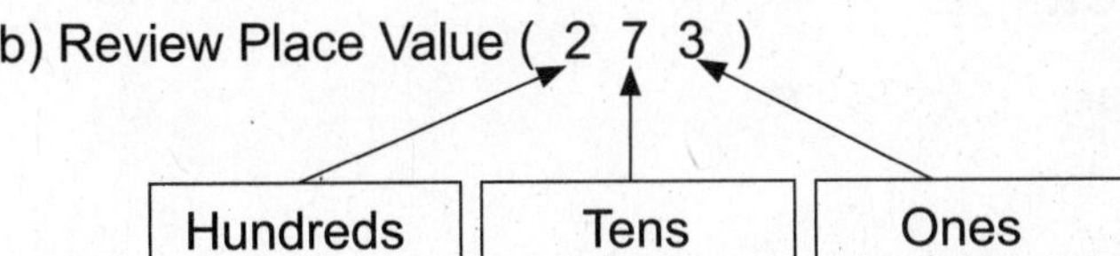

Write down a few questions. Check your child's work.

Step 2 – Binary Code Introduction

Talk about the fact that we represent numbers using numerical symbols (i.e., 2 = two). However, computers do it differently. They use a SECRET electricity CODE!!

electricity = 1; no electricity = 0

You're going to teach them how to CRACK THE CODE!!

Step 3 – Binary Code Exercises

Set up the following chart:

	Eights	Fours	Twos	Ones
a)				
b)				
c)				

Explain to your child that if you put a "1" in a column, it means that the number contains the value at the heading of the column.

For example:

	Eights	Fours	Twos	Ones	
a)	0	0	0	1	$1 = 1$
b)	0	0	1	1	$2 + 1 = 3$
c)	0	0	1	0	$2 = 2$

Explanation:

a) There are 0 eights, 0 fours, 0 twos, 1 one. Therefore, the code 0001 = 1

b) There are 0 eights, 0 fours, 1 two, 1 one. Therefore, the code 0011 = 2 + 1 = 3

c) There are 0 eights, 0 fours, 1 two, 0 ones. Therefore, the code 0010 = 2

Write down a few questions. Check your child's work.

Binary Code *(continued)*

NOTE TO PARENT:
All numbers can be coded in this manner by adding columns to the left of the chart as follows:

32s	16s	8s	4s	2s	1s
1	0	1	0	1	1

$32 + 8 + 2 + 1 = 43$

JUMP Binary Code Game (A.K.A. MIND-READING TRICK!!):

Here are the boxes you need for the final part of the game.

Copy the following charts.

Have your child pick a number between 1 and 15. They should NOT reveal this number to you.

Then, have your child tell you which charts contain their number.

If a chart contains the number, then think of it as a "1." If it doesn't, think of it as a "0."

D			
8	9	10	11
12	13	14	15

C			
4	5	6	7
12	13	14	15

B			
2	3	6	7
10	11	14	15

A			
1	3	5	7
9	11	13	15

Chart A represents 1s.

Chart B represents 2s.

Chart C represents 4s.

Chart D represents 8s.

Example:

They choose "14."

14 is in Chart D $= 1$

14 is in Chart C $= 1$

14 is in Chart B $= 1$

14 is NOT in Chart A $= 0$

Therefore, the code is 1110, or $8 + 4 + 2 = 14$!!

Always/Sometimes/Never True (Numbers)

A If you multiply a 3-digit number by a one-digit number, the answer will be a three-digit number.	**B** If you subtract a three-digit number from 999, you will not have to regroup.	**C** The product of two numbers is greater than the sum.
D If you divide a number by itself, the answer will be 1.	**E** The product of 0 and a number is 0.	**F** Mixed fractions are larger than improper fractions.
G The product of 2 even numbers is an even number.	**H** The product of 2 odd numbers is an odd number.	**I** A number that ends with an even number is divisible by 4.
J When you round to the nearest thousands place, only the thousands digit changes.	**K** When you divide, the remainder is less than the number you are dividing by.	**L** The sum of the digits of a multiple of 3 is divisible by 3.
M The multiples of 5 are divisible by 2.	**N** Improper fractions are greater than 1.	**O** If you have two fractions, the one with the smaller denominator is the larger fraction.

1. Choose a statement from the chart above and say whether it is **always** true, **sometimes** true, or **never** true. Give reasons for your answer.

   What statement did you choose? Statement Letter _________

   This statement is…

   Always True **Sometimes True** **Never True**

   Explain: ____

   ____

   ____

2. Choose a statement that is sometimes true, and reword it so that it is always true.

   What statement did you choose? Statement Letter _________

   Your reworded statement: ____

   ____

3. Repeat the exercise with another statement.

Pattern Puzzles

1. One of the most famous sequences in mathematics is the **Fibonacci sequence**.

   a) In the circles, write the amount added between the terms of the Fibonacci sequence. Then use the pattern in the steps to continue the sequence.

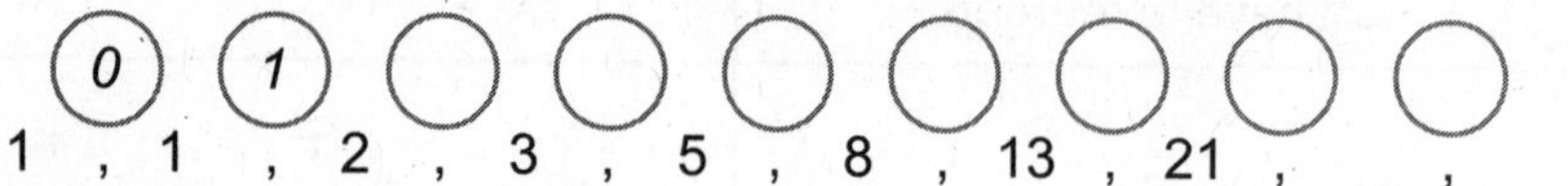

1 , 1 , 2 , 3 , 5 , 8 , 13 , 21 , ____ , ____

   b) Complete the table by writing whether each number in the sequence is even (E) or odd (O).

Number	1	1	2	3	5	8	13	21		
Even or Odd	O	O	E	O						

   c) Describe the odd-even pattern in the Fibonacci sequence.

   d) Is the 38th term in the Fibonacci sequence even or odd? Explain.

   e) Add the first four odd Fibonacci numbers. Then add the first two even Fibonacci numbers. What do you notice?

   f) Add the first six odd Fibonacci numbers. Then add the first three even Fibonacci numbers. What do you notice?

2. Describe any patterns you see in the chart:

HINT: Look at the rows, columns and diagonals.

1	2	3	4	5	6
12	11	10	9	8	7
13	14	15	16	17	18
24	23	22	21	20	19
25	26	27	28	29	30
36	35	34	33	32	31

3.

$$2 = 1 \times 2$$
$$2 + 4 = 2 \times 3$$
$$2 + 4 + 6 = 3 \times 4$$
$$2 + 4 + 6 + 8 = 4 \times 5$$

   a) Describe any patterns you see in the sums shown.

   b) Using the patterns you found in part a), find the sum of the first ten even numbers.

2-Dimensional Patterns

PARENT: For this worksheet, your child will need the hundreds charts on page xliv.

1. 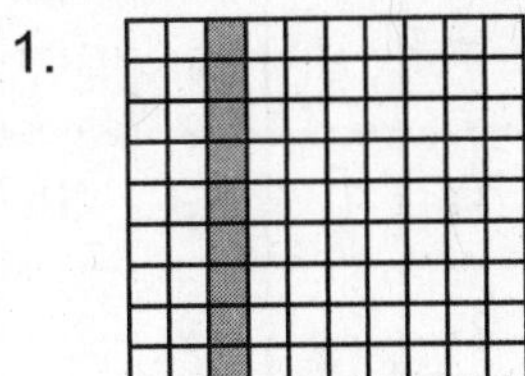

Shade the numbers along any column of a hundreds chart.
Write a rule for the pattern you see.
Look at any other column. How do you explain what you see?

2. This picture shows part of a hundreds chart:
Fill in the missing numbers using the pattern you found in Question 1.

	56	

3. Shade a 2 × 2 square as shown.
Then add the pair of numbers on the "left to right" diagonal:
Then add the pair on the "right to left" diagonal.
Try this again with different 2 × 2 squares.
What do you observe?

"left to right" diagonal

4. Shade a 4-point square around any number on the chart (as shown).
Add the pair of shaded numbers above and below the middle number.
Add the pair of shaded numbers to the right and left of the middle number.
Try this with several different 4 point squares.
Can you explain what you notice?

	15	

5. Shade a 3 × 3 square as shown at left.

a) Take the average of the two numbers above and below the centre square.
What do you notice?

	×	
	×	

b) Add the six numbers that lie in the columns shown:
Repeat this with several 3 × 3 squares.
What relation does the sum have to the number in the centre box?

×		×
×		×
×		×

BONUS:

6. a) Using a calculator, find the sums of the first 3 columns:
b) Why are the sums equal?
c) Describe any patterns you see in the hundreds chart.

1	2	3	4	5	6	7	8	9	10
11	12	13	14	15	16	17	18	19	20
21	22	23	24	25	26	27	28	29	30
31	32	33	34	35	36	37	38	39	40
41	42	43	44	45	46	47	48	49	50
51	52	53	54	55	56	57	58	59	60
61	62	63	64	65	66	67	68	69	70
71	72	73	74	75	76	77	78	79	80
81	82	83	84	85	86	87	88	89	90
91	92	93	94	95	96	97	98	99	100

Hundreds Charts

1	2	3	4	5	6	7	8	9	10
11	12	13	14	15	16	17	18	19	20
21	22	23	24	25	26	27	28	29	30
31	32	33	34	35	36	37	38	39	40
41	42	43	44	45	46	47	48	49	50
51	52	53	54	55	56	57	58	59	60
61	62	63	64	65	66	67	68	69	70
71	72	73	74	75	76	77	78	79	80
81	82	83	84	85	86	87	88	89	90
91	92	93	94	95	96	97	98	99	100

1	2	3	4	5	6	7	8	9	10
11	12	13	14	15	16	17	18	19	20
21	22	23	24	25	26	27	28	29	30
31	32	33	34	35	36	37	38	39	40
41	42	43	44	45	46	47	48	49	50
51	52	53	54	55	56	57	58	59	60
61	62	63	64	65	66	67	68	69	70
71	72	73	74	75	76	77	78	79	80
81	82	83	84	85	86	87	88	89	90
91	92	93	94	95	96	97	98	99	100

1	2	3	4	5	6	7	8	9	10
11	12	13	14	15	16	17	18	19	20
21	22	23	24	25	26	27	28	29	30
31	32	33	34	35	36	37	38	39	40
41	42	43	44	45	46	47	48	49	50
51	52	53	54	55	56	57	58	59	60
61	62	63	64	65	66	67	68	69	70
71	72	73	74	75	76	77	78	79	80
81	82	83	84	85	86	87	88	89	90
91	92	93	94	95	96	97	98	99	100

1	2	3	4	5	6	7	8	9	10
11	12	13	14	15	16	17	18	19	20
21	22	23	24	25	26	27	28	29	30
31	32	33	34	35	36	37	38	39	40
41	42	43	44	45	46	47	48	49	50
51	52	53	54	55	56	57	58	59	60
61	62	63	64	65	66	67	68	69	70
71	72	73	74	75	76	77	78	79	80
81	82	83	84	85	86	87	88	89	90
91	92	93	94	95	96	97	98	99	100

Sudoku

1. Each row, column or box should contain the numbers 1, 2, 3, and 4. Find the missing number in each set.

a) b)

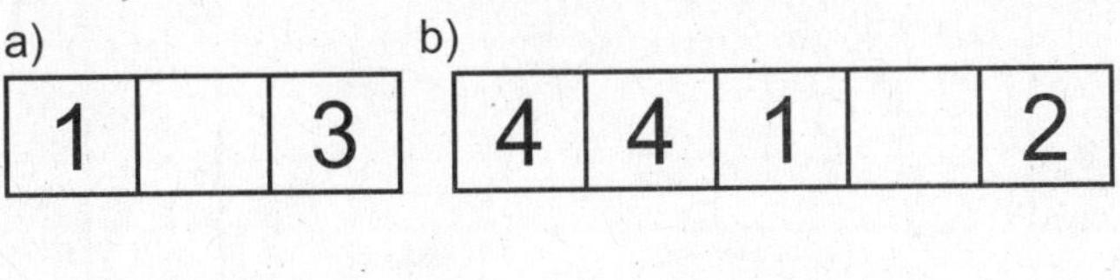

c) d)

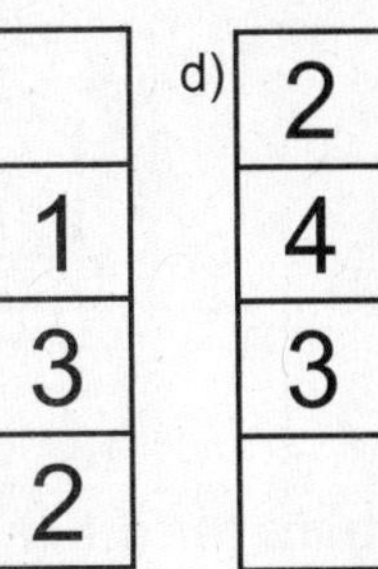

e)

4	
1	3

f)

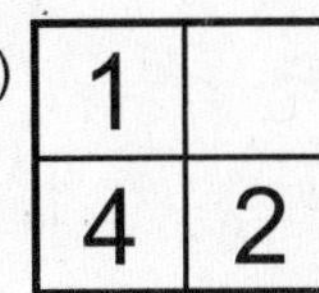

2. Circle the pairs of sets that are missing the SAME number.

a)

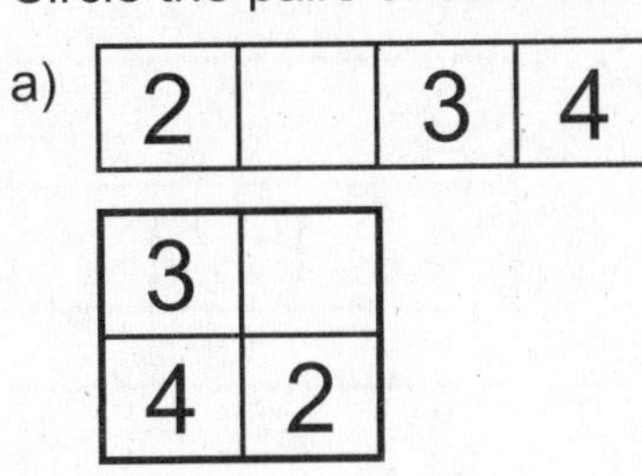

b)

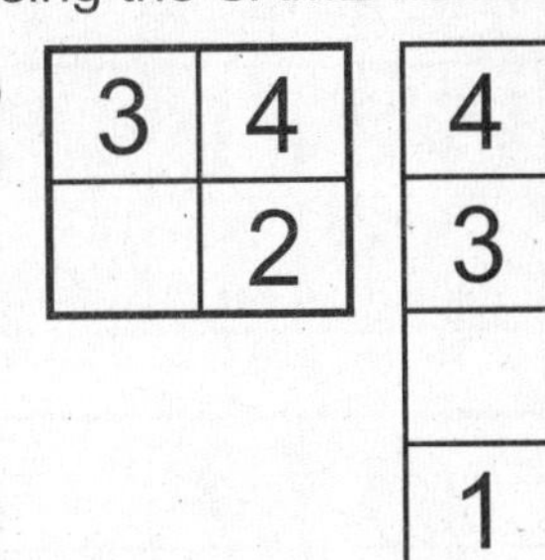

c)

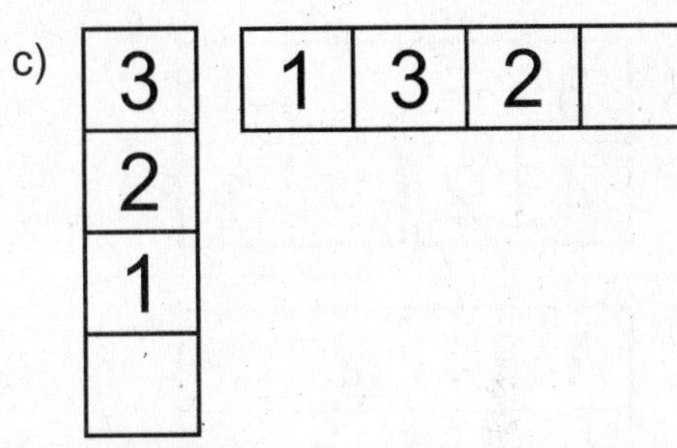

3. Find the number that should be in each shaded square below. **REMEMBER: In Sudoku puzzles a number can appear only once in each row, column, or box.**

a)

b)

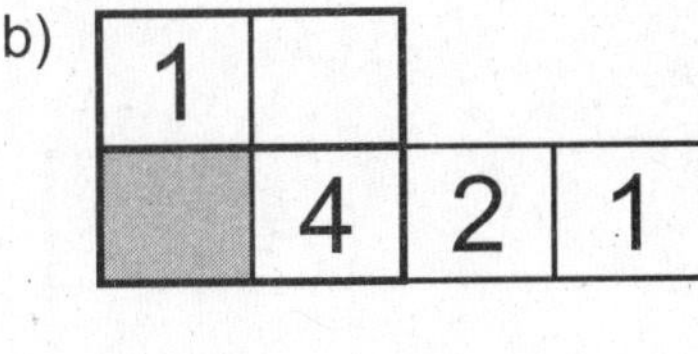

c)

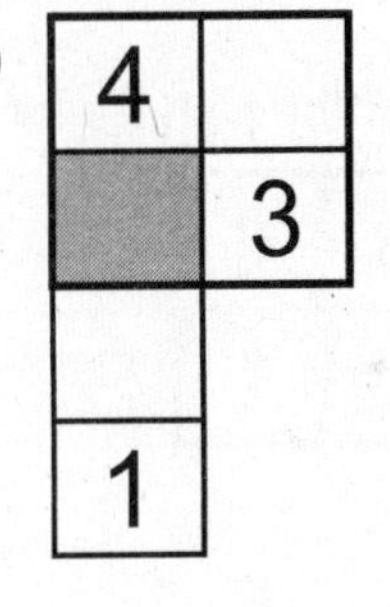

d)

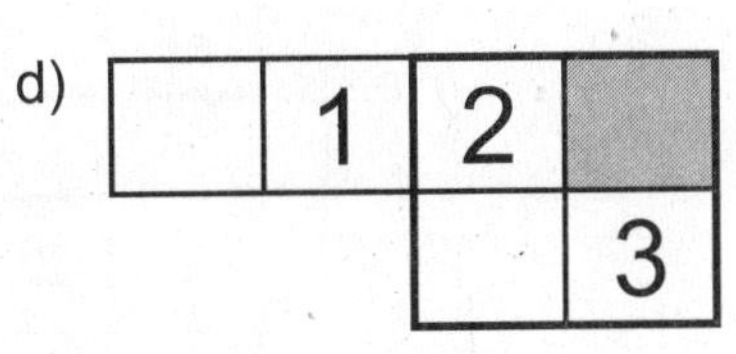

e)

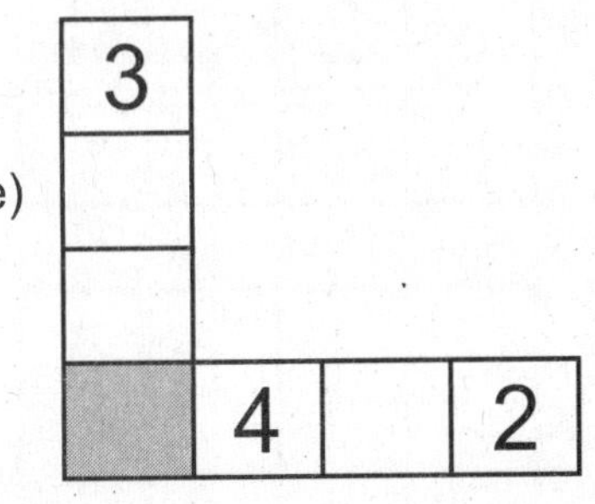

f)

	1
	(shaded)
3	4

4. Fill in the shaded number. Remember that each row, column, and box must have the numbers 1, 2, 3, and 4.

a)

		1	2
2	1	(shaded)	3
		3	
		2	

b)

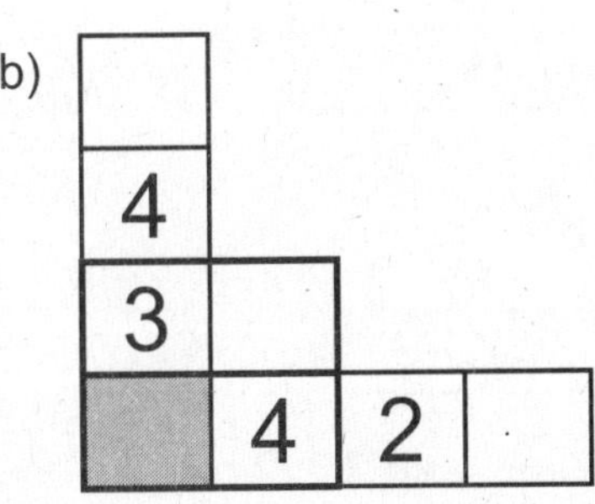

c)

	4		
(shaded)		2	1
1			

Sudoku *(continued)*

d)

1			3
		2	

e)

	1		
			2
4			

f)

			1
		3	
4			

BONUS: Can you find the numbers for other empty squares (besides the shaded ones)?

5. Try to solve the following puzzles using the skills you've learned.

a)

3		2	4
4	2		1

b)

4	2	1	
	1		2

c)

2			4
4	1	2	

d)

1	4	2	
3			4

e)

	1	3	
4		2	

f)

3			1
	2	4	

6. Find the missing numbers in these puzzles.

a)

1		3	4
4	3		1
	1		
2	4		

b)

		4	
		3	1
3	2		4
	1	2	

c)

3		2	4
	2		
		1	2
		4	

d)

2	3		
1	2	4	
	4	2	

e)

2	1		4
3			1
	3		
4			

e)

			4
			2
4		2	
3			1

Now go back and solve the mini Sudoku puzzles!

In the sudoku pattern blocks, the numbers 1, 2, 3, and 4 are used.

Each number must appear in each row, column, and 2×2 box.

Sudoku *(continued)*

When solving Sudoku problems:

1. Start with a row or square that has more than one number.
2. Look along rows, columns, and in the 2 × 2 boxes to solve.
3. Only put in numbers when you are sure the number belongs there (use a pencil with an eraser in case you make a mistake).

Example:

1			
	2		
			3
	4		

1	3	2	4
4	2	3	1
2	1	4	3
3	4	1	2

Here's how you can find the numbers in the shaded second column:
The 2 and 4 are given, so we have to decide where to place 1 and 3.
There is already a 3 in the third row of the puzzle, so we must place a 3 in the first row of the shaded column and a 1 in the third row.

Continue in this way by placing the numbers 1, 2, 3, and 4 throughout the Sudoku. Before you try the problems below, try the Sudoku warm-up on the following Worksheet.

1.

a)

1			4
4	3	2	
	4	1	3
3		4	

b)

	2	1	
1	4		3
4		3	2
	3	4	

c)

1			4
	4	1	
	2	3	
3			2

d)

	4	2	
2			4
4			1
	3	4	

2.

a)

2		1	
	3		
		4	

b)

1			
		2	
4		3	

c)

	4		3
1			
	2		

d)

		4	
3			
	2		2

Sudoku *(continued)*

Try these Sudoku Challenges with numbers from 1 to 6. The same rules and strategies apply!

BONUS:

3.

1	4			3	5
	6	4	5		1
	2	3		6	
4	1	6	2		3
		5		1	2
2	5		3	4	6

4.

5	4		2	1	
	1		5		6
3	6	4		5	
6			4		
		2	3		1
	2			3	

5.

4				3	
6		4		5	2
			6		
5					1
1			5	2	3
		2			

6.

	2				
4		1			2
	6		5	1	
	4				3
				6	
	3	5			1

Sudoku *(continued)*

Try these Sudoku puzzles in the original format 9 × 9.

You must fill in the numbers from 1 through 9 in each row, column, and box. Good luck!

BONUS:

4		2		1	8	3		9
	7	1	4				6	
		6		7	3	2		
	3			6			9	5
6	2		8	4	5		1	3
8					7	6		
	9				4		8	
1		8		3	6		5	7
5		7			1	4		2

SUPER BONUS:

5		3		6			7	8
		2		8			6	
		4	7		3	9		
	7			1			3	4
1				4	5		2	
4		9				1		
	2		4		6	8		7
8			3	9			5	1
9					1		4	

For more Sudoku puzzles, check the puzzle section of your local newspaper!

Sudoku *(continued)*

The following special situation is useful to look for. Suppose you have a complete line (row or column) within a given box and you have a number which

a) is in another box either on the same level as the original box, or above it or below it (not diagonally);

b) is a different number from the three numbers in the completed line; and

c) is not in the same row or column as the threesome.

For example, in the sample partial grid below, we can see that the number 9 satisfies the above criteria.

9								
						5	1	8

As such, you can pencil in the small number 9s in the same row (different box) as the threesome, and again in the third row of the box with the threesome. This means that 9 might go in any of these places. It cannot go anywhere else in those boxes. Can you see why?

Hint: there must be a 9 in the middle row. Can it be in the first box? In the third box?

9								
			9	9	9	5	1	8
						9	9	9

If there is more information, you might be able to narrow down the position of the number 9 to a single cell. For example, if there were already the numbers 3 and 7 in the middle box:

9								
			3	9	7	5	1	8
						9	9	9

Or, the numbers 2 and 6 in the right-most box:

9								
			9	9	9	5	1	8
						9	2	6

Sudoku *(continued)*

Or, the number 3 in the middle box and a 9 in the right-most cell in the box below:

9								
			3	9		5	1	8
						9	9	9

					9			

Now you have a new strategy to add to your other ones. Hopefully, this will help make solving Sudokus even more fun. Try to solve the following Sudoku and use the new strategy when you can.

HINT: find the numbers in the dotted cells first, then the ones in the lighter highlighted cells, using the strategy, then try to fill in the rest of the puzzle:

	4			1				6
5	9	7					4	
2			5	8				
	8			5		9		
4			7	6	3			1
		2					7	
3	7			4	9		8	2
			6			3	1	5
1	6			2				

Models of Fractions

1. Give your child a ruler and ask them to solve the following puzzles:
   a) Draw a line 1 cm long. If the line represents $\frac{1}{4}$ show what a whole line what look like.

   b) Line: 1 cm long. The line represents $\frac{1}{6}$. Show the whole.

   c) Line: 2 cm long. The line represents $\frac{1}{3}$. Show the whole.

   d) Line: 3 cm long. The line represents $\frac{1}{4}$. Show the whole.

   e) Line: $1\frac{1}{2}$ cm long. The line represents $\frac{1}{2}$. Show the whole.

   f) Line: $1\frac{1}{2}$ cm long. The line represents $\frac{1}{4}$. Show the whole.

   g) Line: 3 cm long. The line represents $\frac{1}{4}$. Show $\frac{1}{2}$.

   h) Line: 2 cm long. The line represents $\frac{1}{8}$. Show $\frac{1}{4}$.

2. Give your child counters to make a model of the following problem:
   Postcards come in packs of 4. How many packs would you need to buy to send 15 postcards? Write a mixed and improper fraction for the number of packs you would use.

   Your child could use a counter of a particular colour to represent the postcards they have used and a counter of a different colour to represent the postcards left over. After they have made their model, they could fill in the following chart:

Number of postcards	15
Number of packs of 4 postcards (improper fraction)	$\frac{15}{4}$
Number of packs of 4 postcards (mixed fraction)	$3\frac{3}{4}$

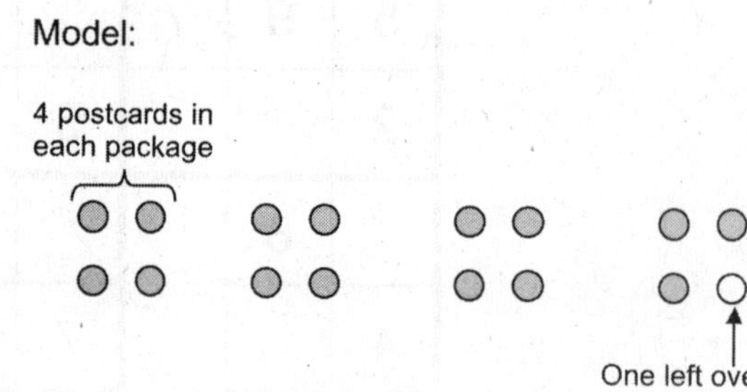

   Here is another sample problem your child could try:

   Juice cans come in boxes of 6. How many boxes would you bring if you needed 20 cans? What fraction of the boxes would you use?

3. Give your child blocks of 2 colours and have them make models of fractions of whole numbers using the method described at the top of the worksheet. Here are some fractions they might try:
   a) $\frac{3}{4}$ of 15 b) $\frac{3}{4}$ of 16 c) $\frac{3}{5}$ of 20 d) $\frac{2}{7}$ of 21

Models of Fractions *(continued)*

4. Ask your child to draw 4 boxes of equal length on grid paper and shade 1 box:

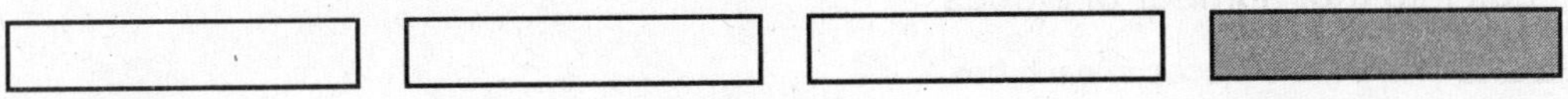

Point out to them that $\frac{1}{4}$ of the area of the boxes is shaded. Now ask them to draw the same set of boxes, but in each box to draw a line dividing the box into 2 parts:

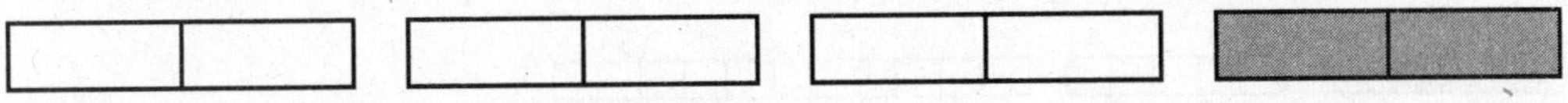

Now $\frac{2}{8}$ of the area is shaded. Repeat the exercise, dividing the boxes into 3 equal parts, (roughly: the sketch doesn't have to be perfectly accurate), then 4 parts, then five parts:

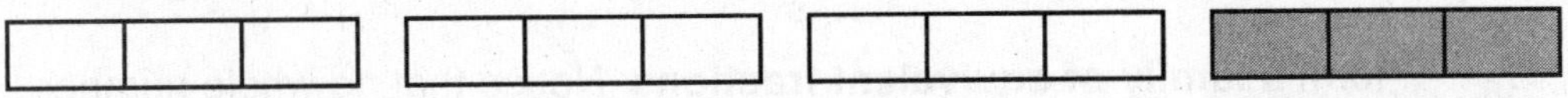

$\frac{3}{12}$ of the area is shaded.

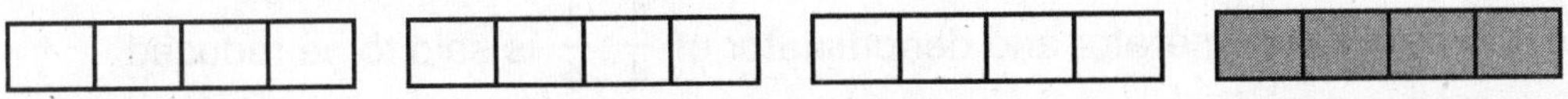

$\frac{4}{16}$ of the area is shaded.

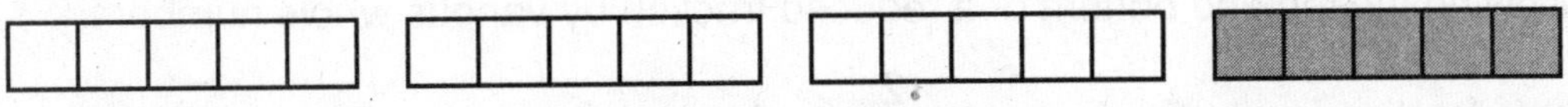

$\frac{5}{20}$ of the area is shaded.

Point out to your child that while the appearance of the fraction changes, the same amount of area is represented:

$\frac{1}{4}$, $\frac{2}{8}$, $\frac{3}{12}$, $\frac{4}{16}$, and $\frac{5}{20}$ all represent the same amount: they are equivalent fractions.

Ask your child how each of the denominators in the fractions above can be generated from the initial fraction of $\frac{1}{4}$:

Answer:
Each denominator is a multiple of the denominator 4 in the original fraction:

$8 = 2 \times 4$ $\quad$ $12 = 3 \times 4$ $\quad$ $16 = 4 \times 4$ $\quad$ $20 = 5 \times 4$

Then ask them how each fraction could be generated from the original fraction.

Answer:
Multiplying the numerator and denominator of the original fraction by the same number:

$\frac{1 \times 2}{4 \times 2} = \frac{2}{8}$ $\quad$ $\frac{1 \times 3}{4 \times 3} = \frac{3}{12}$ $\quad$ $\frac{1 \times 4}{4 \times 4} = \frac{4}{16}$ $\quad$ $\frac{1 \times 5}{4 \times 5} = \frac{5}{20}$

Models of Fractions *(continued)*

Point out that multiplying the top and bottom of the original fraction by any given number, say 5, corresponds to cutting each box into that number of pieces:

$\frac{1 \times 5}{4 \times 5}$

- 1×5 ← There are 5 pieces in each box.
- 4×5 ← There are 4×5 pieces altogether.

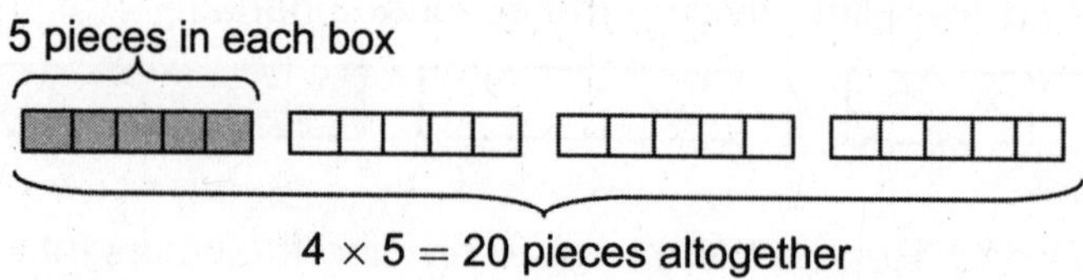

The fractions $\frac{1}{4}, \frac{2}{8}, \frac{3}{12}, \frac{4}{16}$ . . . form a **family of equivalent fractions**. Notice that no whole number greater than 1 will divide into both the numerator and denominator of $\frac{1}{4}$: $\frac{1}{4}$ is said to be reduced to lowest terms. By multiplying the top and bottom of a reduced fraction by various whole numbers, you can generate an entire fraction family. For instance, $\frac{2}{5}$ generates this family:

$$\frac{2 \times 2}{5 \times 2} = \frac{4}{10} \qquad \frac{2 \times 3}{5 \times 3} = \frac{6}{15} \qquad \frac{2 \times 4}{5 \times 4} = \frac{8}{20}$$

Models of Decimals

Children often make mistakes in comparing decimals where one of the decimals is expressed in tenths and the other in hundredths. (For instance, they will say that .17 is greater than .2.) The following activity will help your child understand the relation between tenths and hundredths.

Give your child a set of play-money dimes and pennies. Explain that a dime is a tenth of a dollar (which is why it is written as $0.10), and a penny is a hundredth of a dollar (which is why it is written as $0.01).

Ask your child to make models of the amounts in the left-hand column of the chart below and to write as many names for the amounts as they can think of in the right-hand columns (sample answers are provided in italics):

Amount	Amount in Pennies	Decimal Names (in words)	Decimal Names (in numbers)
2 dimes	*20 pennies*	*2 tenths (of a dollar)* *20 hundredths*	*.2* *.20*
3 pennies	*3 pennies*	*3 hundredths*	*.03*
4 dimes and 3 pennies	*43 pennies*	*4 tenths and 3 hundredths* *43 hundredths*	*.43* *.43*

You should also write various amounts of money on a sheet of paper and have your child make models of the amounts (e.g., make models of .3 dollars, .27 dollars, .07 dollars, etc.). Also challenge them to make models of amounts that have 2 different decimal representations (e.g., 2 dimes can be written as .2 dollars or .20 dollars).

When you feel your child is able to translate between money and decimal notation, ask them to say whether they would rather have .2 dollars or .17 dollars. In their answer, they should say exactly how many pennies each amount represents (e.g., they must articulate that .2 represents 20 pennies and so it is actually the larger amount).

Amount (in dollars)	Amount (in pennies)
.2	
.15	

For extra practice, ask your child to fill in the right-hand column of the chart and then circle the greater amount. (Create several charts of this sort for them.)

Magic Trick

In the magic trick below, the magician can always predict the result of a sequence of operations performed on any chosen number. Try the trick with your child, then encourage them to figure out how it works using a block to stand in for the mystery number (give lots of hints).

The Trick	The Algebra	
Pick any number.	□	Use a square block to represent the mystery number.
Add 4.	□ ○○○○	Use 4 circles to represent the 4 ones that were added.
Multiply by 2.	□ ○○○○ □ ○○○○	Create 2 sets of blocks to show the doubling.
Subtract 2.	□ ○○○ □ ○○○	Take away 2 circles to show the subtraction.
Divide by 2.	□ ○○○	Remove one set of blocks to show the division.
Subtract the mystery number.	○○○	Remove the square.

The answer is 3!

No matter what number you choose, after performing the operations in the magic trick, you will always get the number 3. The model above shows why the trick works.

Encourage your child to make up their own trick of the same type.

Models for Algebra

Give your child two containers to represent the two balance scales in the problems that follow. Your child will place blocks into each container according to the picture (e.g., circle = red block, triangle = blue block). Your child must solve the problem by isolating the block that represents the solution (for instance, in the first **EXAMPLE** they must isolate the triangle). Your child can add or remove blocks from the containers, but they must follow two rules. Start with the first rule:

RULE 1: You may add or remove one or more blocks from one container as long as you add or remove the same number of blocks from the other container. (This mirrors the algebraic rule that whatever you add or subtract from one side of an equation you must add or subtract from the other side.)

EXAMPLE:

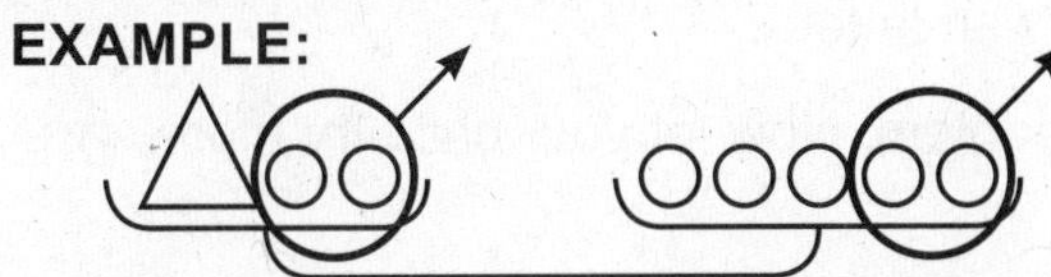

If 2 blocks are taken from the left side of the scale, then 2 blocks must be taken from the right side as well.

Let your child practice with problems such as:

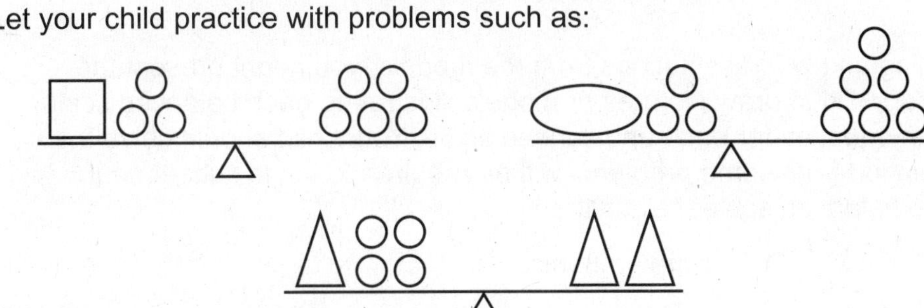

Ask your child to write an equation that represents each scale. What did they do to solve the problem? Ask them to write down the solution. In the **EXAMPLE** above, the equation and the solution will look like:

$\triangle + 2 = 5$ remove (subtract) two from both sides: $\triangle = 5 - 2 = 3$

Present the second rule:

RULE 2: If all the blocks in one container are of a particular type, and all blocks in the other container are of a particular type, and if you can group the blocks in each container equally (and into exactly the same number of sets), you may remove all but one of the sets of blocks from each container.

EXAMPLE:

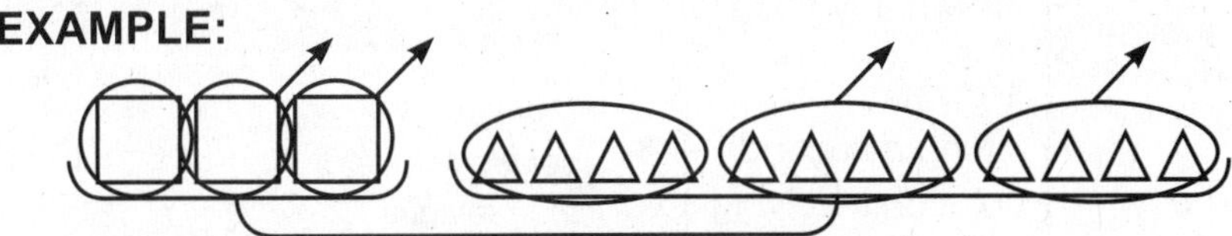

The blocks are placed into 3 equal sets on either side. So 2 sets can be removed from each side.

In the picture above, the blocks are grouped into three equal sets of squares (1 square in each set) and three equal sets of triangles (4 triangles in each set). Each square must weigh the same as 4 triangles. So you can remove all but one group of squares and triangles without unbalancing the scale.

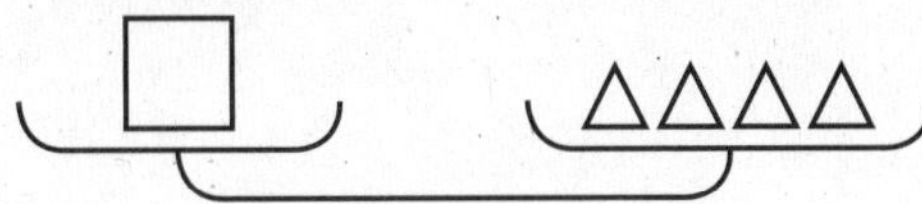

Models for Algebra *(continued)*

This rule mirrors the algebraic rule that you may divide both sides of an equation by the same number. The equation and the solution for the example above would be written as:

$3 \times \square = 12$, divide both sides by 3, so $\square = 12 \div 3 = 4$.

Let your students practice with problems such as:

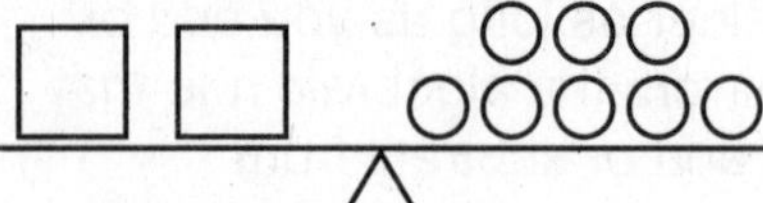

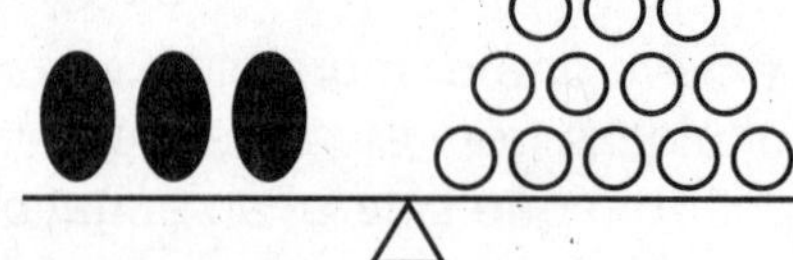

Encourage your child to replace the symbols in the equations with letters.

Your child should write the equations and solutions for each problem. Now let your child try more complicated problems that require the use of both rules, such as:

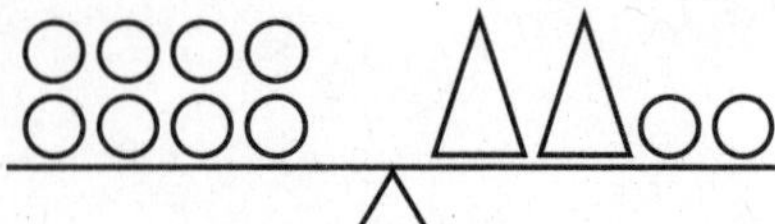

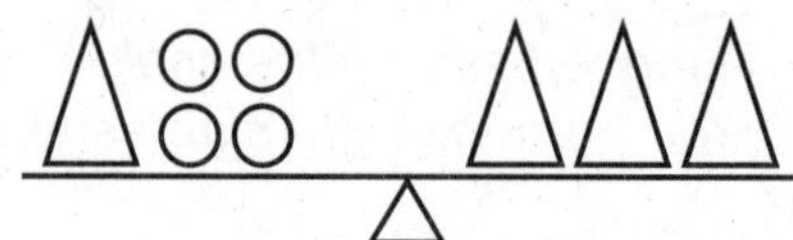

When your child is comfortable finding and writing solutions from the models, you might present the sample problems below and ask your child to draw pictures or models illustrating each balanced scale. Next, ask them to write and solve an equation for each unbalanced scale. Your child should solve the problems in sequence, since information from some problems will be required to solve subsequent problems. For example, the first two balanced scales tell us that:

1 puppy = 1 cat + 3 mice　　　　1 puppy = 8 mice

This information will be necessary to find the weight of the cat in mice.

SAMPLE PROBLEMS:

The scales on the left are balanced perfectly. Can you balance the scales on the right?

Balanced Scales	
A puppy and 2 mice	A cat and 5 mice
A puppy and 2 mice	10 mice
A dog	5 puppies
Two cows	5 dogs

Unbalanced Scales	
A puppy	How many cats and mice?
A puppy	How many mice?
A cat	How many mice?
A dog and a mouse	How many mice?
A cow	How many cats? Find a second solution involving dogs, puppies and mice.

← *Use your solution to the previous problems.*

Give your child several puzzles of the form: $36 + 2\square = 61$. Which digit is missing? Encourage your child to use a systematic search or to solve the equations by subtraction. (**NOTE:** The square here represents the missing digit, not a number as it did earlier.)

UNIT 1

Number Sense 1

NS7-1 Place Value

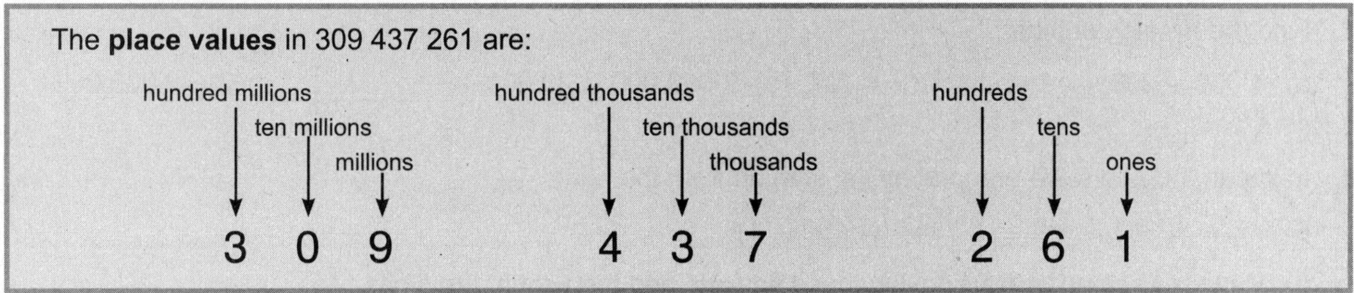
The **place values** in 309 437 261 are:

1. Write the next three place values greater than hundred millions, from largest to smallest.

__________ __________ *billions*

2. Underline the digit with the given place value.

a) 250 329 120 ten millions b) 791 250 329 120 ten billions

c) 791 250 329 120 hundred millions d) 791 250 329 120 thousands

e) 791 250 329 120 billions f) 791 250 329 120 hundred thousands

3. Write the place value of the bold digit.

a) 8**6**1 359 746 323 *ten billions* b) 861 35**9** 746 323 *millions*

c) 861 **3**59 746 323 __________ d) **8**61 359 746 323 __________

e) 861 3**5**9 746 323 __________ f) 86**1** 359 746 323 __________

4. Write the number with the correct spacing, then write the place value of the digit 5.

a) 1405897660213 = *1* *405* *897* *660* *213* place value: *billions*

b) 76312098532 = ____ ____ ____ ____ ____ place value: ________

c) 995132498763 = ____ ____ ____ ____ ____ place value: ________

d) 3542706 = ____ ____ ____ ____ ____ place value: ________

e) 5410328 = ____ ____ ____ ____ ____ place value: ________

f) 841073521960347 = ____________________ place value: ________

5. Write each number in expanded form. Example: 74 512 = 70 000 + 4 000 + 500 + 10 + 2

a) 378 403 ____________________

b) 16 025 ____________________

c) 721 803 ____________________

6. Write the number for each expanded form. Example: 50 000 + 600 + 40 = 50 640

a) 30 000 + 4 000 + 50 + 3 b) 600 000 + 30 c) 40 000 + 200 + 5

__________ __________ __________

NS7-1 Place Value *(continued)*

7. Find the missing number.

a) 4 000 + 300 + ______ + 7 = 4 327   b) 2 000 000 + 30 000 + __________ + 2 = 2 035 002

8. In Japan, numbers are grouped by 4s, starting from the right.

Example: 52341 is written 5 2341 (not 5234 1)

a) Rewrite each number using Japanese spacing and then count the digits.

89034582367121 = ____________________________ ______ digits

8904358239121 = ____________________________ ______ digits

b) Does Japanese spacing make it easier to count the digits? ______________________

c) Circle the number from part a) that is larger. How do you know? ______________________

____

When two numbers have the same number of digits, we can compare the numbers by looking at the first digit that is different, starting from the left. Example: 764 322   769 303

this number is larger

9. Underline the left-most digits that are different and then circle the larger number in each pair.

a) (84 312)   84 065

b) 74 312 908   74 314 873

c) 7 860 432   5 860 432

d) 531 658   531 662

10. Circle the larger number in each pair. First count the digits. Then, if necessary, look for the left-most digit that is different.

a) 543 806   5 412 679

b) 983 152 801   984 125 108

c) 654 009 280   654 092 800

d) 45 678 098 531   45 679 908

11. In the number 36, the 3 is worth 30 and the 6 is worth 6, so the 3 is worth 5 times as much as the 6. How many times more is the first bold digit worth than the second?

a) **84**   b) **84**0   c) **8 4**23   d) **84** 502   e) **84**7 631   f) **8 4**30 601

______ ______ ______ ______ ______ ______

g) **8**0**4**   h) **8** 32**4**   i) **8**3 20**4**   j) 9**8**3 20**4**   k) 2**8**3 651 **4**09   l) 5**8**7 03**4**

______ ______ ______ ______ ______ ______

BONUS▸ **3**7 215 48**6**

12. Write each number in words.

Example: 41 832 107   forty-one million eight hundred thirty-two thousand one hundred seven

a) 5 210 354   b) 573 312 400   c) 576 401 311 212   d) 31 485 620 417

NS7-2 Order of Operations

We add and subtract the way we read: from left to right.

1. Add or subtract from left to right.

a) $7 + 3 - 2$
$= 10 - 2$
$= 8$

b) $7 - 3 + 2$

c) $8 + 4 + 2$

d) $6 + 4 - 5$

2. a) Do the addition in brackets first.

i) $(4 + 6) + 5$
$=$ ____ $+ 5$
$=$ ____

ii) $4 + (6 + 5)$
$= 4 +$ ____
$=$ ____

b) Does the answer change depending on which addition you did first?

____

3. a) Do the subtraction in brackets first.

i) $(7 - 4) - 2$
$=$ ____ $-$ ____
$=$ ____

ii) $7 - (4 - 2)$
$=$ ____ $-$ ____
$=$ ____

b) Does the answer change depending on which subtraction you did first?

____

If there are brackets in an equation, do the operations in brackets first.
Example: $7 - 3 + 2 = 4 + 2 = 6$ but $7 - (3 + 2) = 7 - 5 = 2$

4. a) Calculate each expression using the correct order of operations.

i) $(15 + 7) - 3 - 1$

ii) $15 + (7 - 3) - 1$

iii) $15 + 7 - (3 - 1)$

iv) $(15 + 7 - 3) - 1$

v) $15 + (7 - 3 - 1)$

vi) $(15 + 7) - (3 - 1)$

b) How many different answers did you get in part a)? ____________

5. a) Add brackets in different ways to get as many different answers as you can.

i) $15 + 7 + 3 + 1$

ii) $15 - 7 + 3 - 1$

iii) $15 + 7 - 3 + 1$

iv) $15 - 7 - 3 - 1$

b) How many different answers did you get in part a)? i) ____ ii) ____ iii) ____ iv) ____

c) Check all that apply. The order of operations affects the answer when the expression consists of…

☐ addition only ☐ subtraction only ☐ addition and subtraction

NS7-2 Order of Operations *(continued)*

Multiplication and division are also done from left to right. If there are brackets, do the operations in brackets first. Example: $15 \div 5 \times 3 = 3 \times 3 = 9$ but $15 \div (5 \times 3) = 15 \div 15 = 1$

6. Evaluate each expression.

a) $4 \times 3 \div 6 \times 7$ b) $6 \times 4 \div 2 \div 3$ c) $30 \div 5 \div (2 \times 3)$ d) $16 \times 2 \div (4 \times 2)$

7. a) Add brackets in different ways to get as many different answers as you can.

i) $2 \times 3 \times 2 \times 5$ ii) $64 \div 8 \div 4 \div 2$ iii) $90 \div 5 \times 6 \div 3$

b) Which expression in part a) gives the same answer, no matter where you place the brackets?

8. Do the operation in brackets first.

a) $10 + (4 \times 2)$
$= 10 + 8$
$= 18$

b) $(10 + 4) \times 2$ c) $(10 + 4) \div 2$ d) $10 + (4 \div 2)$

e) $10 - (4 \times 2)$ f) $(10 - 4) \times 2$ g) $(10 - 4) \div 2$ h) $10 - (4 \div 2)$

9. Check all that apply. The order of operations affects the answer when the expression combines…

- ☐ addition and multiplication
- ☐ addition and division
- ☐ subtraction and multiplication
- ☐ subtraction and division
- ☐ addition and subtraction
- ☐ multiplication and division

Mathematicians have ordered the operations to avoid writing brackets all the time. The order is:
1. Operations in brackets.
2. Multiplication and division, from left to right.
3. Addition and subtraction, from left to right.

Example: $3 \times 5 + 3 \times 6 = (3 \times 5) + (3 \times 6)$
$= 15 + 18$
$= 33$

but $3 \times (5 + 3) \times 6$
$= 3 \times 8 \times 6$
$= 24 \times 6$
$= 144$

10. Evaluate each expression. Use the correct order of operations.

a) $4 \times 2 - 7$ b) $2 + 4 \div 2$ c) $6 - 2 \times 3$ d) $20 \div 2 + 8$

e) $4 + 3 \times 6 - 5$ f) $6 + 6 \div 3 - 7$ g) $4 \times 3 \div 6 + 5$ h) $3 \times 7 - 6 \div 2$

i) $4 \div (2 - 1)$ j) $(5 - 1) \times 3$ k) $20 - (14 - 7)$ l) $(12 - 4) \div 4$

NS7-2 Order of Operations *(continued)*

11. Turn the written instructions into mathematical expressions.

a) Add 8 and 3.
Then subtract 4.
Then multiply by 3.
(8 + 3 − 4) × 3

b) Subtract 6 from 9.
Then multiply by 2.
Then add 4.
____

c) Multiply 6 and 5.
Then subtract from 40.
Then add 5.
____

d) Divide 4 by 2.
Then add 10.
Then subtract 4.
____

e) Divide 6 by 3.
Then add 5.
Then subtract 3.
____

BONUS ▶
Divide 8 by 4 and then add 2.
Add 5 and 3 together.
Multiply the two results.
____

12. Write the mathematical expressions in words.

a) $(6 + 2) \times 3$ *Add 6 and 2. Then multiply by 3.*

b) $(6 + 1) \times 2$ __________

c) $4 \times (3 - 1 + 5)$ __________

d) $(5 - 2) \times (4 + 17)$ e) $(24 - 2 \times 6) \div 4$ f) $24 - 2 \times 6 \div 4$

13. a) Add brackets in different ways to get as many different answers as you can.

i) $3 + 1 \times 7 - 2$ ii) $16 - 4 \times 2 + 8$ iii) $16 \div 4 \times 2 + 8$

b) How many different answers did you get in part a)? i) _____ ii) _____ iii) _____

14. a) Calculate the expression in the box. Which expression without brackets gives the same answer?

i) $\boxed{8 - (5 + 2)} = 8 - 5 - 2$ or $8 - 5 + 2$ ii) $\boxed{7 - (3 - 2)} = 7 - 3 - 2$ or $7 - 3 + 2$

iii) $\boxed{7 + (5 - 2)} = 7 + 5 - 2$ or $7 + 5 + 2$ iv) $\boxed{6 + (2 + 4)} = 6 + 2 + 4$ or $6 + 2 - 4$

15. How would you write the expressions below without brackets? Justify your answer.

a) $24 \div (6 \times 2)$ b) $5 \times 8 \div (4 \div 2)$ c) $5 \times 8 \div (4 \times 2)$

16. a) The expressions on the left have brackets and the expressions on the right do not. Calculate the expressions, then match by the same answer.

$4 \times 6 \div (3 \times 2)$	$4 \times 6 \times 2 + 4 \times 3 \times 2$
$4 \times (6 + 3) \times 2$	$4 \times 3 + 4 \times 2 + 6 \times 3 + 6 \times 2$
$(4 + 6) \times (3 + 2)$	$4 \times 6 \div 3 \div 2$

b) Which expression with brackets from part a) needs the most writing to write without brackets and still get the same answer? __________

NS7-3 Equations

A **numeric expression** is a combination of numbers, operation signs, and sometimes brackets, that represents a quantity. Example: These expressions all represent 10:

$7 + 3$ $12 - 2$ $100 \div 10$ $(4 + 1) \times 2$

1. Calculate each expression.

a) $1 + 3 + 4$ ______ b) 3×4 ______ c) $2 \times 2 \times 2$ ______ d) $5 + 2$ ______

An **equation** is a mathematical statement that has two expressions representing the same quantity separated by an equal sign. Example: $12 - 2 = 100 \div 10$

2. a) Circle two expressions in Question 1 that represent the same quantity.

b) Write an equation using those two expressions.

______ = ______

3. Verify that each equation is true.

a) $(4 + 3) \times 2 = 5 \times 3 - 1$ b) $3 \times 4 \times 5 = 6 \times 10$ c) $1 + 2 + 3 + 4 + 5 + 6 = 7 \times 3$

$(4 + 3) \times 2$ and $5 \times 3 - 1$

$= 7 \times 2$ $= 15 - 1$

$= 14$ $= 14$

4. Verify that each equation is true.

a) $5 + 12 = (5 + 1) + (12 - 1)$ b) $5 + 12 = (5 + 2) + (12 - 2)$ c) $5 + 12 = (5 + 3) + (12 - 3)$

5. Rewrite each pair of equations as a single equation by leaving out the number on the right.

a) $(5 + 4) + (6 - 4) = 11$ $5 + 6 = 11$ b) $(7 - 2) + (4 + 2) = 11$ $7 + 4 = 11$

$(5 + 4) + (6 - 4) = 5 + 6$ ______

c) $(8 + 2) + (7 - 2) = 15$ $8 + 7 = 15$ d) $(8 - 5) + (9 + 5) = 17$ $8 + 9 = 17$

______ ______

6. Write the correct number to make the equation true. Verify your answer by calculating both sides.

a) $(12 - 3) + (8 + \underline{3}) = 12 + 8$ b) $(11 + 7) + (9 - \_\_\_) = 11 + 9$ c) $(8 - 2) + (5 + \_\_\_) = 8 + 5$

$= 9 + 11$ *$= 20$*

$= 20$ ← equal ↗

NS7-3 Equations *(continued)*

7. Verify that each equation is true.

a) $(9 + 2) - (4 + 2) = 9 - 4$ b) $(10 - 3) - (7 - 3) = 10 - 7$ c) $(8 - 3) - (6 - 3) = 8 - 6$

8. Write the correct number to make the equation true. Verify your answers.

a) $(12 - 3) + (8 +$ ____ $) = 12 + 8$ b) $(12 - 5) - (8 -$ ____ $) = 12 - 8$

c) $(15 + 2) - (8 +$ ____ $) = 15 - 8$ d) $(11 + 7) + (9 -$ ____ $) = 11 + 9$

9. Write the correct operation to make the equation true. Verify your answers.

a) $(13 - 3) + (7 \bigcirc 3) = 13 + 7$ b) $(8 + 2) + (7 \bigcirc 2) = 8 + 7$

c) $(6 + 5) - (4 \bigcirc 5) = 6 - 4$ d) $(9 - 3) - (5 \bigcirc 3) = 9 - 5$

10. a) Write the correct operation and number to make the statement true.

i) $(26 + 3) + (35$ <u>-3</u> $) = 26 + 35$ ii) $(18 + 4) - (7$ ____ $) = 18 - 7$

iii) $(17 - 4) + (26$ ____ $) = 17 + 26$ iv) $(24 - 3) - (9$ ____ $) = 24 - 9$

v) $(134$ ____ $) - (38 + 7) = 134 - 38$ vi) $(287$ ____ $) + (41 + 6) = 287 + 41$

b) Choose one of the equations you made and verify that it is true by calculating both sides.

BONUS▶ Add brackets where necessary to the following equations to make them true.

a) $3 + 1 \times 7 - 2 = 20$ b) $3 + 1 \times 7 - 2 = 26$ c) $3 + 1 \times 7 - 2 = 8$

d) $6 - 3 \times 2 = 6$ e) $16 \div 2 \times 2 = 4$ f) $4 + 8 \div 2 = 6$

g) $8 - 4 \times 2 + 5 = 28$ h) $8 - 4 \times 2 + 5 = 13$ i) $5 \times 4 - 3 + 2 = 7$

NS7-4 Properties of Operations

The area of a rectangle is the number of square units that cover it.

1. Find the area of each rectangle.

a) 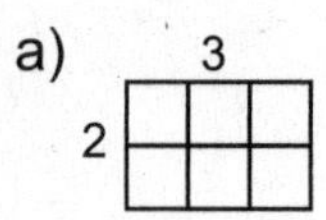

$2 \times 3 = 6$

b) 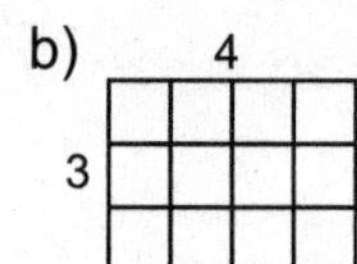

c) 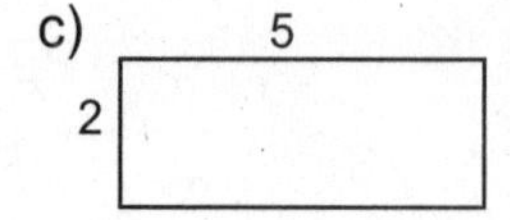

d) 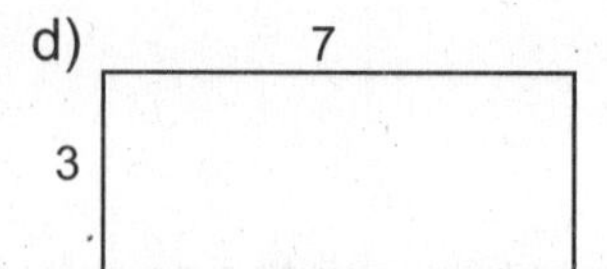

e) 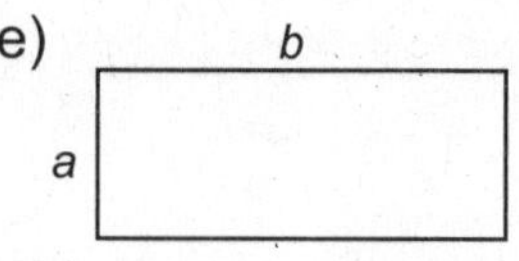

2. A rectangle is cut in half in two different ways. How long are the resulting sides?

a) 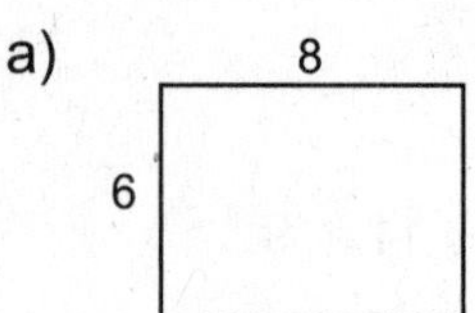

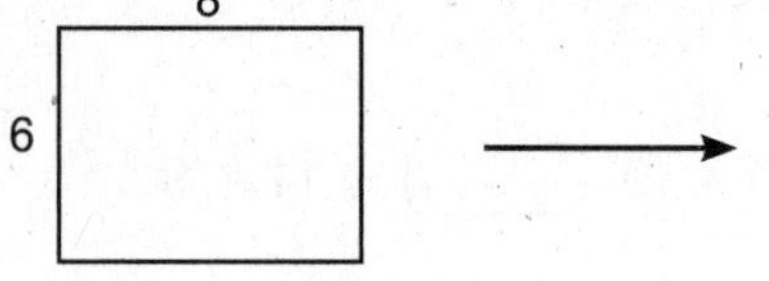
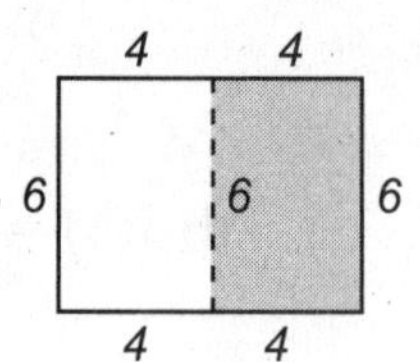

and
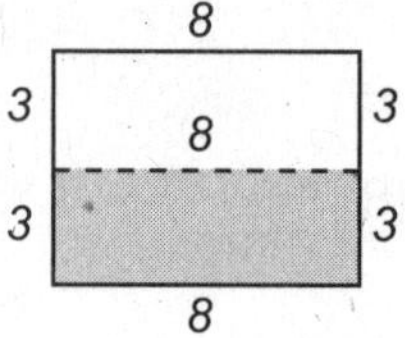

b) 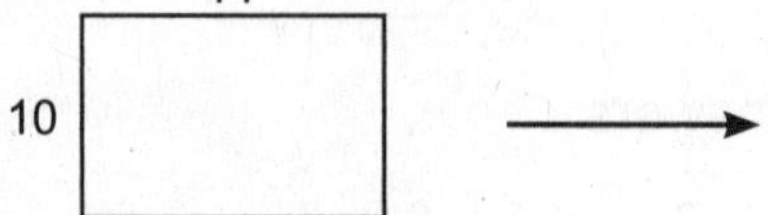

and
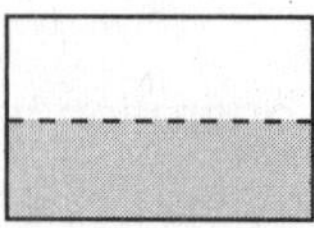

c) 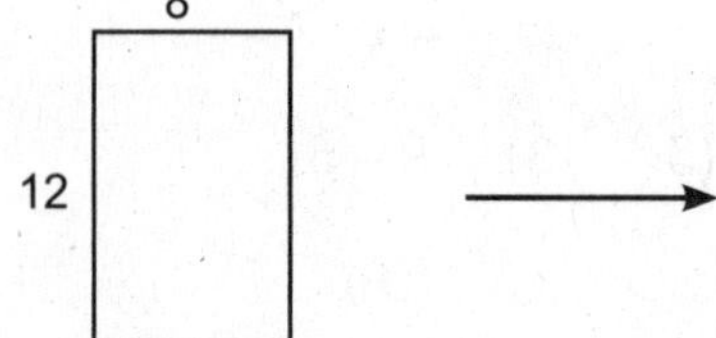

and
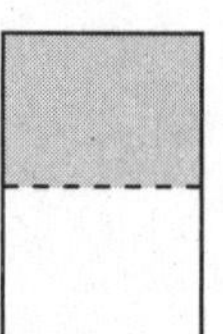

3. A rectangle is cut in half and rearranged. How long are the resulting sides?

a) 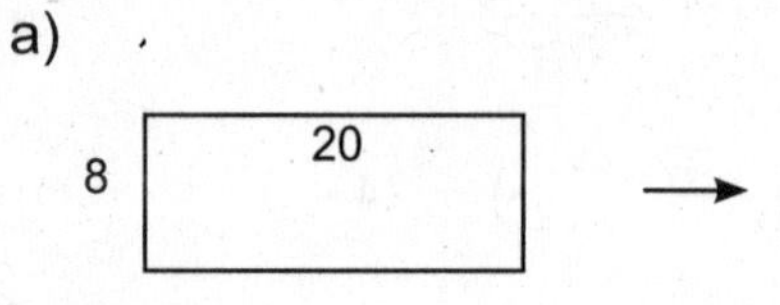

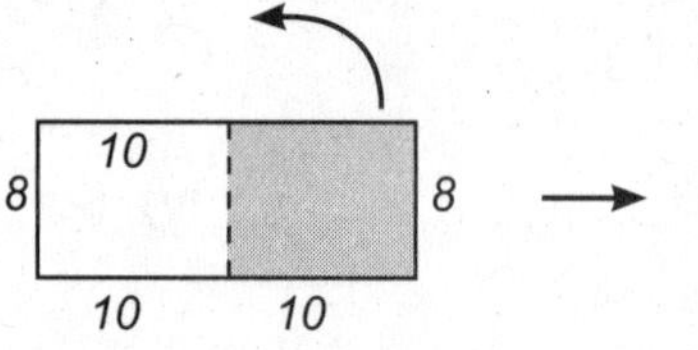

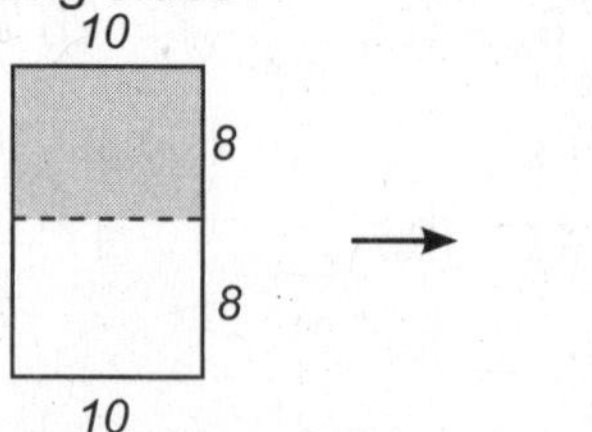

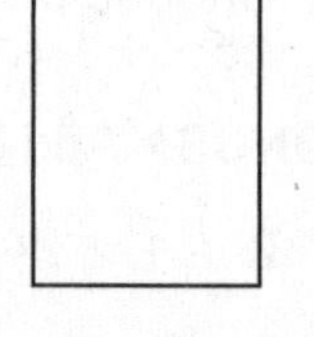

b) 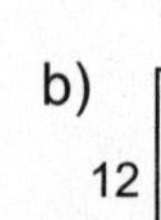
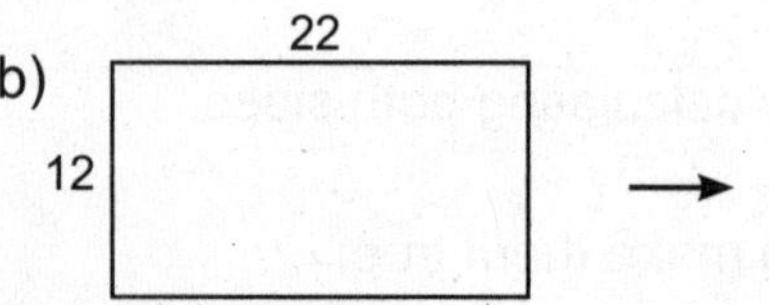

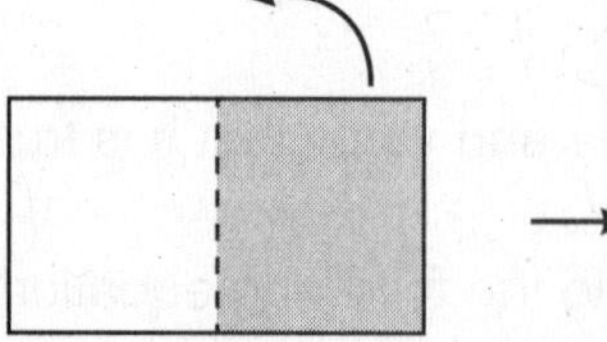
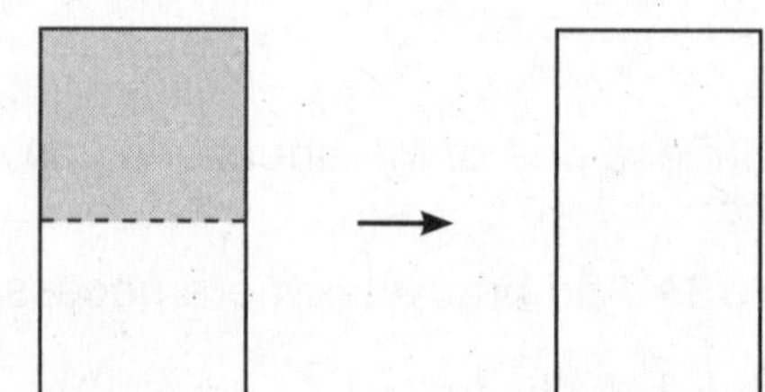

c) 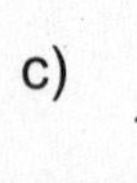
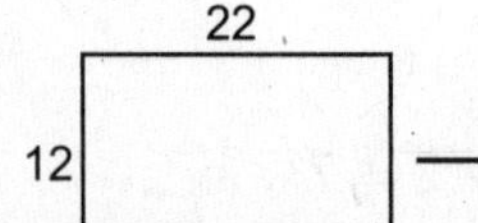

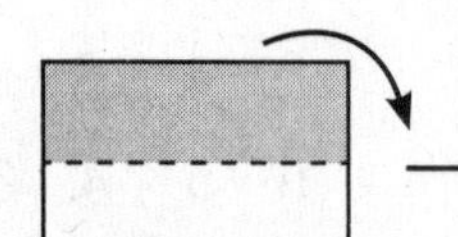
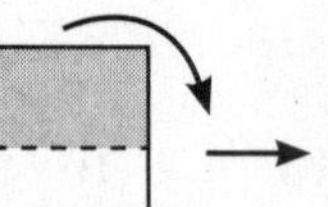
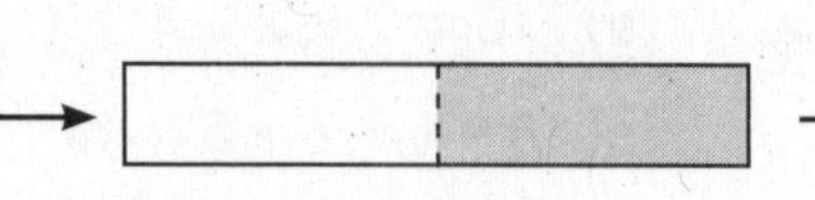

NS7-4 Properties of Operations *(continued)*

4. A rectangle is cut in half and rearranged. Make another product with the same answer to complete the equation.

a) 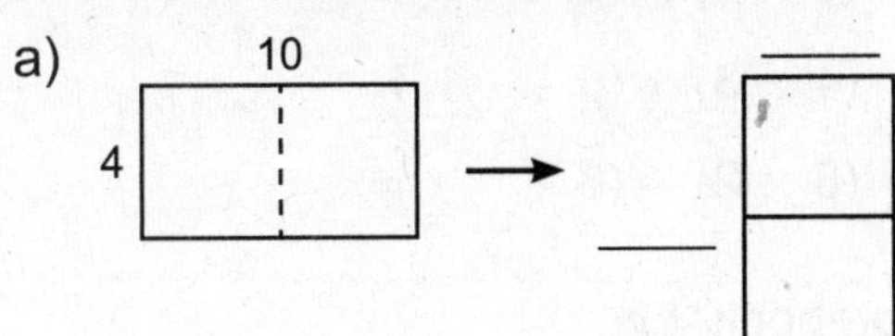

$4 \times 10 =$ ____ $\times$ ____

b) 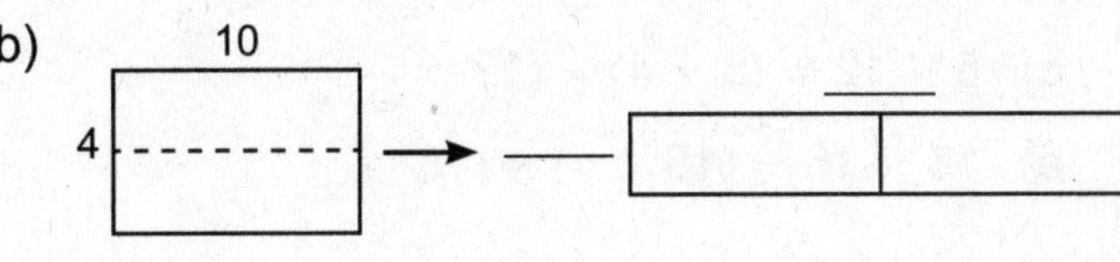

$4 \times 10 =$ ____ $\times$ ____

5. Imagine cutting the rectangle in half and rearranging. Make two more products with the same answer.

a) 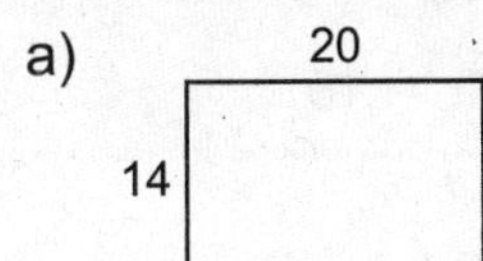

b) 12, 8

c) 124, 42

$20 \times 14 =$ ____ $\times$ ____
$=$ ____ $\times$ ____

$8 \times 12 =$ ____ $\times$ ____
$=$ ____ $\times$ ____

$124 \times 42 =$ ____ $\times$ ____
$=$ ____ $\times$ ____

6. Cut the rectangle in thirds and rearrange. Make two more products with the same answer.

a) 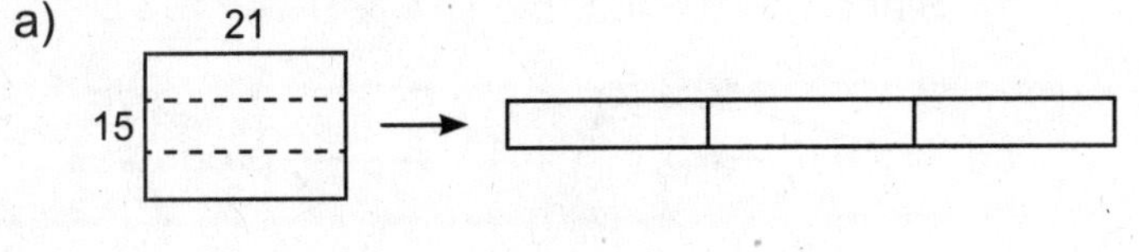

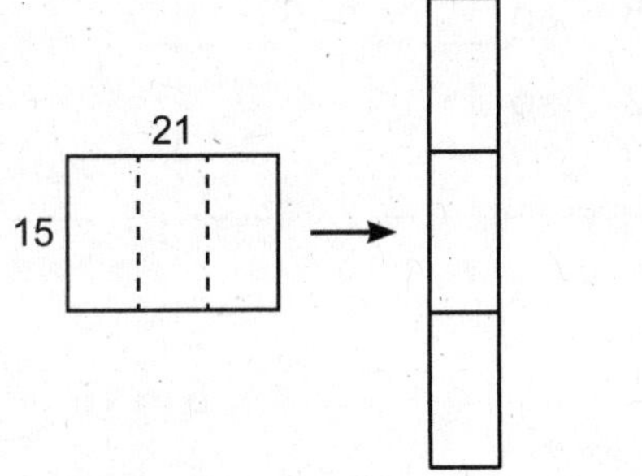

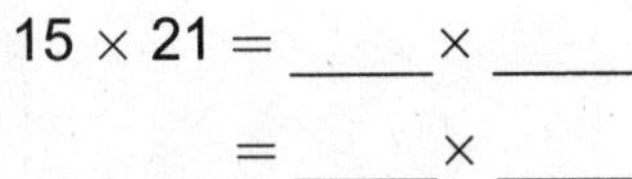

$15 \times 21 =$ ____ $\times$ ____
$=$ ____ $\times$ ____

b) 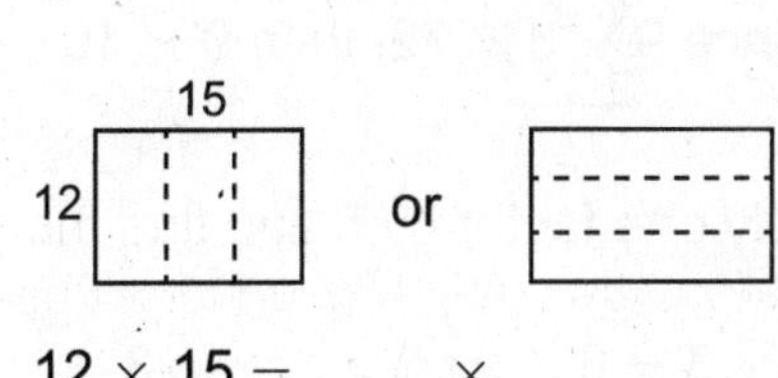

$12 \times 15 =$ ____ $\times$ ____
$=$ ____ $\times$ ____

c) 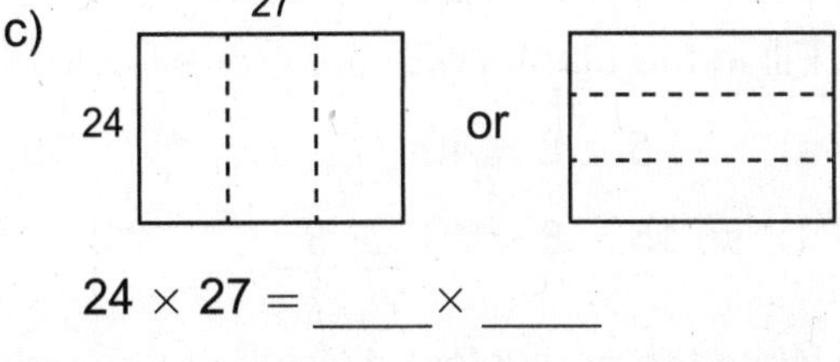

$24 \times 27 =$ ____ $\times$ ____
$=$ ____ $\times$ ____

7. Draw rectangles to show why:

a) $5 \times 6 = 10 \times 3$
b) $5 \times 9 = 15 \times 3$
c) $5 \times 12 = 20 \times 3$

NS7-4 Properties of Operations *(continued)*

8. Write the correct number to make the equation true.

a) $5 \times 6 = (5 \times 2) \times (6 \div$ ___)   b) $5 \times 9 = (5 \times 3) \times (9 \div$ ___)

c) $5 \times 12 = (5 \times 4) \times (12 \div$ ___)   d) $4 \times 6 = (4 \times 3) \times (6 \div$ ___)

e) $15 \times 16 = (15 \times 4) \times (16 \div$ ___)   f) $8 \times 8 = (8 \times 2) \times (8 \div$ ___)

9. Write the correct operation. Then verify your answers in your notebook, by calculating both sides.

a) $3 \times 4 = (3 \times 2) \times (4 \bigcirc 2)$ b) $4 \times 15 = (4 \times 3) \times (15 \bigcirc 3)$ c) $9 \times 21 = (9 \times 7) \times (21 \bigcirc 7)$

Start with any multiplication statement. To find another multiplication statement with the same answer **multiply one factor and divide the other by the same number**.

Example: **5** × **30** = 150   10 × 15 = 150 (**5** × 2, **30** ÷ 2)   50 × 3 = 150 (**5** × 10, **30** ÷ 10)

10. Write the correct operation and number. Then verify your answers in your notebook.

a) $5 \times 18 = (5 \times 2) \times (18$ _÷ 2_)   b) $7 \times 60 = (7 \times 10) \times (60$ ___)   c) $8 \times 25 = (8 \times 5) \times (25$ ___)

11. Explain why these problems have the same answer. Then choose the easiest one and solve it.

25×16 50×8 100×4

12. Multiply.

a) Since $3 \times 5 = 15$, then $6 \times 5 =$ _____   b) Since $4 \times 3 = 12$, then $8 \times 3 =$ _____

c) Since $9 \times 8 = 72$, then $9 \times 16 =$ _____   d) Since $7 \times 9 = 63$, then $14 \times 9 =$ _____

13. Multiply one factor by 5 and find the products.

factors → 3 × 5 = 15 ← product

a) $2 \times 3 = 6$ so _____ $\times 3 =$ _____   b) $3 \times 5 = 15$ so _____ $\times 5 =$ _____

c) $4 \times 5 = 20$ so $4 \times$ _____ = _____   d) $2 \times 6 = 12$ so $2 \times$ _____ = _____

When you multiply one factor by 5, what happens to the product? ______________________

14. Fill in the blanks with the correct operation and number.

a) $5 \times 8 = 40$ so $15 \times 8 = 40$ _× 3_   b) $5 \times 9 = 45$ so $5 \times 18 = 45$ _____   c) $3 \times 6 = 18$ so $21 \times 6 = 18$ _____

15. Write the equivalent division statement for each multiplication statement.

$6 \times 5 = 30$ so _30_ ÷ _6_ = 5

$(6 \times 2) \times 5 = 30 \times 2$ so (_30 × 2_) ÷ (_6 × 2_) = 5

$(6 \times 3) \times 5 = 30 \times 3$ so (________) ÷ (________) = 5

$(6 \times 4) \times 5 = 30 \times 4$ so (________) ÷ (________) = 5

NS7-4 Properties of Operations *(continued)*

16. Write the correct operation and number.

$30 \div 6 = (30 \times 2) \div (6$ ______ $)$
$= (30 \times 3) \div (6$ ______ $)$
$= (30 \times 4) \div (6$ ______ $)$

17. Fill in the blanks with the correct operation and number. Verify your answers in your notebook.

a) $12 \div 3 = (12 \times 2) \div (3$ _____ $)$ b) $20 \div 5 = (20 \times 2) \div (5$ _____ $)$ c) $90 \div 6 = (90 \times 5) \div (6$ _____ $)$

18. Explain why these problems have the same answer. Then choose the easiest one and solve it.

$35 \div 5$ $70 \div 10$ $105 \div 15$

19. Fill in the blanks to solve the problems.

a) $135 \div 5 =$ *270* $\div 10$
$=$ ______

b) $120 \div 5 =$ ______ $\div 10$
$=$ ______

c) $65 \div 5 =$ ______ $\div 10$
$=$ ______

Start with any division statement. To find another division statement with the same answer, **multiply both terms (the dividend and the divisor) by the same number.**

Example: $\mathbf{6} \div \mathbf{2} = 3$ $12 \div 4 = 3$ ($\mathbf{6} \times 2$, $\mathbf{2} \times 2$) $18 \div 6 = 3$ ($\mathbf{6} \times 3$, $\mathbf{2} \times 3$) $24 \div 8 = 3$ ($\mathbf{6} \times 4$, $\mathbf{2} \times 4$)

20. Write the equivalent division statement for each multiplication statement.

$12 \times 5 = 60$ so *60* $\div$ *12* $= 5$
$(12 \div 2) \times 5 = 60 \div 2$ so (*60 ÷ 2*) $\div$ (*12 ÷ 2*) $= 5$
$(12 \div 3) \times 5 = 60 \div 3$ so (________) $\div$ (________) $= 5$
$(12 \div 4) \times 5 = 60 \div 4$ so (________) $\div$ (________) $= 5$

21. Write the correct operation and number.

$60 \div 12 = (60 \div 2) \div (12$ ______ $)$
$= (60 \div 3) \div (12$ ______ $)$
$= (60 \div 4) \div (12$ ______ $)$

22. Write the correct operation and number. Verify your answers in your notebook.

a) $20 \div 4 = (20 \div 2) \div (4$ ______ $)$ b) $24 \div 6 = (24 \div 3) \div (6$ ______ $)$

23. Write an operation and a number to make the equation true.

a) $9 - 5 = (9 + 2) - (5$ _____ $)$ b) $9 + 5 = (9 + 2) + (5$ _____ $)$ c) $18 \times 6 = (18 \times 3) \times (6$ _____ $)$
d) $18 \div 6 = (18 \times 3) \div (6$ _____ $)$ e) $5 \times 12 = (5 \times 3) \times (12$ _____ $)$ f) $7 \times 9 = ($ _____ $3) \times (9 \div 3)$
g) $8 + 7 = (8 - 4) + (7$ _____ $)$ h) $30 \div 6 = (30 \div 2) \div (6$ _____ $)$ i) $12 \times 10 = (12 \div 2) \times (10$ _____ $)$

BONUS▶
j) $m \div n = (m \times p) \div (n$ _____ $)$ k) $a \times d = (a \div m) \times (d$ _____ $)$ l) $r + s = (r - t) + (s$ _____ $)$

NS7-5 Breaking Multiplication into Simpler Problems

Mathematicians often break problems into simpler problems.
In multiplication, this often means using multiplication by 10, 100, or 1 000.

1. Find each product.

a) $3 \times 20 = 3 \times$ ____ tens
$=$ ____ tens
$=$ ____

b) $3 \times 200 = 3 \times$ ____ hundreds
$=$ ____ hundreds
$=$ ____

c) $3 \times 2\,000 =$ ______
d) $3 \times 20\,000 =$ ______
e) $3 \times 200\,000 =$ ______

f) $3 \times 700 =$ ______
g) $5 \times 4\,000 =$ ______
h) $15 \times 40\,000 =$ ______

2. Use multiples of 10 or 100 to break each problem into simpler problems.

a) $5 \times 23 = 5 \times 20 + 5 \times$ ______
$=$ ______ $+$ ______
$=$ ______

b) $2 \times 432 = 2 \times$ ______ $+ 2 \times$ ______ $+ 2 \times$ ______
$=$ ______ $+$ ______ $+$ ______
$=$ ______

c) $3 \times 312 =$ ________________ $+$ ________________ $+$ ________________
$=$ ______ $+$ ______ $+$ ______
$=$ ______

3. Multiply in your head.

a) $3 \times 12 =$ ______
b) $3 \times 52 =$ ______
c) $6 \times 31 =$ ______
d) $7 \times 21 =$ ______

e) $5 \times 31 =$ ______
f) $3 \times 621 =$ ______
g) $5 \times 411 =$ ______
h) $3 \times 632 =$ ______

4. Use the 2 times table and the 10 times table to write the 12 times table.

	1	**2**	**3**	**4**	**5**	**6**	**7**	**8**	**9**	**10**
× 2	2	4	6							
× 10	10	20	30							
× 12	12	24	36							

5. Use the 3 times table and the 20 times table to write the 23 times table.

	1	**2**	**3**	**4**	**5**	**6**	**7**	**8**	**9**	**10**
× 3	3	6	9							
× 20	20	40	60							
× 23	23	46								

NS7-6 Long Multiplication

How to solve $3 \times 42 = 3 \times 40 + 3 \times 2$

$= 3 \times 4$ tens $+ 3 \times 2$ ones

Step 1:

Multiply the ones digit by 3 (3×2 ones $= 6$ ones).

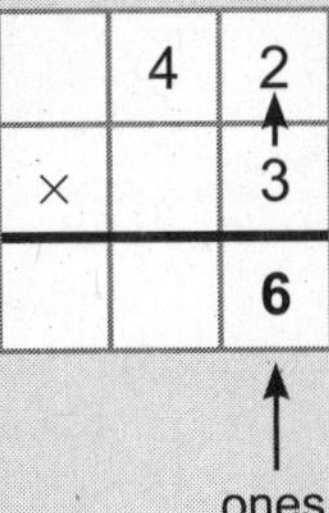

Step 2:

Multiply the tens digit by 3 (3×4 tens $= 12$ tens).

Regroup 10 tens as 1 hundred.

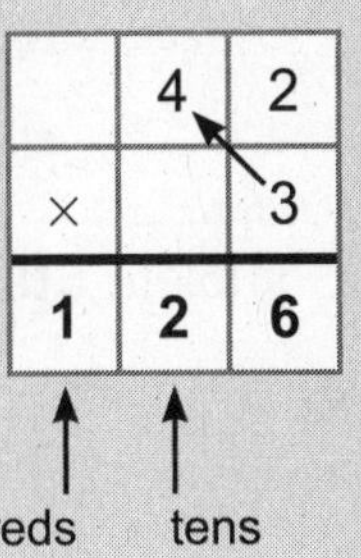

1. Use Steps 1 and 2 to find the products.

a) b) c)

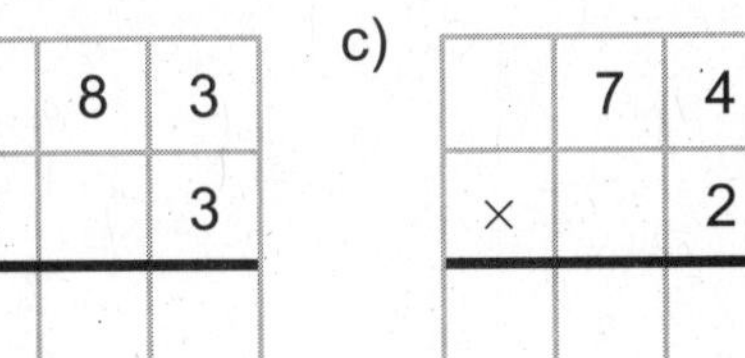

d) e)

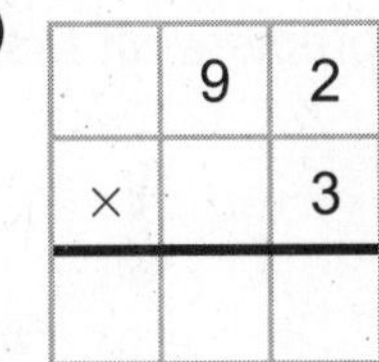

How to solve $7 \times 43 = 7 \times 40 + 7 \times 3$

$= 7 \times 4$ tens $+ 7 \times 3$ ones

Step 1:

Multiply 3 ones by 7 ($7 \times 3 = 21$).

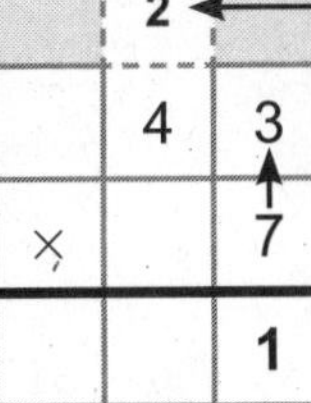

Step 2:

Regroup 20 ones as 2 tens.

2. Complete **Steps 1** and **2** of the multiplication.

a)

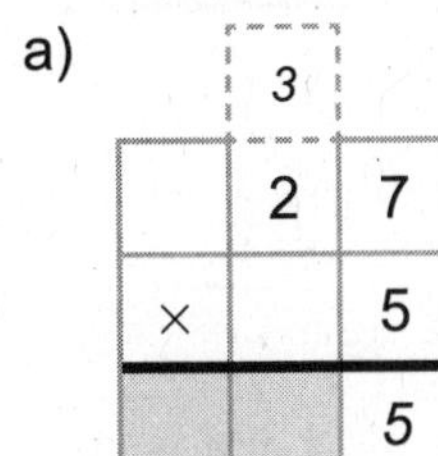

b)

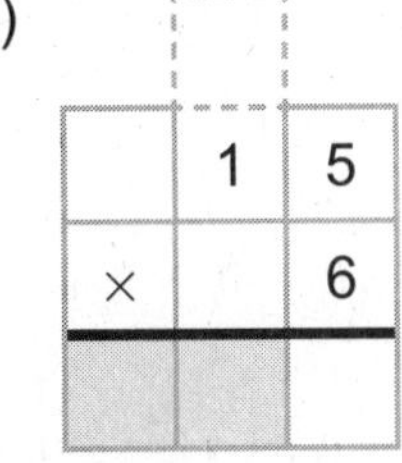

c)

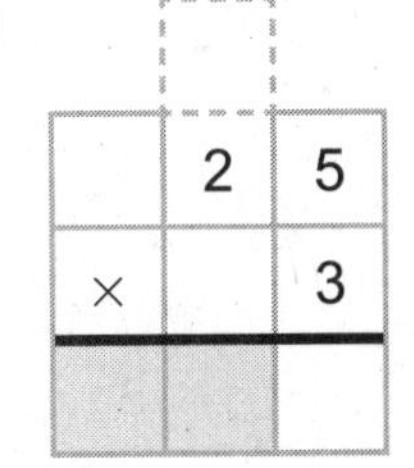

d)

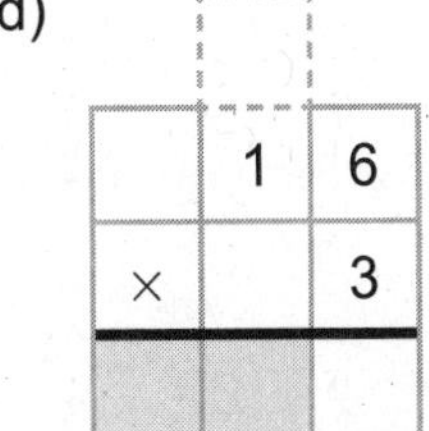

e)

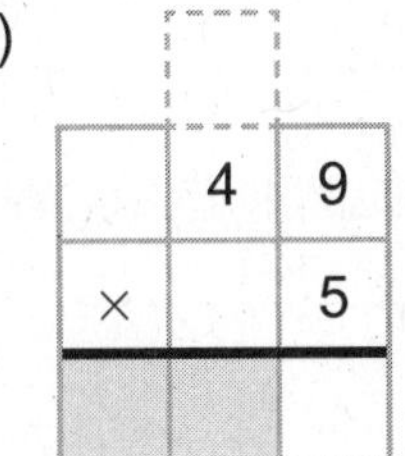

NS7-6 Long Multiplication *(continued)*

Step 3:

Multiply 4 tens by 7
(7 × 4 tens = 28 tens).

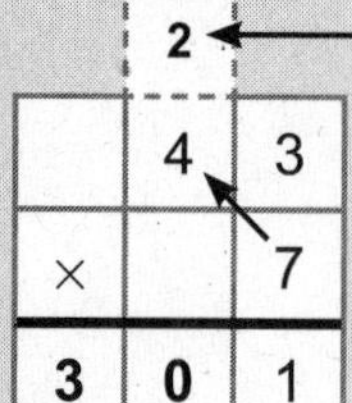

	2	
	4	3
×		7
3	**0**	1

Step 4:

Add 2 tens to the result
(28 + 2 = 30 tens).

3. Complete **Steps 3** and **4** of the multiplication.

a) regrouped: 1; 2 4 × 3; answer: _ 7 2

b) regrouped: 4; 3 5 × 9; answer: _ _ 5

c) regrouped: 2; 1 5 × 5; answer: _ _ 5

d) regrouped: 1; 7 3 × 5; answer: _ _ 5

e) regrouped: 4; 8 9 × 5; answer: _ _ 5

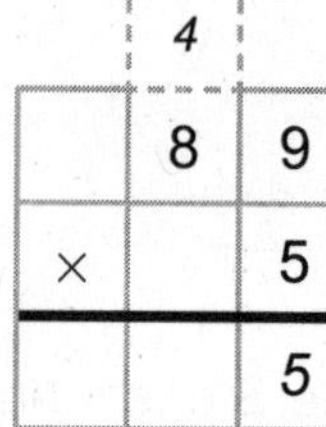

4. Complete **all steps** of the multiplication.

a) 3 5 × 9

b) 3 5 × 6

c) 1 5 × 7; answer: _ _ 5

d) 2 5 × 8

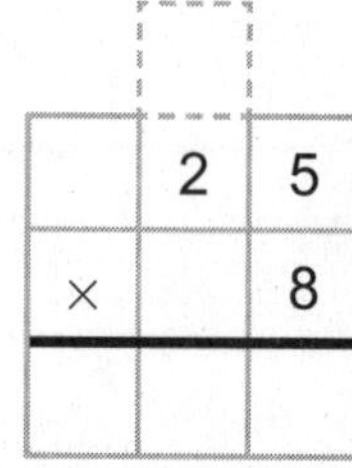

e) 2 4 × 5

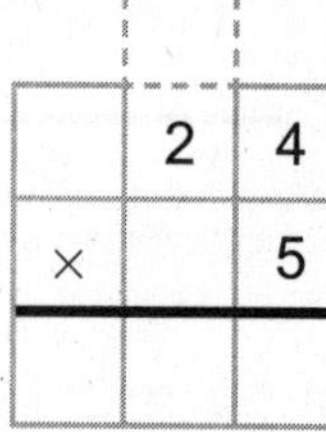

5. Multiply.

a) 4 1 × 5

b) 4 3 4 × 2

c) 3 1 2 × 3

d) 1 2 4 × 2

e) 3 2 3 × 3

6. Multiply by regrouping ones as tens.

a) 2 2 7 × 3

b) 1 1 6 × 5

c) 2 2 4 × 3

d) 1 1 9 × 5

e) 3 2 8 × 3

7. Multiply by regrouping when you need to.

a) 2 3 7 × 5

b) 7 5 6 × 3

c) 5 2 8 × 2

d) 5 3 2 × 7

e) 2 1 3 × 8

f) 5 × 174 g) 7 × 321 h) 6 × 132 i) 9 × 532 **BONUS▸** 8 × 31 245

NS7-6 Long Multiplication *(continued)*

To multiply a 2-digit number by any multiple of ten, first multiply by the number of tens, then multiply by 10. Example: to find 37 × 20, find 37 × 2, then multiply by 10.

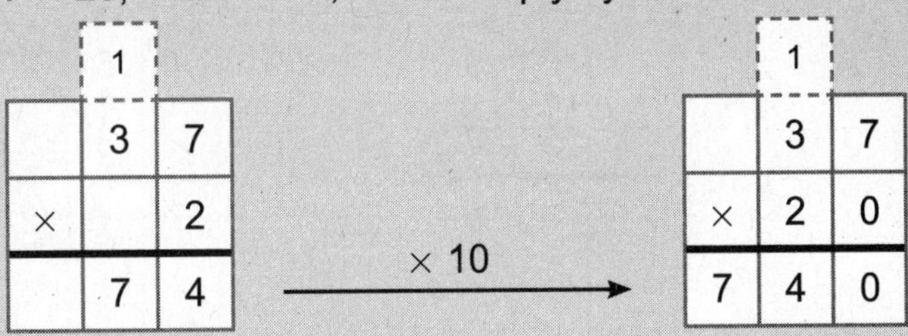

8. Multiply.

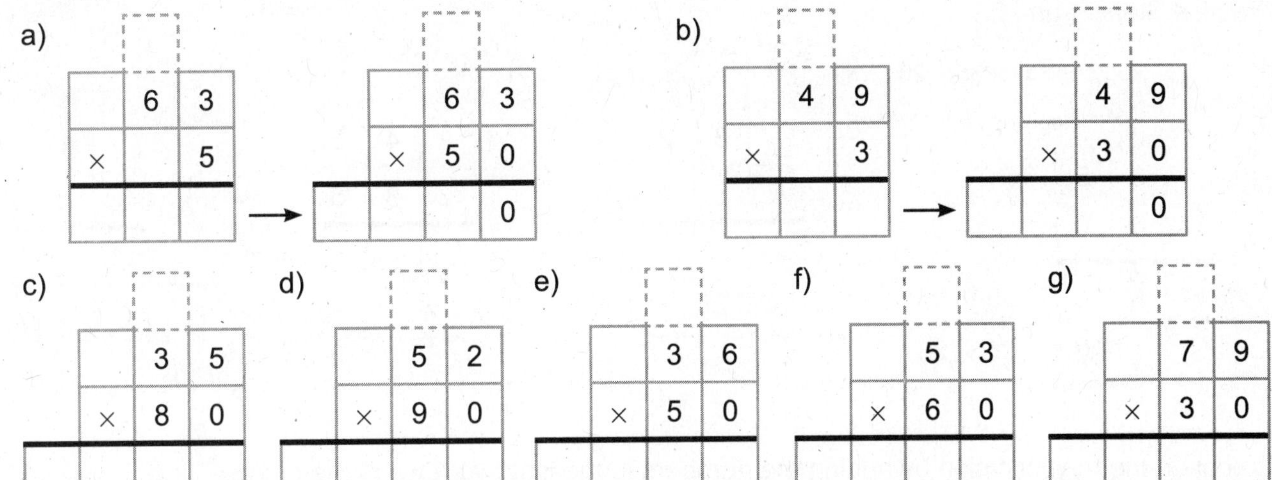

To multiply 2-digit numbers, split the product into a sum of two easier products.

Example: 37 × 25 = 37 × a multiple of ten + 37 × a 1-digit number

37 × **25** = 37 × **20** + 37 × **5**

= 740 + 185

= 925

Keep track using a grid:

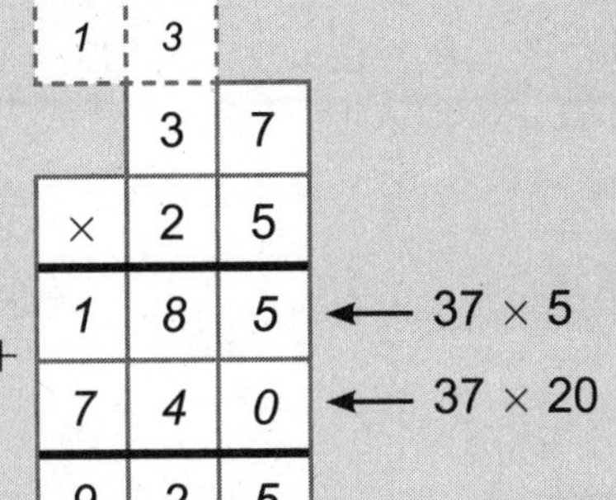

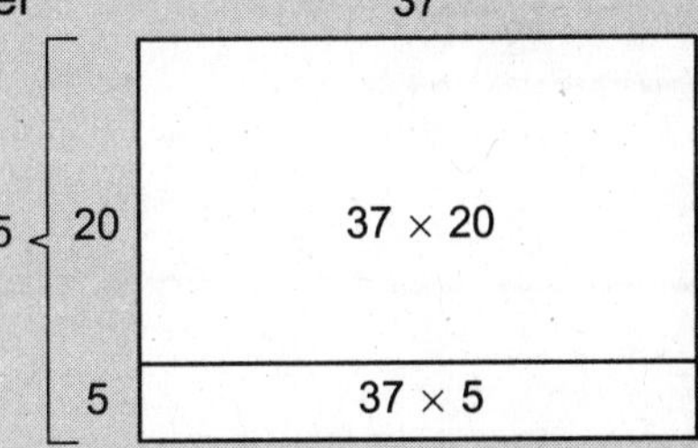

Step 1: Calculate 37 × 5

Step 2: Calculate 37 × 20

Step 3: Add the results

9. Practise Step 1.

a) 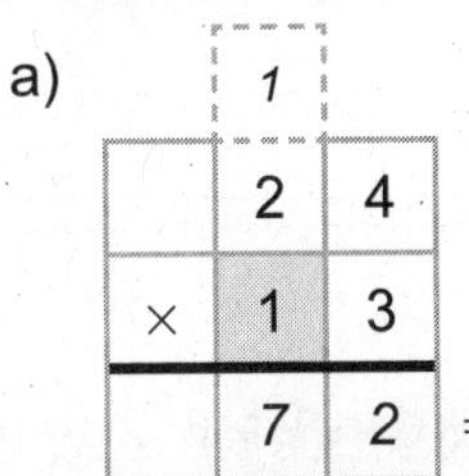

b) 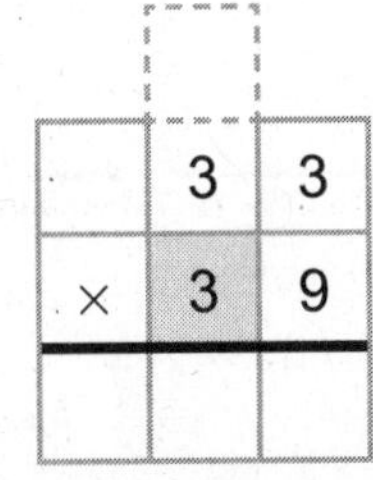

c) 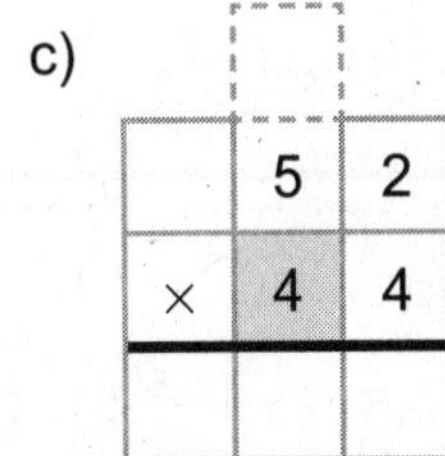

d) 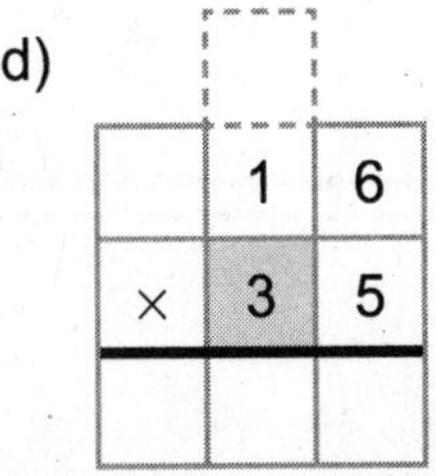

NS7-6 Long Multiplication *(continued)*

10. Practise Step 2.

a) 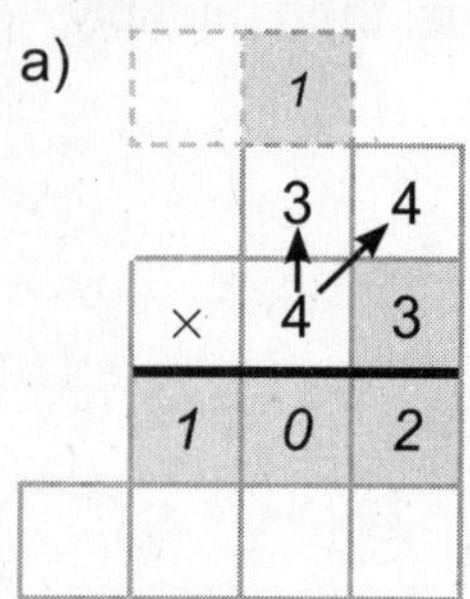
= 34 × 40

b) 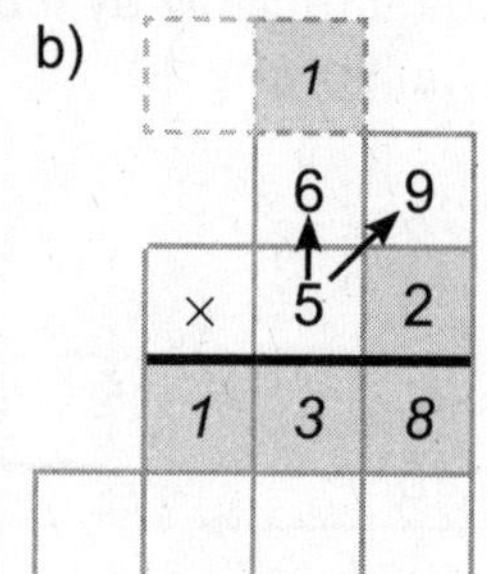

c)

d) 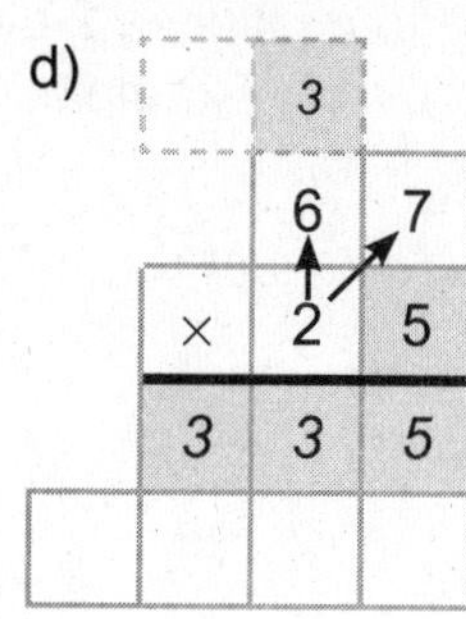

11. Practise Steps 1 and 2.

a) 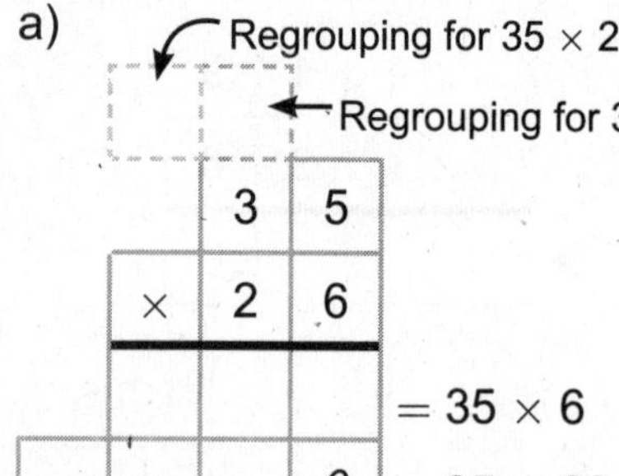

b) 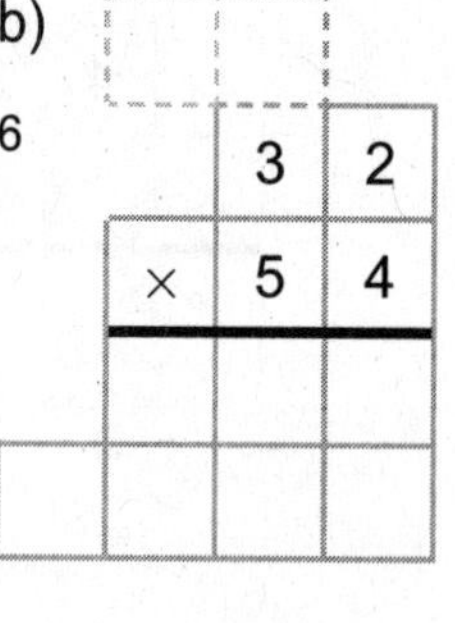

c) 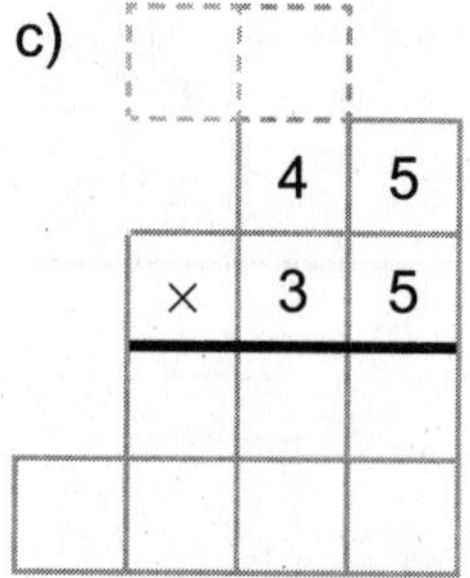

d) 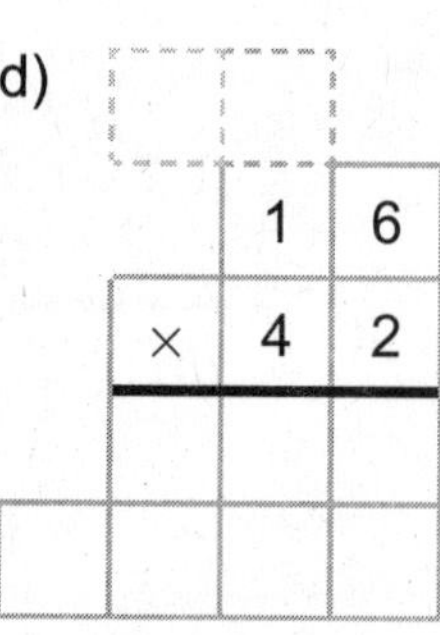

12. Complete the multiplication by adding the numbers in the last two rows of the chart.

a) 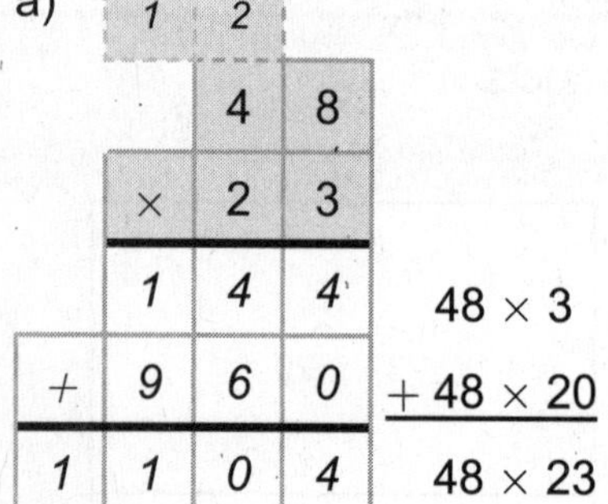

b)

c)

d)

13. Multiply.

a) b) c) d) e)

f) 35 × 23 g) 64 × 51 h) 25 × 43 i) 12 × 87 **BONUS ▶** 652 × 473

UNIT 2

Patterns and Algebra 1

PA7-1 Extending Patterns

1. These sequences were made by adding the same number to each term. Find the number, then extend the pattern.

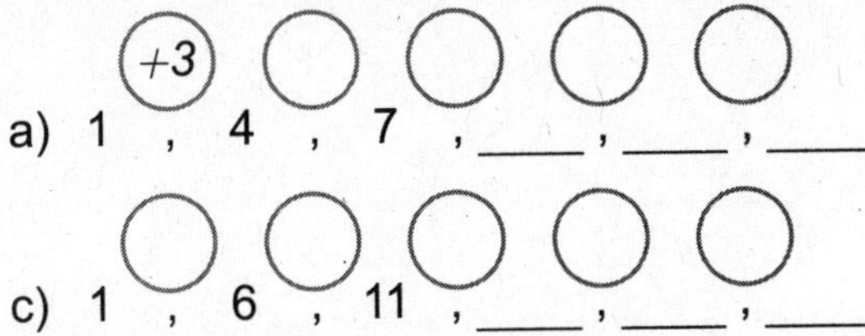

a) 1 , 4 , 7 , ____, ____, ____

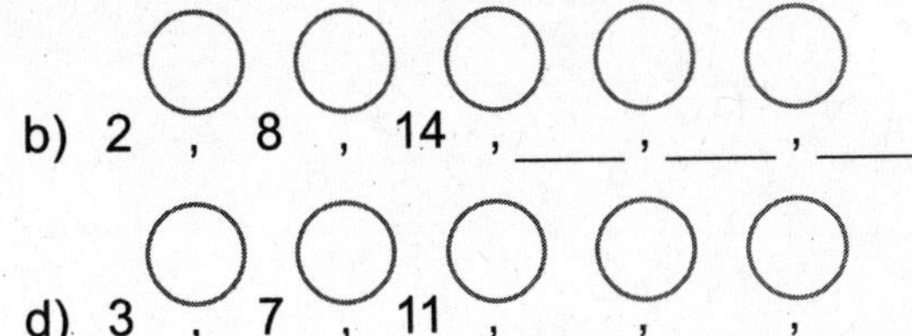

b) 2 , 8 , 14 , ____, ____, ____

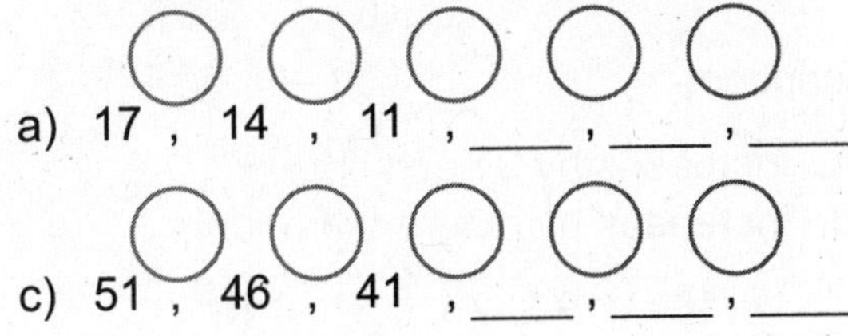

c) 1 , 6 , 11 , ____, ____, ____

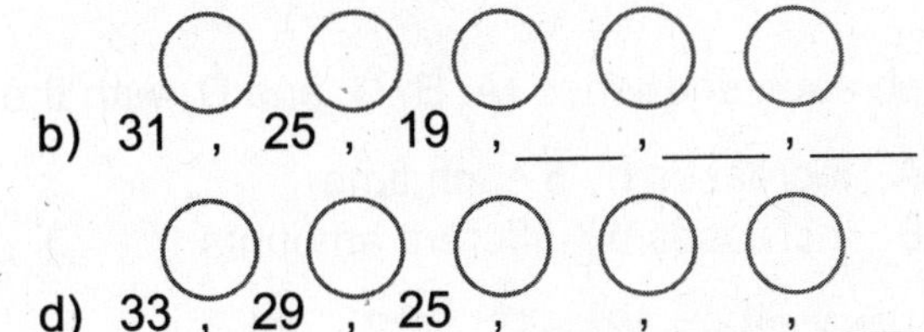

d) 3 , 7 , 11 , ____, ____, ____

2. These sequences were made by subtracting the same number from each term. Find the number, then extend the pattern.

a) 17 , 14 , 11 , ____, ____, ____

b) 31 , 25 , 19 , ____, ____, ____

c) 51 , 46 , 41 , ____, ____, ____

d) 33 , 29 , 25 , ____, ____, ____

3. Find the numbers that are added or subtracted, then extend the pattern. Write a plus sign (+) if you add the number and a minus sign (−) if you subtract the number.

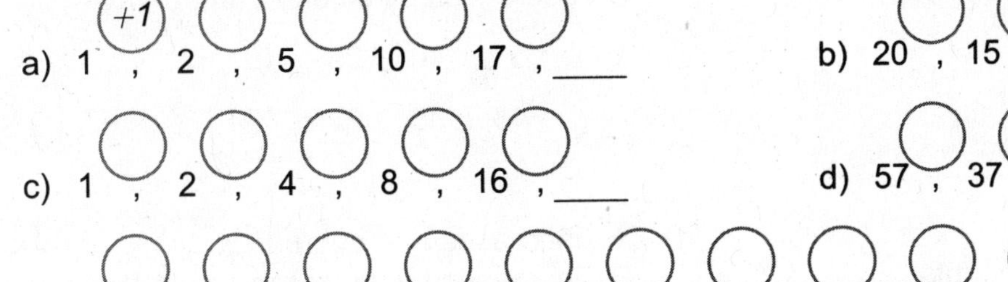

a) 1 , 2 , 5 , 10 , 17 , ____

b) 20 , 15 , 11 , 8 , 6 , ____

c) 1 , 2 , 4 , 8 , 16 , ____

d) 57 , 37 , 22 , 12 , 7 , ____

e) 1 , 1 , 2 , 3 , 5 , 8 , 13 , 21 , 34 , ____, ____, ____

4. The sequence in Question 3e) is called the **Fibonacci sequence**.

How can you get each term from the previous two terms? ________________________________

____.

5. Find the gaps between the gaps and extend the patterns.

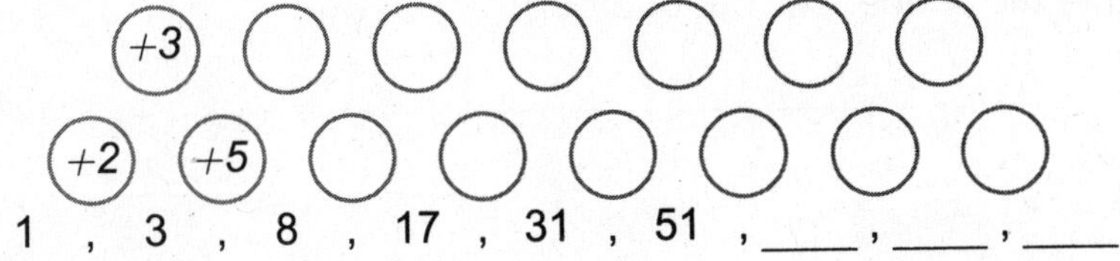

1 , 3 , 8 , 17 , 31 , 51 , ____, ____, ____

PA7-2 Describing Patterns

1. Write the amount by which each term in the sequence increases (goes up) or decreases (goes down). Use a plus sign (+) if the sequence increases and a minus sign (–) if it decreases.

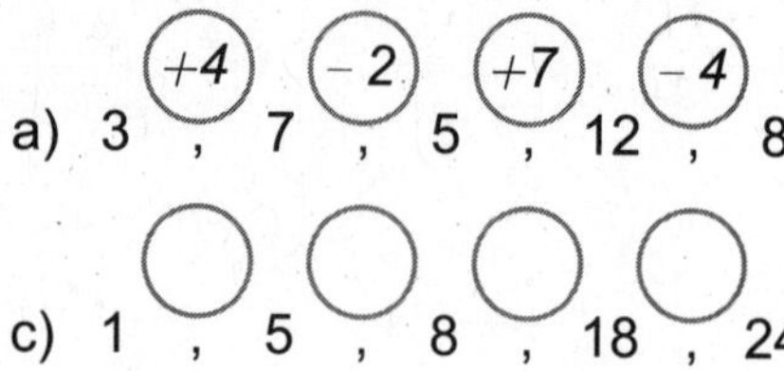

a) 3 (+4) 7 (–2) 5 (+7) 12 (–4) 8

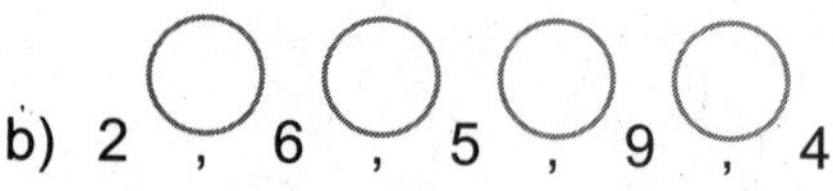

b) 2 , 6 , 5 , 9 , 4

c) 1 , 5 , 8 , 18 , 24

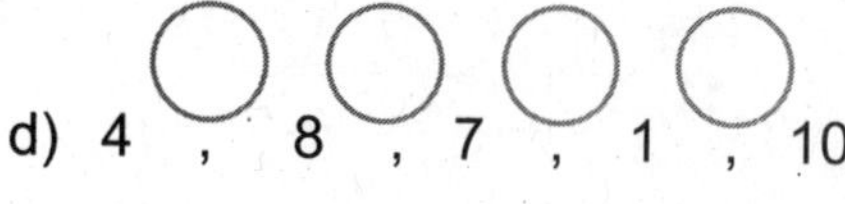

d) 4 , 8 , 7 , 1 , 10

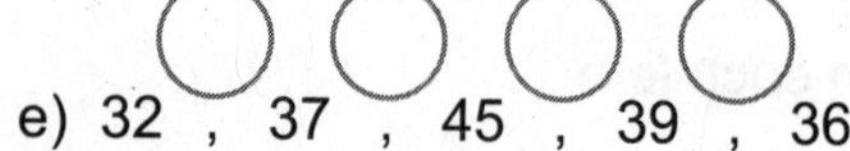

e) 32 , 37 , 45 , 39 , 36

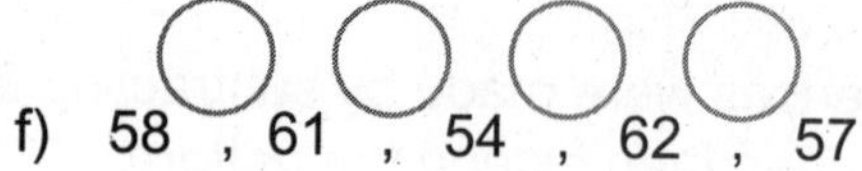

f) 58 , 61 , 54 , 62 , 57

2. Match each sequence (A, B, C, and D) with the correct description.

a) A. increases by 5 each time
B. increases by different amounts

_B_ 8 , 12 , 18 , 22 , 24

_A_ 7 , 12 , 17 , 22 , 27

b) A. increases by 9 each time
B. increases by different amounts

____ 10 , 19 , 28 , 37 , 46

____ 6 , 13 , 18 , 26 , 31

c) A. decreases by different amounts
B. decreases by the same amount

____ 21 , 20 , 18 , 15 , 11

____ 13 , 10 , 7 , 4 , 1

d) A. decreases by 11 each time
B. decreases by different amounts

____ 51 , 40 , 29 , 18 , 7

____ 48 , 35 , 22 , 15 , 3

e) A. increases by 5 each time
B. decreases by different amounts
C. increases by different amounts

____ 18 , 23 , 29 , 33 , 35

____ 27 , 24 , 20 , 19 , 16

____ 24 , 29 , 34 , 39 , 44

f) A. increases and decreases
B. increases by the same amount
C. decreases by different amounts
D. decreases by the same amount

____ 31 , 29 , 25 , 13 , 9

____ 10 , 14 , 9 , 6 , 5

____ 18 , 16 , 14 , 12 , 10

____ 8 , 11 , 14 , 17 , 20

3. Make 3 sequences that match the descriptions. Ask a partner to match each sequence with the correct description. (Write the sequences out of order!)

A. increases by 4 each time ____ ______________________

B. decreases by different amounts ____ ______________________

C. increases and decreases ____ ______________________

PA7-2 Describing Patterns *(continued)*

4. These sequences were made by multiplying each term by the same number. Find the number, then extend the pattern.

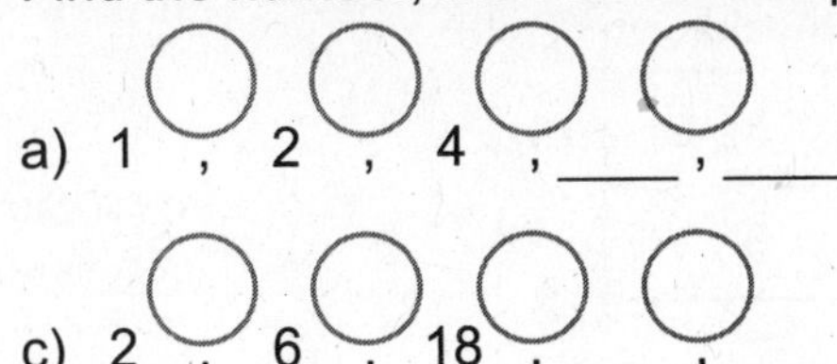

a) 1 , 2 , 4 , ____ , ____

c) 2 , 6 , 18 , ____ , ____

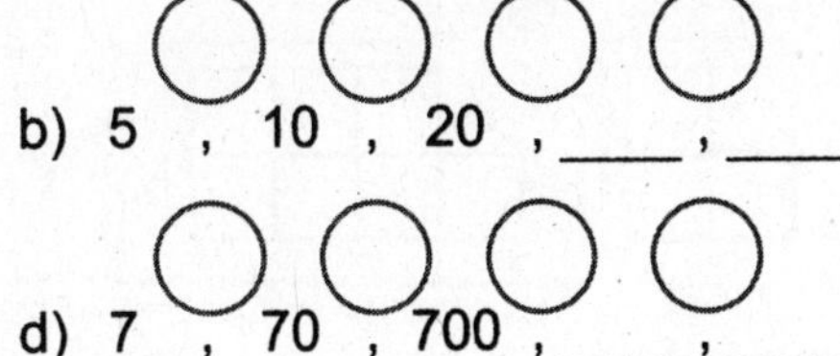

b) 5 , 10 , 20 , ____ , ____

d) 7 , 70 , 700 , ____ , ____

5. These sequences were made by dividing each term by the same number. Find the number, then extend the pattern.

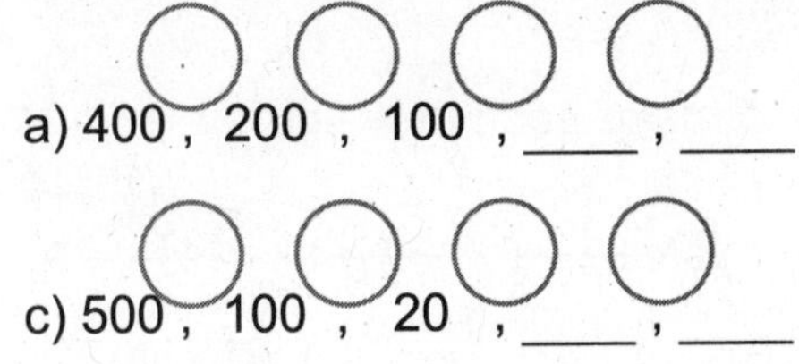

a) 400 , 200 , 100 , ____ , ____

c) 500 , 100 , 20 , ____ , ____

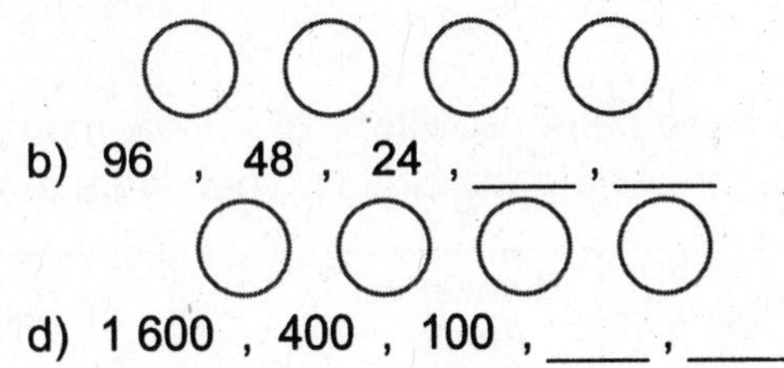

b) 96 , 48 , 24 , ____ , ____

d) 1 600 , 400 , 100 , ____ , ____

6. Write a rule for each pattern. Use the words **add**, **subtract**, **multiply**, or **divide**.

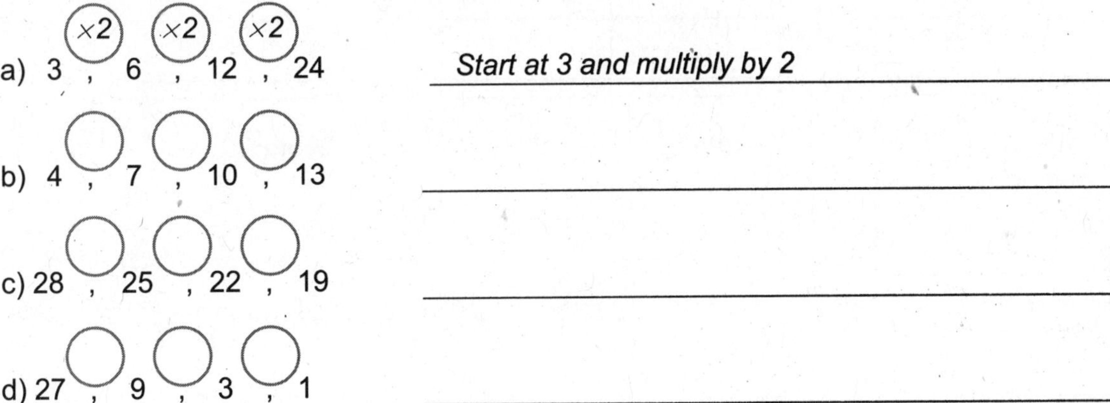

a) 3 , 6 , 12 , 24 (×2, ×2, ×2) *Start at 3 and multiply by 2*

b) 4 , 7 , 10 , 13 ____________________

c) 28 , 25 , 22 , 19 ____________________

d) 27 , 9 , 3 , 1 ____________________

e) 2, 10, 50, 250 f) 32, 16, 8, 4 g) 30 000, 3 000, 300, 30 h) 10, 200, 4 000, 80 000

7. Describe each pattern as **increasing, decreasing,** or **repeating**.

a) 2 , 4 , 8 , 16 , 32 , 64 ____________ b) 3 , 7 , 1 , 3 , 7 , 1 ____________

c) 29 , 27 , 25 , 23 , 22 ____________ d) 2 , 6 , 10 , 14 , 17 ____________

e) 11 , 9 , 6 , 11 , 9 , 6 ____________ f) 61 , 56 , 51 , 46 , 41 ____________

8. Write the rule for each repeating pattern.

a) 3, 7, 1, 3, 7, 1 *3, 7, 1, then repeat* b) 0, 5, 0, 5, 0, 5 ____________

c) 11, 9, 6, 11, 9, 6 ____________ d) M, M, N, M, M, N ____________

PA7-3 T-tables

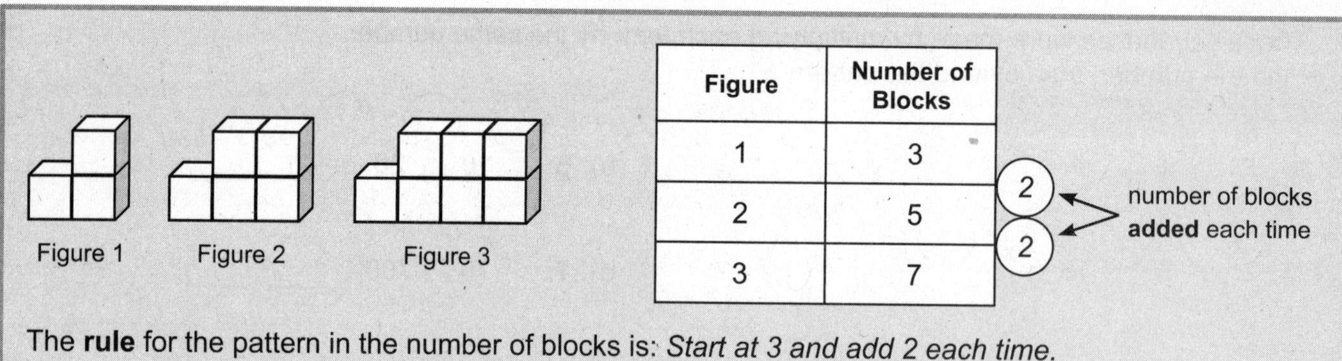

Figure	Number of Blocks
1	3
2	5
3	7

The **rule** for the pattern in the number of blocks is: *Start at 3 and add 2 each time.*

1. Here are more patterns with blocks. How many blocks do you add to make each new figure? Write your answer in the circles. Then write a rule for the pattern.

a)

Figure	Number of Blocks
1	3
2	7
3	11

Rule: *Start at* ____ *and add* ____.

b)

Figure	Number of Blocks
1	2
2	6
3	10

Rule:

c)

Figure	Number of Blocks
1	2
2	4
3	6

Rule:

d)

Figure	Number of Blocks
1	1
2	6
3	11

Rule:

e)

Figure	Number of Blocks
1	5
2	9
3	13

Rule:

f)

Figure	Number of Blocks
1	12
2	18
3	24

Rule:

PA7-3 T-tables *(continued)*

2. Extend the pattern. How many blocks would be used in Figure 6?

a)

Figure	Number of Blocks
1	2
2	7
3	12

b)

Figure	Number of Blocks
1	4
2	7
3	10

c)

Figure	Number of Blocks
1	3
2	8
3	13

3. Amy makes an increasing pattern with blocks. After making the 3rd figure, she has only 14 blocks left. Does she have enough blocks to complete the 4th figure?

a)

Figure	Number of Blocks
1	8
2	10
3	12

Yes No

b)

Figure	Number of Blocks
1	7
2	10
3	13

Yes No

c)

Figure	Number of Blocks
1	1
2	5
3	9

Yes No

4. Make a table to show how many squares are needed to make the 5th figure in each pattern.

a)

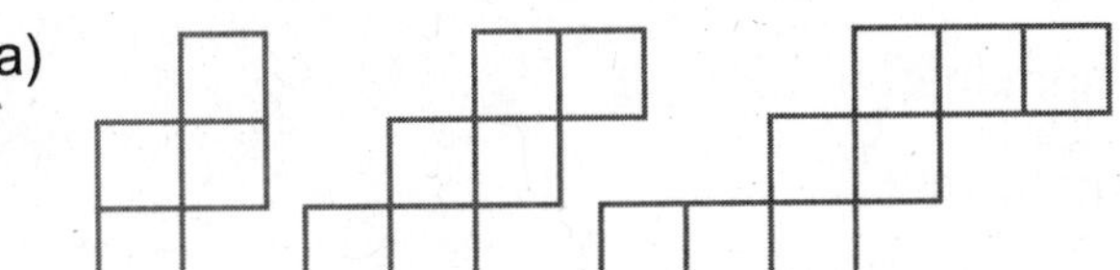

b)

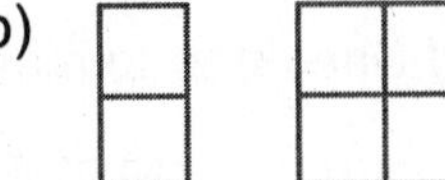

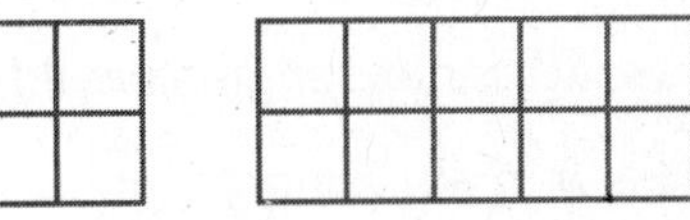

5. Claude buys a plant that is 12 cm high. After 1 week, it is 17 cm high. After 2 weeks it is 22 cm high.

a) How much does the plant grow each week?

____

b) How high will it be after 3 weeks?

____

c) After how many weeks will the plant be 42 cm high?

____

Weeks	Height of Plant (cm)
0	12
1	17
2	22

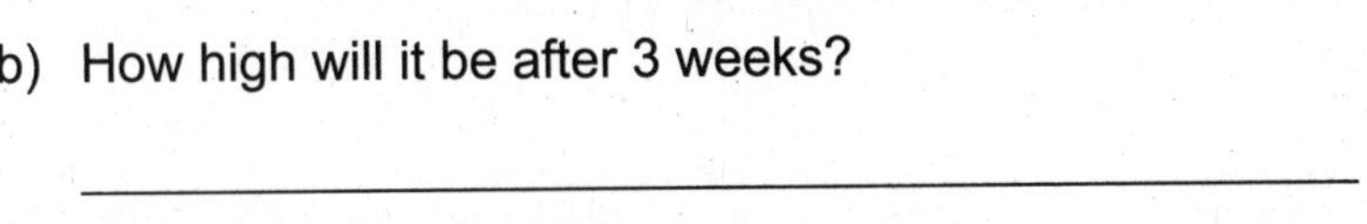

PA7-3 T-tables *(continued)*

6. Claude's fish tank is leaking. At 6 p.m., there are 24 L of water in the tank. At 7 p.m., there are 20 L and at 8 p.m. there are 16 L.

   a) How many litres of water leak out each hour?

   ____

   b) How many litres will be left in the tank at 10 p.m.?

   ____

   c) How many hours will it take for all the water to leak out?

   ____

Time	Amount of Water in the Tank (L)
6 p.m.	24
7 p.m.	20
8 p.m.	16
9 p.m.	
10 p.m.	

7. The snow is 19 cm deep at 4 p.m. Snow falls at a rate of 5 cm per hour. How deep is the snow at 8 p.m.?

8. A marina rents sailboats at a rate of $8 for the first hour and $4 for every hour after that. How much does it cost to rent a sailboat for 5 hours?

9. Use a table of values to find out how many toothpicks will be required to make the 5th figure in each pattern.

   a) b)

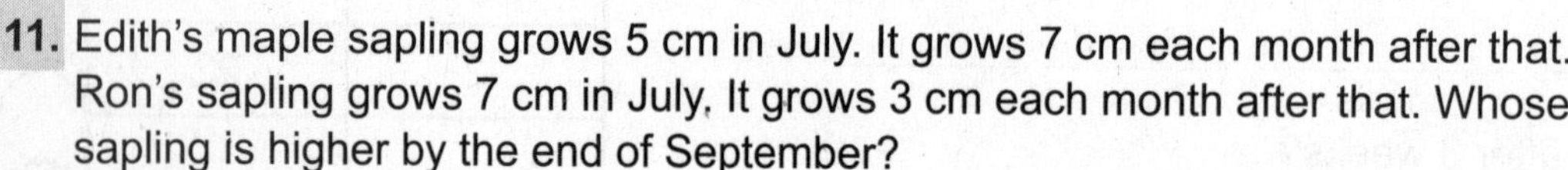

10. Sue makes an ornament using a hexagon (the white figure), rhombuses (the striped figures), triangles, and squares.

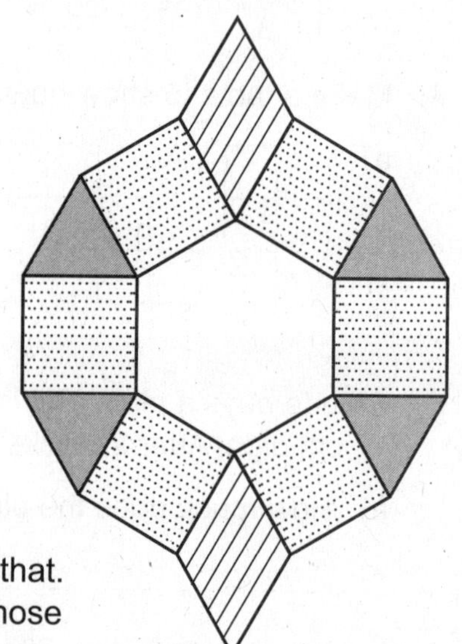

   a) How many triangles would Sue need to make 9 ornaments?

   b) How many squares would Sue need to make 6 ornaments?

   c) Sue used 4 hexagons to make ornaments. How many rhombuses and how many triangles did she use?

   d) How many triangles would Sue need to make ornaments with 12 rhombuses?

11. Edith's maple sapling grows 5 cm in July. It grows 7 cm each month after that. Ron's sapling grows 7 cm in July. It grows 3 cm each month after that. Whose sapling is higher by the end of September?

12. Wang has $79 and spends $3 per week. Kam has $84 and spends $4 per week. How many weeks will it take for them to have the same amount left?

PA7-4 Constant Rates

A **variable** is a letter or symbol (such as x, n, or h) that represents a number. An **algebraic expression** is a combination of one or more variables that may include numbers and operation signs.

Examples of algebraic expressions: $5 \times t + 7$ $n \div 5$ $3 + z + 5y$

1. Make your own example of an algebraic expression. ______

In the product of a number and a variable, the multiplication sign is usually dropped.

Example: $3 \times t$ and $t \times 3$ are both written as $3t$.

2. Write these expressions without multiplication signs.

a) $3 \times s =$ $3s$ b) $n \times 5 + 2 =$ $5n + 2$ c) $12 - 4 \times r =$ ______

d) $7 \times a - 3 =$ ______ e) $b \times 4 - 3 =$ ______ f) $5 + 6 \times w =$ ______

3. Write these expressions with multiplication signs.

a) $3h =$ $3 \times h$ b) $2 - 3g =$ ______ c) $3f + 4 =$ ______

d) $5 + 7t =$ ______ e) $7a - 4 =$ ______ f) $3x + 4y =$ ______

4. It costs \$3 per hour to rent a pair of skates. Write a numeric expression for the cost of renting skates for…

a) 2 hours: 3 2 b) 5 hours: ______ c) 6 hours: ______

5. It costs \$5 per hour to rent a pair of skis. Write an algebraic expression for the cost of renting skis for…

a) h hours: $5 \times h$ or $5h$ b) t hours: ______ or ______ c) x hours: ______ or ______

6. Write an expression for the distance a car would travel at…

a) Speed: 60 km per hour
Time: 2 hours
Distance: 60×2 km

b) Speed: 80 km per hour
Time: 3 hours
Distance: ______ km

c) Speed: 70 km per hour
Time: 5 hours
Distance: ______ km

7. A car is travelling at a speed of 70 km per hour. Write an algebraic expression for the distance it would travel in...

a) h hours: $70h$ km b) t hours: ______ km c) z hours: ______ km

PA7-4 Constant Rates *(continued)*

A **flat fee** is a fixed charge that does not depend on how long you rent an item.

Example: It costs a flat fee of \$7 to rent a boat, plus \$3 for each hour you use the boat.

8. Write an expression for the amount you would pay to rent a boat for…

a) 2 hours
Flat fee: \$9
Hourly rate: \$5 per hour
$2 \times 5 + 9$

b) 3 hours
Flat fee: \$4
Hourly rate: \$6 per hour
____

c) 7 hours
Flat fee: \$5
Hourly rate: \$4 per hour
____

d) *h* hours
Flat fee: \$5
Hourly rate: \$4
$4h + 5$

e) *t* hours
Flat fee: \$8
Hourly rate: \$3
____

f) *w* hours
Flat fee: \$6
Hourly rate: \$5
____

9. Match the fee for renting a windsurf board (left) to the correct algebraic expression (right).

A \$15 flat fee and \$7 for each hour — $15h + 7$

\$15 for each hour, no flat fee — $7h + 15$

A \$7 flat fee and \$15 for each hour — $15h$

10. Underline the variable — the quantity that changes. Then write an expression for each cost. Use *n* for the variable.

	Cost (\$)
a) Umbrellas are on sale for \$2 each.	$2n$
b) A copy shop charges \$0.79 for each copy.	
c) A bus company charges a \$10 flat fee plus \$5 per passenger.	
d) A boat company charges a \$20 flat fee plus \$7 per passenger.	

11. Sara has \$*n*. How much money, in dollars, will she have if her mother gives her…

a) \$7 $n + 7$ b) \$5 __________ c) \$12 __________ d) \$31 __________

12. Sara has \$5 ($n =$ \$5). Replace *n* with 5 in Question 11 to calculate Sara's money in dollars.

a) $5 + 7 = 12$ b) c) d)

PA7-4 Constant Rates *(continued)*

13. Socks cost \$2 per pair. The cost of n pairs is \$$2n$.

John says that the cost of 6 pairs is \$26 and the cost of 7 pairs is \$27.

Is this correct? ______ What did John do wrong? ____________________

____

When replacing a variable with a number, we use brackets.

Example: 3(7) is another way to write 3×7.

14. Write the number 2 in the brackets and evaluate.

a) $5(\ 2\ ) = \underline{\ 5 \times 2\ } = \underline{\ 10\ }$　b) $3(\quad) =$ ______ = ____　c) $4(\quad) =$ ______ = ____

d) $2(\quad) + 5$ = ______ = ______

e) $4(\quad) - 2$ = ______ = ______

f) $6(\quad) + 3$ = ______ = ______

15. Replace n with 2 in each expression.

a) $4n + 3$

$4(2) + 3$

$= 8 + 3$

$= 11$

b) $5n + 1$

c) $3n - 2$

d) $2n + 3$

16. A company charges a \$6 flat fee to rent a pair of skis plus \$3 for each hour you use the skis. The total is given by the expression $3h + 6$. Find the cost of renting a pair of skis for…

a) 4 hours

$3(4) + 6$

$= 12 + 6$

$= 18$

b) 2 hours

c) 5 hours

d) 7 hours

17. Replace the variable with the given value and evaluate — this is called **substitution**.

a) $5h + 2,\ \ h = 3$

$5(3) + 2$

$= 15 + 2$

$= 17$

b) $2n + 3,\ \ n = 6$

c) $5t - 2,\ \ t = 4$

d) $3m + 9,\ \ m = 8$

e) $9 - 2z,\ \ z = 4$

f) $3n + 2,\ \ n = 5$

PA7-4 Constant Rates *(continued)*

18. Evaluate each expression.

a) $2n + 3$, $n = 5$

$2(5) + 3$

$= 10 + 3 = 13$

b) $2t + 3$, $t = 5$

c) $2w + 3$, $w = 5$

19. What do you notice about your answers to Question 18? ____________________

Why is that so? ____________________

20. Evaluate each expression.

a) $2x + 7$, $x = 6$

b) $7 + 2x$, $x = 6$

21. What do you notice about your answers to Question 20? ____________________

Why is that so? ____________________

22. Circle all the expressions that mean the same thing as $4n + 7$.

$7 + 4n$	$7n + 4$	$4m + 7$	$7t + 4$
$7 + 4w$	$7 + 4 \times p$	$4 + 7s$	$n \times 4 + 7$

23. Sandwiches cost \$3 and drinks \$2. The cost of s sandwiches and d drinks is: $3s + 2d$.

Find the cost of the following items.

a) 5 sandwiches and 4 drinks

$3s + 2d = 3(5) + 2(4)$

$= 15 + 8$

$= 23$

The cost is \$23

b) 6 sandwiches and 6 drinks

The cost is ______

c) 2 sandwiches and 7 drinks

The cost is ______

24. A company charges a \$5 flat fee to rent a bike plus \$8 for each hour you use the bike.

a) Write an expression for the cost of renting a bike for h hours.

b) Sara has \$61. How many hours can she rent the bike for? (Can you write an equation to help you solve the problem?)

PA7-5 Solving Equations — Guess and Check

1. a) Calculate $x + 3$ for each value of x.

x	0	1	2	3	4	5	6	7	8	9	10
$x + 3$	3	4									

b) In each equation below, only one value of x will make the equation true. Find the value of x that will make the equation true.

i) $x + 3 = 10$ ii) $x + 3 = 4$ iii) $x + 3 = 12$ iv) $x + 3 = 7$ v) $x + 3 = 3$

$x =$ 7 $x =$ ____ $x =$ ____ $x =$ ____ $x =$ ____

Finding the value of a variable that makes an equation true is called **solving for the variable.** In Question 1, you **solved for *x*.**

2. a) Calculate $3n$ ($= 3 \times n$) and $3n - 5$ for each value of n.

n	2	3	4	5	6	7	8	9	10	11	12
$3n$	6	9	12								
$3n - 5$	1	4	7								

b) Solve for n.

i) $3n - 5 = 16$ ii) $3n - 5 = 25$ iii) $3n - 5 = 10$ iv) $3n - 5 = 31$

$n =$ ____ $n =$ ____ $n =$ ____ $n =$ ____

3. Substitute $n = 5$ into the expression on the left side of the equation. Does n need to be **greater than**, **less than**, or **equal to** 5 to make the equation true?

a) $3n + 2 = 20$

$3(5) + 2 =$ 17 is less than 20.

So n should be greater than 5.

b) $5n + 6 = 26$

$5(5) + 6 =$ ____ is ____ 26.

So n should be ____ 5.

c) $2n + 3 = 13$

$2(5) + 3 =$ ____ is ____ 13.

So n should be ____ 5.

d) $4n + 3 = 27$

$4(5) + 3 =$ ____ is ____ 27.

So n should be ____ 5.

4. Solve for n by guessing small values for n, checking, and revising. Do your rough work in your notebook.

a) $3n + 2 = 8$ b) $5n - 2 = 13$ c) $4n - 1 = 15$ d) $6n - 5 = 31$

$n =$ ____ $n =$ ____ $n =$ ____ $n =$ ____

e) $7n - 2 = 19$ f) $2n + 3 = 9$ g) $3n + 5 = 14$ h) $2n - 5 = 3$

$n =$ ____ $n =$ ____ $n =$ ____ $n =$ ____

PA7-5 Solving Equations — Guess and Check *(continued)*

5. Sara solves $7x + 11 = 67$ and gets $x = 8$.

a) Verify Sara's answer.

b) What value for t solves $7t + 11 = 67$? ______

c) What value for x solves $11 + 7x = 67$?

How do you know? ______

d) What value for x solves $67 = 7x + 11$? ______

How do you know? ______

6. Circle the equations that mean the same thing as $8x + 3 = 51$.

$3 + 8x = 51$	$8t + 3 = 51$	$3w + 8 = 51$	$8 + 3x = 51$
$51 = 3 + 8x$	$51 = 8w + 3$	$r \times 8 + 3 = 51$	$51 = 3 + 8t$
$3 + 8r = 51$	$51 + 8r = 3$	$8z + 3 = 51$	$8z + 51 = 3$

7. Solve these equations by guessing, checking, and revising. Do your rough work in your notebook.

a) $3t + 4 = 13$ $t =$ ______	b) $4h + 5 = 13$ $h =$ ______	c) $2w + 9 = 17$ $w =$ ______	d) $10p = 30$ $p =$ ______
e) $2 + 7x = 23$ $x =$ ______	f) $3 + 5x = 38$ $x =$ ______	g) $8 + 2x = 26$ $x =$ ______	h) $5 + 3n = 20$ $n =$ ______
i) $10 = 3x + 1$ $x =$ ______	j) $15 = 4x - 1$ $x =$ ______	k) $20 = 4x$ $x =$ ______	l) $32 = 5w + 2$ $w =$ ______
m) $3 + 5x = 18$ $x =$ ______	n) $23 = 7u + 2$ $u =$ ______	o) $7u + 5 = 40$ $u =$ ______	p) $30 = 3 + 9n$ $n =$ ______

8. Find another equation from Question 7 that means the same thing as the equation in part e).

BONUS▶ Solve for x and y: $2x + 1 = 7 = 4y - 1$

PA7-6 Modelling Equations

1. Each bag contains the same unknown number of apples. Let x stand for the number of apples in one bag. Write a mathematical expression for the total number of apples.

a) 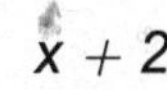

$x + 2$ ________

b) 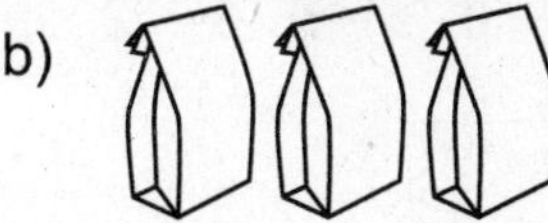

____

c) 

____

2. Write an **expression** for the total number of apples. Write an **equation** by making the expression equal to the total number of apples.

a) There are **7 apples** in total.

Expression $x + 2$

Equation $x + 2 = 7$

b) There are **10 apples** in total.

Expression ________

Equation ________

c) There are **15 apples** in total.

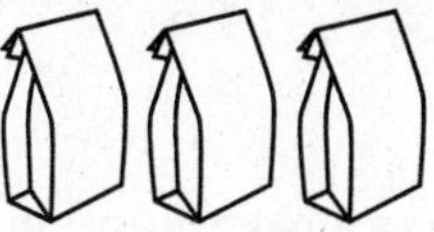

Expression ________

Equation ________

3. Write an equation and find the number of apples in each bag.

a) 10 apples in total

b) 13 apples in total

c) 17 apples in total

d) 11 apples in total

e) 14 apples in total

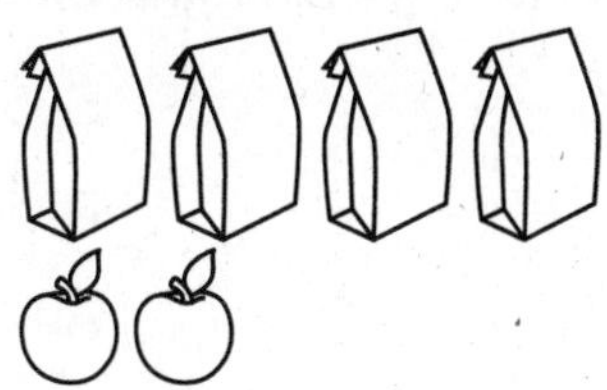

f) 31 apples in total

4. Solve each equation for x by guessing and checking, then draw a model to verify your answer.

a) $3x + 4 = 19$

b) $2x + 5 = 13$ c) $4x + 2 = 14$ d) $3x + 8 = 14$ e) $5x + 2 = 27$ f) $4x + 3 = 15$

5. Does this type of model work for the equation $3x - 4 = 14$? ______. Explain in your notebook.

PA7-7 Solving Equations — Preserving Equality

1. Write the number that makes each equation true.

a) $8 + 4 - \square = 8$ b) $8 \times 3 \div \square = 8$ c) $8 \div 2 \times \square = 8$ d) $8 - 5 + \square = 8$

e) $12 \div 4 \times \square = 12$ f) $13 - 6 + \square = 13$ g) $3 \times 5 \div \square = 3$ h) $19 + 3 - \square = 19$

2. Write the operation that makes each equation true.

a) $7 + 2 \bigcirc 2 = 7$ b) $8 \times 3 \bigcirc 3 = 8$ c) $12 \div 2 \bigcirc 2 = 12$ d) $15 - 4 \bigcirc 4 = 15$

e) $18 \div 3 \bigcirc 3 = 18$ f) $8 - 2 \bigcirc 2 = 8$ g) $5 \times 3 \bigcirc 3 = 5$ h) $6 + 4 \bigcirc 4 = 6$

3. Write the operation and number that make each equation true.

a) $17 + 3$ *−3* $= 17$ b) $20 \div 4$ ______ $= 20$ c) 18×2 ______ $= 18$

d) $11 - 4$ ______ $= 11$ e) 4×3 ______ $= 4$ f) $15 + 2$ ______ $= 15$

g) 15×2 ______ $= 15$ h) $5 + 3$ ______ $= 5$ i) 5×3 ______ $= 5$

j) $6 \div 2$ ______ $= 6$ k) 6×2 ______ $= 6$ l) $6 - 2$ ______ $= 6$

4. How could you undo each operation and get back to the number you started with?

a) add 4 *subtract 4* b) multiply by 3 ______

c) divide by 2 ______ d) subtract 7 ______

5. Start with the number 3. Do the operations and then undo them in backwards order.

Add 7.	*10*	Subtract 7.	______
Multiply by 2.	*20*	Divide by 2.	______
Subtract 5.	______	Add 5.	______
Divide by 3.	______ →	Multiply by 3.	______

Did you finish with the number you started with? ______

6. Start with the number 11. Do the operations and then undo them in backwards order.

Add 4.	*15*	______	______
Divide by 3.	______	______	______
Subtract 1.	______	______	______
Multiply by 4.	______ →	*Divide by 4.*	______

Did you finish with the number you started with? ______

PA7-7 Solving Equations — Preserving Equality *(continued)*

Remember: The variable x represents a number, so you can treat it like a number.

Operation	Result	Operation	Result
Add 3 to x	$x + 3$	Multiply 3 by x	$3 \times x = 3x$
Add x to 3	$3 + x$	Multiply x by 3	$x \times 3 = 3x$
Subtract 3 from x	$x - 3$	Divide x by 3	$x \div 3$
Subtract x from 3	$3 - x$	Divide 3 by x	$3 \div x$

7. Show the result of each operation.

a) Multiply x by 7 ___*7x*___ b) Add 4 to x ___*x + 4*___ c) Subtract 5 from x ______

d) Subtract x from 5 ______ e) Divide x by 10 ______ f) Divide 9 by x ______

g) Multiply 8 by x ______ h) Add x to 9 ______ **BONUS▶** Add x to y ______

8. What happens to the variable x?

a) $2x$ ___*Multiply by 2.*___ b) $3x$ ______ c) $x + 4$ ______

d) $x - 5$ ______ e) $x \div 3$ ______ f) $6 \div x$ ______

g) $4 - x$ ______ **BONUS▶** $x + x$ ______

9. Start with the variable. Write the correct operation and number to get back where you started.

a) $n + 3$ ___*− 3*___ $= n$ b) $n \times 3$ ______ $= n$ c) $5m$ ______ $= m$

d) $x - 5$ ______ $= x$ e) $x + 7$ ______ $= x$ f) $x - 14$ ______ $= x$

g) $z \div 5$ ______ $= z$ h) $7y$ ______ $= y$ i) $r + 8$ ______ $= r$

j) $x + 4$ ______ $= x$ k) $6x$ ______ $= x$ l) $x + 7 - 3$ ______ $= x$

10. Circle the expressions that get you back to m.

$7m - 7$ $7m \div 7$ $m \div 7 \times 7$ $7 \div m \times 7$ $7 + m - 7$ $7 - m + 7$

11. Solve for x by doing the same thing to both sides of the equation. Check your answer.

a) $3x = \mathbf{12}$

$3x \div 3 = 12 \div 3$

$x = 4$

Check by replacing x with your answer:
$3(4) = 12$ ✓

b) $x - 4 = \mathbf{11}$

c) $4x = 20$ d) $3 + x = 9$ e) $x + 5 = 8$

f) $x \div 6 = 3$ g) $5x = 15$ h) $x - 7 = 10$

i) $2x = 18$ j) $x \div 2 = 3$ k) $x + 1 = 20$

l) $10x = 90$ m) $9x = 54$ n) $x + 26 = 53$

PA7-8 Solving Equations — Two Operations

1. Jason does some operations to the secret number x. He gets 37 every time. Write an equation and then work backwards to find x.

a) **Jason's operations**

Start with x. x

Multiply by 5. $5x$

Add 7. $5x + 7$

The answer is 37. $5x + 7 = 37$

Work backwards to find x

Write the equation again. $5x + 7 = 37$

Undo adding 7 by subtracting 7. $5x + 7 - 7 = 37 - 7$

Write the new equation. $5x = 30$

Undo multiplying by 5 by dividing by 5. $5x \div 5 = 30 \div 5$

Write the new equation. $x = 6$

You solved for x!

Check your answer by doing the operations in order, the way Jason did them.

Start with your answer: 6 Multiply by 5: 30 Add 7: 37 Do you get 37? Yes

b) **Jason's operations**

Start with x. x

Multiply by 8. ______

Add 5. ______

The answer is 37. ______

Work backwards to find x

Write the equation again. ______

Undo adding 5 by subtracting 5. ______

Write the new equation. ______

Undo multiplying by 8 by dividing by 8. ______

Write the new equation. ______

You solved for x!

Check your answer by doing the operations in order, the way Jason did them.

Start with your answer: ______ Multiply by 8: ______ Add 5: ______ Do you get 37? ______

c) **Jason's operations**

Start with x. x

Multiply by 4. ______

Subtract 3. ______

The answer is 37. ______

Work backwards to find x

Write the equation again. ______

Undo subtracting 3 by adding 3. ______

Write the new equation. ______

Undo multiplying by 4 by dividing by 4. ______

Write the new equation. ______

You solved for x!

Check your answer by doing the operations in order, the way Jason did them.

Start with your answer: ______ Multiply by 4: ______ Subtract 3: ______ Do you get 37? ______

PA7-8 Solving Equations — Two Operations *(continued)*

2. Solve for the variable by undoing each operation in the equation.

a) $8x + 3 = 27$

$8x + 3 - 3 =$ 27 − 3

$8x =$ ______

$8x \div 8 =$ ______ ÷ ______

$x =$ ______

b) $4h - 3 = 37$

$4h - 3 + 3 = 37 +$ ______

$4h =$ ______

$4h \div 4 =$ ______ ÷ ______

$h =$ ______

c) $3s - 4 = 29$ d) $2t + 3 = 11$ e) $2m - 7 = 13$ f) $5a + 2 = 47$

g) $4z + 3 = 19$ h) $7w - 2 = 26$ i) $8x + 3 = 3$ j) $9r - 3 = 6$

3. A store charges you $3 per hour to rent a pair of roller blades.

a) Write an expression for the cost of renting the roller blades. Use *h* for hours. ______

b) Mary rented the roller blades for 4 hours. How much did she pay? ______

c) Sue paid $15 to rent the roller blades. How many hours did she rent the roller blades for? ______

4. Kim has $36 in savings. She earns $9 an hour. She saves all the money she makes.

a) Write an expression for the amount Kim will have saved after working *h* hours.

b) How much will she have saved after working 3 hours?

c) How many hours does she have to work to buy a shirt that costs $90?

5. a) In which part of Question 4 did you **substitute** for *h*? ______

b) In which part of Question 4 did you **solve** for *h*? ______

6.

	Company A	Company B	Company C
Rental fee for boat	$100	$120	$70
Fee for each person	$3	$5	$7

a) Write an expression that gives the total amount each company would charge for a boat carrying *n* people.

b) A group chose Company C and paid $126. How many people were in the group?

c) How much would the group have paid with Companies A and B?

d) Was Company C the best choice for the group? Why or why not?

PA7-9 Modelling Equations — Advanced

Scale A is balanced. A triangle has mass x kg and a circle has mass 1 kg. $\triangle = x$ kg $\bigcirc = 1$ kg

1. Write the equation for each balance.

a) 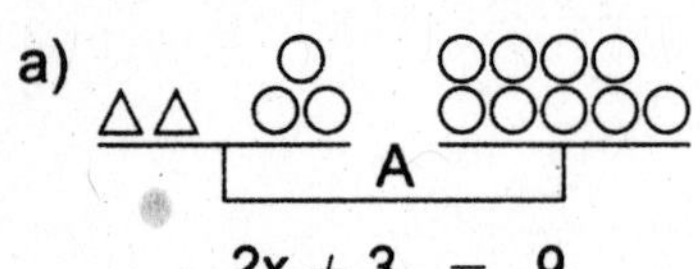

$2x + 3 = 9$

b) 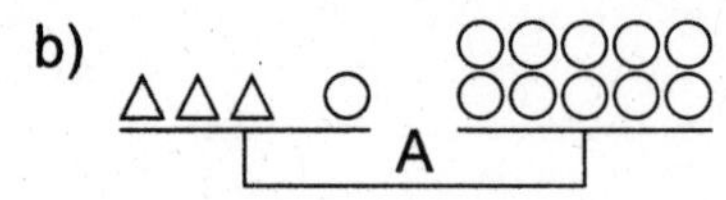

c) 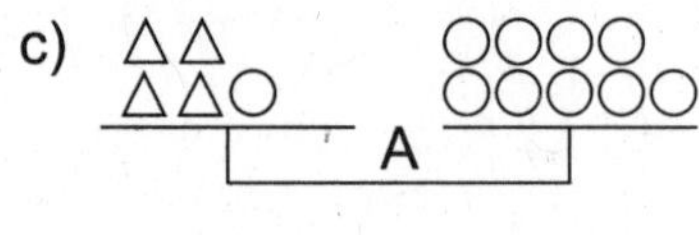

2. Write the equation that Scale A shows. Draw Scale B so that it balances only the triangles from Scale A, and write the new equation.

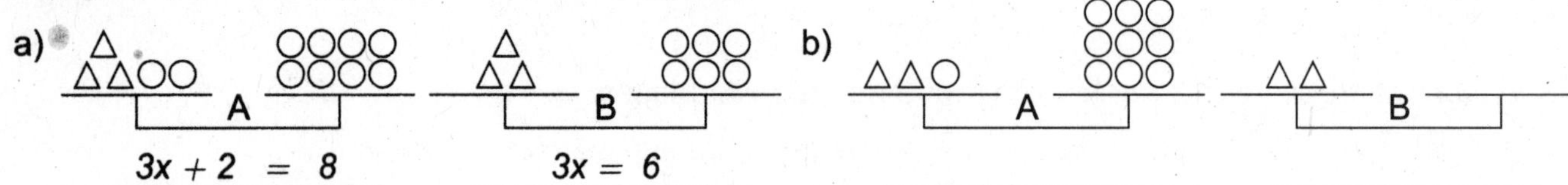

a) $3x + 2 = 8$ $3x = 6$

b)

3. Scale B is balanced and has only triangles on one side and only circles on the other. Put the circles into the number of groups given by the number of triangles. Show on Scale C what balances 1 triangle.

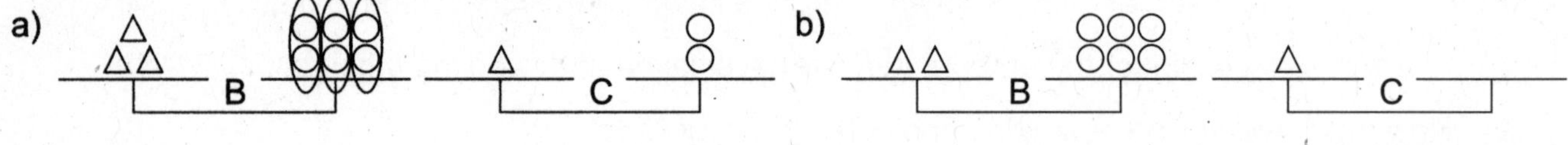

a) b)

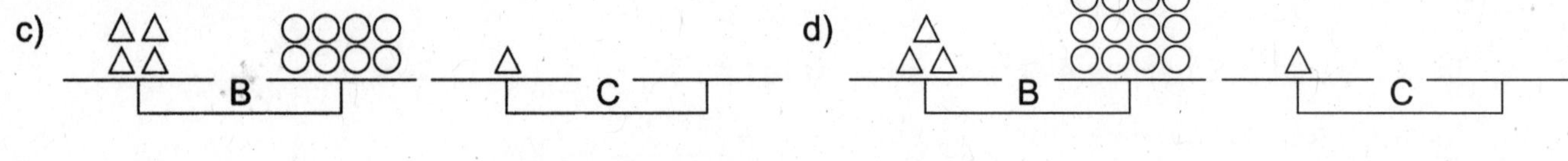

c) d)

4. Scale A is balanced perfectly. Draw scales B and C as in Questions 2 and 3. Write the new equations.

a) 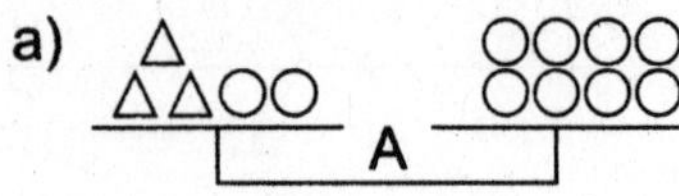 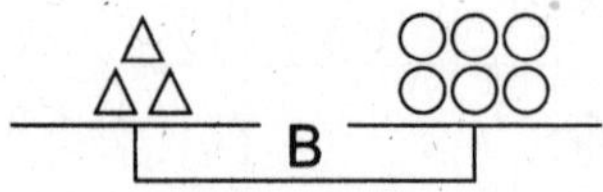 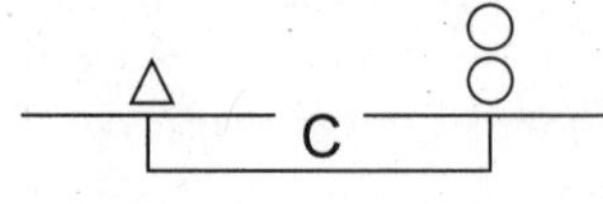

b) 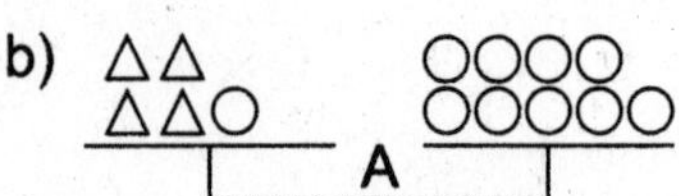 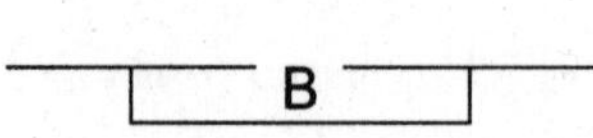 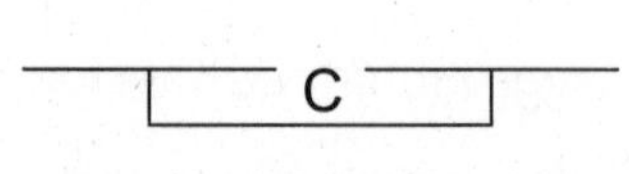

5. Draw Scales A, B, and C to model the process of solving the equation $3x + 5 = 11$.

PA7-10 Solving Equations — Advanced

The expression 3×2 is short for $2 + 2 + 2$. Similarly, the expression $3x$ is short for $x + x + x$.

1. Write $6x$ in three ways.

a) $6x = \underbrace{x + x + x}_{3x} + \underbrace{x + x + x}_{3x}$ $6x = 3x + 3x$

b) $6x = \underbrace{x + x}_{} + \underbrace{x + x + x + x}_{}$ $6x = \_\_\_ + \_\_\_$

c) $6x = \underbrace{x}_{} + \underbrace{x + x + x + x + x}_{}$ $6x = \_\_\_ + \_\_\_$

2. Add.

a) $3x + x =$ 4x b) $5x + 2x =$ ______ c) $7x + x =$ ______ d) $4x + 2x + 3x =$ ______

3. Group the x's together, then solve the equation for x.

a) $2x + 5x = 21$ b) $5x + 4x + 2 = 20$ c) $6x + x + 4 = 32$ d) $3x + 2x + 2 = 22$

4. Fill in the blanks.

a) $3 - 3 =$ ______ b) $8 - 8 =$ ______ c) $132 - 132 =$ ______ d) $x - x =$ ______

e) $3 + 3 - 3 =$ ______ f) $7 + 7 - 7 =$ ______ g) $5 + 5 - 5 =$ ______ h) $x + x - x =$ ______

Every time you see a number or variable subtracted by itself in an equation (Examples: $3 - 3$, $5 - 5$, $8 - 8$, $x - x$), you can cross out both numbers or variables because they will add to 0. Crossing out parts of an equation that make 0 is called **cancelling**.

5. Fill in the blanks by crossing out numbers or variables that add to 0.

a) $4 + \cancel{3} - \cancel{3} =$ 4 b) $5 + 2 - 2 =$ ____ c) $7 + 1 - 1 =$ ____

d) $8 + 6 - 6 =$ ____ e) $3 + 7 - 3 =$ ____ f) $2 + 9 - 2 =$ ____

g) $4 + 3 - 3 + 7 - 7 + 6 - 6 =$ ____ h) $5 + 2 - 2 + 4 - 5 =$ ____ i) $7 + x - x =$ ____

j) $x + 12 - x =$ ____ k) $x + x - x =$ ____ l) $x + x + x - x =$ ____

m) $x + x - x + x + x + x - x - x =$ ____

6. Rewrite these expressions as sums of individual variables and then cancel. Write what's left.

a) $5x - 2x =$ ______
$x + x + x + \cancel{x} + \cancel{x} - \cancel{x} - \cancel{x}$

b) $4x - x =$ ______ c) $5x - x + 2x =$ ______

7. Add or subtract without writing the expressions as sums of individual x's.

a) $7x - 5x =$ 2x b) $8x - 4x =$ ______ c) $4x - 2x + 3x =$ ______ d) $9x - 3x + 4x =$ ______

8. Group the x's together, then solve for x.

a) $8x - 3x + x - 2 = 28$ b) $5x + x - x - 2x + 4 = 19$ c) $7x + 4 - 2x - 3 = 26$

UNIT 3

Number Sense 2

NS7-7 Factors and Multiples

The **multiples** of a number are the numbers you say when counting by that number.

$3 \times 5 = 15$ ← 15 is a **multiple** of both 3 and 5
3 and 5 are both **factors** of 15

$0 \times 4 = 0$ ← 0 is a **multiple** of both 0 and 4
0 and 4 are both **factors** of 0

1. List the first few multiples of these numbers.

a) 3: 0, 3, 6, 9, ____, ____, ____. b) 4: ____, ____, ____, ____, ____, ____, ____.

c) 5: ____, ____, ____, ____, ____, ____, ____.

2. Look at the lists you made in Question 1.

a) Is 12 a multiple of 4? ____ b) Is 17 a multiple of 5? ____ c) Is 0 a multiple of 3? ____ Of 4? ____ Of 5? ____

3. a) Write 0 as a multiple of 17. $0 = 17 \times$ ____

b) Which whole numbers is 0 a multiple of? Explain. ____

4. Rewrite each statement in a way that means the same thing but uses the word "factor."

a) 20 is a multiple of 5. *5 is a factor of 20.* b) 9 is a multiple of 1. ____

c) 0 is a multiple of 8. ____ d) 11 is not a multiple of 4. ____

INVESTIGATION 1 ▶ What are the factors of 12?

A. Count by each number until you either reach 12 or pass it.

a) by 1s: 0, 1, 2, 3, 4, 5, 6, 7, 8, *9, 10, 11, 12* b) by 2s: 0, 2, 4, ____

c) by 3s: 0, 3, 6, ____ d) by 4s: 0, 4, ____

e) by 5s: 0, 5, ____ f) by 6s: 0, 6, ____

g) by 7s: 0, 7, ____ h) by 8s: 0, 8, ____

i) by 9s: 0, 9, ____ j) by 10s: 0, 10, ____

k) by 11s: 0, 11, ____ l) by 12s: 0, 12, ____

m) by 13s: 0, ____

B. How do you know that any number greater than 12 cannot be a factor of 12?

____

C. a) List all the factors of 12. ____ b) Is 12 a factor of 12? ____

NS7-7 Factors and Multiples *(continued)*

5. a) Count by 0s from 0. 0, 0, 0, ____, ____, ____.

b) Is 8 a multiple of 0? _______

c) Is 0 a factor of 8? _______

d) What is the only number that is a multiple of 0? _______

e) What is the only number that has 0 as a factor? _______

6. a) Show that 13 is a factor of 13 by counting by 13s starting at 0.

b) Which whole numbers are factors of themselves? Explain. ____________________

____

7. a) Show that 1 is a factor of 8 by counting by 1s starting at 0.

b) Which whole numbers have 1 as a factor? Explain. ____________________

____

8. a) Fill in the blanks:

$0 \times 1 =$ _______ $0 \times 2 =$ _______ $0 \times 3 =$ _______ $0 \times 4 =$ _______

b) What numbers will fit in the blank here: $0 \times$ _______ $= 0$?

Can you find a number that does not fit? ____________________

c) We know that 0 is a factor of 0. What are the other factors of 0? Explain. ____________________

____

9. Rewrite each statement in a way that means the same thing but uses the word "factor."

a) 5 is a multiple of 1. ____________________

b) Every number is a multiple of 1. ____________________

c) 8 is a multiple of 8. ____________________

d) Every number is a multiple of itself. ____________________

e) 0 is a multiple of 7. ____________________

f) 0 is a multiple of any number. ____________________

10. Rewrite each statement in a way that means the same thing but uses the word "multiple."

a) 5 is a factor of 15.

b) 3 is a factor of 0.

c) Any factor of 12 is at most 12.

d) Any factor of a number (except 0) is at most the number.

e) 6 is a factor of 6.

f) Any number is a factor of itself.

NS7-8 Organized Search

1. Alana uses a chart to find all the factors of 10 by pairing up numbers that multiply to give 10. She lists numbers 1 to 10 in the 1st column, and the number you multiply each one by to get 10 in the 2nd column. If there is no number that multiplies to 10, she leaves the box in the 2nd column blank.

1st	2nd
1	10
2	5
3	
4	
5	2
6	
7	
8	
9	
10	1

a) Why did Alana not list any 1st number greater than 10?

____

b) Why did Alana not list 0 as a 1st number?

____

2. Use Alana's method to find all the pairs of numbers that multiply to give the number in bold.

a) **6**

1st	2nd
1	
2	
3	
4	
5	
6	

b) **8**

1st	2nd
1	
2	
3	
4	
5	
6	
7	
8	

c) **9**

1st	2nd
1	
2	
3	
4	
5	
6	
7	
8	
9	

3. Cross out the pairs of numbers that are repeated in Question 2.

4. Connor makes a chart to list all the factors of 24. He does not want to write and check all the numbers from 1 to 24. He starts his list as shown.

1st	2nd
1	24
2	12
3	8
4	6
5	
6	4

a) Connor knows that $6 \times 4 = 24$. He thinks that if $7 \times \square = 24$, then $\square$ must be less than 4. Explain his thinking.

b) Explain why Connor's list is complete.

5. Connor used this chart to help him identify pairs that multiply to 16. Why did he know that his search was complete as soon as he found a pair with both numbers the same?

1st	2nd
1	16
2	8
3	
4	4

NS7-8 Organized Search *(continued)*

To list all the factors of a given number (the pairs of numbers that multiply to give that number), stop when you get a number that is already part of a pair.

6. Make a chart to find all the pairs of numbers that multiply to give each number.

a) 20   b) 12   c) 15   d) 14   e) 25   f) 5

g) 26   h) 30   i) 42   j) 72

k) 63   l) 100   m) 64   n) 91

A **factor rainbow** for a number, such as 9 or 10, pairs the factors that multiply to give that number.

Factor rainbow for 9

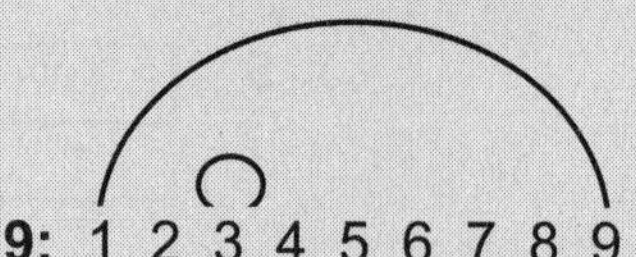

9: 1 2 3 4 5 6 7 8 9

Factor rainbow for 10

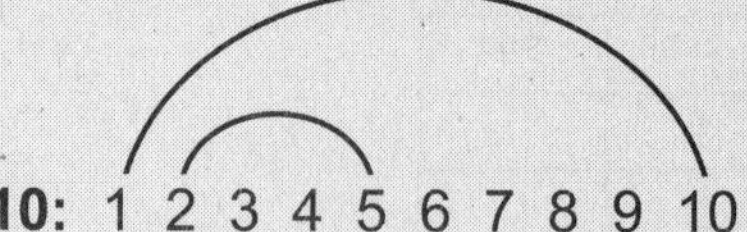

10: 1 2 3 4 5 6 7 8 9 10

7. Finish the factor rainbow for each number.

6: 1 2 3 4 5 6   **8:** 1 2 3 4 5 6 7 8   **12:** 1 2 3 4 5 6 7 8 9 10 11 12

8. As a shortcut to making a factor rainbow, we can leave out all numbers that are not factors. Using this shortcut, make a factor rainbow for each number.

Example: **6:** 1 2 3 6

a) 4   b) 8   c) 12   d) 15   e) 7   f) 24   g) 42

9. a) Tom knows that 3 is a factor of 144. Is $144 \div 3$ also a factor of 144? ______

b) Tom's teacher tells him that 1, 2, 3, 4, 6, and 12 are all factors of 144. Find 6 more factors of 144 by division.

$144 \div 1 =$ ______ $144 \div 2 =$ ______ $144 \div 3 =$ ______

$144 \div 4 =$ ______ $144 \div 6 =$ ______ $144 \div 12 =$ ______

c) As n gets larger, what happens to $144 \div n$? ______

d) List the factors of 144 you found so far in order. Have you found all of them? How do you know?

10. 1 is a factor of every number. What is the next smallest factor of 3 256? What is the largest factor of 3 256, other than 3 256? How do you know?

NS7-9 LCMs and GCFs

The multiples of 2 and 3 are marked with X on the number lines.

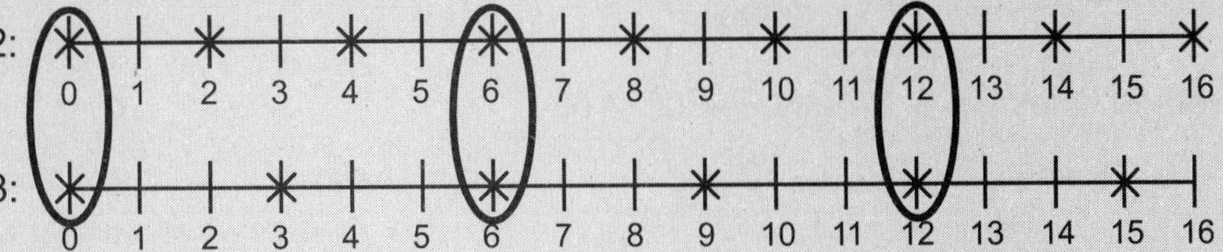

The numbers marked with X on both number lines are 0, 6, and 12. These numbers are called **common multiples** of 2 and 3.

1. Predict the next common multiple of 2 and 3, then check by extending the number sequences.

2. Mark the multiples of each number on the number lines.

2: 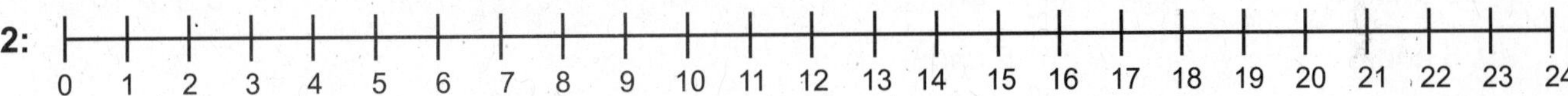

3: 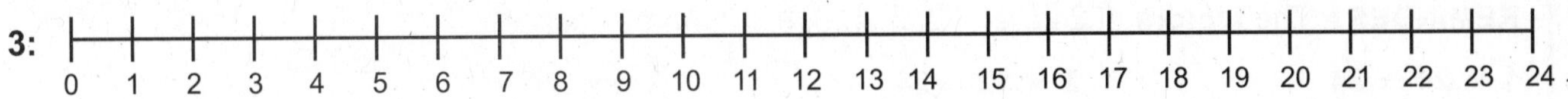

4: 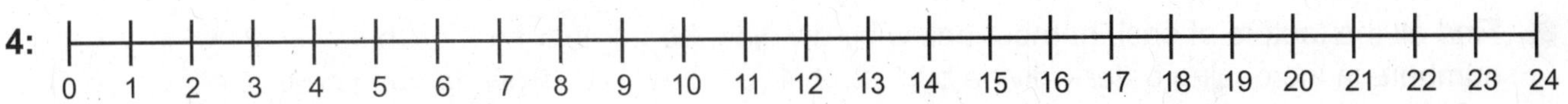

5: 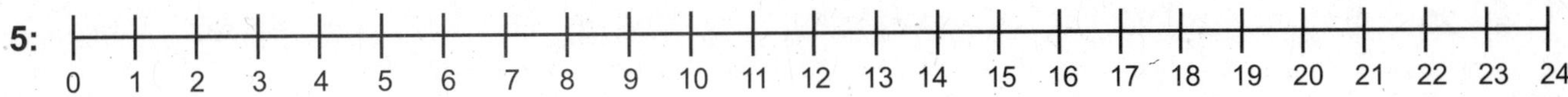

6: 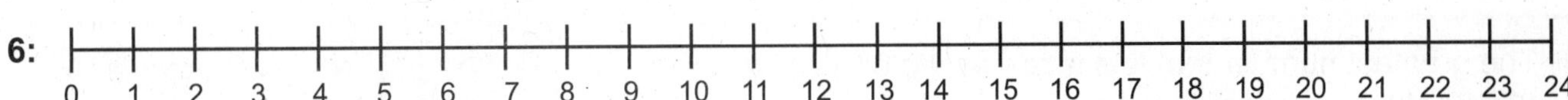

3. Find the first 2 common multiples (after 0) of…

   a) 2 and 5: ______, ______ b) 3 and 6: ______, ______ c) 2 and 4: ______, ______

   d) 3 and 4: ______, ______ e) 4 and 6: ______, ______ f) 3, 4, and 6: ______, ______

4. a) How can you find the second common multiple of two numbers from the first?

   b) The first common multiple of 18 and 42 is 126. What is the second common multiple?

5. a) Write the first 4 common multiples of 2 and 3, after 0. ______ ______ ______ ______.

   b) Extend the pattern from part a). Predict the fifth common multiple of 2 and 3. ______

NS7-9 LCMs and GCFs *(continued)*

The **lowest common multiple (LCM)** of two numbers is the smallest number (not 0) that is a multiple of both numbers.

6. Look at your answers to Question 3. What is the LCM of…

a) 2 and 5 b) 3 and 6 c) 2 and 4 d) 3 and 4 e) 4 and 6

7. Find the lowest common multiple of each pair of numbers.

a) 3 and 5
*3: 3, 6, 9, 12, **15**, 18*
*5: 5, 10, **15**, 20*
LCM = ***15***

b) 4 and 10
LCM = ______

c) 3 and 9
LCM = ______

d) 2 and 6
LCM = ______

e) 2 and 10 f) 2 and 7 g) 3 and 12 h) 4 and 8

i) 8 and 10 j) 5 and 15 k) 6 and 10 l) 3 and 10

m) 6 and 8 n) 6 and 9

REMINDER▶ The **factors** of 24 are 1, 2, 3, 4, 6, 8, 12, and 24, since:

1 × 24 = 24 **2 × 12 = 24** **3 × 8 = 24** **4 × 6 = 24**

8. Find all the factors of each number below by dividing the number by the whole numbers in increasing order—divide by 1, 2, 3, 4, 5, and so on. How do you know when to stop dividing?

a) 20 b) 22 c) 26 d) 65 e) 66

The greatest number that is a factor of two or more numbers is called the **greatest common factor (GCF)** of the numbers.

9. Use your answers to Question 8. Find the greatest common factor of…

a) 20 and 22 b) 22 and 66 c) 20 and 65 d) 65 and 66

e) 26 and 65 f) 22 and 65 g) 20, 26, and 65 h) 20, 22, and 66

10. i) List the factors of each number below in order from least to greatest.
ii) Circle all the **common factors** for each pair.
iii) Put a double circle around the **GCF** of the pair.

a) 10 and 15 b) 18 and 24 c) 20 and 30 d) 28 and 42

NS7-9 LCMs and GCFs *(continued)*

11. a) Find the factors of each number and then the greatest common factor (GCF) of each pair.

i) 2 and 10	ii) 5 and 15	iii) 6 and 30	iv) 10 and 50
2: *1, 2*	**5:**	**6:**	**10:**
10: *1, 2, 5, 10*	**15:**	**30:**	**50:**
GCF = 2	GCF = ______	GCF = ______	GCF = ______

b) If *a* is a factor of *b*, what is the **GCF** of *a* and *b*? ______

Two numbers are called **consecutive** if one number is the next number after the other.
Example: 13 and 14 are consecutive because 14 is the next number after 13.

INVESTIGATION 1 ▶ What is the GCF of two consecutive numbers?

A. Find the factors of each number and then the GCF of each pair.

a) 14 and 15	b) 20 and 21	c) 15 and 16	d) 35 and 36
14: *1, 2, 7, 14*	**20:**	**15:**	**35:**
15: *1, 3, 5, 15*	**21:**	**16:**	**36:**
GCF = 1	GCF = ______	GCF = ______	GCF = ______

B. Make a conjecture about the GCF of any two consecutive numbers.

____

C. Test your conjecture on two more consecutive numbers of your choice: ______ and ______

INVESTIGATION 2 ▶ How are the GCF, the LCM, and the product of two numbers related?

A. Find the **GCF**, the **LCM**, and the **product** of each pair of numbers. Do rough work in your notebook.

a) 3 and 4	b) 2 and 5	c) 4 and 6	d) 10 and 15
GCF = ______	GCF = ______	GCF = ______	GCF = ______
LCM = ______	LCM = ______	LCM = ______	LCM = ______
$3 \times 4 =$ ______	$2 \times 5 =$ ______	$4 \times 6 =$ ______	$10 \times 15 =$ ______

e) 5 and 10	f) 3 and 5	g) 4 and 5	h) 6 and 9
GCF = ______	GCF = ______	GCF = ______	GCF = ______
LCM = ______	LCM = ______	LCM = ______	LCM = ______
$5 \times 10 =$ ______	$3 \times 5 =$ ______	$4 \times 5 =$ ______	$6 \times 9 =$ ______

B. Circle the questions from part A where the LCM is the product of the two numbers.

C. Make a conjecture: When the LCM is the product of the two numbers, the GCF is ______.

NS7-10 Perfect Squares and Square Roots

1. Find the factors of each number by drawing all non-congruent rectangles (with whole-number sides) that have an area equal to the number.

Example:

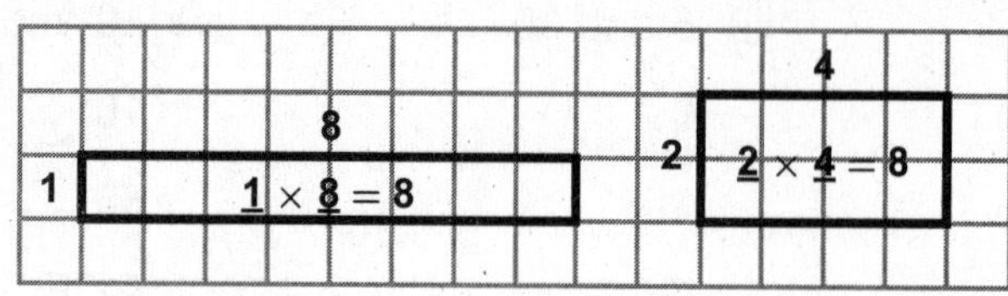

So the factors of 8 are 1, 2, 4, and 8.

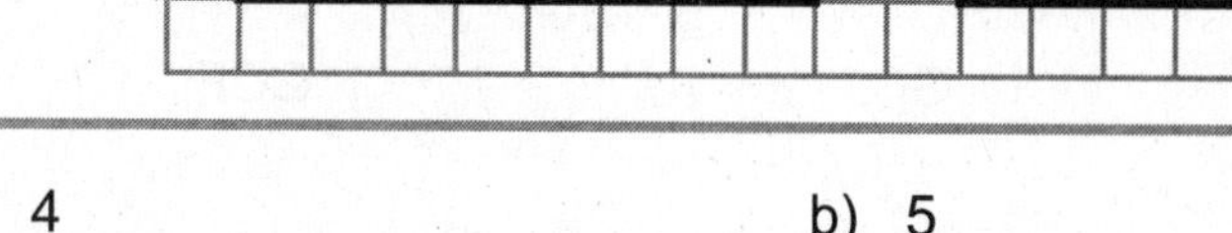

a) 4 b) 5 c) 6

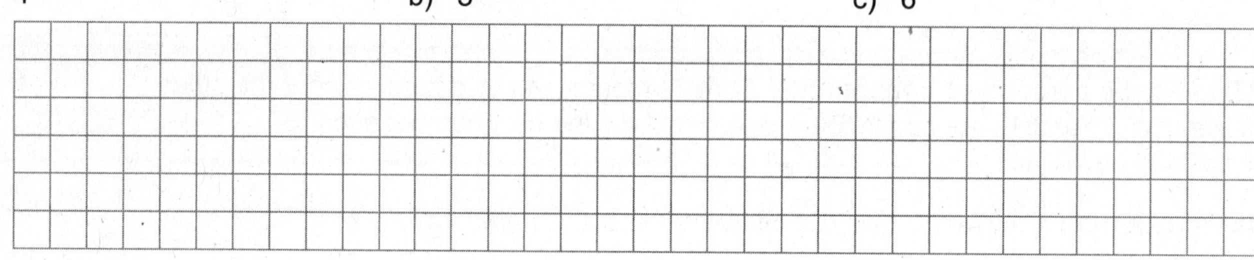

d) 7 e) 8 f) 9

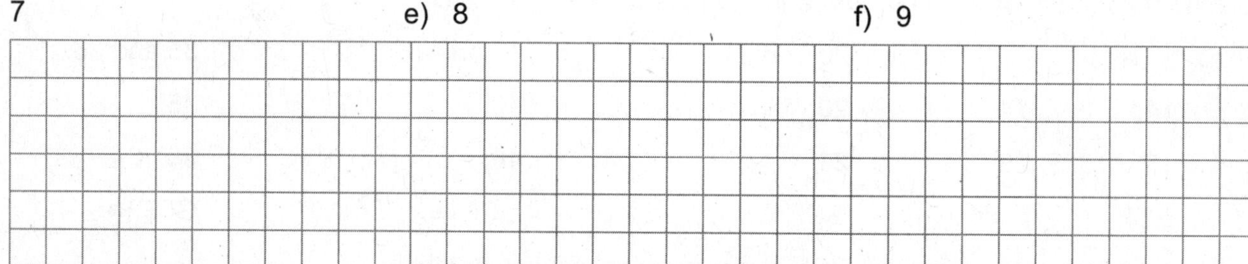

A number larger than 1 is called a **prime number** if you can draw only 1 rectangle with an area equal to that number.

A number larger than 0 is called a **perfect square** if you can draw a square with whole-number side lengths having that area.

2. Which numbers from Question 1 are prime numbers? ______________________

3. Which numbers from Question 1 are perfect squares? ______________________

4. Can a prime number be a perfect square? Explain. ______________________

____

5. a) Draw squares with side lengths 1, 2, 3, 4, and 5 on the grid below.

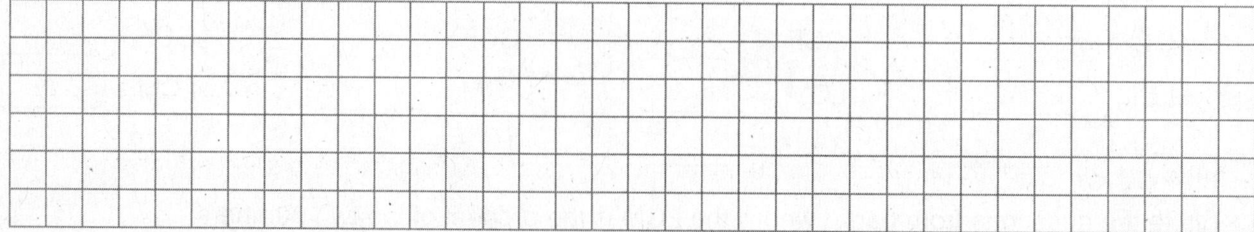

b) Write the first 5 perfect squares larger than 0. _____ _____ _____ _____ _____

NS7-10 Perfect Squares and Square Roots *(continued)*

6. Show that 36 is a perfect square by drawing a square with area 36.

7. Show that 10 is not a perfect square by drawing all non-congruent rectangles with area 10.

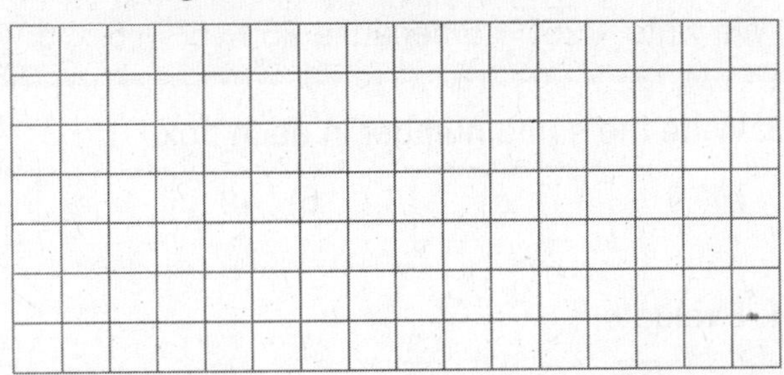

Any perfect square can be written as a product of a whole number with itself.

Example: $25 = 5 \times 5$ 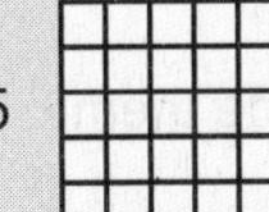 Area $= 5 \times 5 = 25$ squares

Note: Since $0 = 0 \times 0$, we say that 0 is a perfect square even though you cannot draw a square with area 0.

8. Write down the first 10 perfect squares larger than 0.

$1 \times 1 =$ ______ $2 \times 2 =$ ______ $3 \times 3 =$ ______ $4 \times 4 =$ ______ $5 \times 5 =$ ______

$6 \times 6 =$ ______ $7 \times 7 =$ ______ $8 \times 8 =$ ______ $9 \times 9 =$ ______ $10 \times 10 =$ ______

When we multiply a number by itself, we get a perfect square. This process is called **squaring the number.** Example: 6 squared is $6 \times 6 = 36$. We write $6^2 = 36$. (The 2 is because we multiplied 2 sixes.)

9. Write each perfect square as a product and evaluate it.

a) $5^2 = 5 \times 5$
$= 25$

b) $3^2 =$

c) $8^2 =$

d) $0^2 =$

e) $7^2 =$

10. a) Will a square of side length 131 cm fit into a square of side length 132 cm? ______________

b) Explain how you know that $131^2 < 132^2$. ______________________________

____

11. Write the numbers from smallest to largest without calculating the perfect squares.

a) 3^2 5^2 4^2

____ ____ ____

b) 10^2 8^2 9^2

____ ____ ____

c) 5^2 12^2 7^2

____ ____ ____

12. Write the numbers from largest to smallest. You will need to calculate the perfect squares.

a) 3^2 5 10 4^2 2^2

____ ____ ____ ____ ____

b) 50 7^2 9^2 8^2 85

____ ____ ____ ____ ____

NS7-10 Perfect Squares and Square Roots *(continued)*

5 is called the **square root** of 25 because 25 is the **square** of 5.

We write $\sqrt{25} = 5$ because $25 = 5^2 = 5 \times 5$.

13. Write the same number in each box.

a) $9 = \square \times \square$ b) $49 = \square \times \square$ c) $0 = \square \times \square$ d) $25 = \square \times \square$

14. Evaluate.

a) $\sqrt{49}$ $= 7$ b) $\sqrt{16}$ c) $\sqrt{9}$ d) $\sqrt{36}$ e) $\sqrt{1}$ f) $\sqrt{100}$ g) $\sqrt{81}$ h) $\sqrt{64}$

15. Square roots are numbers, so you can add, subtract, multiply, and divide them. Evaluate.

a) $\sqrt{25} + \sqrt{4}$ $= 5 + 2 = 7$ b) $\sqrt{36} \times \sqrt{25}$ c) $\sqrt{64} - \sqrt{9}$ d) $\sqrt{100} \div \sqrt{4}$ e) $\sqrt{49} + \sqrt{64}$

f) $\sqrt{36} - \sqrt{25}$ g) $\sqrt{36} \div \sqrt{4}$ h) $\sqrt{36} + \sqrt{25} - \sqrt{1}$ **BONUS▶** $\sqrt{25} + \sqrt{16} \times \sqrt{9}$

16. Evaluate.

a) $\sqrt{3^2}$ $= \sqrt{3 \times 3} = \sqrt{9} = 3$ b) $\sqrt{5^2}$ c) $\sqrt{9^2}$ d) $\sqrt{4105^2}$ e) $\sqrt{n^2}$

17. The side length of a square is the square root of the area. Find the side lengths.

a)

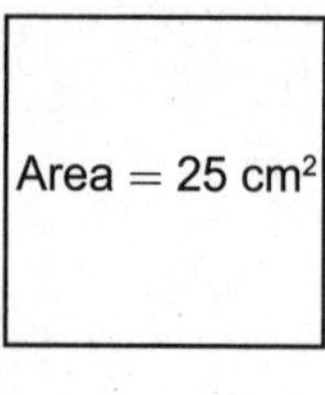

_______ cm

b)

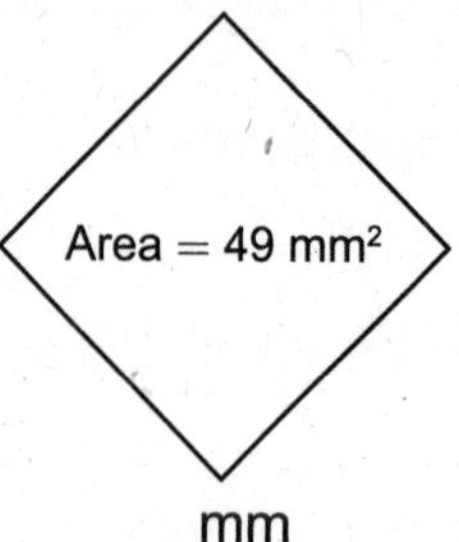

_______ mm

c)

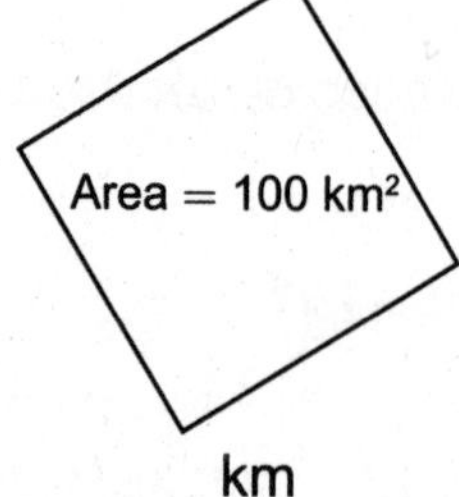

_______ km

18. One square has area 64 cm² and another square has area 36 cm².

a) Which square has a larger side length? How do you know?

b) Write > or <. $\sqrt{64}$ _______ $\sqrt{36}$

19. Order these numbers from smallest to largest.

a) $\sqrt{49}$ $\sqrt{64}$ $\sqrt{25}$ $\sqrt{9}$ $\sqrt{16}$

b) $\sqrt{100}$ 3^2 5 4^2 $\sqrt{4}$ $\sqrt{8^2}$

c) $\sqrt{100} \div \sqrt{4}$ $\sqrt{16}$ $\sqrt{4} \times \sqrt{9}$ 3^2 $\sqrt{100}$ $\sqrt{36} + \sqrt{4}$ $\sqrt{81} - \sqrt{49}$

20. How is the notation for units of area similar to the notation for square numbers?

NS7-11 Divisibility by 2, 5, and 10

. In math, there are sometimes many ways to say the same thing. Example: These statements all mean the same thing:

8 is a multiple of 2 | 2 is a factor of 8 | 2 divides 8 | 8 is divisible by 2

8 leaves no remainder when divided by 2 | You say 8 when counting by 2s from 0

INVESTIGATION 1 ▶ Are all whole numbers with ones digit 0 multiples of 10?

A. Rewrite the question using the word "divisible."

____

B. Choose 3 numbers with ones digit 0 and write them as multiples of 10.
Example: 4 700 = 470 × 10

_____ = _____ × 10   _____ = _____ × 10   _____ = _____ × 10

C. In the first row of the chart, write the first 15 whole numbers greater than 0 that have ones digit 0. Then write each number as a multiple of 10.

	10	20	30												
= _____ × 10	*1*	*2*	*3*												

D. Look for a pattern. The 1st number with ones digit 0 is _____ × 10.

The 2nd number with ones digit 0 is _____ × 10.

The 3rd number with ones digit 0 is _____ × 10.

The 12th number with ones digit 0 is _____ × 10.

The *n*th number with ones digit 0 is _____ × 10.

E. Are all whole numbers with ones digit 0 divisible by 10? _____

INVESTIGATION 2 ▶ Is any number with ones digit divisible by 2 also divisible by 2?

A. Write the first 15 numbers larger than 0 with ones digit divisible by 2 and complete the chart. Then look for a pattern.

	2	4	6	8	10	12	14			20					
= _____ × 2	*1*	*2*	*3*												

B. The *n*th number with ones digit divisible by 2 is _____ × 2.

INVESTIGATION 3 ▶ Is any number with ones digit divisible by 3 also divisible by 3?

A. Write down the first 10 numbers larger than 0 with ones digit divisible by 3.
Then divide each number by 3. Do you get a remainder?

	3	6	9	10	13					
÷ 3	*1*	*2*	*3*	3R___	4R___					

NS7-11 Divisibility by 2, 5, and 10 *(continued)*

B. Write the smallest counter-example to this statement: Any number with ones digit divisible by 3 is also divisible by 3. ____________________

1. The statement "Any number that has ones digit divisible by 2 is also divisible by 2" is true.

a) Write the reverse.

Any number that is ____________________ has ____________________.

b) Write the first fifteen numbers that are divisible by 2 (the multiples of 2) and then their ones digits.

divisible by 2	0	2	4	6	8	10	12								
ones digit	*0*	*2*	*4*												

c) What type of pattern do you see in the ones digits — increasing, decreasing, or repeating? Describe it.

____

d) Is the statement in part a) true? ____________________

2. The statement "Any number with ones digit divisible by 3 is also divisible by 3" is false.

a) Write the reverse.

Any number that is ____________________ has ____________________.

b) Is the reverse statement true? ______ In your notebook, describe the pattern or the counter-example.

3. Write the reverse of each statement, then decide whether the statements are true or false.

a) Any number whose ones digit is divisible by 4 is also divisible by 4.
b) Any number whose ones digit is divisible by 5 is also divisible by 5.

4. How can looking at the ones digit of a number tell you if the number is…

a) divisible by 2? ____________________
b) divisible by 5? ____________________
c) divisible by 10? ____________________

5. Circle the numbers that are divisible by 2.

17 3 418 312 64 76 234 89 94 167 560

6. Circle the numbers that are multiples of 5.

83 17 45 37 150 64 190 65 71 235 618 1 645

7. Underline the numbers in Question 6 that are divisible by 10.

NS7-12 Divisibility by 3, 6, and 9

A number is divisible by 3 if it can be divided into equal groups of three. For instance, 12 is divisible by 3 because it can be divided into four groups of three.

$12 =$ 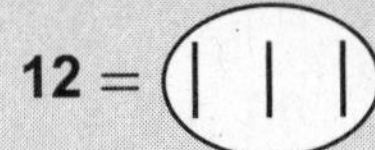   $= 3 + 3 + 3 + 3$

1. Group lines into sets of 3 to show that each number is divisible by 3.

6:  **12:** | | | | | | | | | | | | **9:** | | | | | | | | |

2. Group lines into sets of 3 to find the remainder.

a) 

$7 \div 3$: Remainder 1

b) | | | | |

$5 \div 3$: Remainder ______

c) 

$11 \div 3$: Remainder ______

3. 6 and 9 are both divisible by 3. Miki draws a picture to show that $6 + 9$ is divisible by 3.

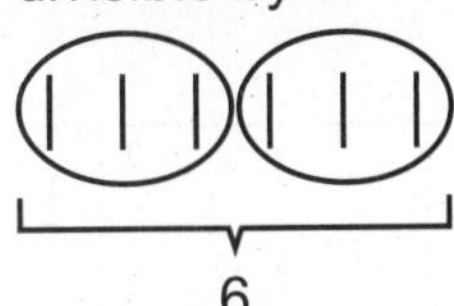
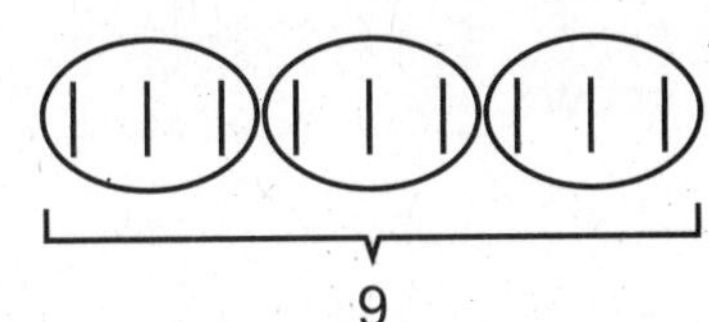

6 + 9

Draw a picture to show that $6 + 12$ is divisible by 3.

4. a) 6 is a multiple of 3. Is $5 \times 6 = 6 + 6 + 6 + 6 + 6$ also a multiple of 3? Explain.

b) Is any multiple of a multiple of 3 also a multiple of 3? ______

5. 12 is divisible by 3 but 5 is not. Ron draws a picture to show that $12 + 5$ is not divisible by 3.

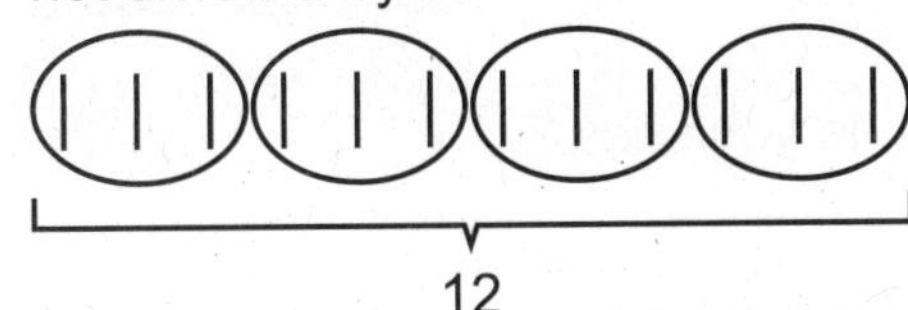
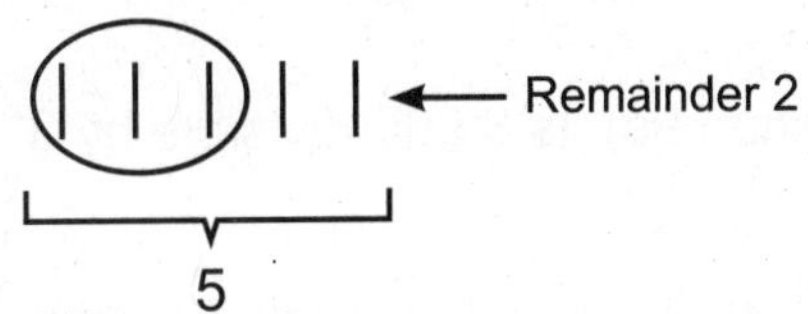

12 + 5

a) Draw a picture to show that $9 + 7$ is not divisible by 3.

b) What is the remainder of $(9 + 7) \div 3$?

c) Explain why the remainder of $(9 + 7) \div 3$ is the same as the remainder of $7 \div 3$.

d) Predict the remainder when each sum is divided by 3. Check your prediction.

i) $12 + 7$ ii) $9 + 5$ iii) $15 + 7$ iv) $33 + 7$ v) $27 + 8$ vi) $33 + 3$

6. Explain why $(12 + 5 + 15 + 2) \div 3$ has the same remainder as $(5 + 2) \div 3$.

NS7-12 Divisibility by 3, 6, and 9 *(continued)*

7. Follow the pattern to predict the answers. Then check your answers by long division in your notebook.

a) 7 ÷ 3 = 2 R 1
70 ÷ 3 = 23 R 1
700 ÷ 3 = 233 R 1
7 000 ÷ 3 = _____ R _____

b) 5 ÷ 3 = 1 R 2
50 ÷ 3 = 16 R 2
500 ÷ 3 = 166 R 2
5 000 ÷ 3 = _____ R _____

c) 8 ÷ 3 = 2 R 2
80 ÷ 3 = 26 R 2
800 ÷ 3 = 266 R 2
8 000 ÷ 3 = _____ R _____

d) 2 ÷ 3 = 0 R 2
20 ÷ 3 = 6 R 2
200 ÷ 3 = 66 R 2
2 000 ÷ 3 = _____ R _____

e) 9 ÷ 3 = 3 R 0
90 ÷ 3 = 30 R 0
900 ÷ 3 = 300 R 0
9 000 ÷ 3 = _____ R _____

f) 4 ÷ 3 = 1 R 1
40 ÷ 3 = 13 R 1
400 ÷ 3 = 133 R 1
4 000 ÷ 3 = _____ R _____

8. Predict the remainder when dividing by 3. Check your prediction in your notebook by long division.

a) 20 000 ÷ 3 has remainder _____

b) 4 000 000 ÷ 3 has remainder _____

9. a) Is 999 × 8 a multiple of 3? _____ How do you know? _____________________

____

b) 8 000 = 1 000 × 8
= 999 × 8 + _____

c) Explain why 8 000 has the same remainder as 8 when you divide both by 3.

d) Explain why 800 and 80 both have the same remainder as 8 when you divide both by 3. Hint: 800 = 99 × 8 + 8.

REMINDER▶ A number is divisible by 3 if the remainder is 0 when you divide by 3.

10. Look at your answer to Question 9c). Is 8 000 divisible by 3? How do you know?

11. Use expanded form and the pattern from Question 7 to find the remainder when dividing by 3. Check your answer by dividing.

a) 52 = 50 + 2, so 52 ÷ 3 has the same remainder as (*5* + *2*) ÷ 3 = *7* ÷ 3 = *2* R *1*
Check: 52 ÷ 3 = *17* R *1*

b) 84 = 80 + 4 has the same remainder as ____ + ____ = ____ which is ____.
Check: 84 ÷ 3 = ____ R ____

c) 47 = 40 + 7 has the same remainder as ____ + ____ = ____ which is ____.
Check: 47 ÷ 3 = ____ R ____

NS7-12 Divisibility by 3, 6, and 9 *(continued)*

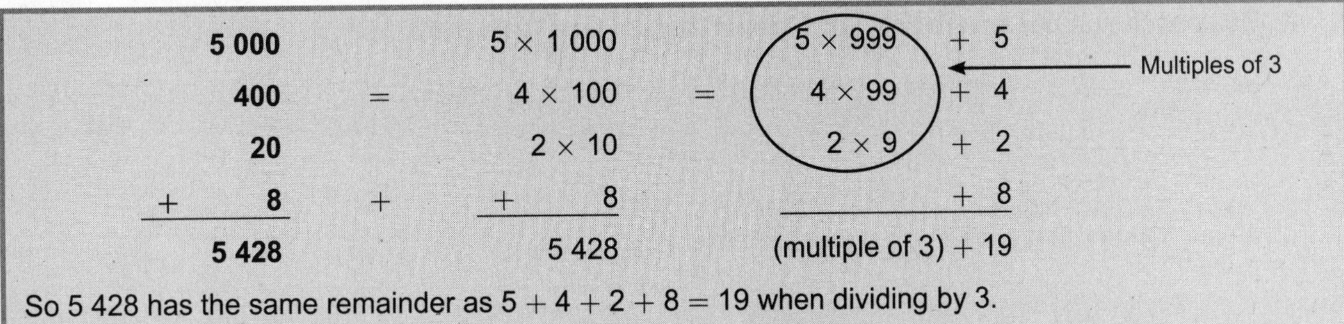

So 5 428 has the same remainder as 5 + 4 + 2 + 8 = 19 when dividing by 3.

12. a) When dividing by 3,

5 428 has the same remainder as: ____ + ____ + ____ + ____ = ____ which is ____.

5 482 has the same remainder as: ____ + ____ + ____ + ____ = ____ which is ____.

2 485 has the same remainder as: ____ + ____ + ____ + ____ = ____ which is ____.

b) Can you rearrange the digits of 5 482 to make a number that is divisible by 3? Explain.

13. Write a rule to determine if a number is divisible by 3, by using the sum of its digits.

14. a) Explain why 5 428 has the same remainder as 5 + 4 + 2 + 8 when dividing by 9.

b) Write a rule to determine if a number is divisible by 9, by using the sum of its digits.

15. a) Find the sum of the digits for each number below.

Number	28	37	42	61	63	87	93	123
Sum of Digits								

b) Sort the numbers in this Venn diagram, using the attributes "divisible by 3" and "divisible by 9."

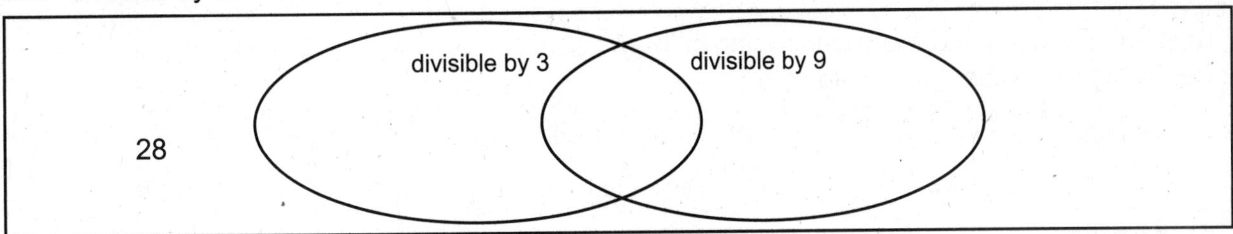

c) Which part of the Venn diagram is empty? Why is it empty?

16. a) Sort the numbers from 0 to 30 in a Venn diagram in your notebook, using the following attributes: divisible by 2; divisible by 3.

b) Where, in the Venn diagram, are the numbers that are divisible by 6? Why did that happen?

c) Use the tests for divisibility by 2 and 3 to make a test for divisibility by 6.

NS7-13 Divisibility by 2, 4, and 8

1. a) Write each number as a multiple of 100 and then as a multiple of 4.

i) 600 = *6* × 100
= *6* × 25 × 4
= *150* × 4

ii) 700 = ____ × 100
= ____ × 25 × 4
= ____ × 4

iii) 3 000 = ____ × 100
= ____ × 25 × 4
= ____ × 4

b) Is any number that ends in two zeros divisible by 4? ________

> If two numbers are divisible by 4, so is their sum. If one number is divisible by 4 and the other is not, their sum is not divisible by 4.

2. Split each number into a number ending in two zeros and another number. Decide if the number is divisible by 4. Divide the 2-digit number in your notebook.

a) 3 464 = 3 400 + *64*
Divisible by 4? *Yes*

b) 782 = 700 + ____
Divisible by 4? ____

c) 560 = 500 + ____
Divisible by 4? ____

d) 32 546 = 32 500 + ____
Divisible by 4? ____

e) 667 = 600 + ____
Divisible by 4? ____

f) 1 984 = 1 900 + ____
Divisible by 4? ____

g) 74 326 = 74 300 + ____
Divisible by 4? ____

h) 43 206 609 841 322 = 43 206 609 841 300 + ____
Divisible by 4? ____

3. Explain why a number is divisible by 4 if its last 2 digits form a number that is divisible by 4.

4. a) 1 000 is divisible by 8. Is any number that ends in 3 zeros divisible by 8? Explain.

b) Explain why a number is divisible by 8 if its last 3 digits form a number that is divisible by 8.

5. Split each number into a number ending in three zeros and another number. Decide if the number is divisible by 8.

a) 34 364 = 34 000 + *364*
Divisible by 8? *No*

b) 54 688 = 54 000 + ____
Divisible by 8? ____

c) 32 408 = 32 000 + ____
Divisible by 8? ____

d) 41 546 = 41 000 + ____
Divisible by 8? ____

e) 58 767 = 58 000 + ____
Divisible by 8? ____

f) 21 936 = 21 000 + ____
Divisible by 8? ____

6. We know that 200 = 8 × 25 is a multiple of 8. Write each number as the sum of a multiple of 200 and a smaller number. Then decide if the number is a multiple of 8.

a) 732 = 600 + *132* Divisible by 8? *No*

b) 432 = 400 + *32* Divisible by 8? *Yes*

c) 236 = 200 + ____ Divisible by 8? ____

d) 746 = ____ + ____ Divisible by 8? ____

e) 976 = ____ + ____ Divisible by 8? ____

f) 672 = ____ + ____ Divisible by 8? ____

NS7-14 Fractions

Fractions name equal parts of a whole.

This pie is cut into 4 equal parts, and 3 of the parts are shaded.

So $\frac{3}{4}$ of the pie is shaded.

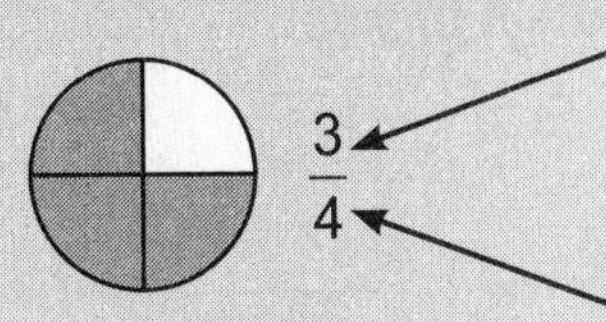

The **numerator** tells you how many parts are counted.

The **denominator** tells you how many equal parts are in a whole.

1. How much of each shape is shaded? Write the fraction.

a) 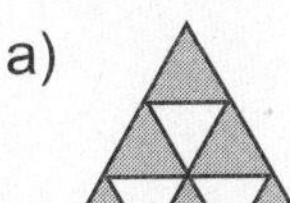 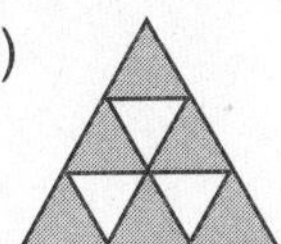

b) 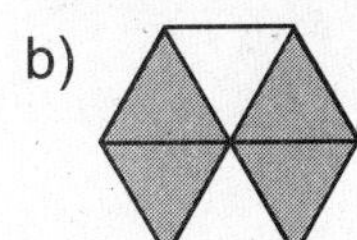

c) 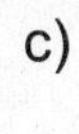 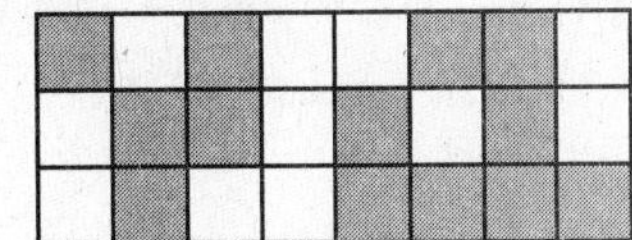

2. Draw lines to divide each figure into equal parts. Then write what fraction of each figure is shaded.

a) 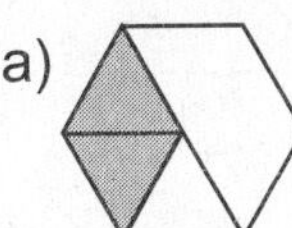

b) 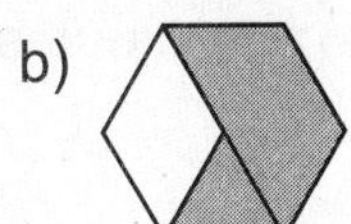

c) 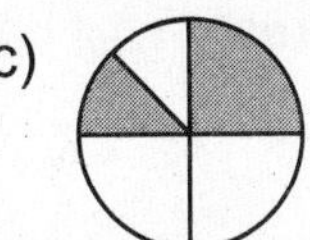

d) 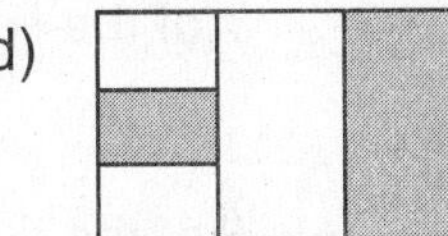

3. Use a ruler to divide each box into…

a) 3 equal parts. 

b) 10 equal parts. 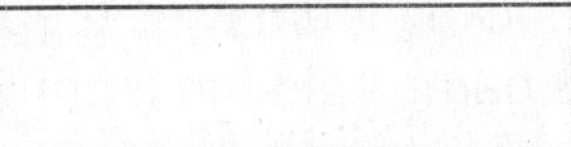

4. This figure represents $\frac{3}{7}$ of a whole. Use a ruler to turn it into a whole. Then fill in the blanks.

$\frac{3}{7}$ is _______ out of _______ parts. _______ more parts make a whole.

5. Divide each line into the given parts.

a) Thirds 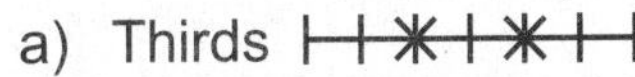

b) Halves

c) Quarters

6. You have $\frac{5}{8}$ of a pie.

a) What does the bottom (denominator) of the fraction tell you?

b) What does the top (numerator) of the fraction tell you?

7. Rectangle A has 5 out of 6 parts shaded.
Rectangle B has 3 out of 4 parts shaded.

A 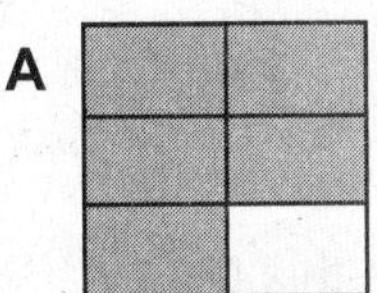

B 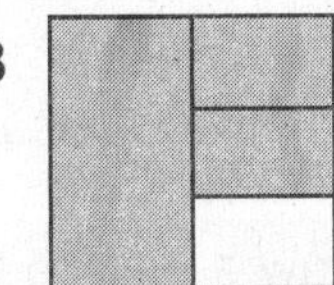

a) Do rectangles A and B have the same amount shaded?

b) What fraction is shaded in each rectangle, $\frac{5}{6}$ or $\frac{3}{4}$? How do you know?

NS7-14 Fractions *(continued)*

Fractions can name parts of a set. In this set, $\frac{3}{5}$ of the figures are pentagons, $\frac{1}{5}$ are squares, and $\frac{1}{5}$ are circles.

8. Fill in the blanks for this set.

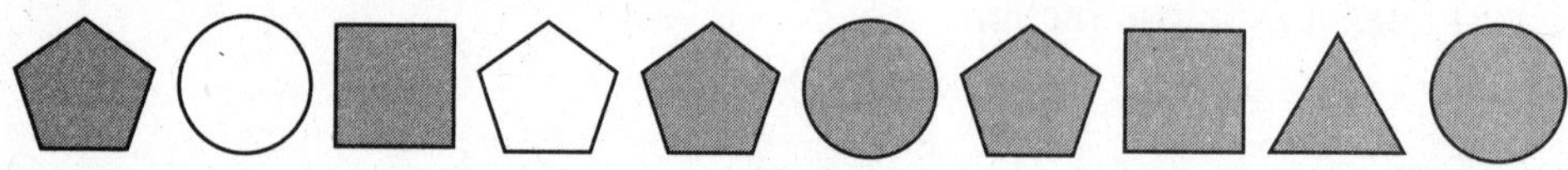

a) $\frac{4}{10}$ of the figures are ______________.

b) ______ of the figures are circles.

c) ______ of the figures are squares.

d) $\frac{1}{10}$ of the figures are ______________.

e) ______ of the figures are shaded.

f) ______ of the figures are unshaded.

9. A hockey team wins 6 games, loses 4 games, and ties 1 game. What fraction of the games did the team…

a) win? ______

b) lose? ______

c) tie? ______

10. A box contains 2 blue marbles, 3 red marbles, and 4 yellow marbles.

What fraction of the marbles are blue? ______

What fraction of the marbles are **not** blue? ______

11. There are 23 students in a class. Each student chose to do a science project on either animals or plants. The chart shows the number of students who chose each topic.

a) Fill in the missing numbers in the chart.

b) What fraction of the children chose to study…

animals? ☐ plants? ☐

c) What fraction of the girls chose to study…

animals? ☐ plants? ☐

	Animals	**Plants**
Boys	7	4
Girls		
Students	12	

12. Draw a picture to solve this puzzle: There are 5 shapes (circles and squares). $\frac{3}{5}$ of the figures are squares. $\frac{3}{5}$ of the figures are shaded. One square is **not** shaded.

NS7-15 Mixed Numbers

Mattias and his friends ate the amount of pie shown.

They ate three and three quarter pies altogether (or $3\frac{3}{4}$ pies).

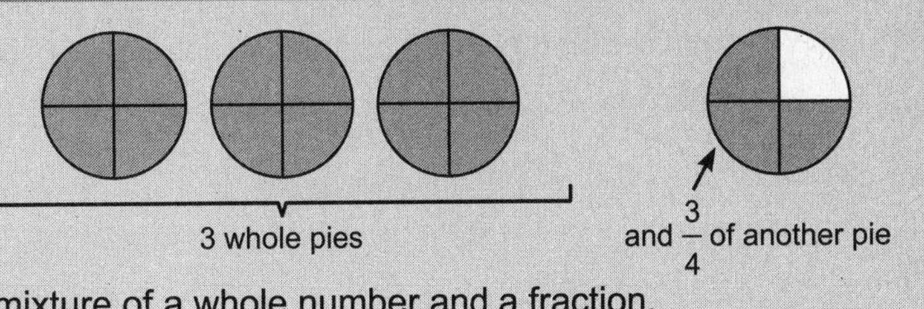

$3\frac{3}{4}$ is called a **mixed number** because it is a mixture of a whole number and a fraction.

1. Find the mixed number for each picture.

a) 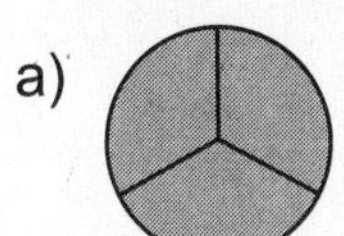 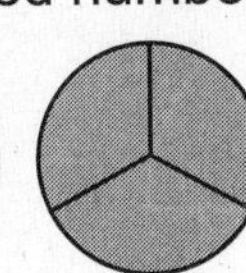 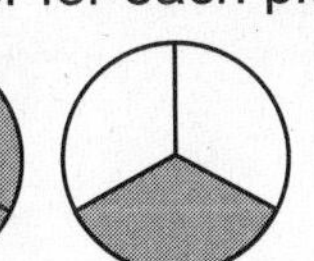 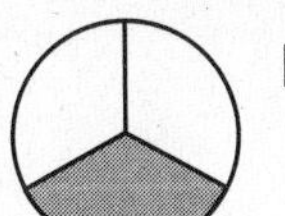

2 whole pies and $\frac{1}{3}$ of another pie = $2\frac{1}{3}$ pies

b) 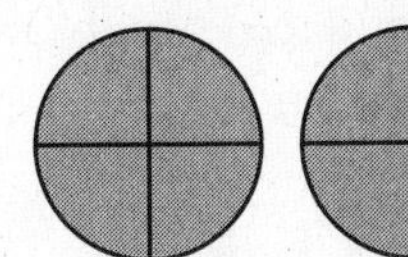

_____ whole pies and _____ of another pie = _____ pies

c) 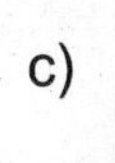 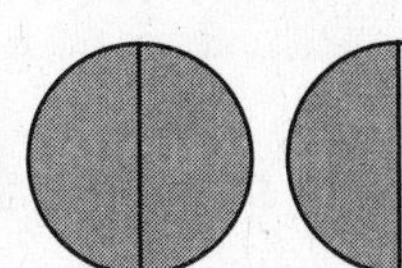

_____ whole pies and _____ of another pie = _____ pies

2. Write the fraction of the shapes that is shaded as a mixed number.

a) 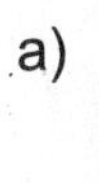 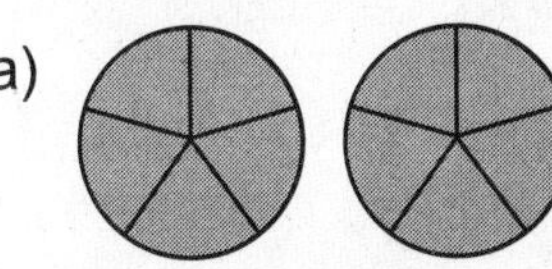 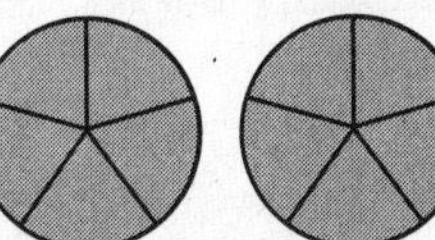 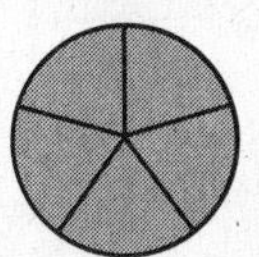 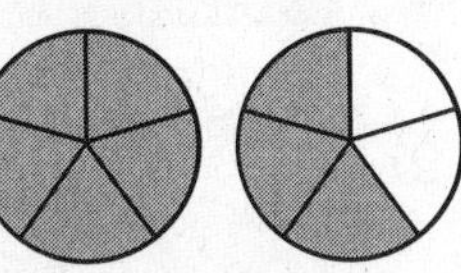 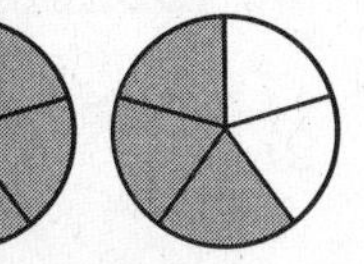

b) 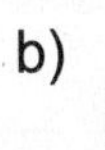 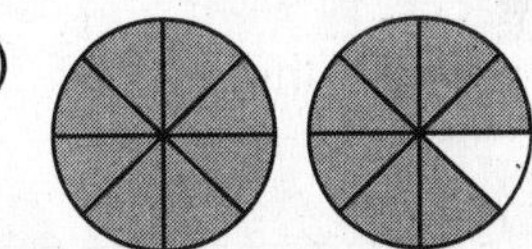

c) 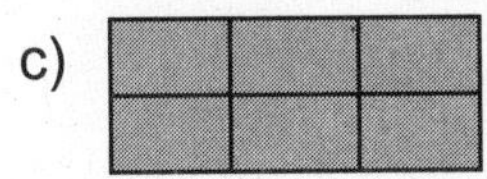 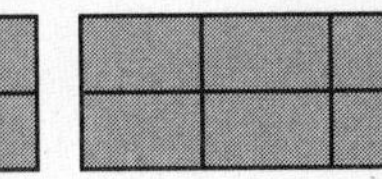 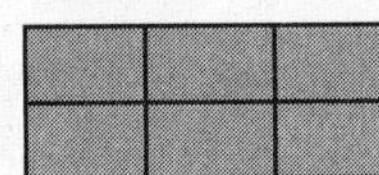 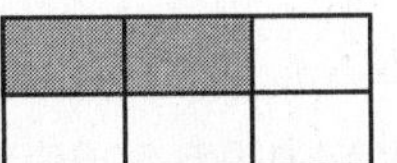

d) 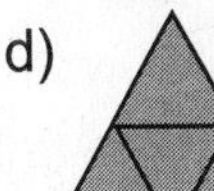 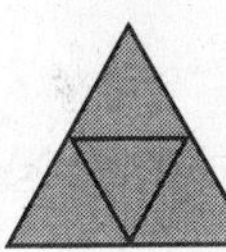 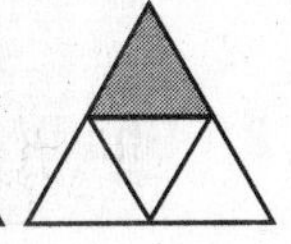

3. Shade the area given by the mixed number. Note: There may be more figures than you need.

a) $2\frac{2}{3}$ 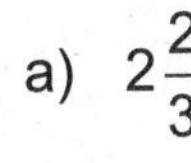  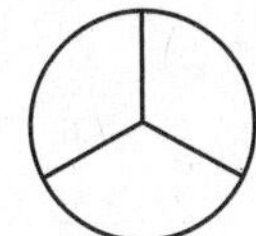 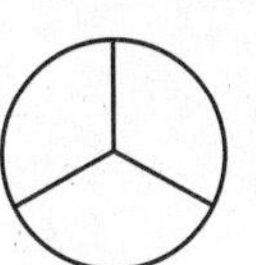 

b) $3\frac{1}{4}$ 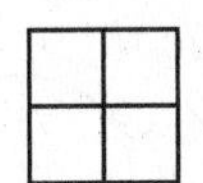 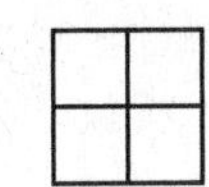 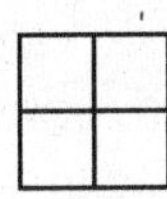 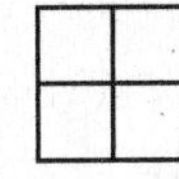

c) $1\frac{5}{6}$  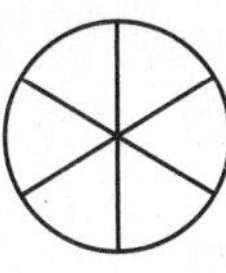 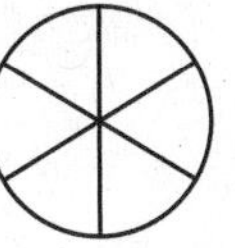 

d) $2\frac{4}{5}$ 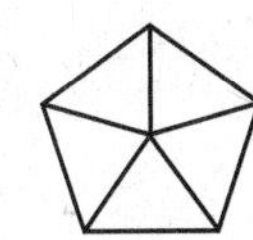 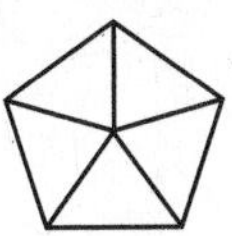 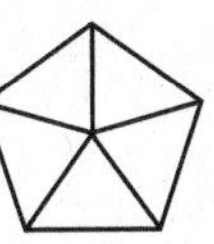 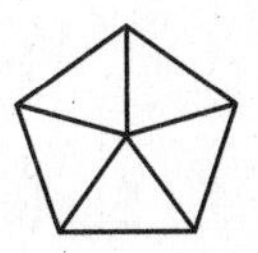

4. Sketch.

a) $3\frac{3}{4}$ pies b) $2\frac{1}{3}$ pies c) $1\frac{3}{5}$ pies d) $2\frac{5}{6}$ pies e) $3\frac{7}{8}$ pies

5. Which fraction represents more pie: $3\frac{2}{3}$, $4\frac{1}{4}$, or $4\frac{3}{4}$? How do you know?

6. Is $5\frac{3}{4}$ closer to 5 or 6?

NS7-16 Improper Fractions

Huan-Yue and her friends ate 9 quarter-sized pieces of pizza.

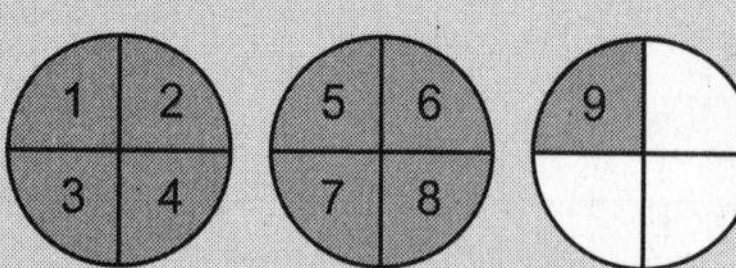

$\frac{9}{4} = 2\frac{1}{4}$

improper fraction — mixed fraction

Altogether, they ate $\frac{9}{4}$ pizzas.

When the numerator of a fraction is larger than the denominator, the fraction represents **more than a whole**. Such fractions are called **improper fractions**.

1. Write these fractions as improper fractions.

a) 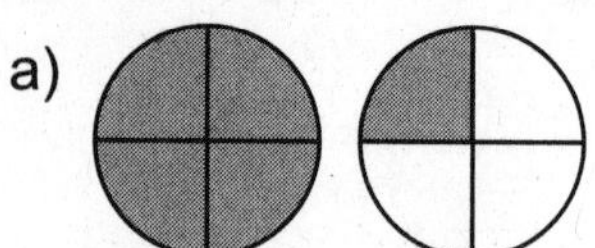

b) 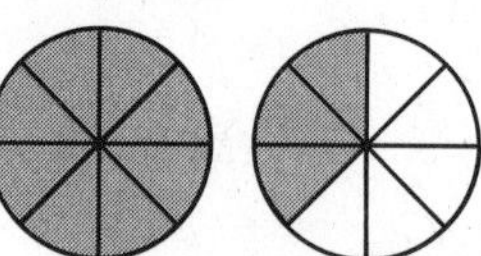

c) 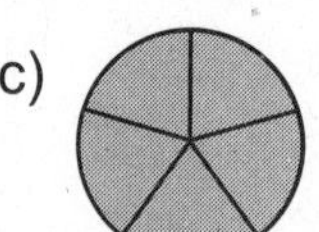 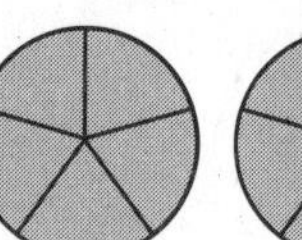

d) 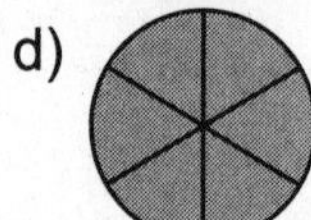 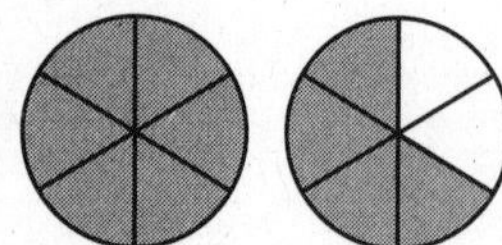

e) 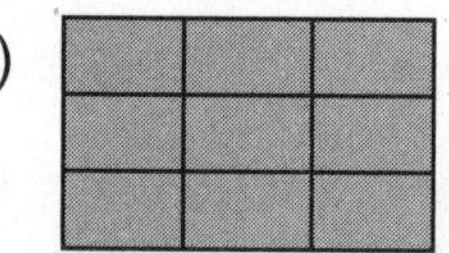  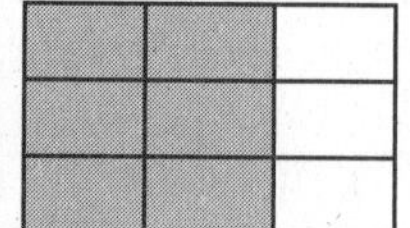

f) 

g) 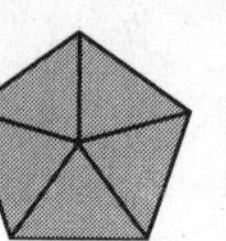 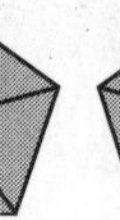 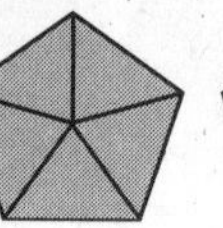 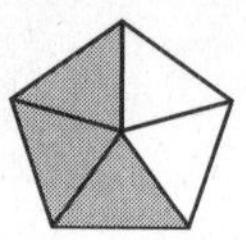

2. Shade one piece at a time until you have shaded the amount of pie given by the improper fraction.

a) $\frac{7}{2}$ 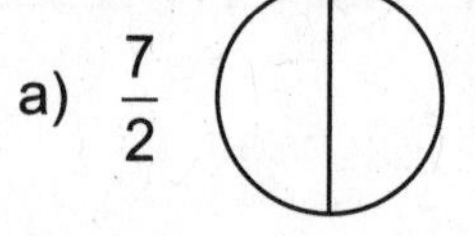  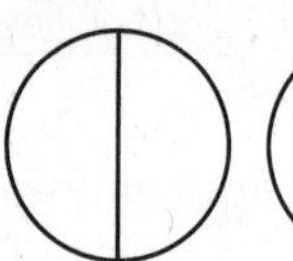  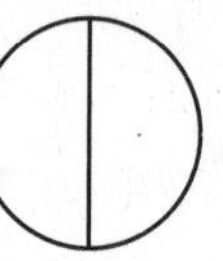

b) $\frac{9}{4}$ 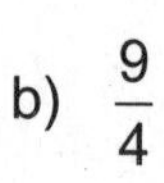 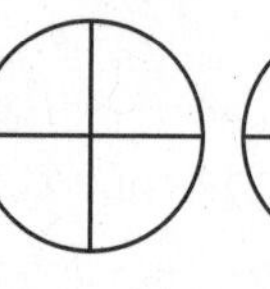 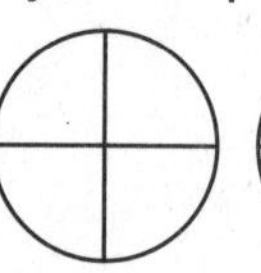 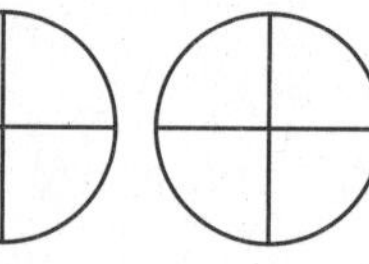

c) $\frac{8}{3}$  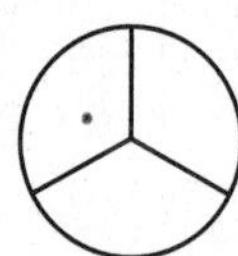  

d) $\frac{15}{5}$ 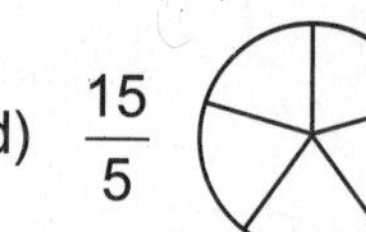  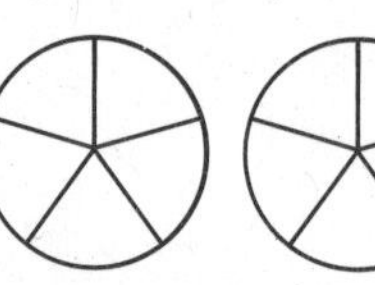

3. Sketch.

a) $\frac{13}{4}$ pies b) $\frac{7}{3}$ pies c) $\frac{9}{2}$ pies d) $\frac{11}{6}$ pies e) $\frac{17}{8}$ pies

4. Which fraction represents more pie: $\frac{7}{4}$, $\frac{9}{4}$, or $\frac{9}{3}$? How do you know?

5. Which fractions are improper fractions? How do you know?

a) $\frac{5}{7}$ b) $\frac{9}{8}$ c) $\frac{13}{11}$

NS7-17 Mixed Numbers and Improper Fractions

1. Write these fractions as mixed numbers and as improper fractions.

a) 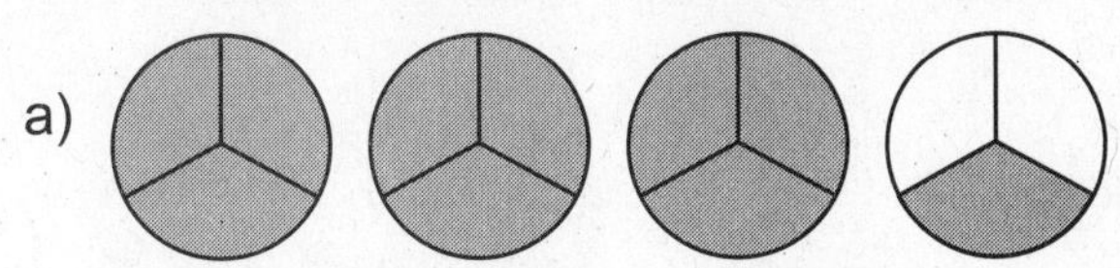

b) 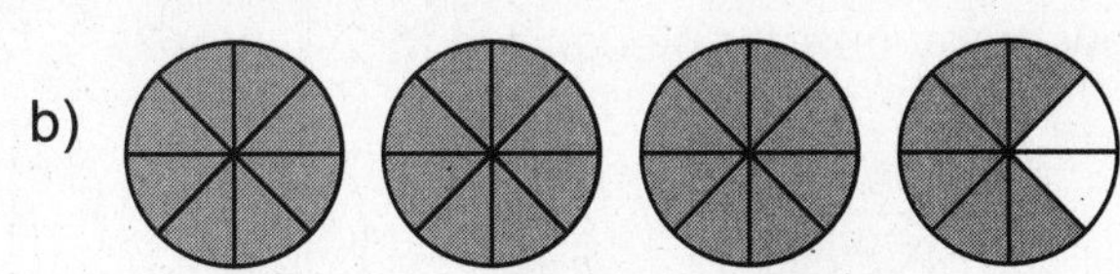

c) 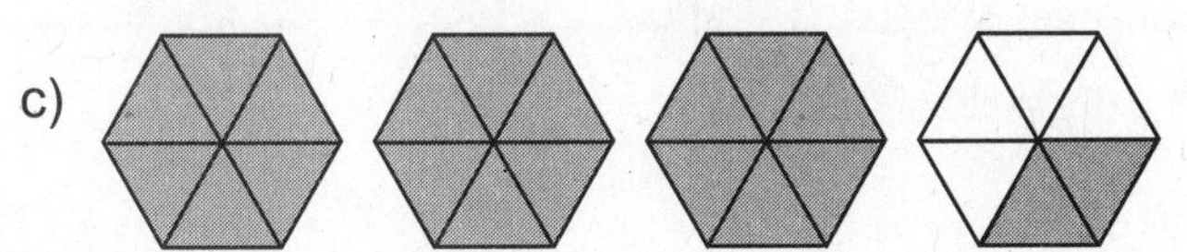

d) 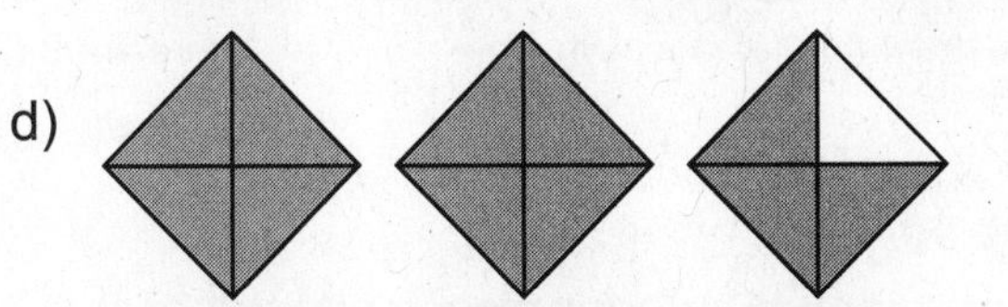

e) 

f) 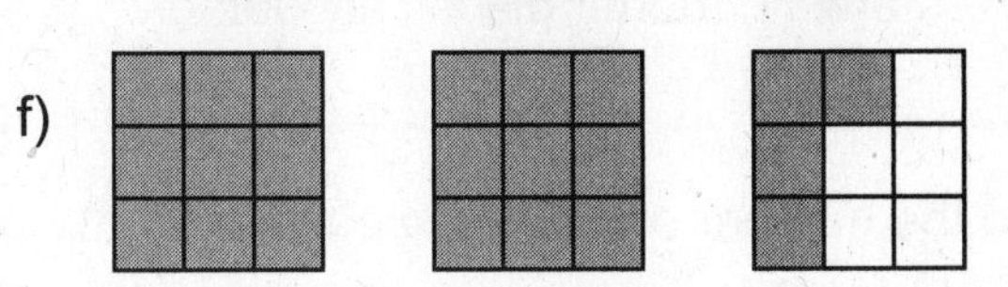

2. Shade the amount of pie given by the mixed number. Then write an improper fraction for the amount.

a) $3\frac{1}{2}$ 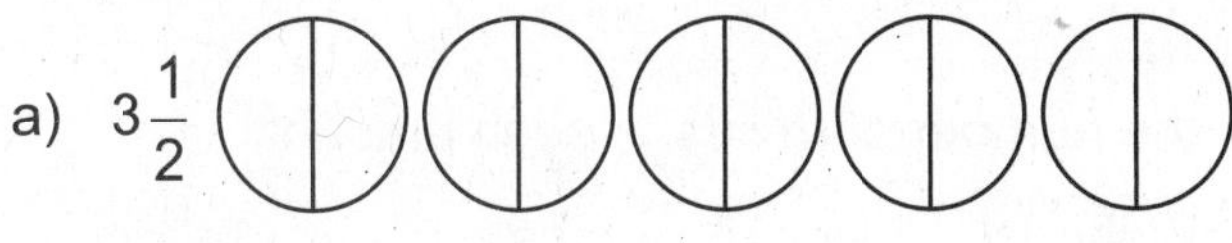

Improper fraction: ______________

b) $4\frac{3}{4}$

Improper fraction: ______________

3. Shade the area given by the improper fraction. Then write a mixed number for the amount of area shaded.

a) $\frac{7}{3}$ 

Mixed number: ______________

b) $\frac{17}{6}$ 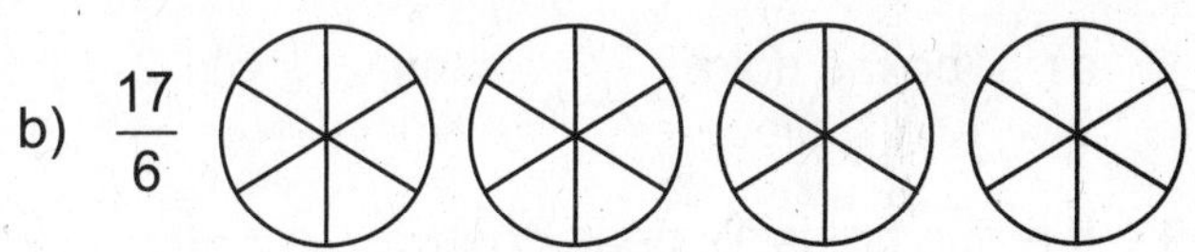

Mixed number: ______________

c) $\frac{13}{5}$ 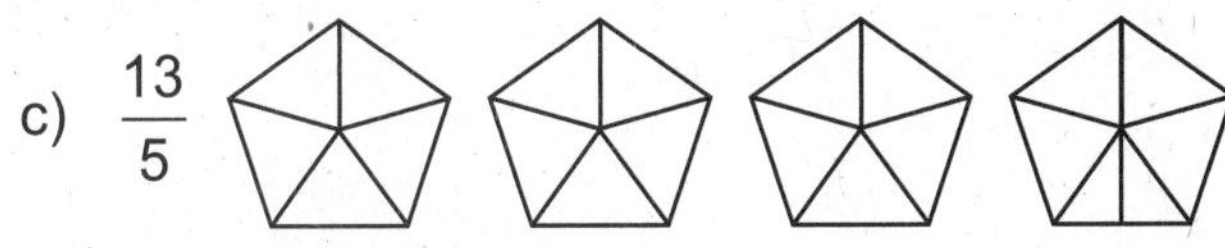

Mixed number: ______________

d) $\frac{21}{8}$ 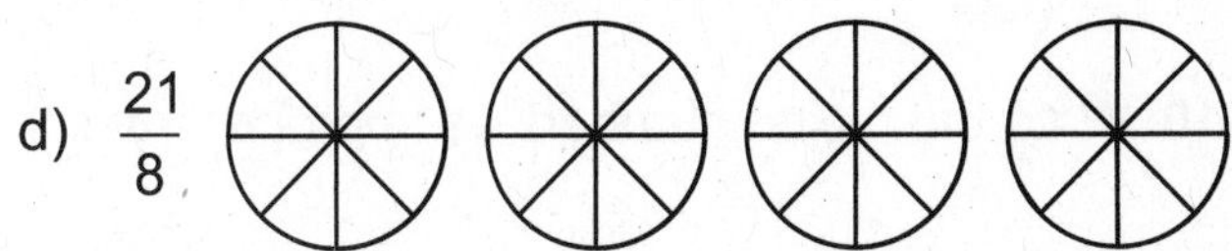

Mixed number: ______________

4. Draw a picture to find out which fraction is greater.

a) $3\frac{1}{2}$ or $\frac{5}{3}$ b) $1\frac{4}{5}$ or $\frac{11}{5}$ c) $\frac{15}{8}$ or $\frac{7}{3}$ d) $\frac{13}{4}$ or $2\frac{2}{3}$

5. How could you use division to find out how many **whole** pies are in $\frac{13}{5}$ of a pie? Explain.

NS7-17 Mixed Numbers and Improper Fractions *(continued)*

How many quarter pieces are in $2\frac{3}{4}$ pies?

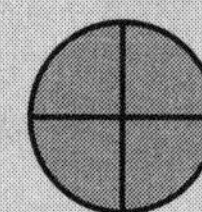

There are 4 quarter pieces in 1 pie.

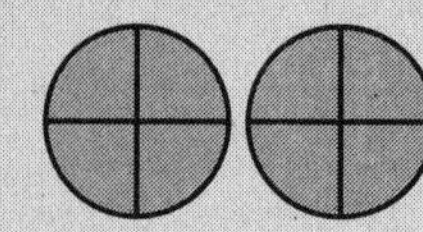

There are 8 (2 × 4) quarters in 2 pies.

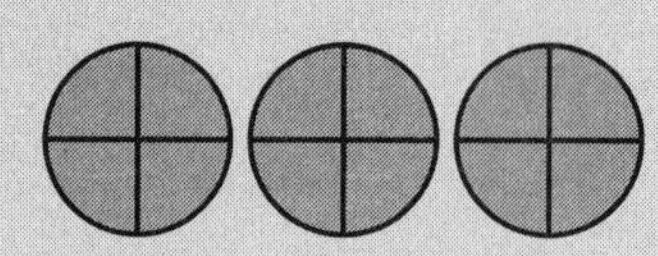

There are 12 (3 × 4) quarters in 3 pies.

8 pieces (2 × 4) + 3 extra pieces = 11

So there are 11 quarter pieces altogether. $2\frac{3}{4} = \frac{11}{4}$

6. Find the number of **halves** in each amount.

a) 1 pie = ______ halves b) 2 pies = ______ halves c) 4 pies = ______ halves

d) $3\frac{1}{2}$ pies = ______ halves e) $4\frac{1}{2}$ pies = ______ halves f) $5\frac{1}{2}$ pies = ______________

7. Each pie has 3 pieces, so each piece is a third. Find the number of **thirds** in each amount.

a) 1 pie = ___3___ thirds b) 2 pies = ______ thirds c) 4 pies = ______ thirds

d) $1\frac{1}{3}$ pies = ______ thirds e) $2\frac{2}{3}$ pies = ____________ f) $5\frac{2}{3}$ pies = ______________

8. A box holds 4 cans, so each can is a fourth. Find the number of **cans** each amount holds.

a) 2 boxes hold ______ cans. b) $2\frac{1}{4}$ boxes hold ______ cans. c) $3\frac{3}{4}$ boxes hold ______ cans.

9. If a bag holds 12 peas, then…

a) $1\frac{1}{12}$ bags hold ______ peas. b) $2\frac{7}{12}$ bags hold ______ peas. c) $3\frac{11}{12}$ bags hold ______ peas.

10. Write the mixed numbers as improper fractions.

a) $2\frac{1}{3} = \frac{}{3}$ b) $5\frac{1}{2} = \frac{}{2}$ c) $4\frac{2}{5} = \frac{}{5}$ d) $7\frac{1}{4} =$ e) $6\frac{3}{7} =$

11. Envelopes come in packs of 6. Alice used $2\frac{5}{6}$ packs. How many envelopes did she use? ______

12. Maia and her friends ate $4\frac{3}{4}$ pizzas. How many quarter-sized pieces did they eat? ______

BONUS ▶ 13. How many quarters are there in $4\frac{1}{2}$ dollars? ______

BONUS ▶ 14. Cindy needs $3\frac{2}{3}$ cups of flour.

a) How many scoops of cup A would she need? ______

b) How many scoops of cup B would she need? ______

A: $\frac{1}{3}$ cups

B: $\frac{1}{6}$ cups

NS7-17 Mixed Numbers and Improper Fractions *(continued)*

How many whole pies are there in $\frac{13}{4}$ pies?

There are 13 pieces altogether, and each pie has 4 pieces.

So you can find the number of whole pies by dividing 13 by 4: **13 ÷ 4 = 3 remainder 1**

There are 3 whole pies and 1 quarter left over: 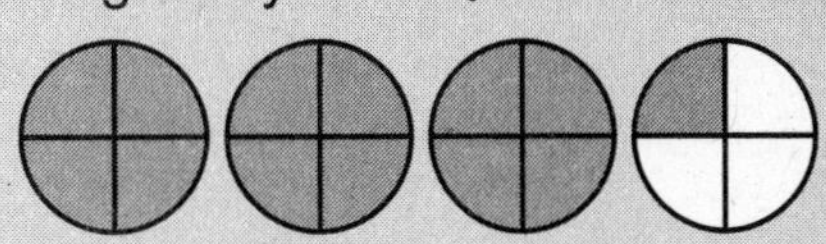 $\frac{13}{4} = 3\frac{1}{4}$

15. Find the number of whole pies in each amount by dividing.

a) $\frac{4}{2}$ pies = _____ whole pies b) $\frac{15}{3}$ pies = _____ whole pies c) $\frac{8}{4}$ pies = _____ whole pies

d) $\frac{21}{7}$ pies = _____ whole pies e) $\frac{20}{5}$ pies = _____ whole pies f) $\frac{24}{6}$ pies = _____ whole pies

16. Find the number of whole pies and the number of pieces remaining by dividing.

a) $\frac{5}{2}$ pies = ___*2*___ whole pies and ___*1*___ half pie = ___$2\frac{1}{2}$___ pies

b) $\frac{9}{2}$ pies = _______ whole pies and _______ half pie = _______ pies

c) $\frac{10}{3}$ pies = _______ whole pies and _______ third = _______ pies

d) $\frac{13}{4}$ pies = _______ whole pies and _______ fourth = _______ pies

17. Divide the numerator by the denominator to write each improper fraction as a mixed number.

a) $\frac{13}{3}$ 13 ÷ 3 = ___*4*___ R ___*1*___ So $\frac{13}{3} = 4\frac{1}{3}$

b) $\frac{13}{6}$ 13 ÷ 3 = ____ R ____ So $\frac{13}{6}$ = _________

c) $\frac{15}{4}$ 15 ÷ 4 = ____ R ____ So $\frac{15}{4}$ = _________

d) $\frac{3}{2}$ = _________ e) $\frac{8}{3}$ = _________ f) $\frac{22}{5}$ = _________

g) $\frac{29}{7}$ = _________ h) $\frac{57}{8}$ = _________ i) $\frac{68}{9}$ = _________

18. Write a mixed number and improper fraction for the total number of litres.

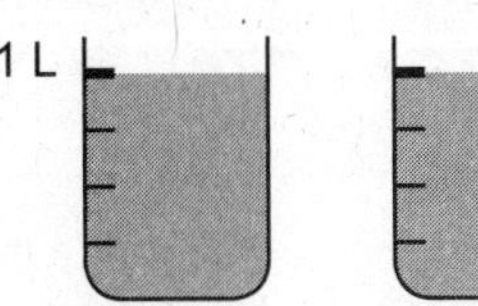

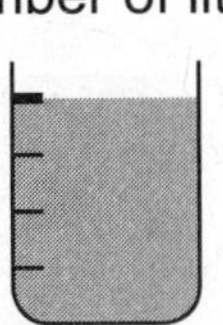
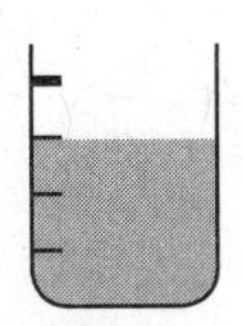

19. Write a mixed number and improper fraction for the length of the rope.

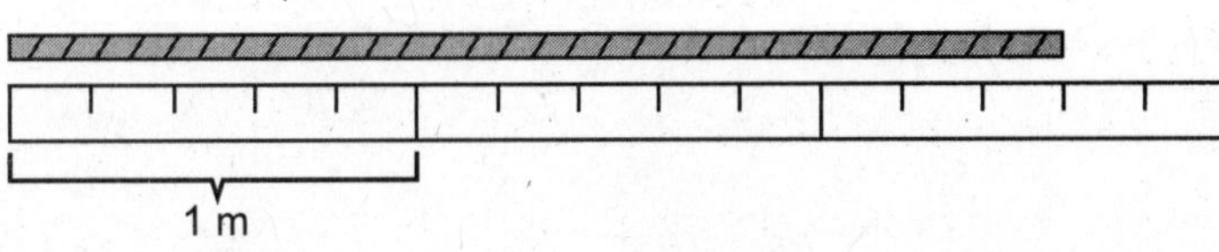

NS7-18 Fractions of Whole Numbers

There are 3 equal groups of dots, so each group is $\frac{1}{3}$ of 6.

There are 2 dots in each group, so $\frac{1}{3}$ of 6 is 2.

There are 4 dots in two groups, so $\frac{2}{3}$ of 6 is 4.

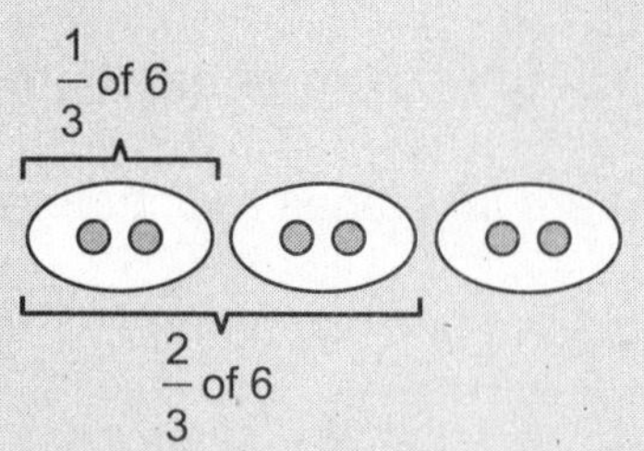

1. Write a fraction for the amount of dots shown.

a)
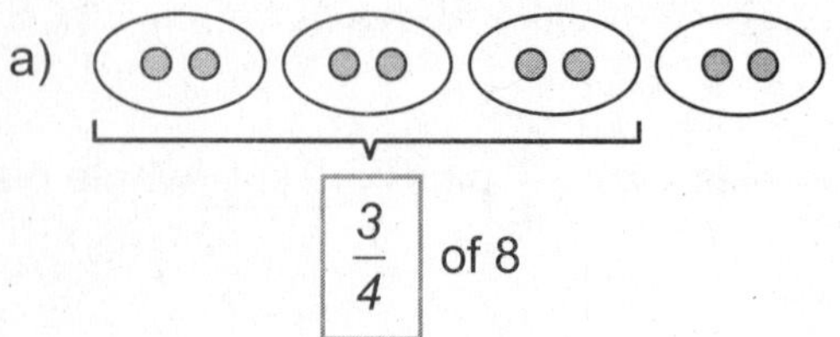

$\frac{3}{4}$ of 8

b)
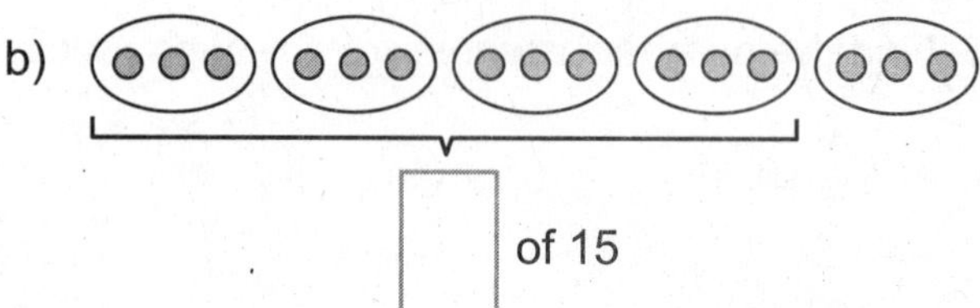

☐ of 15

2. Fill in the missing numbers.

a) $\frac{1}{3}$ of 6 =

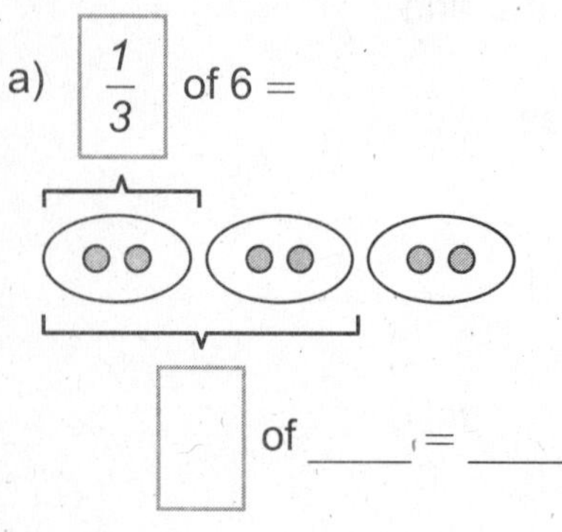

☐ of ____ = ____

b) ☐ of 8 = ______

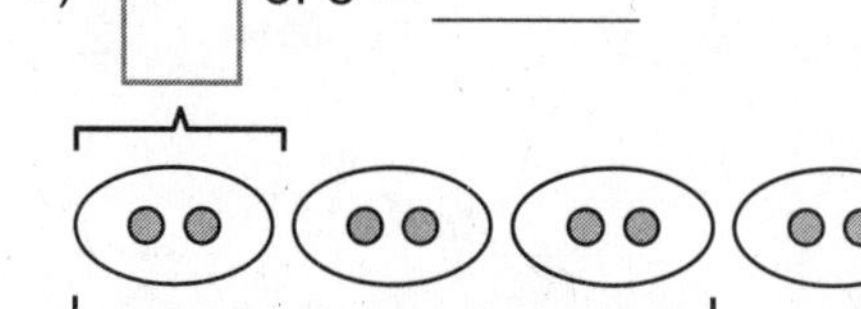

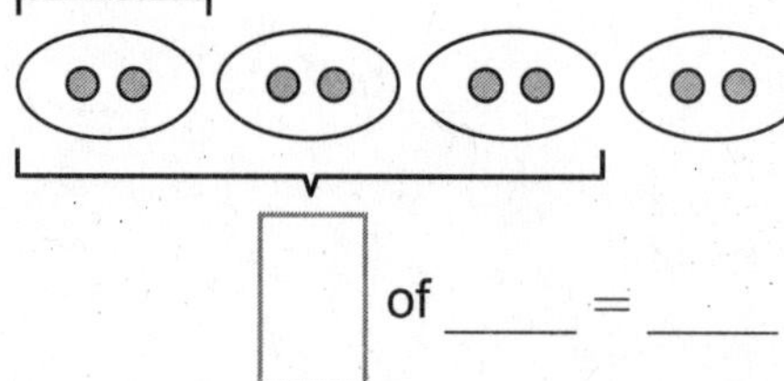

☐ of ____ = ____

c) ☐ of 9 = ______

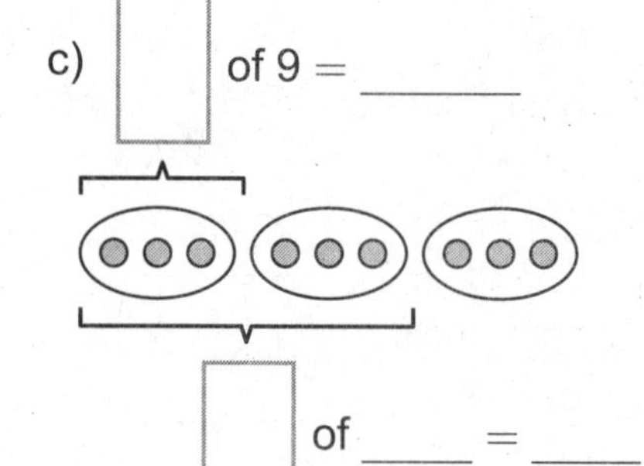

☐ of ____ = ____

d)
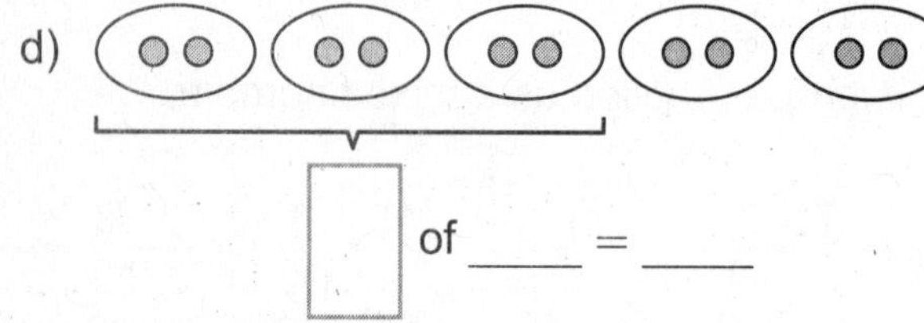

☐ of ____ = ____

e)
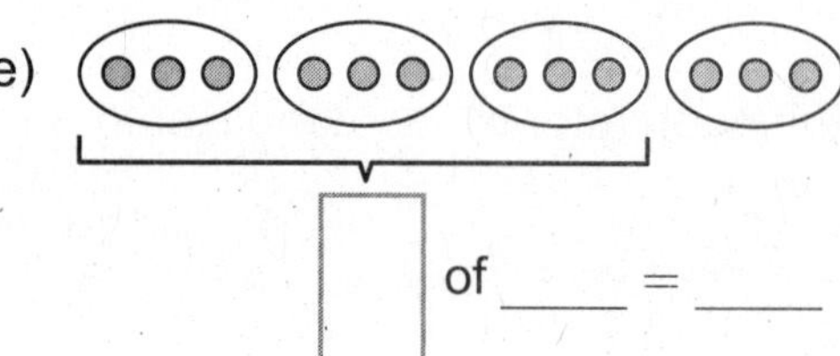

☐ of ____ = ____

3. Draw a circle to show the given amount.

a) $\frac{2}{3}$ of 6

b) $\frac{3}{4}$ of 8

4. Draw the correct number of dots in each circle, then draw a larger circle to show the given amount.

a) $\frac{2}{3}$ of 12

b) $\frac{1}{3}$ of 15

NS7-18 Fractions of Whole Numbers *(continued)*

5. Find the fraction of the whole amount by drawing the correct number of circles and then filling in the correct number of dots in each circle.

   a) $\frac{2}{3}$ of 9 is ______________.   b) $\frac{3}{5}$ of 10 is ______________.

6. This is how Andy finds $\frac{2}{3}$ of 12.

Step 1: He finds $\frac{1}{3}$ of 12 by dividing 12 by 3.	**Step 3:** Then he multiplies the result by 2.
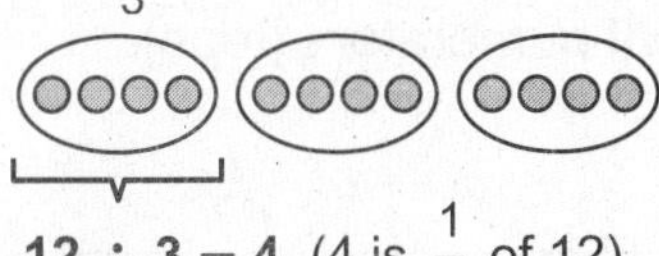	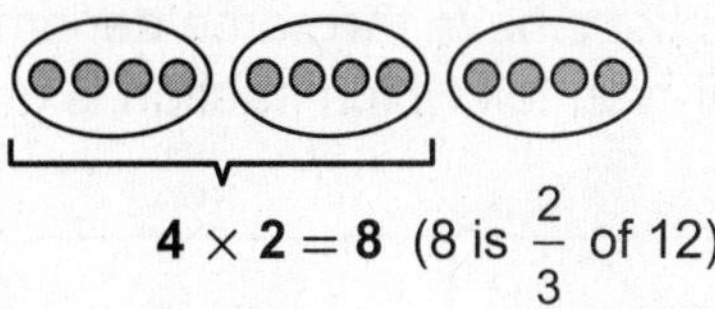
12 ÷ 3 = 4 (4 is $\frac{1}{3}$ of 12)	**4 × 2 = 8** (8 is $\frac{2}{3}$ of 12)

Find the following amounts using Andy's method.

a) $\frac{1}{3}$ of 9 = ____ So $\frac{2}{3}$ of 9 = ____   b) $\frac{1}{4}$ of 8 = ____ So $\frac{3}{4}$ of 8 = ____

c) $\frac{1}{3}$ of 15 = ____ So $\frac{2}{3}$ of 15 = ____   d) $\frac{1}{5}$ of 25 = ____ So $\frac{3}{5}$ of 25 = ____

e) $\frac{1}{3}$ of 27 = ____ So $\frac{2}{3}$ of 27 = ____

7. 20 students are on a bus. $\frac{3}{5}$ are boys. How many boys are on the bus? ______________

8. A store had 15 watermelons. They sold $\frac{2}{3}$ of the watermelons. How many watermelons were sold? ______________ How many were left? ______________

9. Shade $\frac{1}{4}$ of the squares. Draw stripes in $\frac{1}{6}$ of the squares. How many squares are blank? ______________

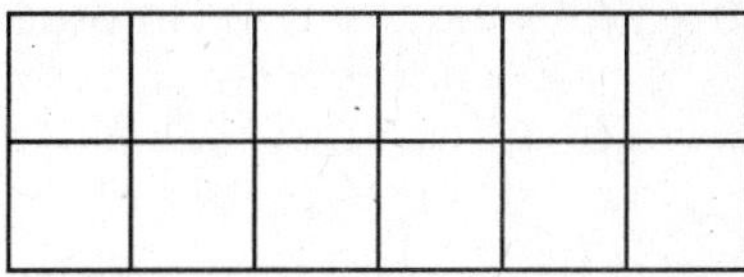

10. Ed has 20 sea shells. $\frac{2}{5}$ are turret shells. $\frac{1}{4}$ are scallops. The rest are conchs. How many shells are conchs?

11. Alan started studying at 8:15. He studied history for $\frac{1}{3}$ of an hour and math for $\frac{2}{5}$ of an hour. At what time did he stop studying?

12. Which is longer, 21 months or $1\frac{5}{6}$ of a year?

BONUS▶ There were 108 grapes. Sara ate $\frac{1}{2}$ of them, Jeff ate $\frac{1}{3}$ of them, and Ron ate $\frac{1}{6}$ of them. How many were left over?

NS7-19 Comparing Fractions — Introduction

1. Shade the given amount in each pie. Then circle the greater fraction in each pair.

a) $\frac{5}{8}$ $\frac{7}{8}$ b) $\frac{6}{9}$ $\frac{4}{9}$ c) $\frac{8}{10}$ $\frac{7}{10}$

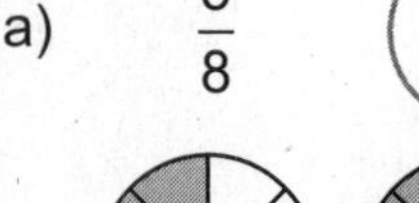
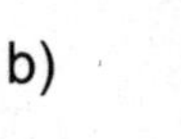
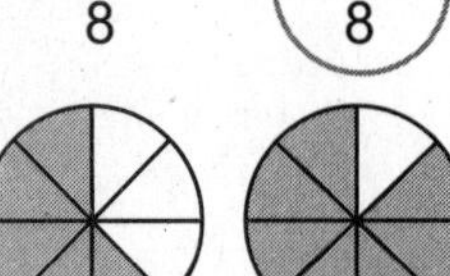

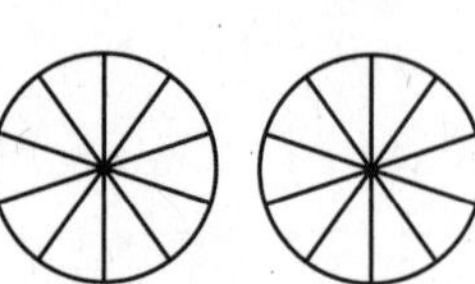

2. Two fractions have the same denominators (bottoms) but different numerators (tops). How can you tell which fraction is greater?

____

____

3. Shade the given amount in each pie. Then circle the greater fraction in each pair.

a) $\frac{1}{3}$ $\frac{1}{4}$ b) $\frac{1}{10}$ $\frac{1}{2}$ c) $\frac{3}{5}$ $\frac{3}{10}$

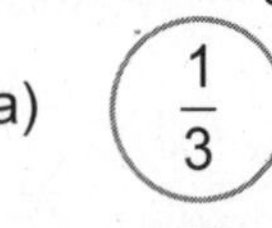
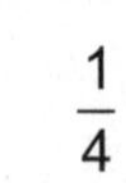
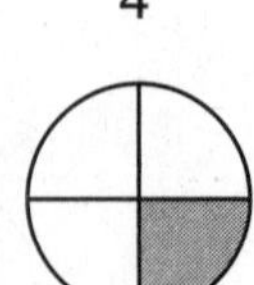

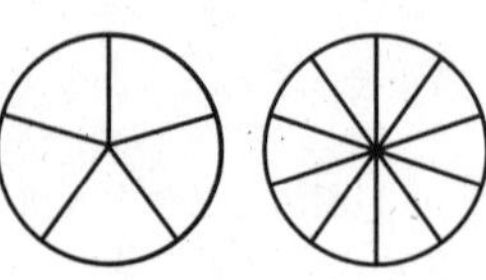

4. Two fractions have the same numerators (tops) but different denominators (bottoms). How can you tell which fraction is greater?

____

____

5. Write the fractions in order from least to greatest.

a) $\frac{1}{9}$ $\frac{1}{4}$ $\frac{1}{17}$ b) $\frac{2}{11}$ $\frac{2}{5}$ $\frac{2}{7}$ $\frac{2}{16}$ c) $\frac{4}{5}$ $\frac{1}{5}$ $\frac{3}{5}$

____ ____ ____ ____ ____ ____ ____ ____ ____ ____

d) $\frac{9}{10}$ $\frac{2}{10}$ $\frac{1}{10}$ $\frac{5}{10}$ e) $\frac{5}{8}$ $\frac{7}{8}$ $\frac{5}{9}$ f) $\frac{3}{7}$ $\frac{2}{7}$ $\frac{3}{5}$

____ ____ ____ ____ ____ ____ ____ ____ ____ ____

BONUS▶ $\frac{15}{19}$ $\frac{9}{23}$ $\frac{11}{21}$ $\frac{11}{19}$ $\frac{6}{23}$ $\frac{9}{22}$ $\frac{15}{17}$ $\frac{9}{21}$

6. Which fraction is greater? How do you know?

a) $\frac{7}{5}$ or $\frac{9}{5}$ b) $4\frac{1}{4}$ or $4\frac{3}{4}$

NS7-19 Comparing Fractions — Introduction *(continued)*

7. a) How much more do you need to shade to make a whole?

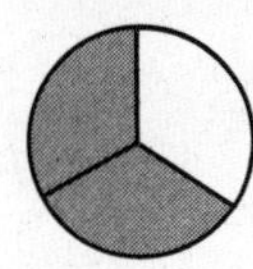 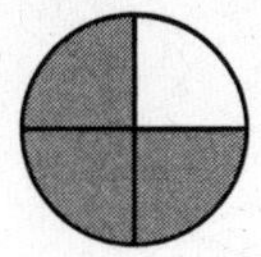 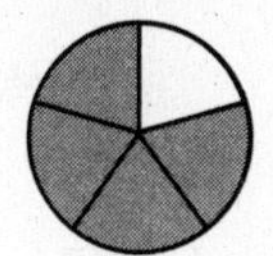 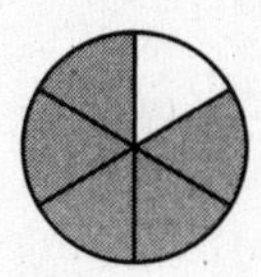

$\frac{2}{3}$ + ______ = 1 $\frac{3}{4}$ + ______ = 1 $\frac{4}{5}$ + ______ = 1 $\frac{5}{6}$ + ______ = 1

b) Which fraction is greater, $\frac{5}{6}$ or $\frac{6}{7}$? How do you know?

____

____

8. How much more do you need to make one whole?

$\frac{11}{13}$ [$\frac{2}{13}$] $\frac{14}{15}$ [ ] $\frac{7}{9}$ [ ] $\frac{19}{20}$ [ ] $\frac{5}{7}$ [ ] $\frac{12}{13}$ [ ]

9. a) Complete the chart.

Improper Fraction				$\frac{11}{5}$		$\frac{13}{3}$
Mixed Number	$6\frac{1}{2}$	$2\frac{3}{4}$	$3\frac{1}{4}$		$1\frac{5}{6}$	

b) Order the improper fractions from least to greatest. ____ ____ ____ ____ ____ ____

c) Order the mixed numbers from least to greatest. ____ ____ ____ ____ ____ ____

d) Explain why the lists in b) and c) should agree. If they do not, find your mistake.

10. Place these numbers on the number line. $\frac{1}{3}$ $\frac{4}{3}$ $2\frac{1}{3}$ $3\frac{1}{3}$ $\frac{13}{3}$

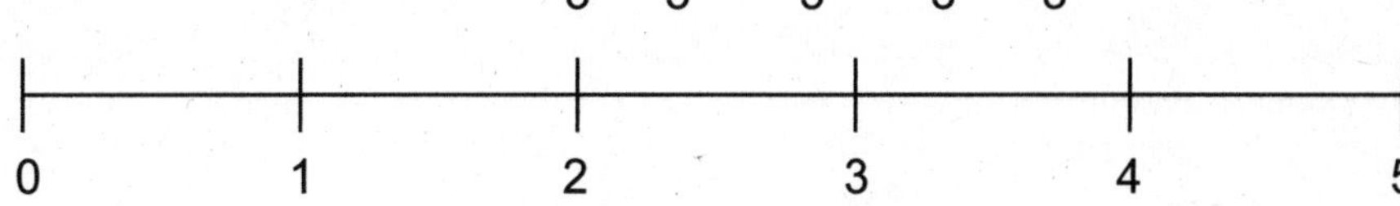

11. Is $2\frac{3}{4}$ closer to 2 or to 3? How do you know? ______________________

12. Place these numbers on the number line. $2\frac{3}{4}$ $\frac{11}{5}$ $\frac{6}{7}$ $\frac{9}{2}$ $\frac{11}{3}$ $\frac{9}{3}$

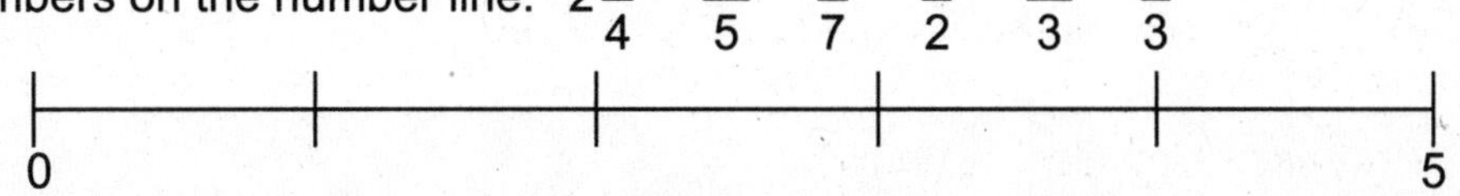

BONUS▸ Write the fractions from Question 8 from greatest to least. Explain how you compared the fractions.

NS7-20 Equivalent Fractions

1. Compare the fractions by shading to see which is more. Write $>$ (more than), $<$ (less than), or $=$ (equal).

a) 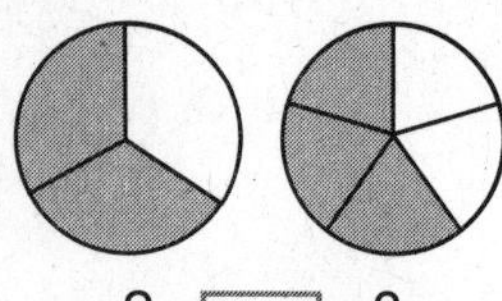

$\frac{2}{3} \ \boxed{>} \ \frac{3}{5}$

b) 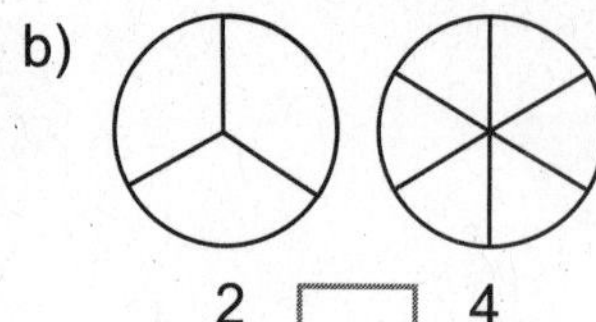

$\frac{2}{3} \ \square \ \frac{4}{6}$

c) 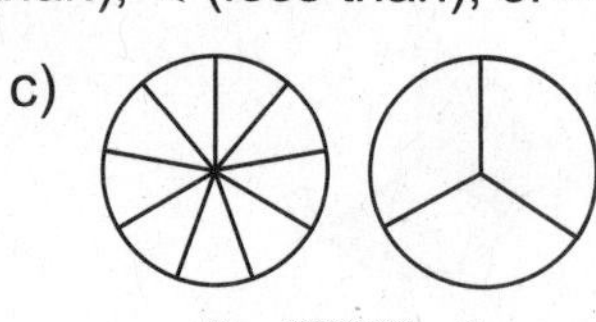

$\frac{5}{9} \ \square \ \frac{2}{3}$

d) 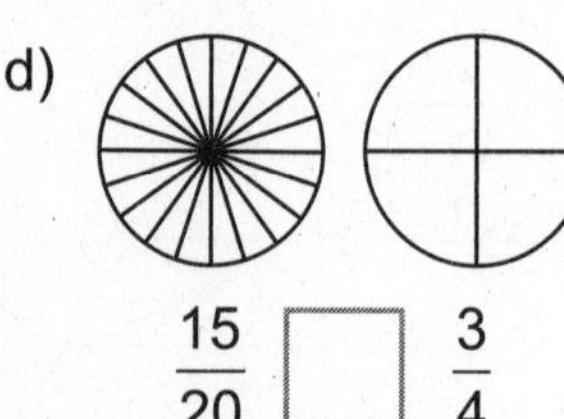

$\frac{15}{20} \ \square \ \frac{3}{4}$

e) 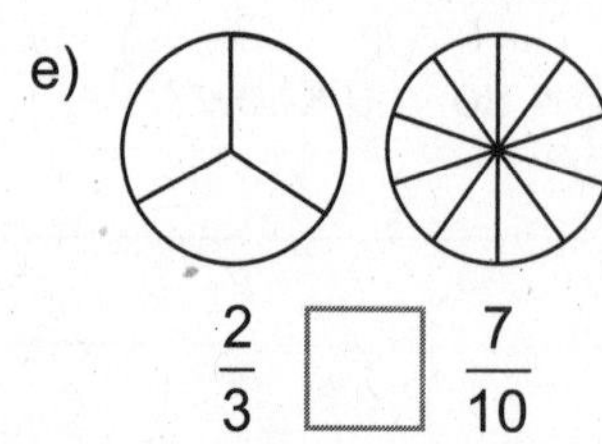

$\frac{2}{3} \ \square \ \frac{7}{10}$

f) 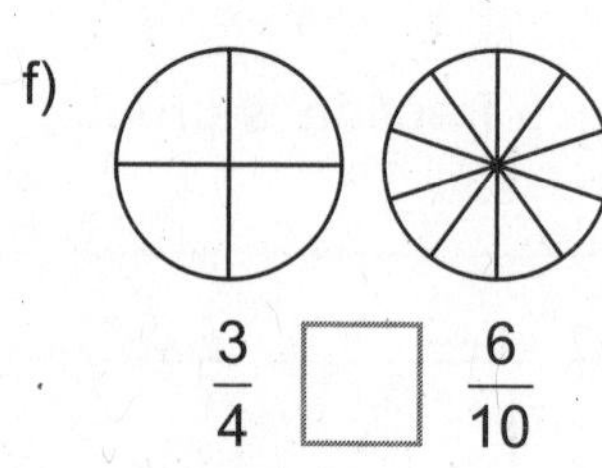

$\frac{3}{4} \ \square \ \frac{6}{10}$

Two fractions are said to be equivalent if they represent the same amount.

2. List two pairs of equivalent fractions from Question 1. _____ = _____ and _____ = _____

3. Group the squares into larger blocks to make an equivalent fraction.

a) 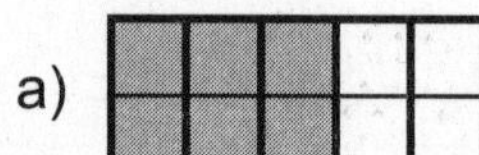 $\frac{6}{10} = \frac{3}{5}$

b) 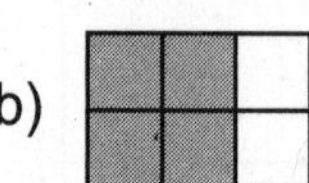 $\frac{4}{6} = \frac{\ }{3}$

c) 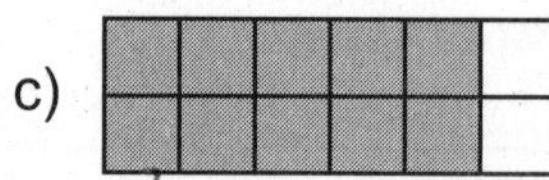 $\frac{10}{12} = \frac{\ }{6}$

4. Write three equivalent fractions for the amount shaded here.

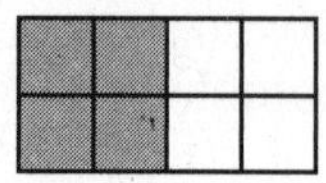

5. a) Draw lines to cut the pies into...

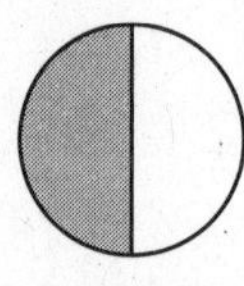

4 equal pieces

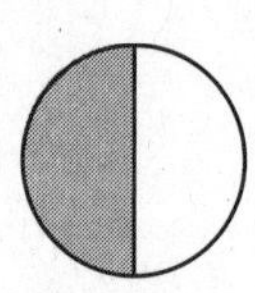

6 equal pieces

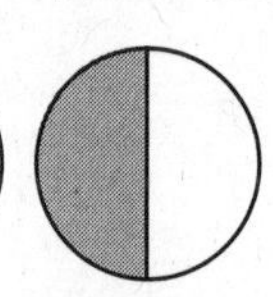

8 equal pieces

b) Fill in the numerators of the equivalent fractions.

$\frac{1}{2} = \frac{\ }{4} = \frac{\ }{6} = \frac{\ }{8}$

6. Make an equivalent fraction by cutting each shaded piece into the same number of equal parts. Then cut the remaining pieces into that number of equal parts.

a) 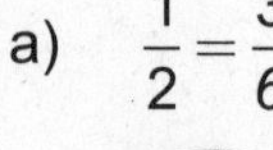

$\frac{1}{2} = \frac{3}{6}$

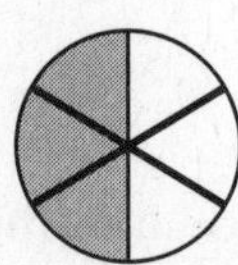

b) $\frac{2}{3} = \frac{4}{\ }$

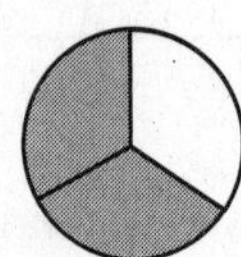

c) $\frac{2}{3} = \frac{6}{\ }$

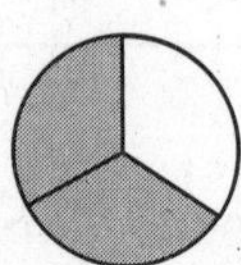

d) $\frac{2}{5} = \frac{8}{\ }$

NS7-21 Comparing Fractions Using Equivalent Fractions

When you multiply the numerator and denominator of a fraction by the same number, you create an equivalent fraction.

$$\frac{1}{2} = \frac{1 \times 5}{2 \times 5} = \frac{5}{10}$$

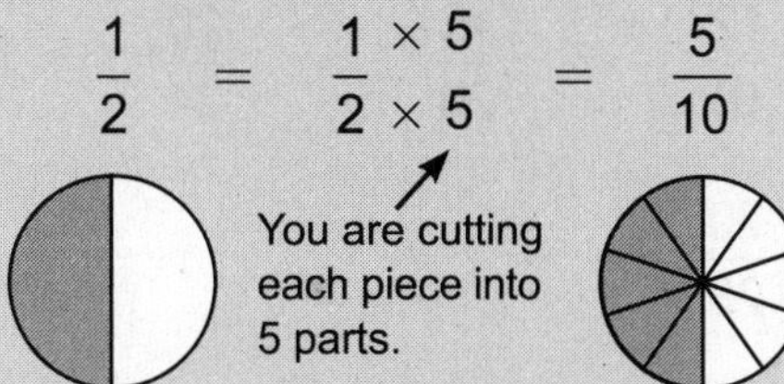

1. Make an equivalent fraction by multiplying the numerator and denominator by the same number.

a) $\frac{3}{5} = \frac{9}{\_\_}$ b) $\frac{2}{5} = \frac{\_\_}{20}$ c) $\frac{3}{10} = \frac{\_\_}{30}$ d) $\frac{5}{6} = \frac{20}{\_\_}$

e) $\frac{2}{3} = \frac{12}{\_\_}$ f) $\frac{2}{5} = \frac{20}{\_\_}$ g) $\frac{2}{3} = \frac{\_\_}{12}$ h) $\frac{3}{3} = \frac{12}{\_\_}$

2. Write six equivalent fractions for each by skip counting to find the numerators.

a) $\frac{2}{3} = \frac{\_\_}{6} = \frac{\_\_}{9} = \frac{\_\_}{12} = \frac{\_\_}{15} = \frac{\_\_}{18} = \frac{\_\_}{21}$

b) $\frac{3}{5} = \frac{\_\_}{10} = \frac{\_\_}{15} = \frac{\_\_}{20} = \frac{\_\_}{25} = \frac{\_\_}{30} = \frac{\_\_}{35}$

3. Which of the fractions in Question 2 is greater, $\frac{2}{3}$ or $\frac{3}{5}$? Find the answer two ways, as follows.

a) Select two fractions with the same denominators from the lists in Question 2. ______ and ______

Which of the two fractions is greater, $\frac{2}{3}$ or $\frac{3}{5}$? ______

How do you know? ______________________________

b) Select two fractions with the same numerators from the lists in Question 2. ______ and ______

Which of the two fractions is greater, $\frac{2}{3}$ or $\frac{3}{5}$? ______

How do you know? ______________________________

c) Did you get the same answer both ways? ______

4. a) Find four equivalent fractions for $\frac{4}{7}$. $\frac{4}{7} = \frac{\_\_}{14} = \frac{\_\_}{21} = \frac{\_\_}{28} = \frac{\_\_}{35}$

b) Write $\frac{2}{3}$, $\frac{3}{5}$, and $\frac{4}{7}$ in order from smallest to largest.

______ ______ ______

NS7-21 Comparing Fractions Using Equivalent Fractions *(cont'd)*

5. List equivalent fractions for each pair in order until you find two with the same denominator. Then compare the fractions.

a) $\frac{3}{4} = \frac{6}{8} = \frac{9}{12} = \frac{12}{16} = \frac{15}{20} = \frac{20}{24} = \frac{25}{28}$

$\frac{5}{7} = \frac{10}{14} = \frac{15}{21} = \frac{20}{28}$

$\frac{3}{4}$ [>] $\frac{5}{7}$

b) $\frac{2}{5}$

$\frac{1}{3}$

$\frac{2}{5}$ [ ] $\frac{1}{3}$

c) $\frac{5}{6}$

$\frac{7}{9}$

$\frac{5}{6}$ [ ] $\frac{7}{9}$

d) $\frac{5}{8}$ and $\frac{3}{4}$

e) $\frac{5}{8}$ and $\frac{7}{12}$

f) $\frac{3}{5}$ and $\frac{5}{9}$

g) $\frac{7}{12}$ and $\frac{8}{15}$

6. a) Write several fractions equivalent to $\frac{1}{2}$.

$\frac{1}{2} = \frac{\_\_}{4} = \frac{\_\_}{6} = \frac{\_\_}{8} = \frac{\_\_}{10} = \frac{\_\_}{12} = \frac{\_\_}{14} = \frac{\_\_}{16} = \frac{\_\_}{18} = \frac{\_\_}{20}$

b) How much more than a half is each fraction below?

$\frac{3}{4}$ is ____ more than $\frac{1}{2}$.

$\frac{4}{6}$ is ____ more than $\frac{1}{2}$.

$\frac{5}{8}$ is ____ more than $\frac{1}{2}$.

c) Write the fractions from part b) in order from smallest to largest.

Does this agree with your answer from Question 5e) ? ______

BONUS▶ Which is bigger, $\frac{187}{372}$ or $\frac{214}{426}$? Explain your choice.

7. Create an equivalent fraction with denominator 24 by multiplying the numerator and denominator by the same number.

a) $\frac{1 \times 12}{2 \times 12} = \frac{12}{24}$

b) $\frac{3}{8} = \frac{\_\_}{24}$

c) $\frac{5}{6} = \frac{\_\_}{24}$

d) $\frac{3}{4} = \frac{\_\_}{24}$

e) $\frac{2}{3} = \frac{\_\_}{24}$

f) $\frac{7}{8} = \frac{\_\_}{24}$

g) $\frac{1}{6} = \frac{\_\_}{24}$

h) $\frac{5}{12} = \frac{\_\_}{24}$

8. Write the fractions from Question 7 in order from smallest to largest.

NS7-22 Problems and Puzzles

1. The chart shows the number of walls in a house painted a particular colour.

   a) What fraction of the walls is painted green?

   b) What colour was used to paint one fifth of the walls?

   c) What colour was used to paint one half of the walls?

Colour	Number of Walls
White	10
Yellow	5
Blue	4
Green	1

2. Subdivide the line into ten equal parts using a ruler and then mark the fractions.

   $\frac{3}{10}$ $\frac{7}{10}$ $\frac{9}{10}$ $\frac{1}{2}$ $\frac{2}{5}$

3. $\frac{5}{6}$ of a pizza is covered in olives:

   $\frac{1}{3}$ of the pizza is covered in mushrooms:

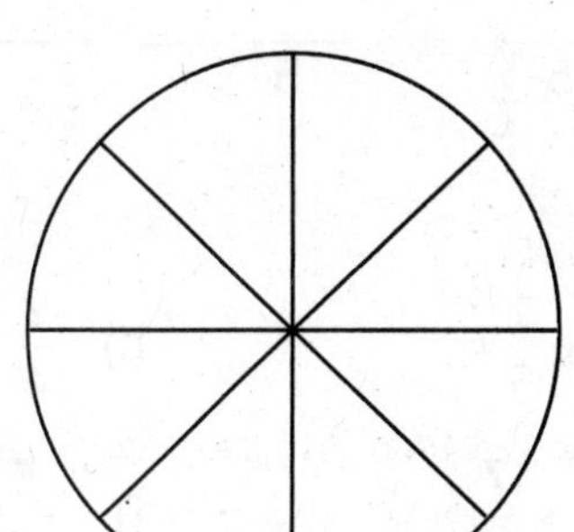

   Each piece has at least one topping. Complete the picture.

   How many pieces are covered in olives **and** mushrooms? _______

4. Equivalent fractions are said to be in the same **family**.
   Write two fractions in the same family as the fraction in each triangle.

   a) 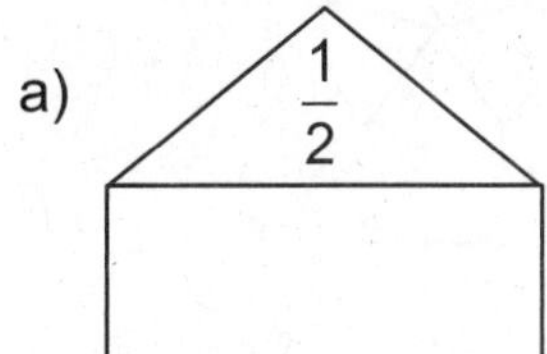

   b) 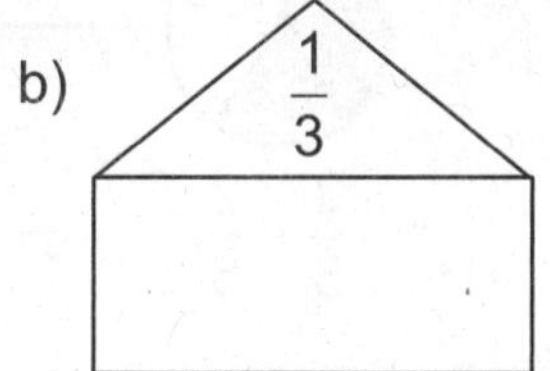

   c) 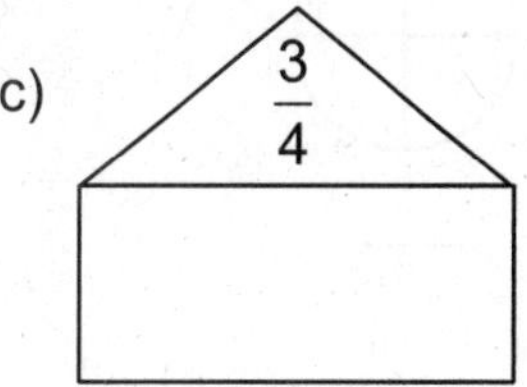

   d) 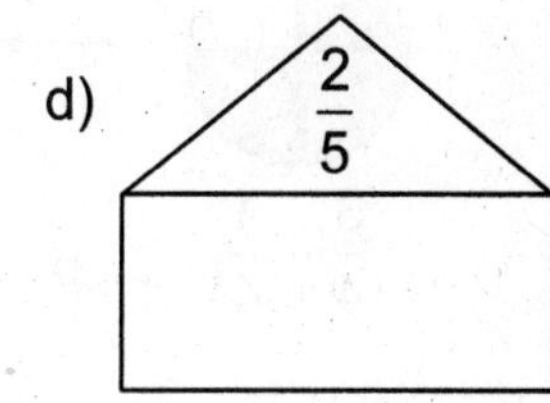

5. In each question, circle the **pair** of fractions that are in the same family.

   a) $\frac{1}{2}$ $\frac{4}{6}$ $\frac{5}{10}$ b) $\frac{3}{15}$ $\frac{16}{20}$ $\frac{4}{5}$ c) $\frac{2}{3}$ $\frac{4}{6}$ $\frac{1}{4}$

6. Find two fractions from the fraction family of $\frac{4}{12}$ with numerators smaller than 4. ____________

7. Find five fractions from the fraction family of $\frac{12}{24}$ with numerators smaller than 12. ____________

NS7-23 Adding and Subtracting Fractions

1. Imagine moving the shaded pieces from pies A and B into pie plate C. Show how much of pie C would be filled, then write a fraction for pie C.

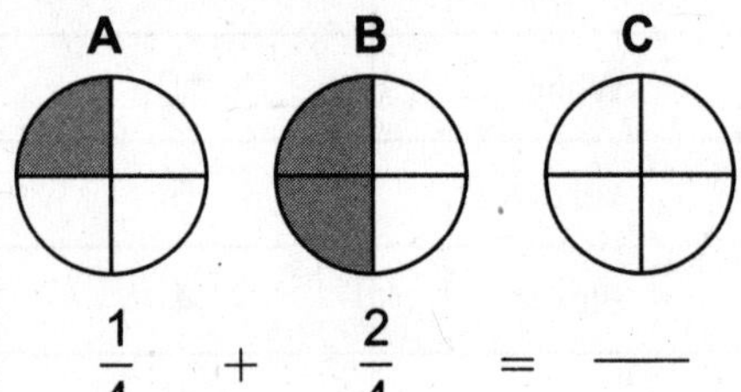

$\frac{1}{4} + \frac{2}{4} = \underline{\quad}$

2. Imagine pouring the liquid from cups A and B into cup C. Shade the amount of liquid that would be in C. Then complete the addition statements.

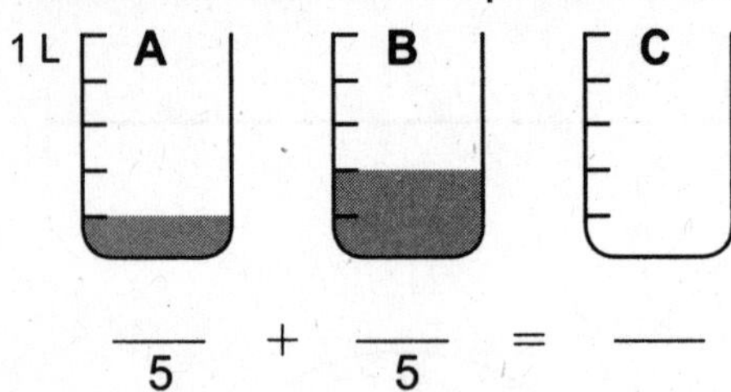

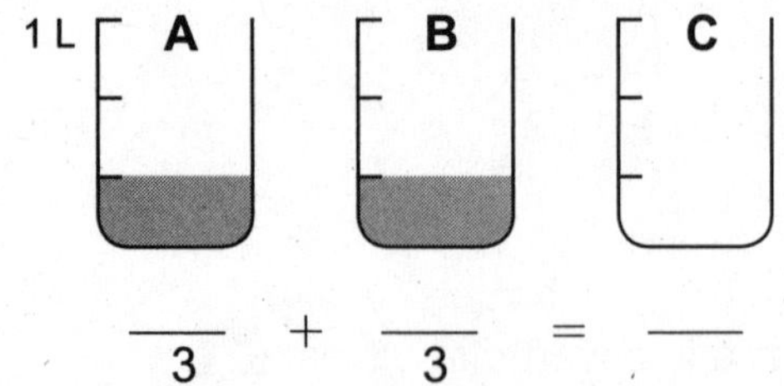

$\frac{\quad}{5} + \frac{\quad}{5} = \underline{\quad}$ $\frac{\quad}{3} + \frac{\quad}{3} = \underline{\quad}$

3. Add.

a) $\frac{3}{5}+\frac{1}{5}=$ b) $\frac{2}{4}+\frac{1}{4}=$ c) $\frac{3}{7}+\frac{2}{7}=$ d) $\frac{5}{8}+\frac{2}{8}=$

e) $\frac{3}{11}+\frac{7}{11}=$ f) $\frac{5}{17}+\frac{9}{17}=$ g) $\frac{11}{24}+\frac{10}{24}=$ h) $\frac{18}{57}+\frac{13}{57}=$

4. Show how much pie would be left if you took away the amount shown. Then complete the fraction statement.

a)

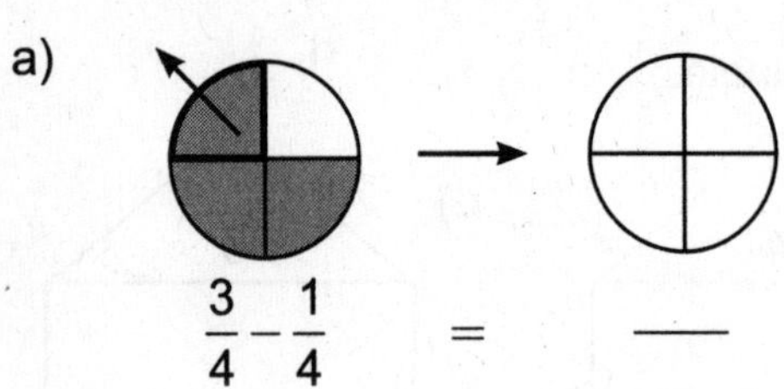

$\frac{3}{4}-\frac{1}{4} = \underline{\quad}$

b)

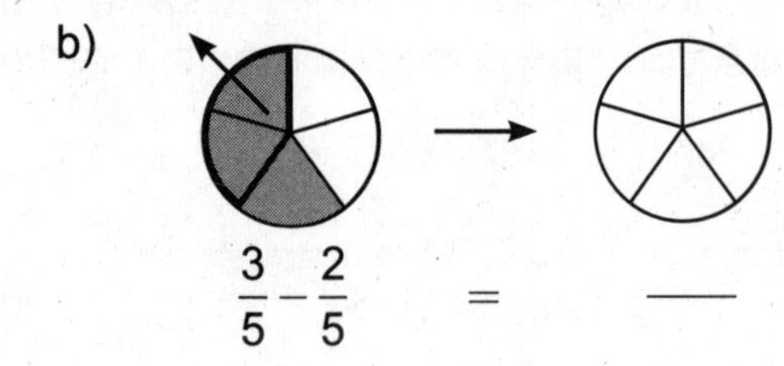

$\frac{3}{5}-\frac{2}{5} = \underline{\quad}$

5. Subtract.

a) $\frac{2}{3}-\frac{1}{3}=$ b) $\frac{3}{5}-\frac{1}{5}=$ c) $\frac{6}{7}-\frac{3}{7}=$ d) $\frac{5}{8}-\frac{2}{8}=$

e) $\frac{9}{12}-\frac{2}{12}=$ f) $\frac{6}{19}-\frac{4}{19}=$ g) $\frac{9}{28}-\frac{3}{28}=$ h) $\frac{17}{57}-\frac{12}{57}=$

6. Calculate.

a) $\frac{2}{7}+\frac{1}{7}+\frac{3}{7}=$ b) $\frac{4}{11}+\frac{5}{11}-\frac{2}{11}=$ c) $\frac{10}{18}-\frac{7}{18}+\frac{5}{18}=$

NS7-23 Adding and Subtracting Fractions *(continued)*

To add fractions that have a common denominator, we can add the numerators.

Example: $\frac{3}{10}+\frac{4}{10}=\frac{7}{10}$

INVESTIGATION 1 ▶ To add fractions that have a common numerator, can we add the denominators?

Look at $\frac{5}{8}+\frac{5}{14}$. Could this equal $\frac{5}{8+14}$?

A. Which is larger, $\frac{5}{8}+\frac{5}{14}$ or $\frac{5}{8}$? How do you know? ____________________

____

B. Which is larger, $\frac{5}{8+14}$ or $\frac{5}{8}$? How do you know? ____________________

____

C. Does $\frac{5}{8}+\frac{5}{14}=\frac{5}{8+14}$? Explain. ____________________

____

INVESTIGATION 2 ▶ How can we add fractions with different denominators, such as $\frac{1}{3}+\frac{2}{5}$?

A. Make equivalent fractions until you find two with the same denominator, 15.

$\frac{1}{3}=\frac{}{6}=\frac{}{9}=\frac{}{12}=\frac{}{15}$

$\frac{2}{5}=\frac{}{10}=\frac{}{15}$

B. Add the two fractions that have the same denominator.

$\frac{}{15}+\frac{}{15}=\frac{}{15}$

C. What is $\frac{1}{3}+\frac{2}{5}$? How do you know? ____________________

NS7-23 Adding and Subtracting Fractions *(continued)*

Adding Fractions with Different Denominators

Step 1: Find the lowest common multiple (LCM) of the denominators. $\frac{1}{3}+\frac{2}{5}$

Multiples of 3: 0, 3, 6, 9, 12, **15**, 18

Multiples of 5: 0, 5, 10, **15**, 20, 25, 30 LCM (3, 5) = 15

Step 2: Create equivalent fractions with that denominator.

$$\frac{1}{3}+\frac{2}{5} = \frac{5\times 1}{5\times 3}+\frac{2\times 3}{5\times 3} = \frac{5}{15}+\frac{6}{15} = \frac{11}{15}$$

The LCM of the denominators is called the **lowest common denominator (LCD)** of the fractions.

7. Find the LCD of each pair of fractions. Then show what numbers you would multiply the numerator and denominator of each fraction by in order to add.

a) $\frac{3\times 1}{3\times 2}+\frac{2\times 2}{3\times 2}$ b) $\frac{3}{4}+\frac{1}{8}$ c) $\frac{1}{20}+\frac{1}{5}$ d) $\frac{3}{4}+\frac{2}{3}$

LCD = *6* LCD = ______ LCD = ______ LCD = ______

e) $\frac{3}{7}+\frac{1}{3}$ f) $\frac{1}{4}+\frac{1}{6}$ g) $\frac{2}{5}+\frac{1}{10}$ h) $\frac{1}{8}+\frac{1}{7}$

LCD = ______ LCD = ______ LCD = ______ LCD = ______

8. Add or subtract the fractions by changing them to equivalent fractions with denominator equal to the LCD of the fractions.

a) $\frac{2}{5}+\frac{1}{4}$ b) $\frac{4}{15}+\frac{2}{3}$ c) $\frac{2}{3}-\frac{1}{8}$ d) $\frac{2}{3}-\frac{1}{12}$

=

=

e) $\frac{3}{4}+\frac{1}{8}$ f) $\frac{1}{6}+\frac{11}{24}$ g) $\frac{5}{28}-\frac{1}{7}$ h) $\frac{2}{7}+\frac{1}{8}$ i) $\frac{4}{9}-\frac{1}{6}$

9. Add or subtract.

a) $\frac{1}{6}+\frac{5}{12}$ b) $\frac{17}{25}-\frac{3}{5}$ c) $\frac{6}{7}-\frac{1}{4}$ d) $\frac{4}{9}+\frac{2}{5}$ e) $\frac{5}{8}-\frac{7}{12}$

f) $\frac{2}{3}+\frac{1}{4}+\frac{1}{2}$ g) $\frac{3}{15}+\frac{2}{3}+\frac{1}{5}$ h) $\frac{7}{15}+\frac{1}{3}-\frac{3}{5}$ i) $\frac{1}{4}+\frac{17}{20}-\frac{3}{5}$

NS7-24 Lowest Terms

A fraction is reduced to **lowest terms** when the greatest common factor (GCF) of its numerator and denominator is the number 1.

$\frac{6}{8}$ is not in lowest terms because the GCF of 6 and 8 is 2.

Factors of 6: 1, **2**, 3, 6
Factors of 8: 1, **2**, 4, 8

$\frac{3}{4}$ is in lowest terms because the GCF of 3 and 4 is 1.

Factors of 3: **1**, 3
Factors of 4: **1**, 2, 4

1. Find the GCF of the numerator and denominator. Is the fraction in lowest terms? Write yes or no.

a) $\frac{3}{6}$ GCF = *3* ______ *no* ______

b) $\frac{2}{5}$ GCF = ______ ______

c) $\frac{4}{5}$ GCF = ______ ______

d) $\frac{5}{10}$ GCF = ______ ______

e) $\frac{6}{10}$ GCF = ______ ______

f) $\frac{7}{10}$ g) $\frac{15}{16}$ h) $\frac{12}{10}$ i) $\frac{9}{5}$ j) $\frac{12}{8}$

Reducing a Fraction to Lowest Terms

Step 1: Find the GCF of the numerator and denominator.

Step 2: Divide both the numerator and denominator by the GCF.

2. Reduce the fractions below by dividing the numerator and the denominator by their GCF.

a) $\frac{2 \div 2}{10 \div 2} = \frac{1}{5}$ b) $\frac{2 \div}{6 \div} =$ ______ c) $\frac{2 \div}{8 \div} =$ ______ d) $\frac{2 \div}{12 \div} =$ ______

e) $\frac{6}{9} =$ ______ f) $\frac{3}{15} =$ ______ g) $\frac{4}{12} =$ ______ h) $\frac{20}{25} =$ ______

3. Add or subtract, then reduce your answer to lowest terms.

a) $\frac{5 \times 1}{5 \times 6} + \frac{1 \times 3}{10 \times 3}$

$= \frac{5}{30} + \frac{3}{30}$

$= \frac{8}{30} = \frac{4}{15}$

b) $\frac{13}{15} - \frac{1}{5}$ c) $\frac{5}{6} + \frac{3}{10}$ d) $\frac{25}{28} - \frac{1}{7}$

e) $\frac{1}{10} + \frac{1}{2} + \frac{1}{5}$ f) $\frac{3}{8} + \frac{1}{5} + \frac{1}{20}$ g) $\frac{4}{7} + \frac{2}{5} - \frac{4}{35}$ h) $\frac{5}{7} - \frac{8}{21} + \frac{2}{3}$

NS7-25 Adding and Subtracting Mixed Numbers

After a party, Chang's class has $2\frac{1}{2}$ pizzas left over.

Alicia's class has $3\frac{1}{3}$ pizzas left over.

Chang's class

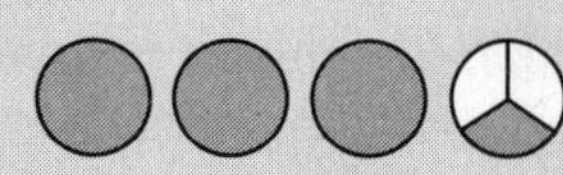
Alicia's class

To find out how much pizza is left over, Chang adds.

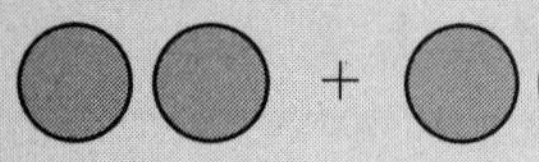

$2 + 3 = 5$

$\frac{1 \times 3}{2 \times 3} + \frac{1 \times 2}{3 \times 2} = \frac{3}{6} + \frac{2}{6} = \mathbf{\frac{5}{6}}$

There are $5\frac{5}{6}$ pizzas left over.

Here is how Chang shows his calculation: $2\frac{1}{2} + 3\frac{1}{3} = 2\frac{1 \times 3}{2 \times 3} + 3\frac{1 \times 2}{3 \times 2} = 2\frac{3}{6} + 3\frac{2}{6} = 5\frac{5}{6}$

1. Add or subtract.

a) $2\frac{1}{5} + 2\frac{2}{5} =$ b) $3\frac{3}{6} + 2\frac{1}{6} =$ c) $5\frac{7}{8} - 3\frac{2}{8} =$ d) $7\frac{9}{15} - 4\frac{4}{15} =$

2. Add or subtract by changing the fractions to equivalent fractions.

a) $2\frac{1 \times 3}{2 \times 3} + 1\frac{1 \times 2}{3 \times 2}$
$= 2\frac{3}{6} + 1\frac{2}{6}$
$= 3\frac{5}{6}$

b) $3\frac{3 \times 3}{4 \times 3} - 1\frac{1 \times 4}{3 \times 4}$
$= 3\frac{9}{12} - 1\frac{4}{12}$
$= 2\frac{5}{12}$

c) $5\frac{2}{3} - 2\frac{3}{5}$

d) $2\frac{2}{7} + 4\frac{1}{2}$

e) $4\frac{2}{5} - 1\frac{1}{6}$

f) $2\frac{3}{8} + 4\frac{1}{3}$

g) $1\frac{1}{4} + 2\frac{3}{7}$

h) $4\frac{1}{5} + 2\frac{4}{7}$

i) $8\frac{4}{5} - 5\frac{5}{9}$

j) $3\frac{2}{3} - 1\frac{1}{2}$

k) $5\frac{3}{4} - 3\frac{2}{3}$

l) $4\frac{4}{5} - 2\frac{3}{4}$

3. If you add $1\frac{1}{2} + 2\frac{2}{3}$ you will find that $1\frac{1}{2} + 2\frac{2}{3} = 3\frac{7}{6}$. How can you simplify this answer?

NS7-25 Adding and Subtracting Mixed Numbers *(continued)*

4. a) Change the improper fractions to mixed numbers.

i) $\frac{7}{6} = 1\frac{1}{6}$ ii) $\frac{11}{5} =$ iii) $\frac{13}{7} =$ iv) $\frac{7}{4} =$

v) $\frac{13}{8} =$ vi) $\frac{13}{10} =$ vii) $\frac{14}{9} =$ viii) $\frac{11}{6} =$

b) Rewrite each mixed number to make the improper fraction a proper fraction. Show the steps.

i) $3\frac{7}{6} = 3 + \frac{7}{6}$
$= 3 + 1\frac{1}{6}$
$= 4\frac{1}{6}$

ii) $2\frac{4}{3} =$ iii) $4\frac{8}{5} =$

iv) $2\frac{5}{4} =$ v) $3\frac{10}{9} =$ vi) $4\frac{12}{7} =$

c) Add by changing the fractions to equivalent fractions. Simplify your answer as in part b).

i) $2\frac{2}{5} + \frac{2}{3}$ ii) $3\frac{2}{3} + \frac{5}{6}$ iii) $4\frac{3}{4} + 2\frac{3}{5}$

iv) $5\frac{1}{6} + 5\frac{7}{8}$ v) $3\frac{5}{8} + 4\frac{1}{2}$ vi) $4\frac{5}{6} + 3\frac{4}{9}$

5. If you know that $\frac{4}{5}$ is greater than $\frac{1}{3}$, how can you subtract $4\frac{1}{3} - 2\frac{4}{5}$? Solve the problems below to find out.

a) Rewrite each mixed number below by regrouping 1 whole as a fraction. Example: $4\frac{1}{3} = 3 + \frac{3}{3} + \frac{1}{3} = 3\frac{4}{3}$

i) $8\frac{1}{4} = 7 + \frac{4}{4} + \frac{1}{4}$
$= 7\frac{5}{4}$

ii) $5\frac{1}{2} = 4 +$

iii) $1\frac{1}{6} =$ iv) $2\frac{3}{4} =$

b) Now try to regroup in your head. Follow the steps from part a).

i) $5\frac{2}{3} = 4\frac{5}{3}$ ii) $7\frac{3}{5} =$ iii) $4\frac{1}{6} =$ iv) $2\frac{7}{10} =$

NS7-25 Adding and Subtracting Mixed Numbers *(continued)*

c) Rewrite the mixed numbers as in part b), then subtract.

i) $3\frac{1}{5}-1\frac{3}{4} = 2\frac{6}{5}-1\frac{3}{4}$

$= 2\frac{24}{20}-1\frac{15}{20}$

$= 1\frac{9}{20}$

ii) $4\frac{1}{3}-2\frac{3}{5}$

iii) $2\frac{1}{4}-1\frac{2}{3}$

iv) $7\frac{1}{2}-3\frac{9}{10}$

6. Add or subtract by first changing the mixed fractions to improper fractions.

a) $3\frac{2}{3}+1\frac{1}{2}$

$= \frac{2 \times 11}{2 \times 3} + \frac{3 \times 3}{2 \times 3}$

$= \frac{22}{6} + \frac{9}{6}$

$= \frac{31}{6}$

$= 5\frac{1}{6}$

b) $1\frac{1}{5}-\frac{2}{3}$

c) $3\frac{1}{4}-2\frac{5}{6}$

d) $5\frac{1}{8}-3\frac{1}{3}$

e) $1\frac{3}{5}+2\frac{1}{6}$

f) $2\frac{4}{7}+3\frac{1}{4}$

g) $4\frac{2}{3}+2\frac{4}{5}$

h) $4\frac{1}{10}-3\frac{4}{5}$

7. Alice walked $1\frac{3}{7}$ km in the first hour and $1\frac{1}{3}$ km in the second hour. How many kilometres did she walk in two hours?

8. Steve bought $2\frac{3}{5}$ kg of apples, $1\frac{2}{3}$ kg of grapes, and $3\frac{4}{5}$ kg of oranges. How many kilograms of fruit did he buy in total?

9. Tom and Andy worked together to paint a $12\frac{1}{6}$ metre fence. On the first day, Tom painted $4\frac{2}{3}$ metres and Andy painted $5\frac{1}{2}$ metres. How many metres of fence needed to be painted on the second day?

NS7-26 Decimal Fractions

1. Write the missing terms in each pattern.

a) 1, 10, 100, ____, 10 000, ...

b) 1, ____, 100, 1 000, ________,

c) 10, 10 × 10, 10 × 10 × 10, ________________, 10 × 10 × 10 × 10 × 10, ...

d) $\frac{1}{10}$, $\frac{1}{100}$, $\frac{1}{\_\_\_\_}$, $\frac{1}{10000}$, ...

e) ..., 1 000, 100, ____, 1, $\frac{1}{10}$, $\frac{1}{\_\_\_\_}$, $\frac{1}{1000}$, ...

f) ..., 1 000, 100, 10, ____, $\frac{1}{10}$, $\frac{1}{100}$, $\frac{1}{\_\_\_\_}$, ...

10, 100, 1 000, ... are **powers of 10**. In a **decimal fraction**, the denominator is a power of ten.

2. Circle the decimal fractions (the denominator is a power of 10).

$\frac{3}{10}$ $\frac{25}{100}$ $\frac{5}{6}$ $\frac{333}{1000}$ $\frac{7}{29}$ $\frac{1}{100}$ $\frac{100}{13}$ $\frac{4}{1000}$ $\frac{1}{55}$ $\frac{48}{10}$ $\frac{16}{101}$

There are 100 squares on a **hundredths grid**.

1 column = $\frac{10}{100} = \frac{1}{10}$ = 1 tenth

1 square = $\frac{1}{100}$ = 1 hundredth

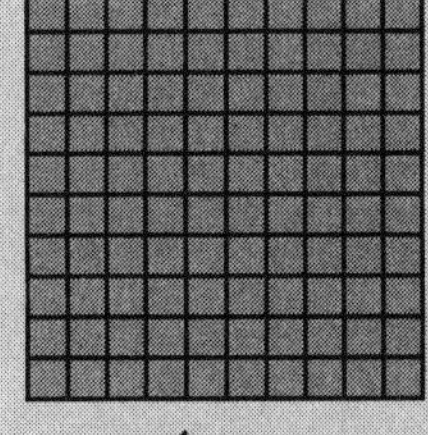

1 one

1 tenth

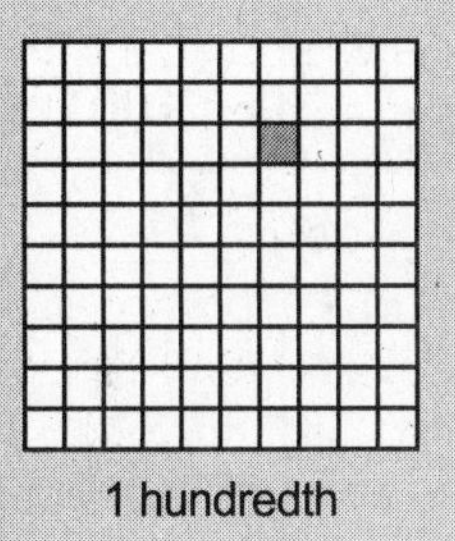

1 hundredth

3. Write two equivalent fractions for the shaded part of the grid. One column on the grid = 1 tenth.

a) $\frac{2}{10} = \frac{\_\_}{100}$

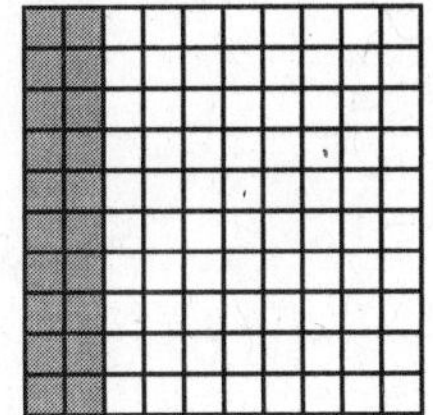

b) $\frac{\_\_}{10} = \frac{\_\_}{100}$

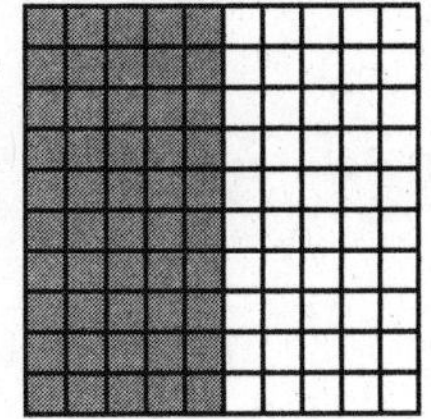

c) $\frac{\_\_}{10} = \frac{\_\_}{100}$

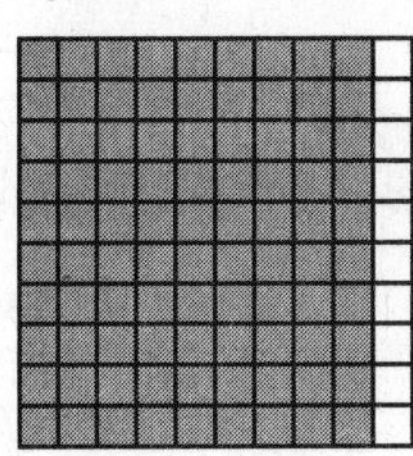

4. Write an equivalent fraction, then shade the grid to show the equivalent fractions.

a) $\frac{6}{10} = \frac{\_\_}{100}$

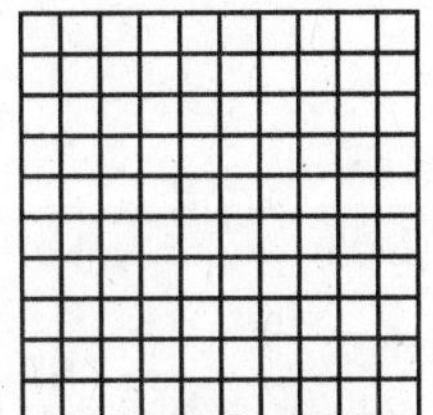

b) $\frac{\_\_}{10} = \frac{70}{100}$

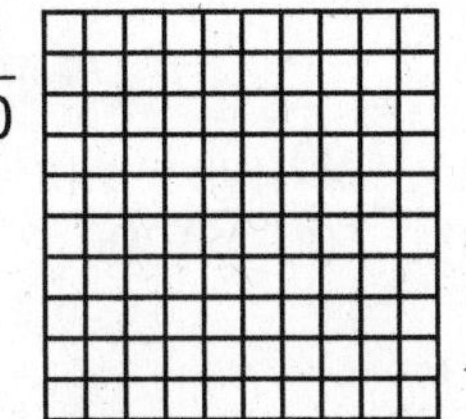

c) $\frac{3}{10} = \frac{\_\_}{100}$

NS7-26 Decimal Fractions *(continued)*

5. Write the fraction shown by the shaded part of the grid in two ways.

a) $\frac{23}{100} =$ $\frac{2}{10} + \frac{\quad}{100}$

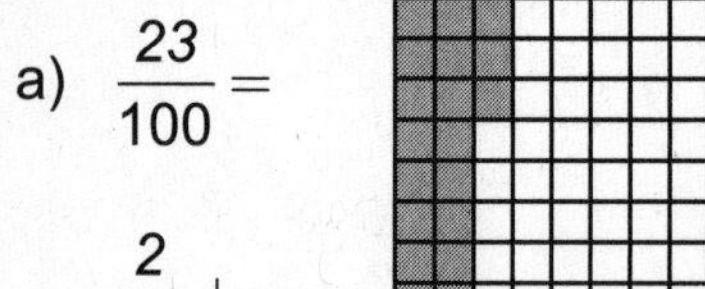
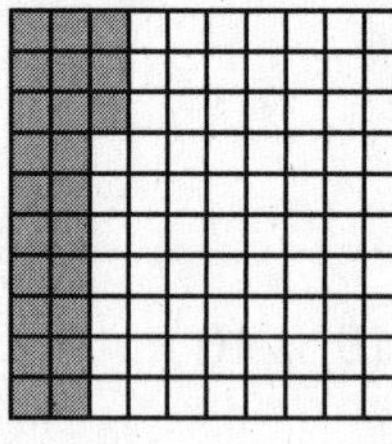

b) $\frac{\quad}{100} =$ $\frac{\quad}{10} + \frac{\quad}{100}$

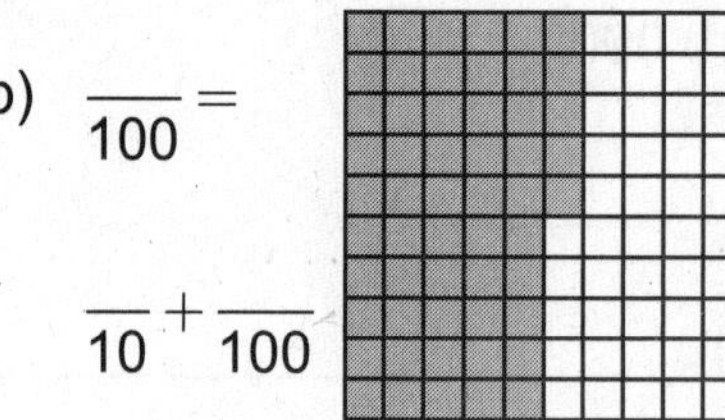
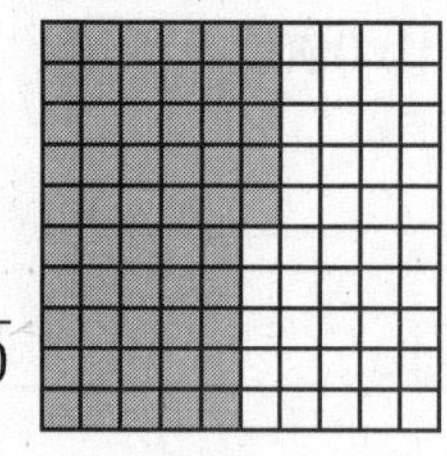

c) $\frac{\quad}{100} =$ $\frac{\quad}{10} + \frac{\quad}{100}$

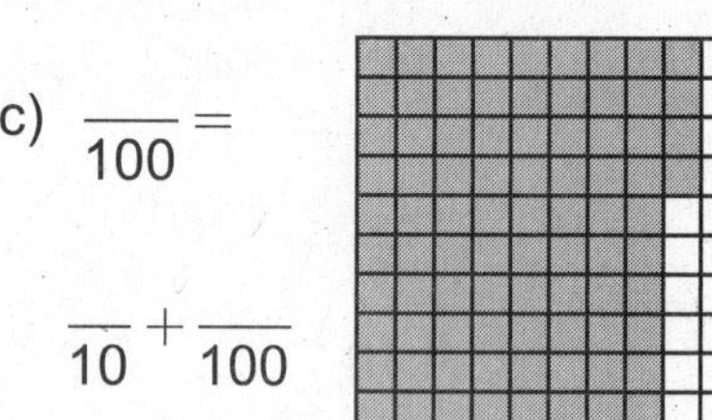

6. Shade the grid to show the fraction. Then write the fraction another way.

a) $\frac{47}{100} =$ $\frac{\quad}{10} + \frac{\quad}{100}$

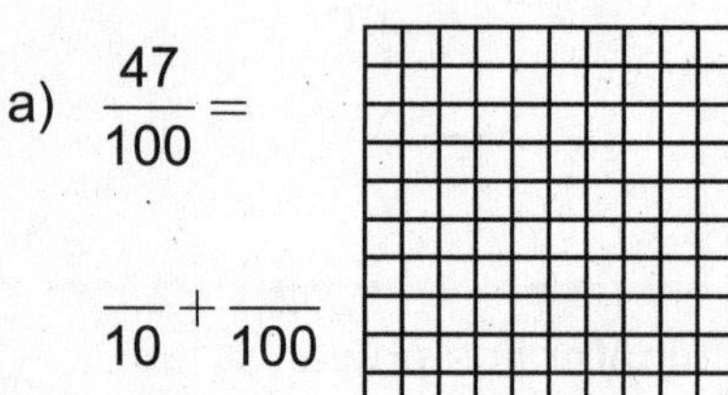
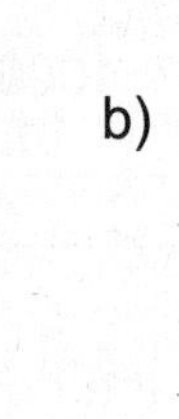

b) $\frac{91}{100} =$ $\frac{\quad}{10} + \frac{\quad}{100}$

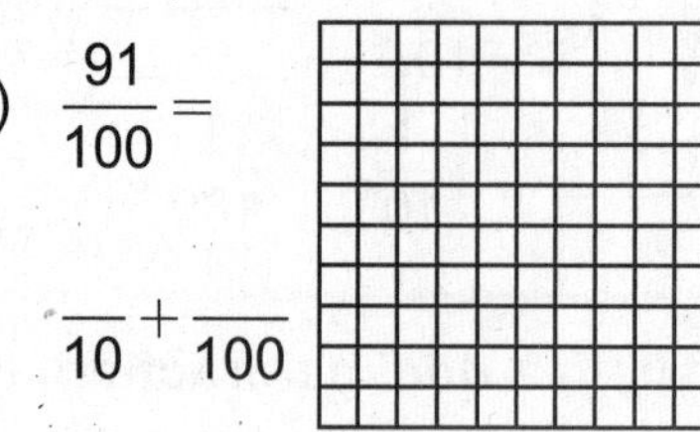
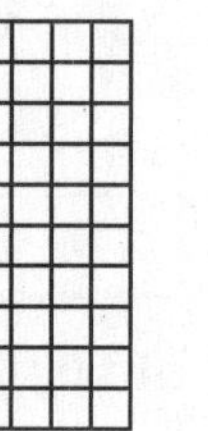

c) $\frac{36}{100} =$ $\frac{\quad}{10} + \frac{\quad}{100}$

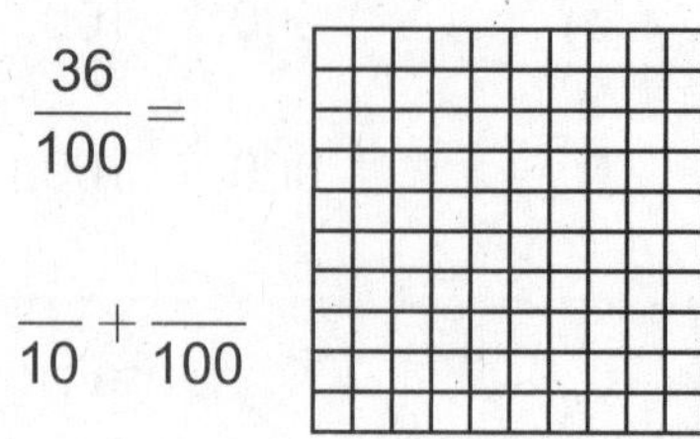

7. Multiply or divide the numerator and denominator by the same number to write an equivalent decimal fraction.

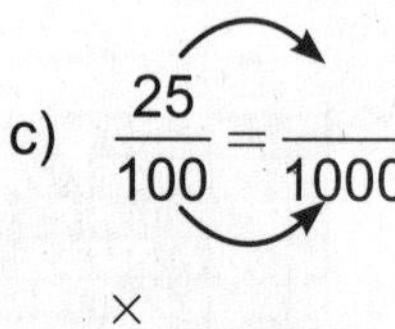

a) × 10: $\frac{2}{10} = \frac{\quad}{100}$ × 10

b) × ___: $\frac{6}{10} = \frac{\quad}{100}$ × 10

c) × ___: $\frac{25}{100} = \frac{\quad}{1000}$ × ___

d) × ___: $\frac{81}{100} = \frac{\quad}{1000}$ × ___

e) × ___: $\frac{9}{10} = \frac{\quad}{1000}$ × ___

f) ÷ ___: $\frac{80}{100} = \frac{\quad}{10}$ ÷ ___

g) ÷ ___: $\frac{360}{1000} = \frac{\quad}{100}$ ÷ ___

h) ÷ ___: $\frac{420}{1000} = \frac{\quad}{100}$ ÷ ___

i) ÷ ___: $\frac{50}{1000} = \frac{\quad}{100}$ ÷ ___

j) ÷ ___: $\frac{30}{100} = \frac{\quad}{10}$ ÷ ___

8. Determine the equivalent fraction.

a) $\frac{6}{10} = \frac{6 \times 10}{10 \times 10} = \frac{\quad}{100}$

b) $\frac{35}{100} = \frac{35 \times \_\_\_}{100 \times \_\_\_} = \frac{\quad}{1000}$

c) $\frac{2}{100} = \frac{2 \times \_\_\_}{100 \times \_\_\_} = \frac{\quad}{1000}$

d) $\frac{4}{10} = \frac{4 \times \_\_\_}{10 \times \_\_\_} = \frac{\quad}{1000}$

e) $\frac{30}{100} = \frac{30 \div \_\_\_}{100 \div \_\_\_} = \frac{\quad}{10}$

f) $\frac{710}{1000} = \frac{710 \div \_\_\_}{1000 \div \_\_\_} = \frac{\quad}{100}$

9. Write the equivalent fractions.

a) $\frac{5}{10} = \frac{\quad}{100} = \frac{\quad}{1000}$

b) $\frac{\quad}{10} = \frac{90}{100} = \frac{\quad}{1000}$

c) $\frac{\quad}{10} = \frac{\quad}{100} = \frac{300}{1000}$

d) $\frac{75}{100} = \frac{\quad}{1000}$

e) $\frac{70}{1000} = \frac{\quad}{100}$

f) $\frac{10}{10} = \frac{\quad}{100} = \frac{\quad}{1000}$

g) $\frac{78}{100} = \frac{\quad}{1000}$

h) $\frac{570}{1000} = \frac{\quad}{100}$

NS7-27 Place Value and Decimals

Decimals are a short way to write decimal fractions.

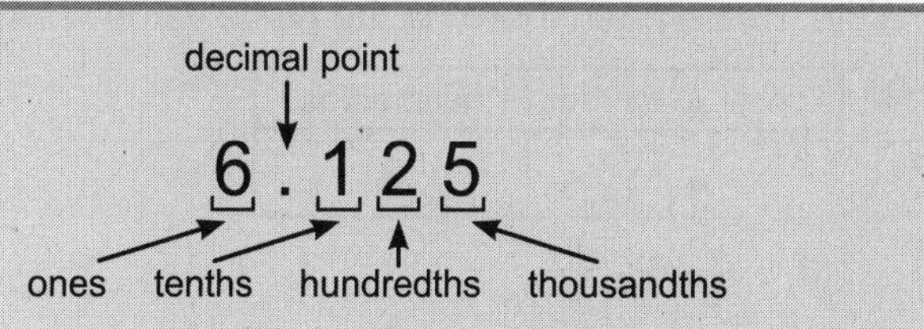

1. Write the decimal fraction in the place value chart. Then write the fraction as a decimal.

a) $\frac{3}{10}$

ones	tenths
0	3

0.___

b) $\frac{6}{10}$

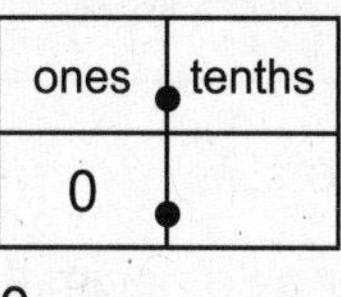

ones	tenths
0	

0.___

c) $\frac{5}{10} + \frac{4}{100}$

ones	tenths	hundredths
0	5	4

___.___ ___

d) $\frac{1}{10} + \frac{8}{100}$

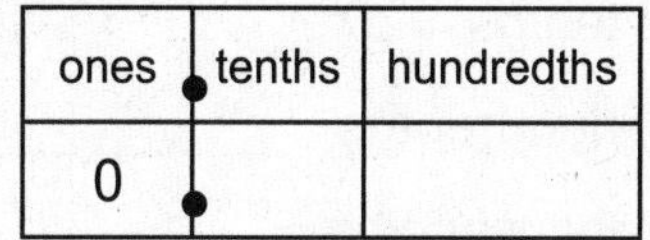

ones	tenths	hundredths
0		

___.___ ___

e) $\frac{9}{10} + \frac{2}{100}$

ones	tenths	hundredths
0		

___.___ ___

f) $\frac{6}{10} + \frac{5}{100}$

ones	tenths	hundredths
0		

___.___ ___

g) $\frac{2}{10} + \frac{4}{100} + \frac{3}{1000} =$ ___.___ ___ ___

ones	tenths	hundredths	thousandths
0	2	4	3

h) $\frac{3}{10} + \frac{1}{100} + \frac{5}{1000} =$ ___.___ ___ ___

ones	tenths	hundredths	thousandths
0			

2. Is the decimal point to the right or the left of the ones place? ☐ to the right ☐ to the left

3. Write the decimal in the place value chart.

	ones	tenths	hundredths	thousandths
a) 0.512	*0*	*5*	*1*	*2*
b) 0.3				
c) 0.763				

	ones	tenths	hundredths	thousandths
d) 0.905				
e) 0.536				
f) 0.8				

4. Write the value of the digit 9 in the decimal in words and as a fraction.

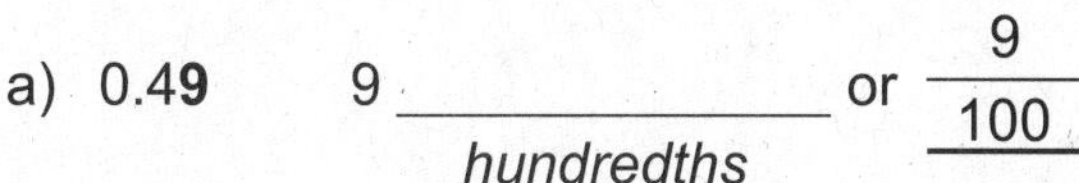

a) 0.4**9**   9 *hundredths* or $\frac{9}{100}$

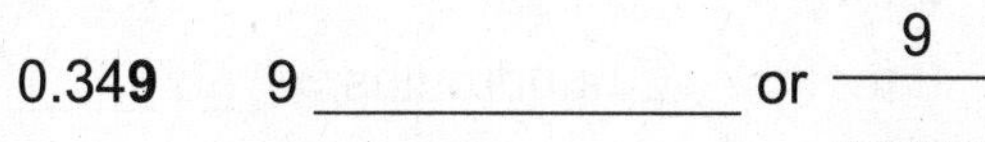

b) 0.34**9**   9 ______________ or $\frac{9}{\_\_\_}$

c) 0.**9**76   9 ______________ or $\frac{9}{\_\_\_}$

d) 0.3**9**   9 ______________ or $\frac{9}{\_\_\_}$

e) 0.**9**5   9 ______________ or $\frac{9}{\_\_\_}$

f) 0.32**9**   9 ______________ or $\frac{9}{\_\_\_}$

NS7-27 Place Value and Decimals *(continued)*

5. Write the number shown in the place value chart as a decimal, using 0 as a placeholder.

a)

ones	tenths	hundredths
		9

0 . *0* *9*

b)

ones	tenths	hundredths	thousandths
			5

___ . ___ ___ ___

c)

ones	tenths	hundredths
		3

___ . ___ ___

d)

ones	tenths	hundredths	thousandths
			1

___ . ___ ___ ___

6. Write the number as a decimal. Use zeros as placeholders.

a) 7 tenths = *0*.___ b) 3 tenths = ___.___ c) 9 tenths = ___.___

d) 7 hundredths = ___.___ ___ e) 5 hundredths = ___.___ ___ f) 4 hundredths = ___.___ ___

g) 7 thousandths = ___.___ ___ ___ h) 2 thousandths = ___.___ ___ ___ i) 6 thousandths = ___.___ ___ ___

7. Underline the smallest place value. Write the decimal in words.

a) 0.<u>6</u> = *six tenths* b) 0.07 = ______________________

c) 0.005 = ______________________ d) 0.02 = ______________________

e) 0.3 = ______________________ f) 0.005 = ______________________

8. Which place is being held by the bolded zero in the decimal?

a) 0.**0**7 *tenths* place b) 0.1**0**5 ______________________ place

c) 0.3**0**6 ______________________ place d) 0.**0**44 ______________________ place

9. Write the decimal in expanded form.

a) 0.407 = *4* tenths + *0* hundredths + *7* thousandths

b) 0.163 = ___ tenths + ___ hundredths + ___ thousandths

c) 0.08 = ___ tenths + ___ hundredths

d) 0.76 = ___ tenths + ___ hundredths

e) 0.201 = ___ tenths + ___ hundredths + ___ thousandths

10. Write the number in expanded form as a decimal.

a) 3 tenths + 5 hundredths + 2 thousandths = *0* . ___ ___ ___

b) 4 tenths + 1 hundredth + 6 thousandths = ___ . ___ ___ ___

c) 5 tenths = ___ . ___

d) 8 tenths + 2 hundredths = ___ . ___ ___

e) 3 hundredths + 5 thousandths = ___ . ___ ___ ___

f) 5 tenths + 3 thousandths = ___ . ___ ___ ___

11. Put a decimal point in the number so the digit 3 has the value $\frac{3}{100}$. Add zeros if you need to.

a) 3 2 b) 1 3 5 c) 9 8 7 3 d) 3

NS7-28 Fractions and Decimals

1. Complete the chart below.

Drawing	Fraction	Decimal	Equivalent Decimal	Equivalent Fraction	Drawing
	$\frac{5}{10}$	0.5	0.50	$\frac{50}{100}$	
	$\frac{\_\_}{10}$	__ . __	__ . __ __	$\frac{\_\_}{100}$	

2. Fill in the missing numbers. Remember: $\frac{1}{10} = \frac{10}{100}$

a) $0.8 = \frac{8}{10} = \frac{\_\_}{100} = 0.80$ b) $0.\_\_ = \frac{\_\_}{10} = \frac{40}{100} = 0.\_\_\ \_\_$ c) $0.\_\_ = \frac{\_\_}{10} = \frac{\_\_}{100} = 0.30$

3. Fill in the missing numbers. Remember: $\frac{1}{100} = \frac{10}{1000}$

a) $0.03 = \frac{3}{100} = \frac{\_\_}{1000} = 0.030$ b) $0.\_\_\ \_\_ = \frac{2}{100} = \frac{\_\_}{1000} = 0.020$

c) $0.\_\_\ \_\_ = \frac{\_\_}{100} = \frac{70}{1000} = 0.\_\_\ \_\_$ d) $0.\_\_\ \_\_ = \frac{\_\_}{100} = \frac{\_\_}{1000} = 0.090$

4. How many tenths and hundreds are shaded? Write a fraction and a decimal to represent them.

a) _47_ hundredths = _4_ tenths _7_ hundredths $\frac{47}{100} = 0.\_\_\ \_\_$

b) __ hundredths = __ tenths __ hundredths $\frac{\_\_}{100} = 0.\_\_\ \_\_$

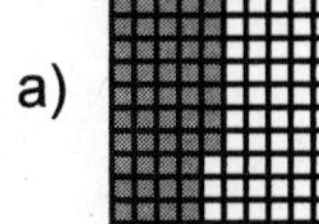

c) __ hundredths = __ tenths __ hundredths $\frac{\_\_}{100} = 0.\_\_\ \_\_$

d) __ hundredths = __ tenths __ hundredths $\frac{\_\_}{100} = 0.\_\_\ \_\_$

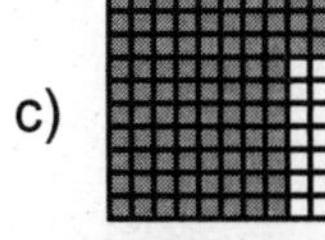

5. Write a decimal for the fraction.

a) $\frac{35}{100} = 0.\_\_\ \_\_$ b) $\frac{61}{100} = 0.\_\_\ \_\_$ c) $\frac{18}{100} = 0.\_\_\ \_\_$ d) $\frac{3}{100} = 0.\_\_\ \_\_$

NS7-28 Fractions and Decimals *(continued)*

6. Describe the decimal in two ways.

a) 0.52 = ___ tenths ___ hundredths = ___ hundredths

b) 0.40 = ___ tenths ___ hundredths = ___ hundredths

c) 0.93 = ___ tenths ___ hundredths = ___ hundredths

7. Write the number as a decimal.

a) 23 hundredths = 0.___ ___ b) 61 hundredths = 0.___ ___ c) 12 hundredths = 0.___ ___

8. Fill in the blanks.

a) 715 thousandths = ___ tenths ___ hundredths ___ thousandths $\frac{715}{1000}$ = 0. ___ ___ ___

b) 164 thousandths = ___ tenths ___ hundredths ___ thousandths $\frac{\quad}{1000}$ = 0. ___ ___ ___

c) 42 thousandths = ___ hundredths ___ thousandths $\frac{\quad}{1000}$ = 0. ___ ___ ___

9. Write a decimal for the fraction.

a) $\frac{275}{1000}$ = 0. ___ ___ ___ b) $\frac{602}{1000}$ = 0. ___ ___ ___

c) $\frac{199}{1000}$ = 0. ___ ___ ___ d) $\frac{56}{1000}$ = 0. ___ ___ ___

10. Describe the decimal in two ways.

a) 0.345 = ___ tenths ___ hundredths ___ thousandths = ___ thousandths

b) 0.629 = ___ tenths ___ hundredths ___ thousandths = ___ thousandths

c) 0.118 = ___ tenths ___ hundredths ___ thousandths = ___ thousandths

11. Write the number as a decimal.

a) 765 thousandths = *0.765* b) 123 thousandths = ______ c) 204 thousandths = ______

d) 42 thousandths = *0.042* e) 18 thousandths = ______ f) 79 thousandths = ______

12. Say the name of the fraction and decimal to yourself. Circle the equalities that are incorrect.

a) $0.36 = \frac{36}{100}$ b) $0.9 = \frac{9}{100}$ c) $0.6 = \frac{6}{10}$ d) $\frac{27}{100} = 0.27$ e) $\frac{125}{1000} = 0.125$

f) $0.75 = \frac{74}{100}$ g) $0.03 = \frac{3}{10}$ h) $\frac{200}{1000} = 0.020$ i) $0.08 = \frac{8}{100}$ j) $0.40 = \frac{40}{10}$

13. Write the decimal as a fraction.

a) 0.3 b) 0.57 c) 0.654 d) 0.45 e) 0.03

f) 0.056 g) 0.002 h) 0.1 i) 0.704 j) 0.069

NS7-29 Decimals, Money, and Measurements

A **dime** is **one tenth** of a dollar. A **penny** is one **hundredth** of a dollar.

1. Express the value of each decimal in four different ways.

a) 0.64

6 dimes and 4 pennies ____

6 tenths and 4 hundredths ____

64 pennies ____

64 hundredths ____

b) 0.31

____

____

____

____

c) 0.73

____

____

____

____

b) 0.31

____

____

____

____

A **decimetre** is **a tenth** of a metre. A **centimetre** is **a hundredth** of a metre.

2. Express the value of each measurement in four different ways.

a) 0.28 m

2 decimetres 8 centimetres ____

____

____

____

b) 0.16 m

____

____

____

____

3. Express the value of each decimal in four different ways.

Hint: Add a zero in the hundredths place if there are no hundredths.

a) 0.32 ____ dimes ____ pennies

____ tenths ____ hundredths

____ pennies

____ hundredths

0.3 ____ dimes ____ pennies

____ tenths ____ hundredths

____ pennies

____ hundredths

b) 0.36 ____ dimes ____ pennies

____ tenths ____ hundredths

____ pennies

____ hundredths

0.4 ____ dimes ____ pennies

____ tenths ____ hundredths

____ pennies

____ hundredths

4. Kieko says 0.73 is greater than 0.9 because 73 is greater than 9. Can you explain her mistake?

5. What unit of measurement does the 5 in 0.725 m represent?

NS7-30 Decimals and Fractions Greater Than 1

The whole-number part of a decimal is the digits to the left of the decimal point.

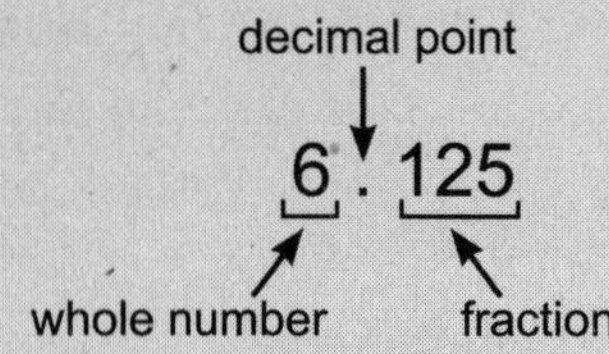

1. Underline the whole-number part of the decimal.

a) 36.497 b) 196.4 c) 25.76

d) 8.036 e) 0.38 f) 10.004

2. Write the decimal in expanded form.

a) 7.5 = ___ ones + ___ tenths

b) 4.32 = ___ ones + ___ tenths + ___ hundredths

c) 36.726 = _3_ tens + _6_ ones + _7_ tenths + ___ hundredths + ___ thousandths

d) 25.04 = ___ tens + ___ ones + ___ tenths + ___ hundredths

e) 7.015 = ___ ones + ___ tenths + ___ hundredths + ___ thousandths

3. Write the number as a decimal.

a) 2 tens + 4 ones + 3 tenths + 5 hundredths + 2 thousandths = ___ ___ . ___ ___ ___

b) 9 ones + 4 tenths + 1 hundredth + 6 thousandths = ____________

c) 4 tens + 8 ones + 7 tenths + 2 hundredths = ____________

d) 3 hundreds + 3 tens + 3 ones + 3 tenths + 3 hundredths = ____________

4. Write the decimal in the place value chart.

	thousands	hundredths	tens	ones	tenths	hundredths	thousands
a) 17.34			1	7	3	4	
b) 8.675							
c) 250.93							
d) 6700.5							
e) 49.007							

5. Write the whole number and how many hundredths or thousandths.

a) 6.45 _six_ and _forty-five_ hundredths

b) 1.32 ________ and ____________ hundredths

c) 36.007 ________________ and ____________________ thousandths

d) 7.052 ________________ and ____________________ thousandths

e) 20.104 ________________ and ____________________ thousandths

NS7-30 Decimals and Fractions Greater Than 1 *(continued)*

6. Fill in the blanks to show how to read the decimal.

a) 6.8 is read as " *six and eight tenths* "

b) 3.02 is read as " ________ and two ________ "

c) 25.79 is read as " twenty-five and seventy-nine ________ "

d) 15.285 is read as " ________ and two hundred eighty-five ________ "

A decimal can be written as a mixed number. Example: $3.75 = 3\frac{75}{100}$

7. Write the number represented on the grids in three ways.

a) 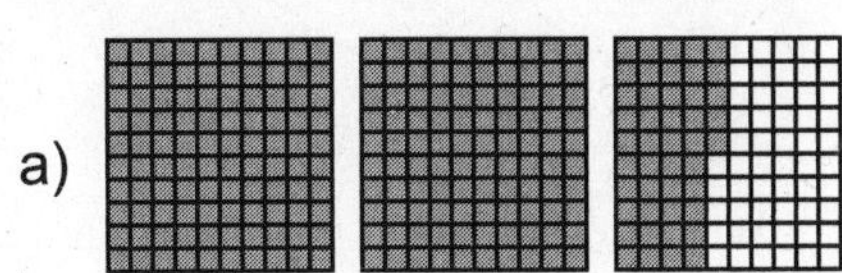 *2* ones *45* hundredths *2* . ___ ___ $2\frac{\quad}{100}$

b) 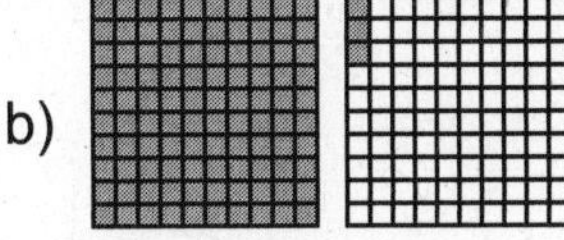 ___ ones ___ hundredths ___ . ___ ___ $\_\frac{\quad}{100}$

c) 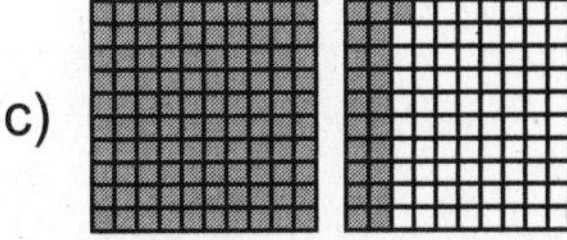 ___ ones ___ hundredths ___ . ___ ___ $\_\frac{\quad}{100}$

d) 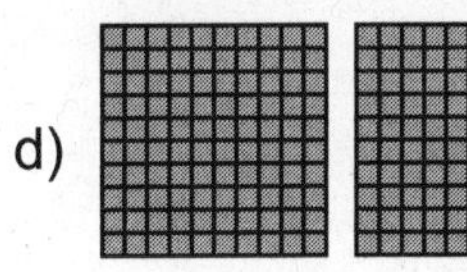 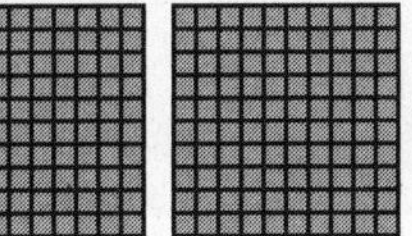 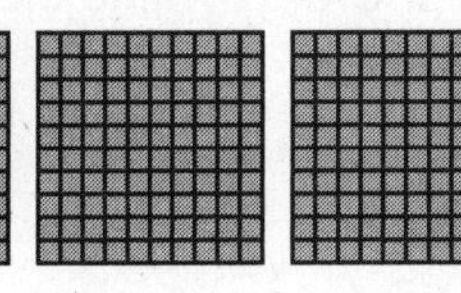 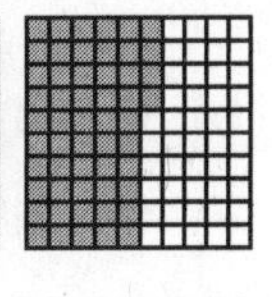

___ ones ___ hundredths ___ . ___ ___ $\_\frac{\quad}{100}$

8. Write a mixed number for the decimal.

a) 3.21 b) 1.62 c) 8.6 d) 9.137

e) 31.76 f) 23.665 g) 1.7 h) 82.505

9. Write a decimal for the mixed number.

a) $2\frac{17}{100}$ b) $1\frac{67}{100}$ c) $76\frac{7}{10}$ d) $5\frac{375}{1000}$ e) $3\frac{9}{100}$ f) $29\frac{5}{1000}$

10. Which is larger, 12.057 or $12\frac{52}{100}$? Explain.

NS7-31 Comparing and Ordering Tenths and Hundredths

This number line is divided into tenths. The number represented by point **A** is $2\frac{3}{10}$ or 2.3.

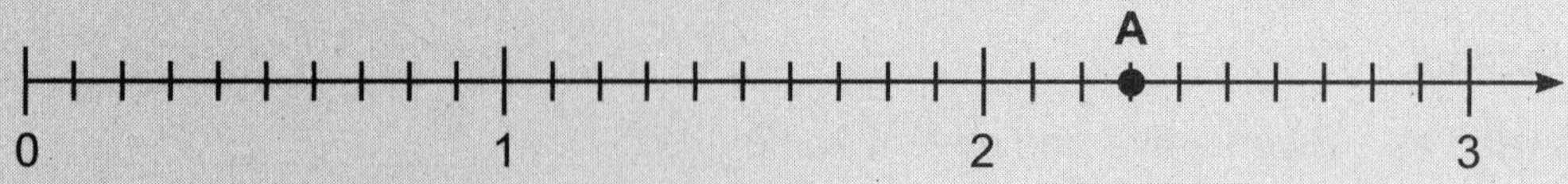

1. Write a fraction or a mixed number for each point.

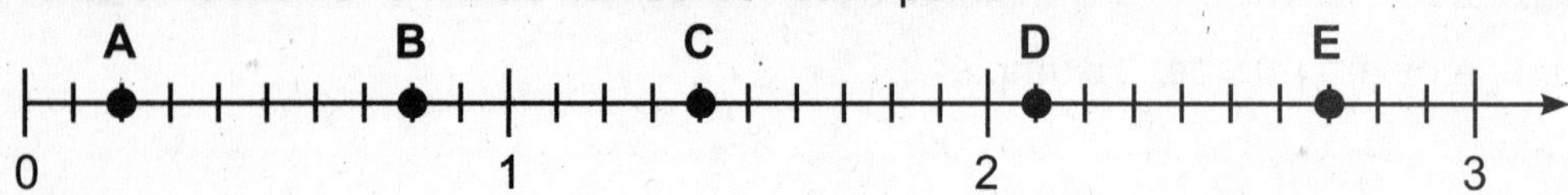

A ______ **B** ______ **C** ______ **D** ______ **E** ______

2. a) Write a decimal for each mark on the number line.

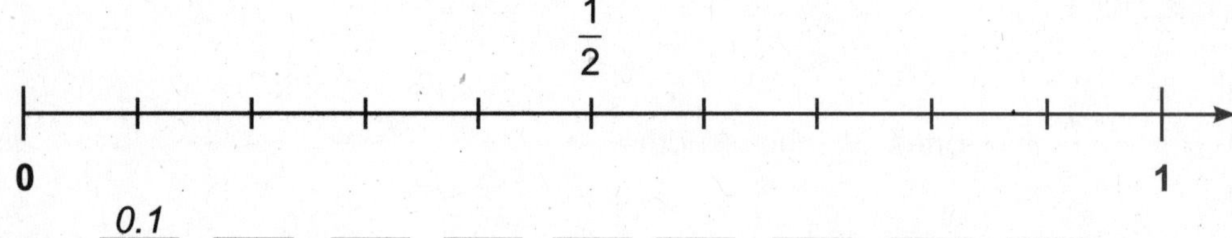

0.1 ____ ____ ____ ____ ____ ____ ____ ____

b) Which decimal is equal to one half? $\frac{1}{2}$ = ______

3. Use the number line in Question 2 to say whether the decimal is closer to 0, $\frac{1}{2}$, or 1.

a) 0.2 is closer to ______ b) 0.8 is closer to ______ c) 0.7 is closer to ______

d) 0.9 is closer to ______ e) 0.3 is closer to ______ f) 0.1 is closer to ______

4. a) Mark each point with a dot and label the point with the correct letter.

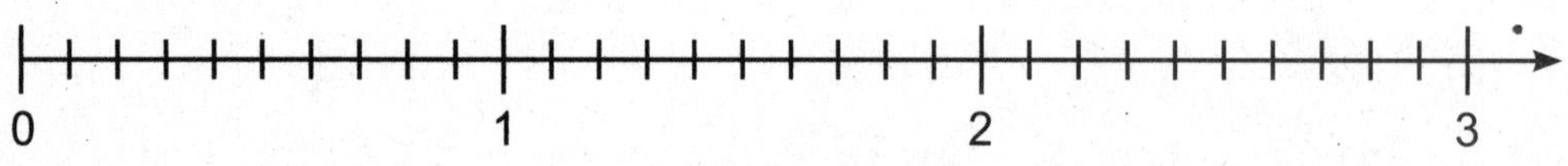

A 1.3 **B** 2.7 **C** 0.7 **D** $2\frac{1}{10}$ **E** $\frac{3}{4}$

F nine tenths **G** one and five tenths

b) Use the number line to order the points from least to greatest. *C*, ___, ___, ___, ___, ___, ___

NS7-31 Comparing and Ordering Tenths and Hundredths *(cont'd)*

5. a) This number line is divided into hundredths. Mark 0.50 on the number line. In your notebook, explain how you decided where to mark this point.

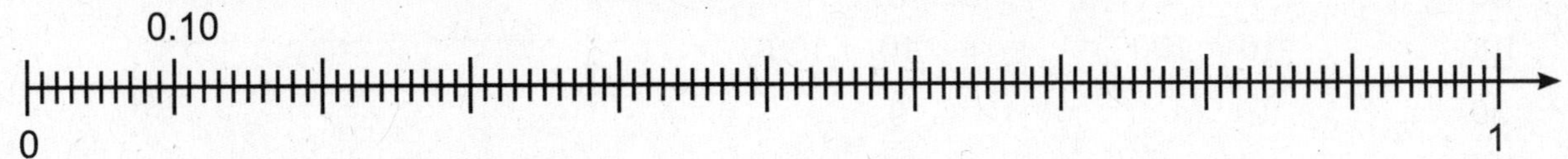

b) Mark and label these points on the number line above. In your notebook, explain the strategy you used to place each number on the line.

A 0.72 **B** $\frac{34}{100}$ **C** 0.05 **D** $\frac{51}{100}$

c) Use the number line to order the points from least to greatest. ___, ___, ___, ___

6.

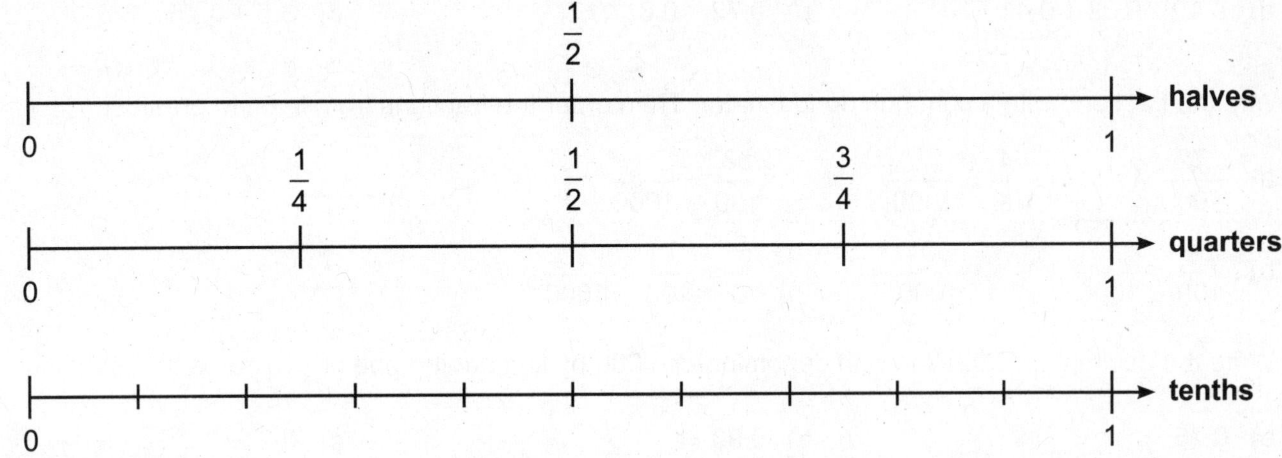

Use the number lines above to compare the pairs of numbers below. Write $<$ (less than) or $>$ (greater than) between each pair of numbers.

a) 0.7 ☐ $\frac{3}{4}$ b) 0.4 ☐ $\frac{7}{10}$ c) 0.8 ☐ $\frac{1}{2}$ d) 0.2 ☐ $\frac{1}{4}$

e) 0.4 ☐ $\frac{1}{2}$ f) 0.35 ☐ $\frac{1}{4}$ g) 0.07 ☐ $\frac{1}{2}$ h) $\frac{3}{4}$ ☐ 65

7. a) Circle the numbers that are placed on the line incorrectly. Draw the correct point(s).

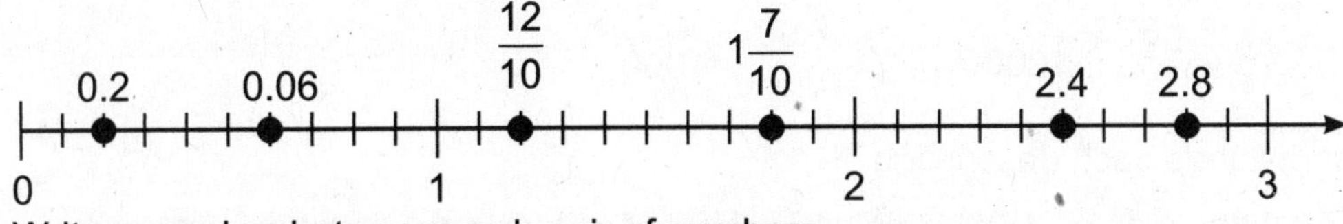

b) Write a number between each pair of numbers.

i) 0.2, ______, $\frac{12}{10}$ ii) $\frac{12}{10}$, ______, $1\frac{7}{10}$ iii) $1\frac{7}{10}$, ______, 2.4 iv) 2.4, ______, 2.8

NS7-32 Ordering Decimals and Fractions to Thousandths

1. Write the fractions with a common denominator. Then order the fractions from least to greatest.

a) $\frac{50}{100}$ $\frac{4}{10} = \frac{}{100}$ $\frac{6}{10} = \frac{}{100}$ _____, _____, _____

b) $\frac{30}{100}$ $\frac{2}{10} =$ $\frac{9}{10} =$ _____, _____, _____

2. Write the decimal as a fraction with denominator 100 by first adding a zero to the decimal.

a) $0.7 = \underline{\ 0.70\ } = \frac{70}{100}$ b) $0.9 = \_\_\_\_ = \frac{}{100}$ c) $0.1 = \_\_\_\_ = \frac{}{100}$

3. Add a zero to change the decimal tenths to hundredths. Then circle the greatest decimal hundredth.

a) 0.4*0* 0.32 (0.41) b) 0.72 0.8 0.7 c) 3.5 3.45 3.6

4. Write the fractions with a common denominator. Then order the fractions from least to greatest.

a) $\frac{72}{1000}$ $\frac{64}{100} = \frac{}{1000}$ $\frac{68}{100} = \frac{}{1000}$ _____, _____, _____

b) $\frac{54}{100} = \frac{}{1000}$ $\frac{504}{1000}$ $\frac{5}{10} = \frac{}{100} = \frac{}{1000}$ _____, _____, _____

5. Write the decimal as a fraction with denominator 1 000 by first adding one or two zeros to the decimal.

a) $0.75 = \_\_\_\_ = \frac{}{1000}$ b) $0.93 = \_\_\_\_ = \frac{}{1000}$ c) $0.2 = \_\_\_\_ = \frac{}{1000}$

6. Add zero(s) to change the decimals to thousandths. Then circle the greatest decimal thousandth.

a) 0.12 0.046 0.4 b) 0.2 0.68 0.092 c) 7.5 7.45 7.6

7. Write each decimal as an improper fraction with the denominator shown. Then order the decimals from greatest to least.

a) $4.6 = \frac{46}{10}$ $3.7 = \frac{}{10}$ $4.4 = \frac{}{10}$ *4.6*, _____, _____

b) $2.97 = \frac{297}{100}$ $3.05 = \frac{}{100}$ $2.76 = \frac{}{100}$ _____, _____, _____

c) $1.3 = \frac{1300}{1000}$ $1.7 = \frac{}{1000}$ $1.4 = \frac{}{1000}$ *0.7*, _____, _____

d) $7.2 = \frac{7200}{1000}$ $7.587 = \frac{}{1000}$ $7.98 = \frac{}{1000}$ _____, _____, _____

8. Write a decimal that matches each description.

a) between 0.83 and 0.89 0. ____ ____ b) between 0.6 and 0.70 0. ________

c) between 0.385 and 0.39 0. ________ d) between 0.457 and 0.5 0. ________

NS7-32 Ordering Decimals and Fractions to Thousandths *(cont'd)*

9. Write the numbers in the place value chart. Order the numbers from greatest to least.

a) 0.242, 1.368, 1.70, 2.05

tens	ones	tenths	hundredths	thousandths
	0	2	4	2

_______, _______, _______, _______

b) 37.03, 7.306, 3.706, 6.73

tens	ones	tenths	hundredths	thousandths

_______, _______, _______, _______

c) 45.25, 45.29, 45.193, 45.210

tens	ones	tenths	hundredths	thousandths

_______, _______, _______, _______

d) 0.654, 0.555, 0.655, 0.554

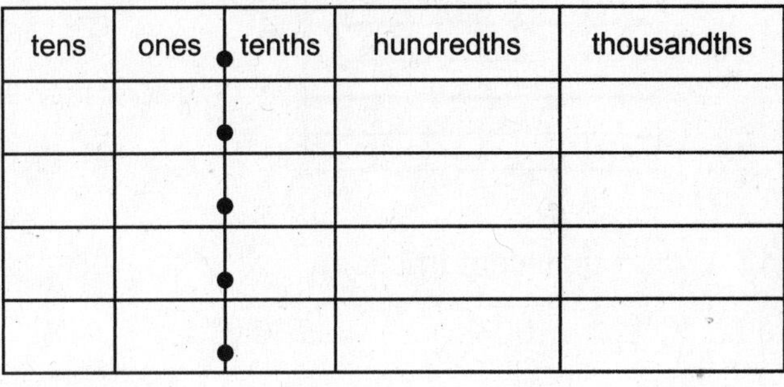

tens	ones	tenths	hundredths	thousandths

_______, _______, _______, _______

10. Complete the number pattern.

a) 7.5, 7.6, 7.___, 7.8, 7.9, 8.___, 8.___

b) 10.5, 11.5, 12.5, ______, ______

c) ______, 9.40, 9.35, ______, 9.25, 9.20

d) 0.005, 0.010, 0.015, ______, 0.025, 0.030

e) 25.6, ________, ________, 28.6, 29.6

f) 50.63, 50.53, ________, 50.33, ________

11. Arrange the numbers in increasing order.

a) 22.546, 22.456, 22.466

_________, _________, _________

b) 60.765, 60.756, 60.657

_________, _________, _________

c) 3.67, 3.076, 367

_________, _________, _________

d) 53.760, 53.670, 53.607

_________, _________, _________

12. Arrange the numbers in decreasing order.

a) 75.240, 75.704, 77.740

_________, _________, _________

b) 0.004, 0.040, 0.041, 4.001

_______, _______, _______, _______

13. Write five decimals greater than 1.32 and less than 1.33.

NS7-32 Ordering Decimals and Fractions to Thousandths *(cont'd)*

14. 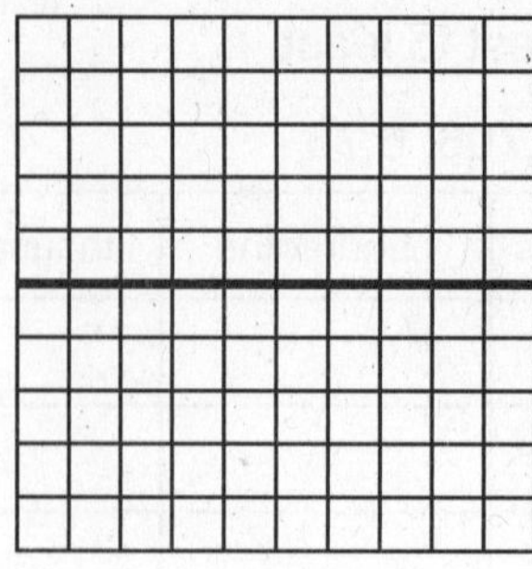

Shade $\frac{1}{2}$ of the squares. Write 2 fractions and 2 decimals for $\frac{1}{2}$.

Fractions: $\frac{1}{2} = \frac{}{10} = \frac{}{100}$

Decimals: $\frac{1}{2} = $ ___._____ = ___._____

15. 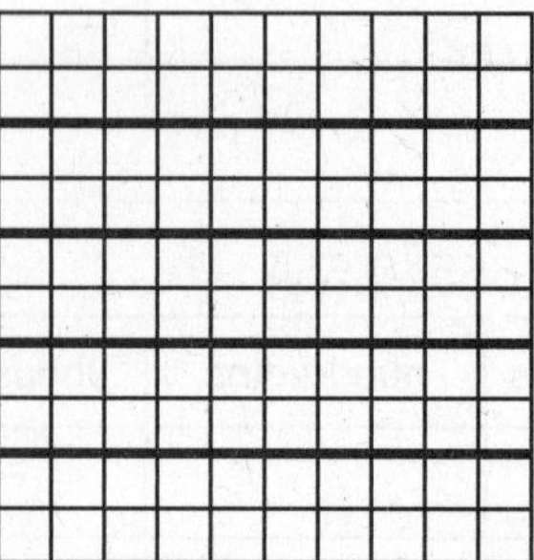

Shade $\frac{1}{5}$ of the boxes. Write 2 fractions and 2 decimals for $\frac{1}{5}$.

Fractions: $\frac{1}{5} = \frac{}{10} = \frac{}{100}$

Decimals: $\frac{1}{5} = $ ___._____ = ___._____

16. Write equivalent fractions.

a) $\frac{2}{5} = \frac{}{10} = \frac{}{100}$ b) $\frac{3}{5} = \frac{}{10} = \frac{}{100}$ c) $\frac{4}{5} = \frac{}{10} = \frac{}{100}$

17. 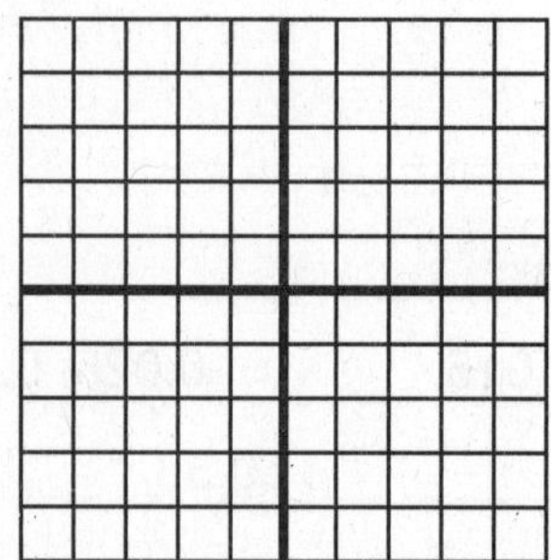

Shade $\frac{1}{4}$ of the squares. Write a fraction and a decimal for $\frac{1}{4}$ and $\frac{3}{4}$.

Fraction: $\frac{1}{4} = \frac{}{100}$ *Fraction:* $\frac{3}{4} = \frac{}{100}$

Decimal: $\frac{1}{4} = $ ___._____ *Decimal:* $\frac{3}{4} = $ ___._____

18. Circle the greater number. Hint: First change all fractions and decimals to fractions with denominator 100 or 1 000. (Note: $4 \times 250 = 1\,000$)

a) $\frac{1}{2}$ 0.51 b) $\frac{4}{5}$ 0.85 c) $\frac{3}{4}$ 0.734

19. Write the numbers in order from least to greatest. Explain how you found your answer.

a) 0.7 0.34 $\frac{3}{5}$ b) 0.817 $\frac{77}{100}$ $\frac{4}{5}$ c) $\frac{3}{5}$ 0.425 $\frac{1}{2}$

20. How does knowing that $\frac{1}{4} = 0.25$ help you find the decimal form of $\frac{3}{4}$?

21. Explain how you know 0.635 is greater than $\frac{1}{2}$.

NS7-33 Regrouping Decimals

A Base Ten Model for Decimal Tenths and Hundredths

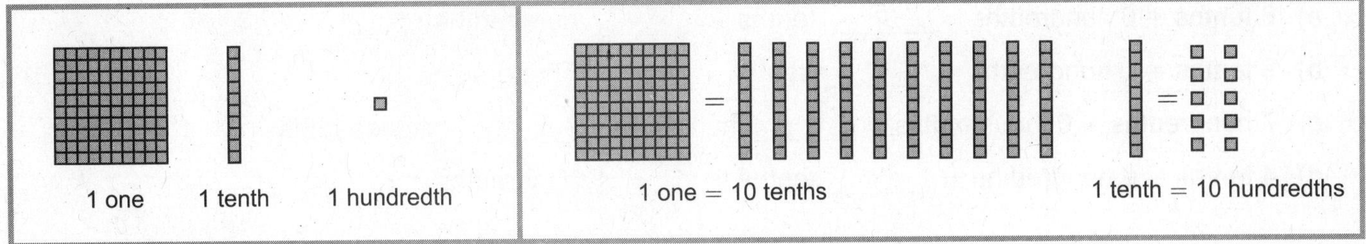

1. a) This model represents the decimal 2.___ ___.

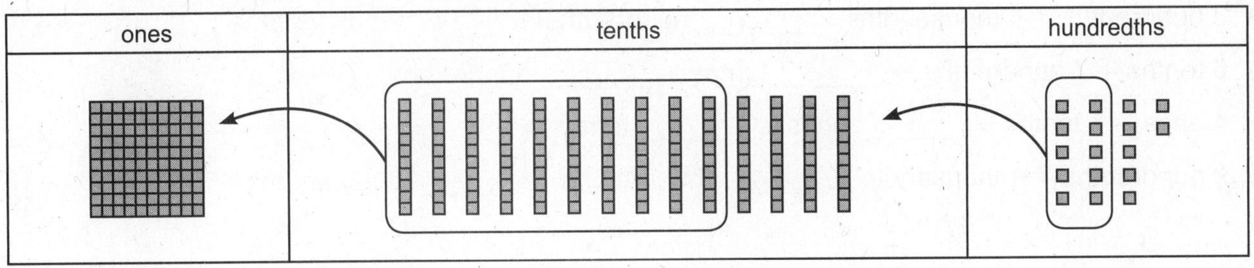

b) Regroup as many of the blocks into bigger blocks as you can. This model represents ___.___ ___.

ones	tenths	hundredths

c) Regroup as many of the blocks into bigger blocks as you can. This model represents ___.___ ___.

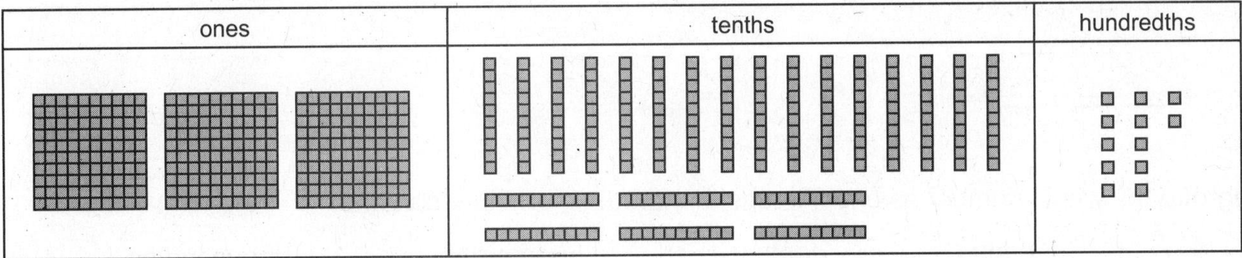

2. Regroup.

a) 27 tenths = 2 ones + ___ tenths

b) 36 tenths = ___ ones + ___ tenths

c) 74 hundredths = ___ tenths + ___ hundredths

d) 19 hundredths = ___ tenths + ___ hundredths

3. Regroup so that each place value has a single digit.

a) 2 ones + 14 tenths = 3 ones + 4 tenths

b) 6 tenths + 17 hundredths = ___ tenths + ___ hundredths

c) 5 hundredths + 11 thousandths = ___ hundredths + ___ thousandth

NS7-33 Regrouping Decimals *(continued)*

4. Exchange 1 tenth for 10 hundredths or 1 hundredth for 10 thousandths.

a) 6 tenths + 0 hundredths = ___5___ tenths + ___10___ hundredths

b) 9 tenths + 0 hundredths = ______ tenths + ______ hundredths

c) 7 hundredths + 0 thousandths = ______ hundredths + ______ thousandths

d) 4 tenths + 0 hundredths = ______ tenths + ______ hundredths

5. Exchange one of the larger unit for 10 of the smaller unit.

a) 3 hundredths + 4 thousandths = ___2___ hundredths + ___14___ thousandths

b) 6 tenths + 7 hundredths = ______ tenths + ______ hundredths

c) 4 ones + 5 tenths = ______ ones + ______ tenths

d) 9 hundredths + 1 thousandth = ______ hundredths + ______ thousandths

6. Underline the smallest place value in the decimal. Then write the decimal as an improper fraction.

a) $2.3 = \frac{23}{10}$ b) $4.5 =$ c) $7.6 =$ d) $3.55 = \frac{\quad}{100}$ e) $6.18 =$

f) $9.76 =$ g) $1.23 =$ h) $1.254 = \frac{\quad}{1000}$ i) $5.355 =$ j) $3.112 =$

7. Add zeros to rewrite the whole number as decimal tenths, hundredths, and thousandths.
Example: 2 = 2.0 = 2.00 = 2.000

a) 7 = ________
= ________
= ________

b) 15 = ________
= ________
= ________

c) 230 = ________
= ________
= ________

8. Regroup the whole number as ones, tenths, hundredths, and thousandths.

a) 8 = ______ ones = ______ tenths = ______ hundredths = ______ thousandths

b) 16 = ______ ones = ______ tenths = ______ hundredths = ______ thousandths

9. Complete the statements.

a) 1.7 = ______ tenths

b) 5.2 = ______ tenths

c) 13.4 = ______ tenths

d) 75.3 = ______ tenths

e) 13.4 = ______ hundredths

f) 75.3 = ______ hundredths

g) 10.36 = ______ hundredths

h) 1.25 = ______ thousandths

i) 10.36 = ______ thousandths

j) 1.25 = ______ thousandths

NS7-34 Addition Strategies for Decimals

1. Write an addition statement that corresponds to the grids.

a) 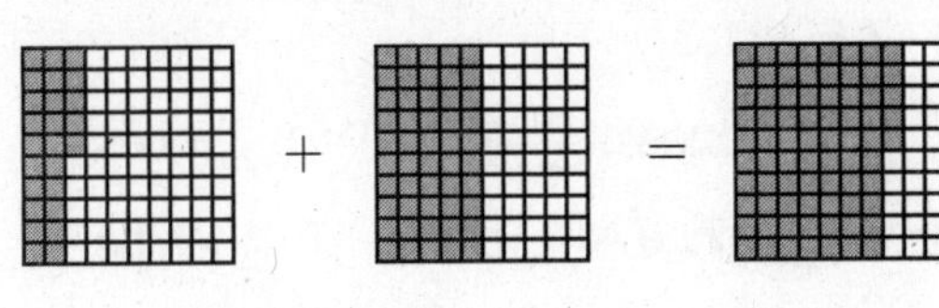

0.______ + 0.______ = 0.______

b) 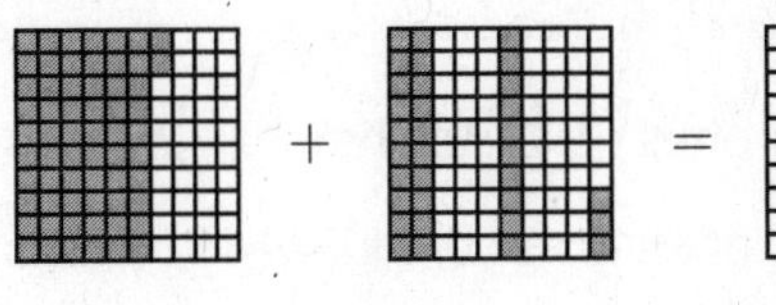

0.______ + 0.______ = 0.______

2. Add by sketching a base ten model. Note: Use a hundreds block for a one and a tens block for a tenth.

a) 1.23 + 1.12

= 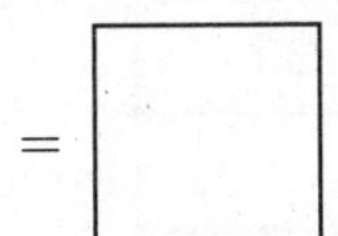 + 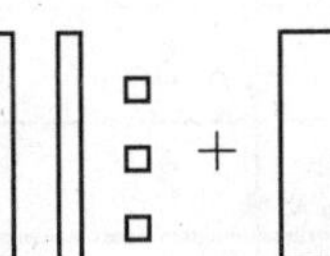

= 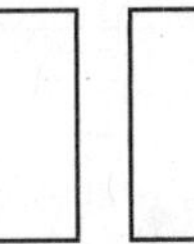  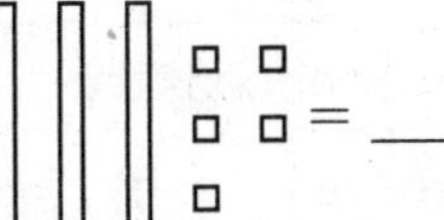 = ______

b) 1.46 + 1.33

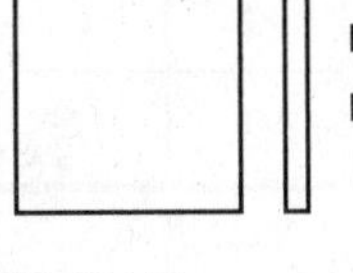

3. Use equivalent fractions to calculate the decimal sums.

a) $0.3 + 0.4 = \frac{3}{10} + \frac{}{10} = \frac{}{10} = 0.$______

b) $0.65 + 0.22 = \frac{}{100} + \frac{}{100} = \frac{}{100} = 0.$______

c) $0.56 + 0.05 = \frac{}{100} + \frac{}{100} = \frac{}{100} = 0.$______

d) $0.123 + 0.44 = \frac{}{1000} + \frac{}{1000} = \frac{}{1000} = 0.$______

4. Write the decimals as fractions with a common denominator to calculate the sums.

a) $0.27 + 0.6 = \frac{27}{100} + \frac{6}{10} = \frac{27}{100} + \frac{}{100} = \frac{}{100} =$ ___.___ ___

b) $0.57 + 0.765 = \frac{57}{100} + \frac{765}{1000} = \frac{}{1000} + \frac{765}{1000} = \frac{}{1000} =$ ___.___ ___ ___

c) $2.025 + 0.99 = \frac{}{1000} + \frac{}{100} = \frac{}{1000} + \frac{}{1000} = \frac{}{1000} =$ ___.___ ___ ___

5. Write both decimals using the smallest place value to calculate the sums.

a) 2.15 + 6.3

= _215_ hundredths + _63_ tenths

= ______ hundredths + ______ hundredths

= ______ hundredths

= ___.___ ___

b) 4.054 + 2.93

= ______ thousandths + ______ hundredths

= ______ thousandths + ______ thousandths

= ______ thousandths

= ___.___ ___

NS7-34 Addition Strategies for Decimals *(continued)*

6. Add by adding each place value.

a) 3.3 + 2.4

= (3 ones + 3 tenths) + (2 ones + 4 tenths)

= (3 ones + 2 ones) + (3 tenths + 4 tenths)

= ___ ones + ___ tenths

= ___.___

b) 7.6 + 1.3

= (___ ones + ___ tenths) + (___ ones + ___ tenths)

= (___ ones + ___ ones) + (___ tenths + ___ tenths)

= ___ ones + ___ tenths

= ___.___

7. Add by adding each place value.

a)

	tens	ones	tenths	hundredths
	3	2	1	
+		6	7	8
	3	8	8	8

b)

	tenths	ones	tenths	thousandths
	4	0	5	3
+	2	7	2	

8. Add by adding each place value. Then regroup wherever necessary.

Example:

	ones	tenths
	1	7
+	4	7
	5	14

14 tenths =

1 one + 4 tenths,

so the sum is

6	4

a)

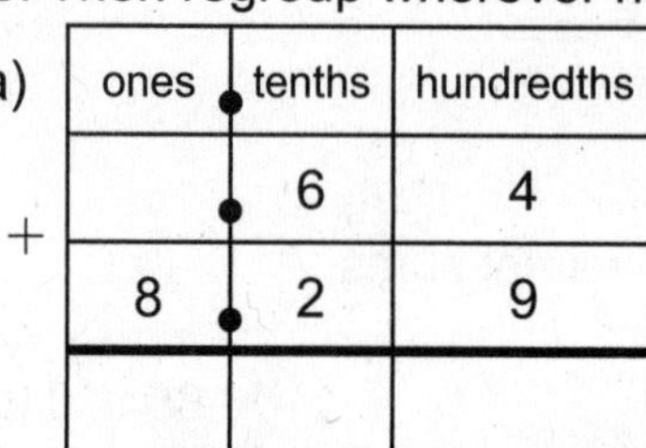

	ones	tenths	hundredths
		6	4
+	8	2	9

___ hundredths =

___ tenths + ___ hundredths,

so the sum is

b)

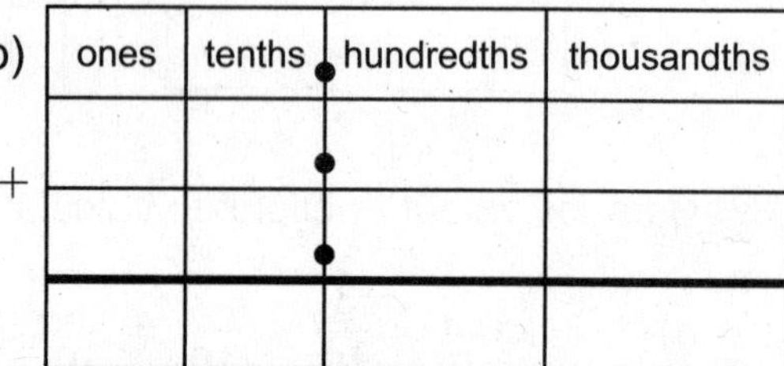

	ones	tenths	hundredths	thousandths
+				

___ thousandths =

___ hundredths + ___ thousandths

so the sum is

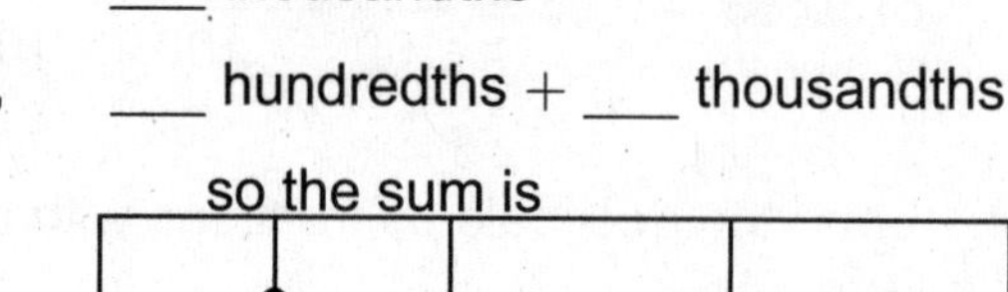

9. Use the place value chart to add the decimals. Then regroup.

a) 0.723 + 3.146 + 0.5

	tens	ones	tenths	hundredths	thousandths
+					

Regroup:

b) 0.23 + 45.652 + 2.4

	tens	ones	tenths	hundredths	thousandths
+					

Regroup:

BONUS ▸ Regroup twice to add: 0.025 + 0.348 + 0.534

NS7-35 Adding and Subtracting Decimals

Adding Decimals

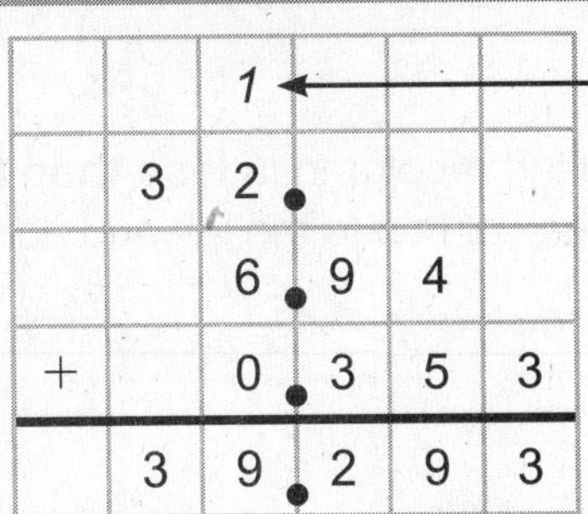

12 tenths were regrouped as 1 one and 2 tenths.

1. Add the decimals.

a) 0.32 + 0.54 b) 5.71 + 3.26 c) 0.416 + 0.573 d) 9.117 + 0.162

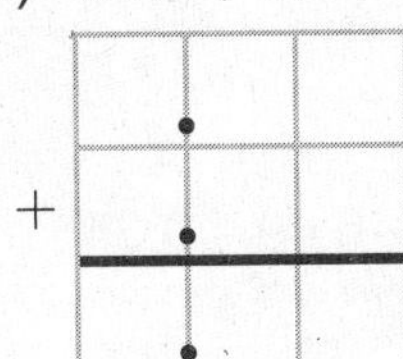

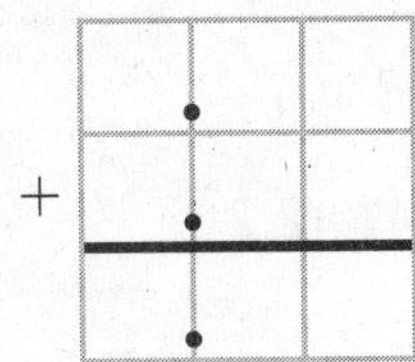

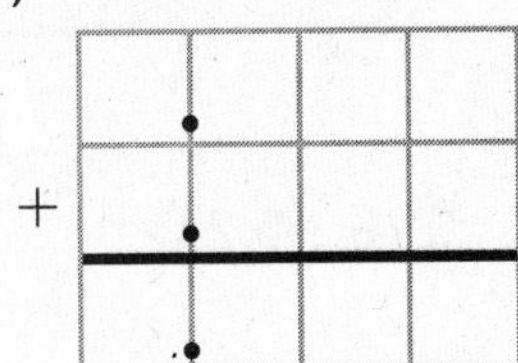

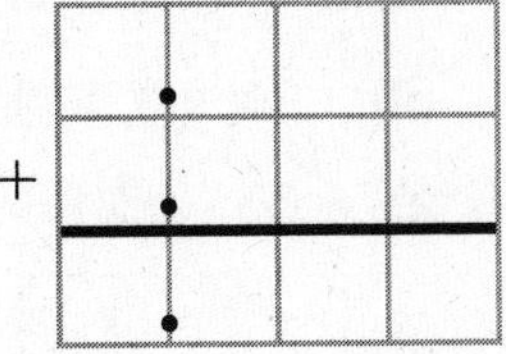

2. Add the decimals by lining up the decimal points.

a) 0.81 + 0.58 b) 2.56 + 7.27 c) 0.583 + 1.251 d) 5.555 + 4.078

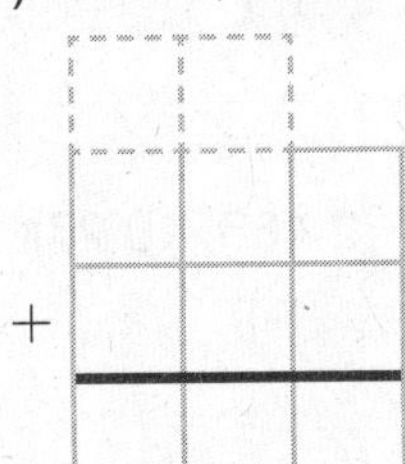

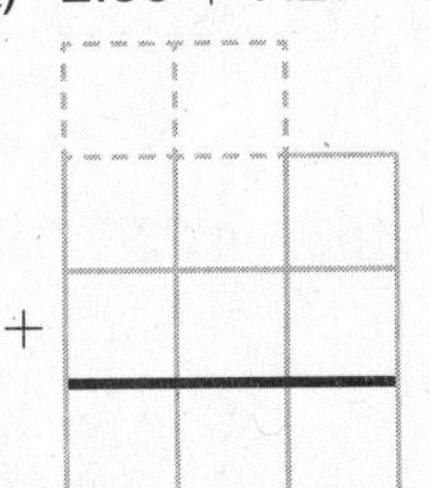

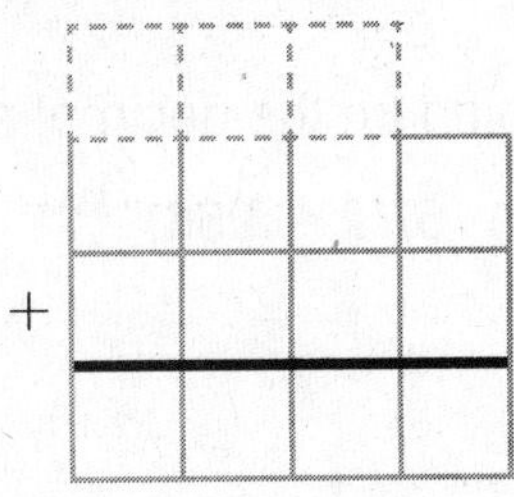

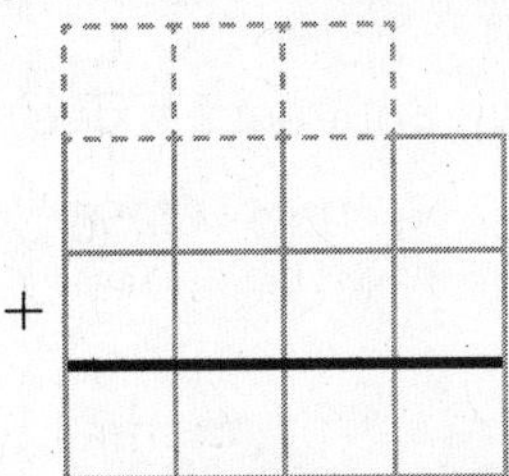

e) 0.45 + 0.08 + 0.32 f) 5.6 + 1.42 + 0.8 g) 1.275 + 0.56 + 6.304 h) 0.9 + 0.99 + 0.999

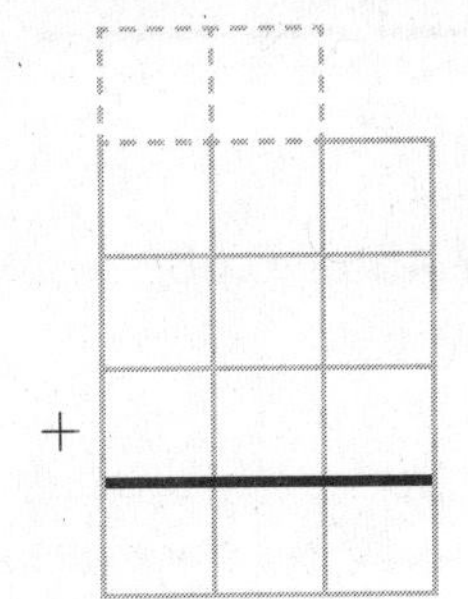

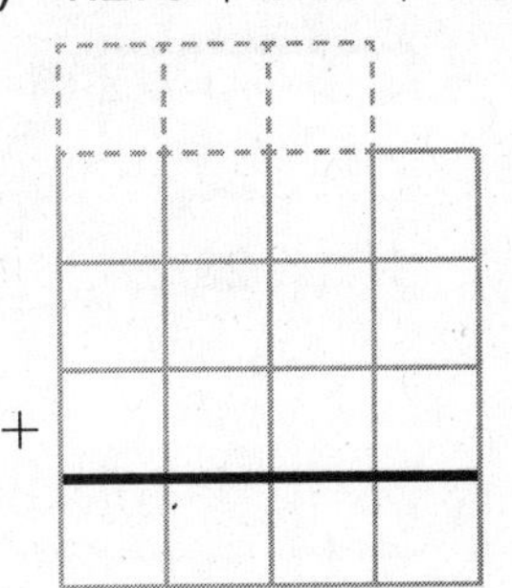

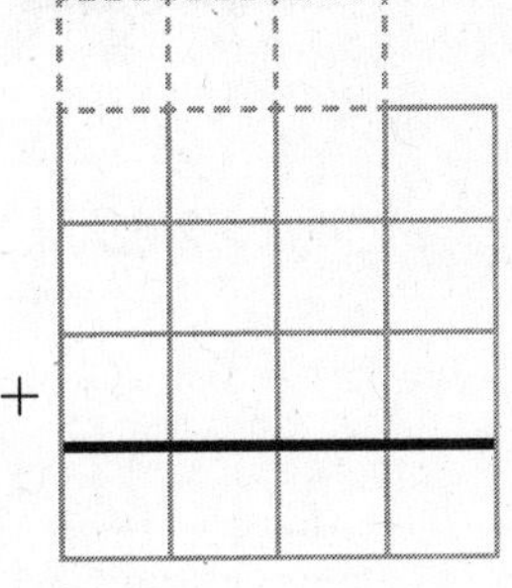

3. Add the decimals on grid paper.

a) 4.32 + 2.77 b) 3.64 + 5.83 c) 9.465 + 3.12 d) 0.87 + 0.026

e) 7.098 + 2.169 + 5.43 f) 0.076 + 2.84 + 0.639 g) 47.5 + 3.003 + 16.87

4. a) The mass of a nickel is 3.95 g and the mass of a penny is 2.35 g. What is the total mass of 1 nickel and 2 pennies?

b) The mass of a dime is 1.75 g, and the mass of a quarter is 4.4 g. What is heavier, five dimes or two quarters?

5. Bill adds 43.4 + 5.65 on grid paper. He gets 99.9. What mistake did he make? Explain.

NS7-35 Adding and Subtracting Decimals *(continued)*

Subtracting Decimals

Add zeros to make each decimal end at the same place value.

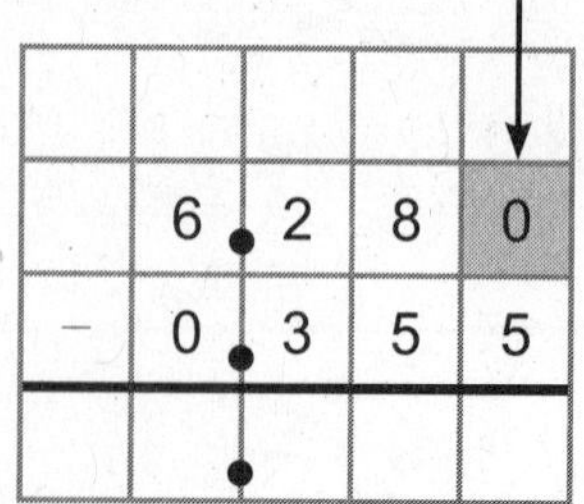

If the top digit in a column is **less than the digit below it**, take 1 from the column to the left and add 10 to the top digit.

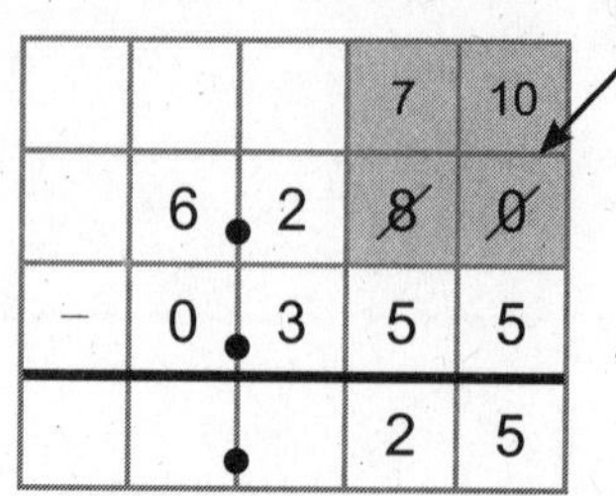

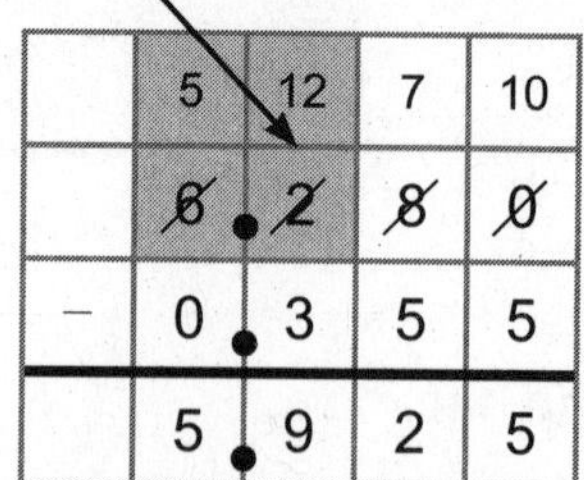

6. Subtract the decimals.

a) 0.53 – 0.21

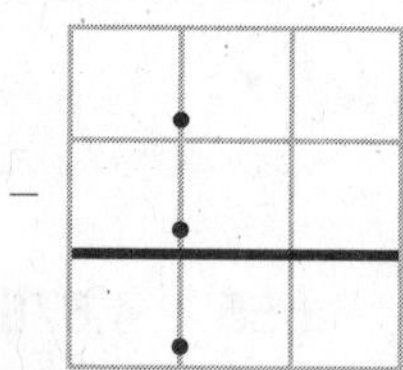

b) 0.76 – 0.24

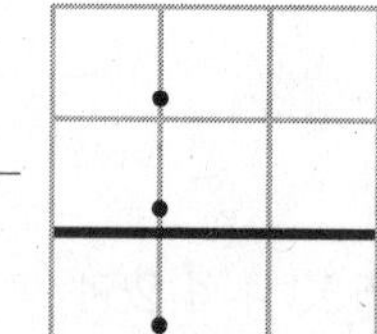

c) 3.47 – 2.2

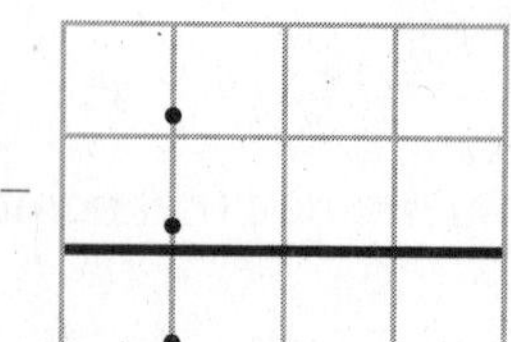

d) 6.49 – 0.35

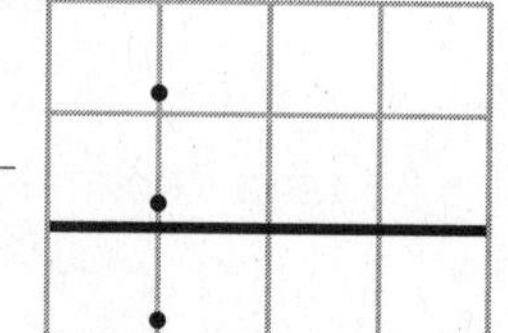

7. Subtract the decimals by lining up the decimal points.

a) 0.81 – 0.58

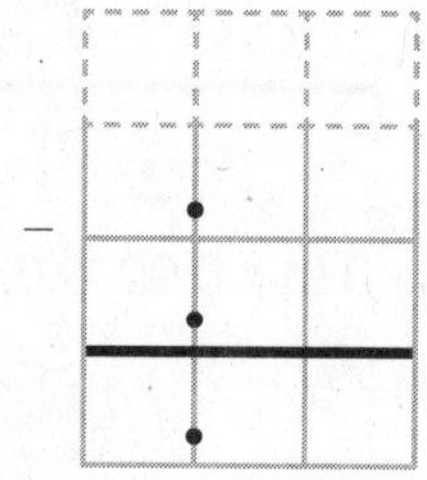

b) 5.72 – 3.56

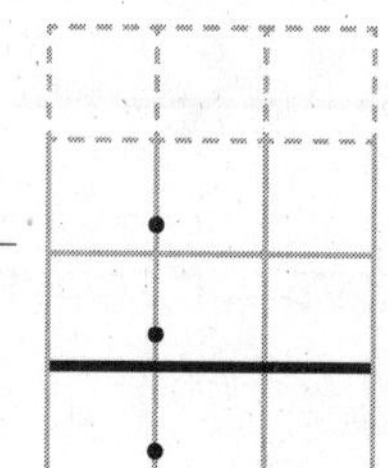

c) 6.156 – 4.25

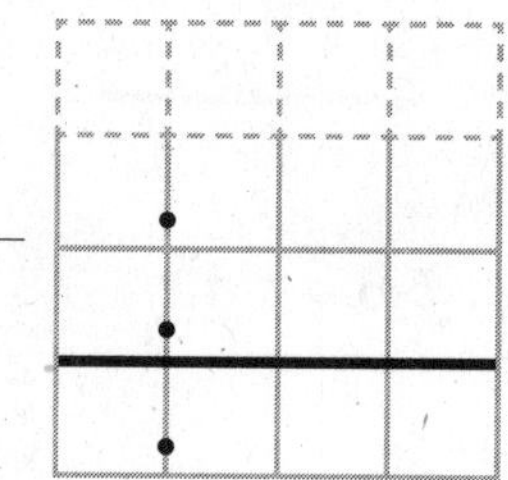

d) 2.463 – 0.271

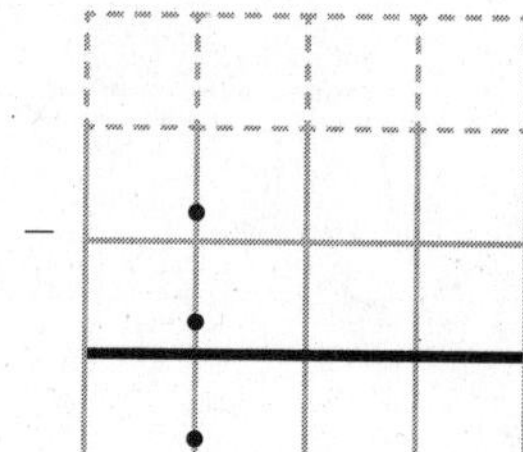

e) 4.5 – 2.65

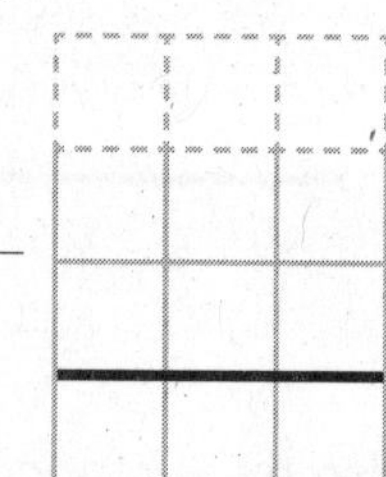

f) 31.1 – 22.2

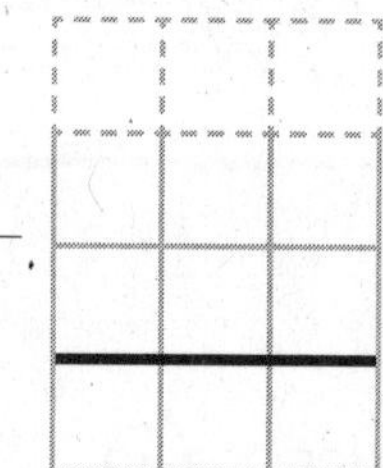

g) 7.455 – 6.68

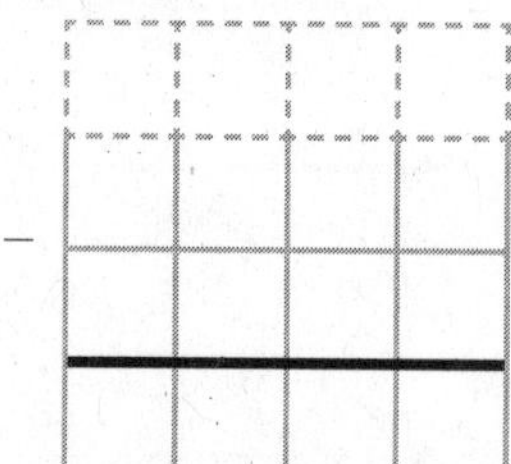

h) 5.207 – 1.238

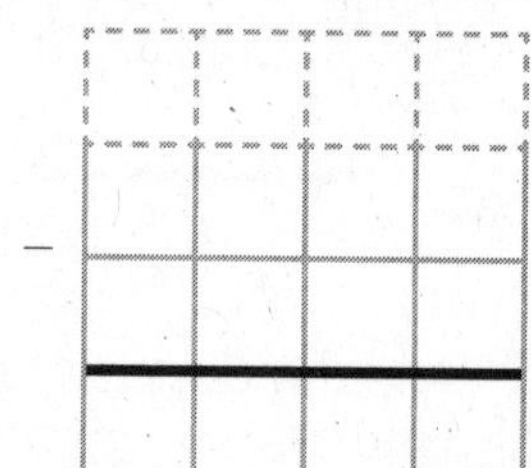

8. Subtract the decimals on grid paper.

a) 0.87 – 0.026 b) 9.465 – 3.12 c) 5.83 – 3.69 d) 4.35 – 2.72

9. What is the difference in thickness of these coins?

a) a penny (1.45 mm) and a dime (1.22 mm)

b) a dollar (1.95 mm) and a quarter (1.58 mm)

NS7-36 Multiplying Decimals by 10

 = 1.0   [tens block] = 0.1 ⟶ 10 × [tens block] = [hundreds block]

If a hundreds block represents 1 whole (1.0), then a tens block represents 1 tenth (0.1).

$10 \times 0.1 = 1.0$

10 tenths make 1 whole

1. Multiply the number of tens blocks by 10. Draw the number of hundreds blocks you would have, then complete the multiplication sentence.

a) 10 × [3 tens blocks] = 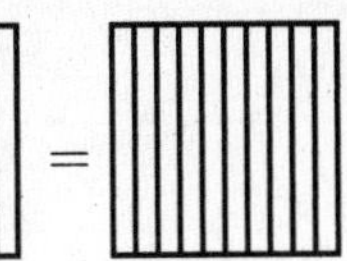  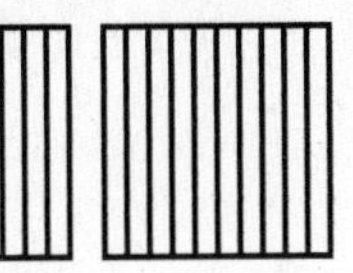

$10 \times 0.3 =$ *3*

b) 10 × [2 tens blocks] =

$10 \times 0.2 =$ _____

c) 10 × [5 tens blocks] =

$10 \times 0.5 =$ _____

2. To multiply by 10, shift the decimal one place to the right.

a) $10 \times 0.5 =$ *5*   b) $10 \times 0.6 =$ _____   c) $10 \times 1.4 =$ _____   d) $10 \times 0.8 =$ _____

e) $10 \times 2.4 =$ _____   f) $3.5 \times 10 =$ _____   g) $14.5 \times 10 =$ _____   h) $11.2 \times 10 =$ _____

i) $10 \times 2.06 =$ *20.6*   j) $10 \times 2.75 =$ _____   k) $10 \times 97.6 =$ _____   l) $52.36 \times 10 =$ _____

To change metres to decimetres, multiply by 10.

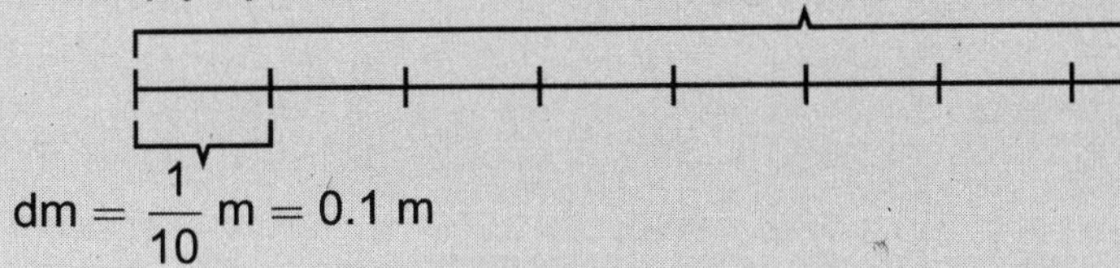

3. Find the answers.

a) 0.4 m = _____ dm   b) 0.8 m = _____ dm   c) 7.5 m = _____ dm

4. 10×4 can be written as a sum: $4 + 4 + 4 + 4 + 4 + 4 + 4 + 4 + 4 + 4$.

Write 10×0.4 as a sum and skip count by 0.4 to find the answer.

5. A dime is a tenth of a dollar (10¢ = \$0.10). Draw a picture or use play money to show that 10 × \$0.30 = \$3.00.

NS7-37 Multiplying Decimals by 100 and 1 000

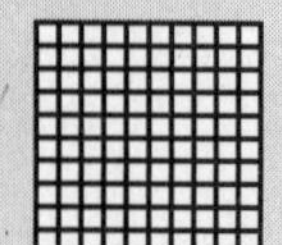

= 1.0 ▫ = 0.01 ⟶ 100 × ▫ =

If a hundreds block represents 1 whole (1.0), then a ones block represents 1 hundredth (0.01).

100 × 0.01 = 1.0

100 hundredths makes 1 whole

1. Write a multiplication sentence for each picture.

a) 100 × 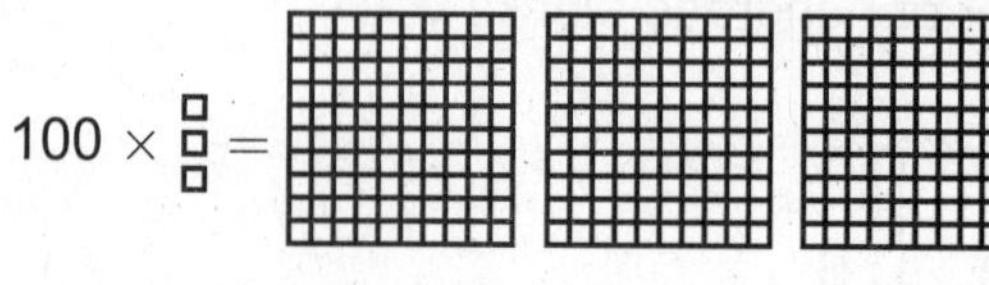 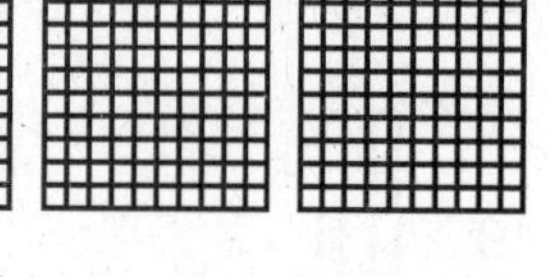

100 × 0.03 = ______

b) 100 × 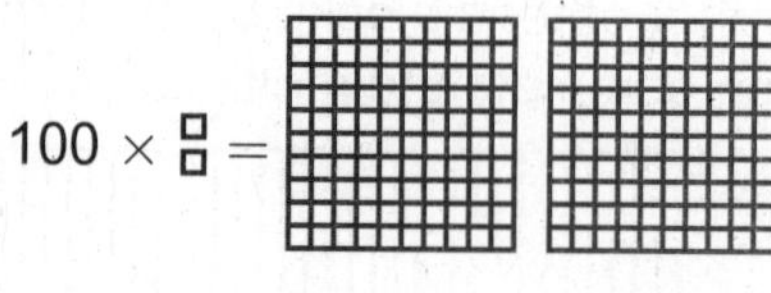

______ = ______

The picture shows why the decimal shifts two places to the right when you multiply by 100.

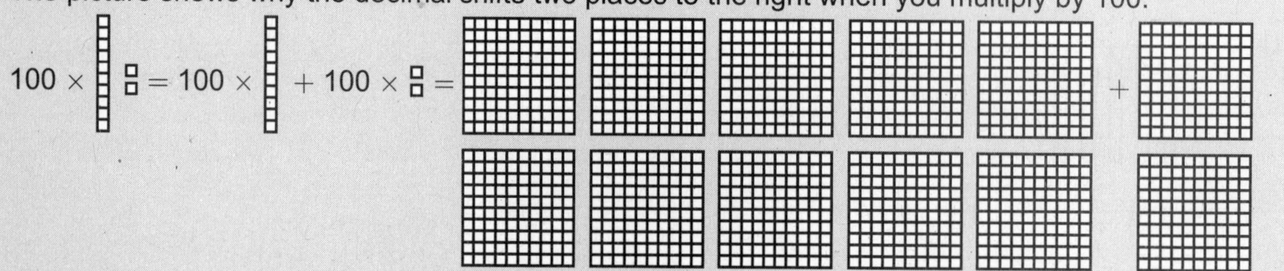

100 × 0.12 = 100 × 0.1 (= 10) + 100 × 0.02 (= 2) = 12

2. To multiply by 100, shift the decimal two places to the right.

a) 100 × 0.8 = *80* b) 100 × 3.5 = ______ c) 7.2 × 100 = ______

d) 6.3 × 100 = ______ e) 100 × 2.1 = ______ f) 6.0 × 100 = ______

g) 100 × 0.34 = ______ h) 0.76 × 100 = ______ i) 100 × 0.07 = ______

3. Multiply.

a) 100 × 0.05 = *5* b) 100 × 0.02 = ______ c) 0.63 × 100 = ______ d) 0.45 × 100 = ______

e) 2.72 × 100 = ______ f) 100 × 3.09 = ______ g) 100 × 0.23 = ______ h) 100 × 0.7 = ______

i) 1.4 × 100 = ______ j) 100 × 0.06 = ______ k) 11.3 × 100 = ______ l) 2.4 × 100 = ______

4. a) What do 1 000 thousandths add up to? ______ b) What is 1 000 × 0.001? ______

5. Look at your answer to Question 4 b).

How many places right does the decimal shift when you multiply by 1 000? ______

6. Multiply the numbers by shifting the decimal.

a) 1 000 × 0.93 = ______ b) 1 000 × 0.726 = ______ c) 6.325 × 1 000 = ______

d) 1 000 × 0.27 = ______ e) 1 000 × 3.21 = ______ f) 2.8 × 1 000 = ______

NS7-38 Dividing Decimals by 100 and 1 000

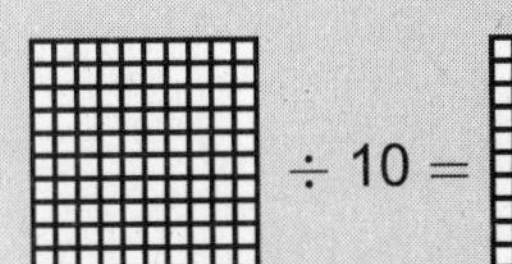

÷ 10 =

Divide 1 whole into 10 equal parts; each part is 1 tenth.

1.0 ÷ 10 = 0.1

÷ 10 =

Divide 1 tenth into 10 equal parts; each part is 1 hundredth.

0.1 ÷ 10 = 0.01

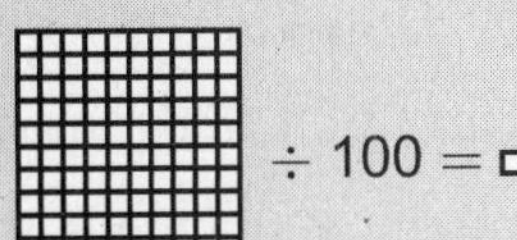

÷ 100 =

Divide 1 whole into 100 equal parts; each part is 1 hundredth.

1.0 ÷ 100 = 0.01

1. Complete the picture and write a division sentence for each picture.

a) 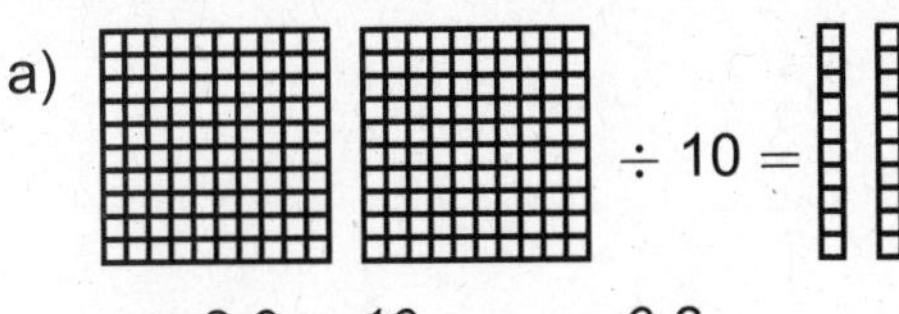 ÷ 10 =

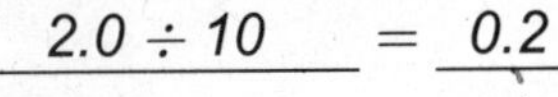

2.0 ÷ 10 = *0.2*

b) 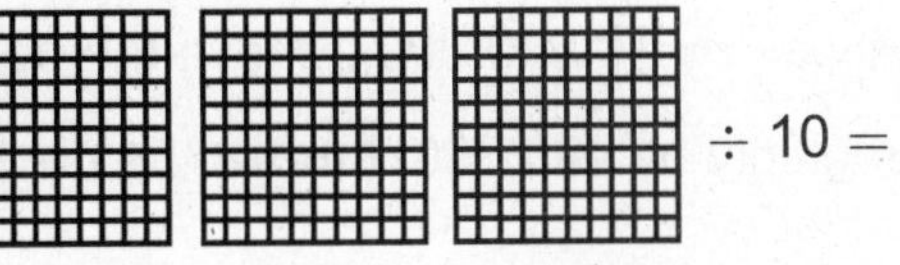 ÷ 10 =

______ = ____

c) ÷ 10 =

0.4 ÷ 10 = ____

d) 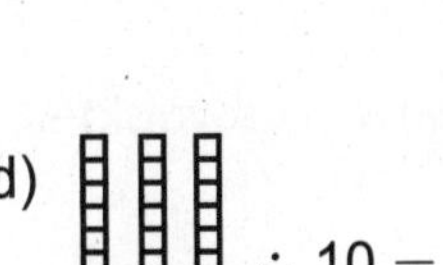 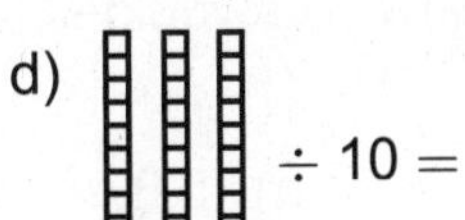 ÷ 10 =

______ = ____

e)  ÷ 10 =

______ = ____

f) 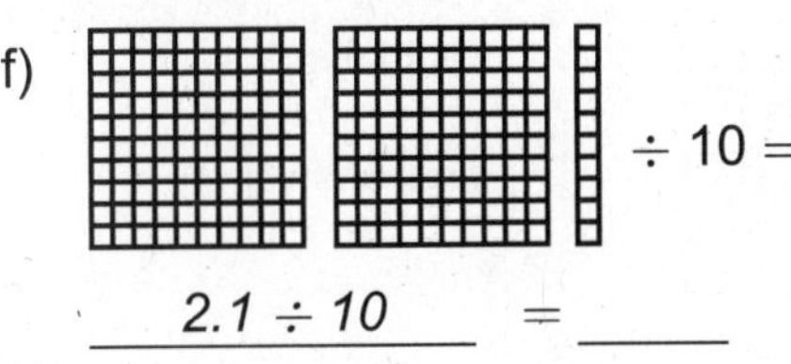 ÷ 10 =

2.1 ÷ 10 = ____

g) 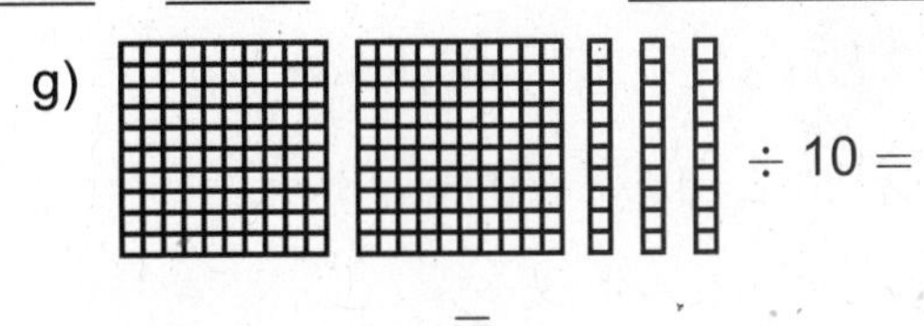 ÷ 10 =

______ = ____

2. Division undoes multiplication. How do you undo multiplying by 10 or 100?

a) To multiply by 10, I move the decimal point ____ places to the ________,
so to divide by 10, I move the decimal point ____ places to the ________.

b) To multiply by 100, I move the decimal point ____ places to the ________,
so to divide by 100, I move the decimal point ____ places to the ________.

3. Shift the decimal one or two places to the left by drawing an arrow, then write the answer in the blank. Hint: If there is no decimal, add one to the right of the number first.

a) 0.4 ÷ 10 = *0.4* b) 0.7 ÷ 10 = ____ c) 0.6 ÷ 10 = ____ d) 3.1 ÷ 10 = ____

e) 26.0 ÷ 10 = ____ f) 81 ÷ 10 = ____ g) 0.3 ÷ 10 = ____ h) 25.4 ÷ 10 = ____

i) 6.0 ÷ 100 = ____ j) 9.1 ÷ 100 = ____ k) 0.5 ÷ 100 = ____ l) 91.3 ÷ 100 = ____

4. Explain why 1.00 ÷ 100 = 0.01, using a dollar coin as a whole.

5. A wall 2.5 m wide is painted with 100 stripes of equal width. How wide is each stripe?

6. 5 × 3 = 15 and 15 ÷ 5 = 3 are in the same fact family. Write a division statement in the same fact family as 10 × 0.1 = 1.0.

NS7-39 Multiplying and Dividing by Powers of 10

1. a) To multiply by 10, I move the decimal ___1___ place(s) to the left ___left___.

b) To multiply by 1 000, I move the decimal _____ place(s) to the __________.

c) To divide by 100, I move the decimal _____ place(s) to the __________.

d) To divide by 10, I move the decimal _____ place(s) to the __________.

e) To __________ by 1 000, I move the decimal _____ places to the left.

f) To __________ by 10, I move the decimal _____ place to the left.

g) To __________ by 100, I move the decimal _____ places to the right.

h) To divide by 10 000 000, I move the decimal _____ places to the __________.

i) To multiply by 100 000, I move the decimal _____ places to the __________.

2. Fill in the blanks. Next, draw arrows to show how you would shift the decimal. Then write your final answer in the grid.

a) 7.325 × 100

I move the decimal ___2___ places ___right___.

		7.	3	2	5			rough work
		7	3	2.	5			final answer

b) 5.3 ÷ 1 000

I move the decimal ___3___ places ___left___.

				5.	3			rough work
		.0	0	5	3			final answer

c) 247.567 × 1 000

I move the decimal _____ places __________.

		2	4	7.	5	6	7			rough work
										final answer

d) 100.45 ÷ 100

I move the decimal _____ places __________.

		1	0	0.	4	5				rough work
										final answer

e) 0.602 × 100 000

I move the decimal _____ places __________.

					.6	0	2			rough work
										final answer

f) 24.682 ÷ 10 000

I move the decimal _____ places __________.

			2	4.	6	8	2			rough work
										final answer

3. Copy the numbers onto grid paper. Show how you would shift the decimal in each case.

a) 2.65 × 1 000 b) 47.001 × 100 c) 0.043 × 10 d) 20.06 × 1 000 e) 0.07 × 10 000

f) 0.643 ÷ 10 g) 170.45 ÷ 100 h) 36.07 ÷ 1 000 i) 17.35 ÷ 10 000 j) 0.05 ÷ 1 000

NS7-40 Multiplying Decimals by Whole Numbers

The picture shows how to multiply a decimal by a whole number.

1.23 → × 3 → 3 × 1.23 = 3.69

1. Multiply mentally. Multiply each digit separately.

a) 3 × 1.32 = ______ b) 2 × 2.4 = ______ c) 6 × 1.01 = ______ d) 3 × 3.2 = ______

e) 4 × 2.12 = ______ f) 5 × 3.1 = ______ g) 2 × 4.21 = ______ h) 7 × 4.11 = ______

2. Multiply by exchanging tenths for ones.

a) 7 × 1.3 = *7* ones + *21* tenths = *9* ones + *1* tenth = *9.1*

b) 3 × 3.4 = ______ ones + ______ tenths = ______ ones + ______ tenths = ______

c) 4 × 4.7 = ______ ones + ______ tenths = ______ ones + ______ tenths = ______

d) 3 × 2.9 = ____

3. Multiply by exchanging tenths for ones or hundredths for tenths.

a) 3 × 3.51 = ______ ones + ______ tenths + ______ hundredths

= ______ ones + ______ tenths + ______ hundredths = ______

b) 4 × 2.34 = ______ ones + ______ tenths + ______ hundredths

= ______ ones + ______ tenths + ______ hundredths = ______

4. Multiply. In some questions you will have to regroup twice.

a)

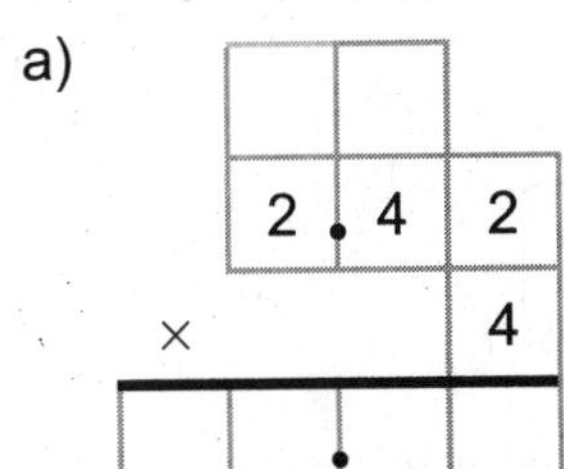

b)

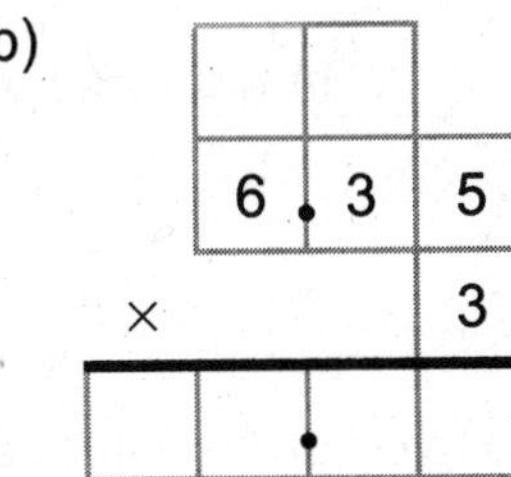

c)

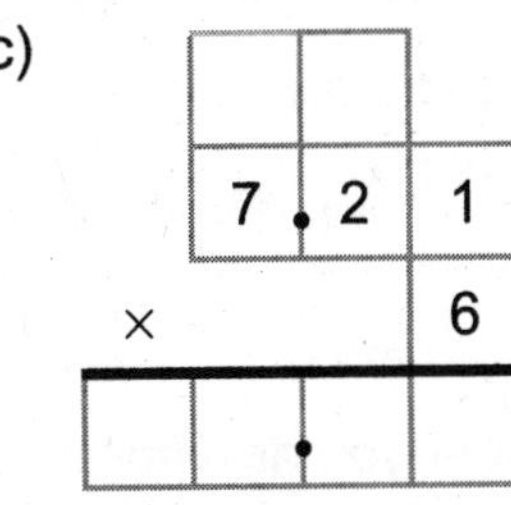

d)

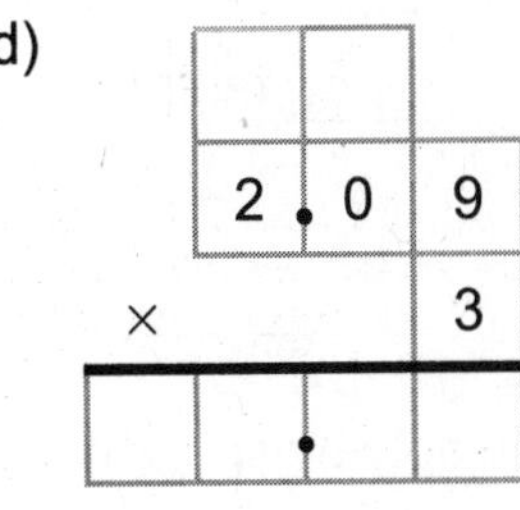

5. Find the products.

a) 5 × 3.6 b) 3 × 0.4 c) 6 × 4.2 d) 9 × 2.27 e) 7 × 34.6 f) 8 × 4.3

g) 4 × 2.7 h) 5 × 9.52 i) 7 × 5.98 j) 8 × 6.29 k) 3 × 46.92 l) 4 × 36.75

6. You can rewrite the product 80 × 3.6 as 10 × 8 × 3.6. Use this method to find these products.

a) 40 × 2.1 b) 60 × 0.7 c) 30 × 9.68 d) 200 × 7.5 e) 500 × 0.2

NS7-41 Multiplying Decimals Using Different Strategies

1. Use the base ten model to multiply the decimal.

a) 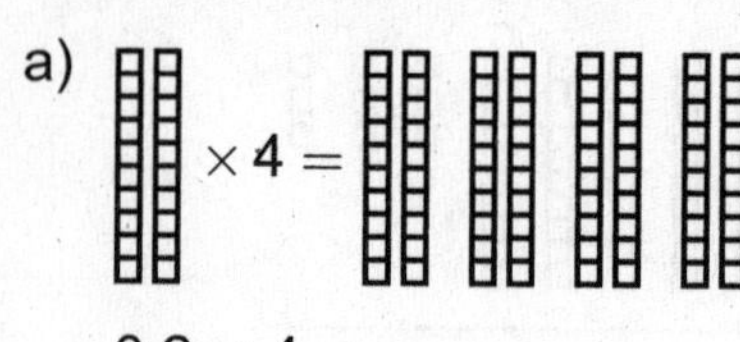

$0.2 \times 4 =$ ___.___

b) 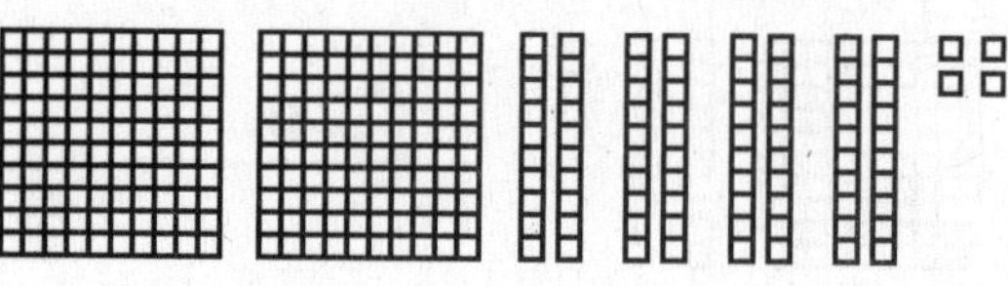

$1.42 \times 2 =$ ___.___ ___

2. Use repeated addition to multiply the decimal.

a) $0.5 \times 3 =$ *0.5 + 0.5 + 0.5*
= ____________

b) $2.4 \times 2 =$ ______ + ______
= ____________

c) $1.6 \times 4 =$ ____________
____

3. Multiply.

a) 0.2×8
= *2* tenths × 8
= *16* tenths
= *1.6*

b) 0.47×5
= ____ hundredths × ____
= ____ hundredths
= 2.___ ___

c) 0.132×3
= ____ thousandths × ____
= ____ thousandths
= ___.___ ___ ___

d) 0.2×44
= ____ tenths × ____
= ____ tenths
= ____ ones + ____ tenths
= ___.___

e) 1.2×4
= ____ tenths × 4
= ____ tenths
= ____ ones + ____ tenths
= ___.___

f) 3.06×3
= ____ hundredths × 3
= ____ hundredths
= ____ ones + ____ hundredths
= ___.___ ___

4. Multiply each place value separately.

a) 0.73×2
= (____ tenths + ____ hundredths) × 2
= (___ tenths × 2) + (___ hundredths × 2)
= ____ tenths + ____ hundredths
= ___.___ + ___.___ ___
= ___.___ ___

b) 0.063×3
= (____ hundredths + ____ thousandths) × 3
= (___ hundredths × 3) + (___ thousandths × 3)
= ____ hundredths + ____ thousandths
= ___.___ ___ + ___.___ ___ ___
= ___.___ ___ ___

5. Multiply by splitting the number you are multiplying into two numbers that are easier to multiply.

a) $4.35 \times 3 =$ (*4* + *0.35*) × *3*
= (*4* × ____) + (*0.35* × ____)
= ____ + ____
= ___.___ ___

b) $6.021 \times 4 =$ (____ + ____) × 4
= (____ × ____) + (____ × ____)
= ____ + ____
= ___.___ ___ ___

6. Multiply. Use the strategy of your choice.

a) 0.4×8 b) 1.5×7 c) 0.32×5 d) 2.9×4 e) 6.02×8 f) 0.047×2 g) 7.91×3

NS7-42 Dividing Decimals Using Different Strategies

1. What division statement does this model show? Fill in the blanks. 0.95 ÷ ____ = ____ R ____

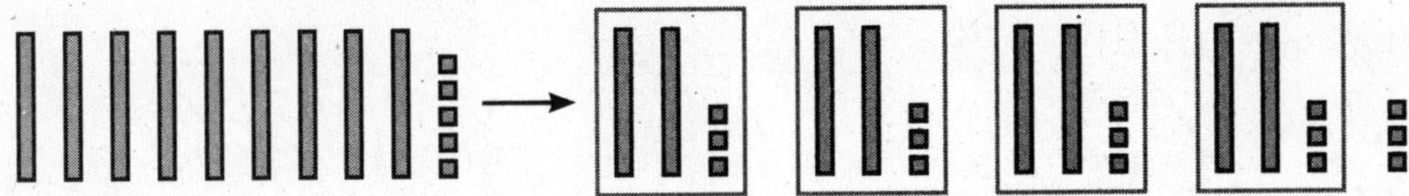

2. Divide.

a) 0.8 ÷ 2
= 8 tenths ÷ 2
= 4 tenths
= 0. 4

b) 2.8 ÷ 7
= 28 tenths ÷ 7
= ____ tenths
= 0.____

c) 0.54 ÷ 9
= ____ hundredths ÷ 9
= ____ hundredths
= 0.____

d) 0.025 ÷ 5
= ____ thousandths ÷ 5
= ____ thousandths
= 0.____

3. Regroup and then divide.

a) 0.3 ÷ 6
= 3 tenths ÷ 6
= 30 hundredths ÷ 6
= 5 hundredths
= 0. 05

b) 0.04 ÷ 5
= ____ hundredths ÷ ____
= ____ thousandths ÷ ____
= ____ thousandths
= 0.____

c) 0.04 ÷ 8
= ____ hundredths ÷ ____
= ____ thousandths ÷ ____
= ____ thousandths
= 0.____

4. Divide one place value at a time.

a) 0.468 = 4 tenths + 6 hundredths + 8 thousandths

So 0.468 ÷ **2** = (4 tenths ÷ **2**) + (6 hundredths ÷ **2**) + (8 thousandths ÷ **2**)
= 2 tenths + 3 hundredths + 4 thousandths
= 0.234

The short way to write this is: $2\overline{)0.468}$ = 0.234

b) $2\overline{)6.4}$ c) $3\overline{)3.9}$ d) $4\overline{)8.4}$ e) $6\overline{)12.6}$ f) $3\overline{)60.93}$ g) $3\overline{)0.396}$

5. Sometimes you can divide by splitting the dividend into two numbers that are easier to divide.

a) 7.2 ÷ 4
= (6.0 + 1.2) ÷ 4
= (6.0 ÷ 4) + (1.2 ÷ 4)
= 1.5 + .3
= 1.8

b) 4.8 ÷ 3
= (3.0 + 1.8) ÷ 3
= (3.0 ÷ 3) + (1.8 ÷ 3)
= ____ + ____
= ____

c) 15.6 ÷ 3
= (____ + ____) ÷ ____
= (____ ÷ ____) + (____ ÷ ____)
= ____ + ____
= ____

6. Divide. Use the strategy of your choice.

a) 0.8 ÷ 4 b) 4.8 ÷ 8 c) 0.54 ÷ 6 d) 0.393 ÷ 3 e) 0.08 ÷ 5 f) 0.7 ÷ 5

g) 7.2 ÷ 8 h) 5.6 ÷ 4 i) 0.54 ÷ 9 j) 27.9 ÷ 3 k) 1.64 ÷ 4 l) 20.4 ÷ 4

NS7-43 Long Division

Problem: Divide 95 objects into 4 groups ($95 \div 4$).

Here is a base ten model of the problem.

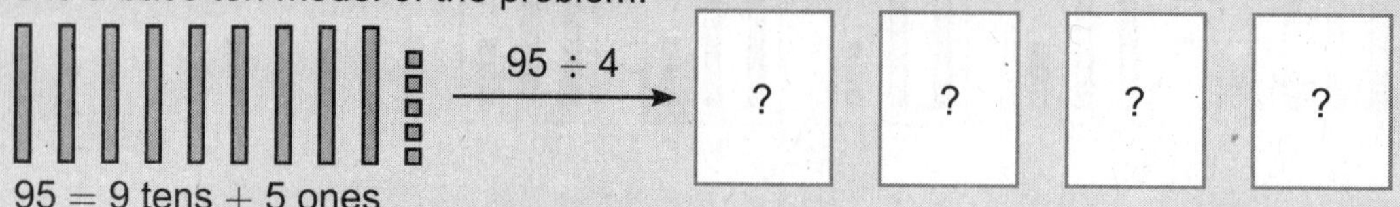

Solve the problem using **long division**.

Step 1: Write the numbers like this: $4\overline{)95}$

the number of groups — the number you are dividing

Step 2: How can you divide 9 tens blocks equally into the 4 groups?

You can divide 8 of the 9 tens blocks into 4 equal groups of size 2:

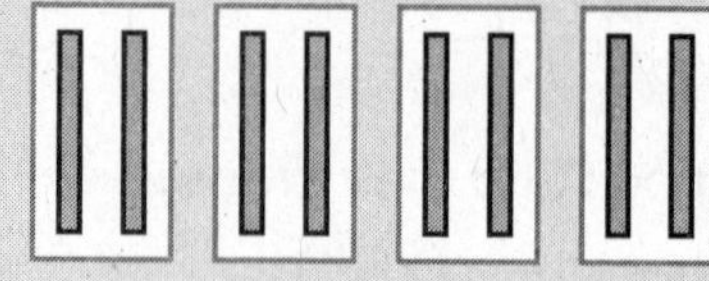

There are 2 tens blocks in each group. → 2

There are 4 groups. $4\overline{)95}$

$$\begin{array}{r} 2 \\ 4\overline{)95} \\ 8 \end{array}$$

8 ← $2 \times 4 = 8$ tens blocks placed

1. How many groups are you going to make? How many tens blocks can you put in each group?

a) $4\overline{)91}$ groups _____ number of tens in each group _____

b) $3\overline{)84}$ groups _____ number of tens in each group _____

c) $6\overline{)75}$ groups _____ number of tens in each group _____

d) $2\overline{)93}$ groups _____ number of tens in each group _____

2. Find out how many tens can be placed in each group. Then multiply to find out how many tens have been placed.

a) $5\overline{)91}$ −

b) $3\overline{)82}$ −

c) $4\overline{)98}$ −

d) $5\overline{)99}$ −

e) $9\overline{)93}$ −

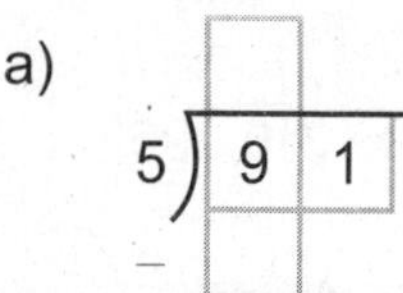

Step 3: How many tens blocks are left?

Subtract to find out. →

$$\begin{array}{r} 2 \\ 4\overline{)95} \\ -\,8 \\ 1 \end{array}$$

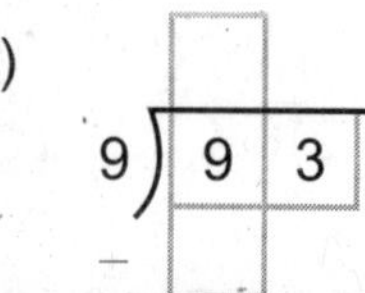

There are $9 - 8 = 1$ left over.

3. For each question, carry out the first **three** steps of long division.

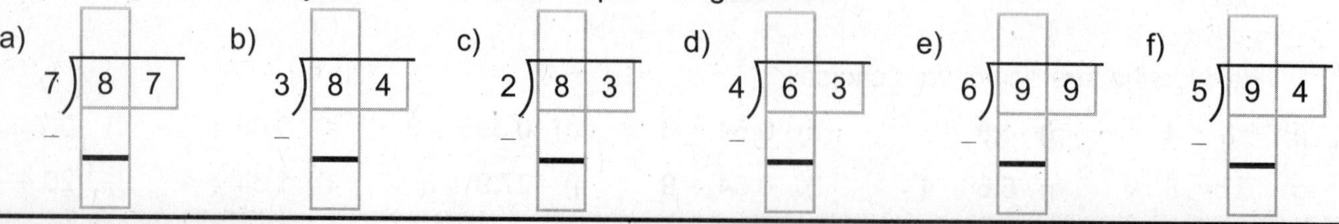

Step 4: There is 1 tens block left over, and there are 5 ones in 95.

So there are 15 ones left in total. Write the 5 beside the 1 to show this.

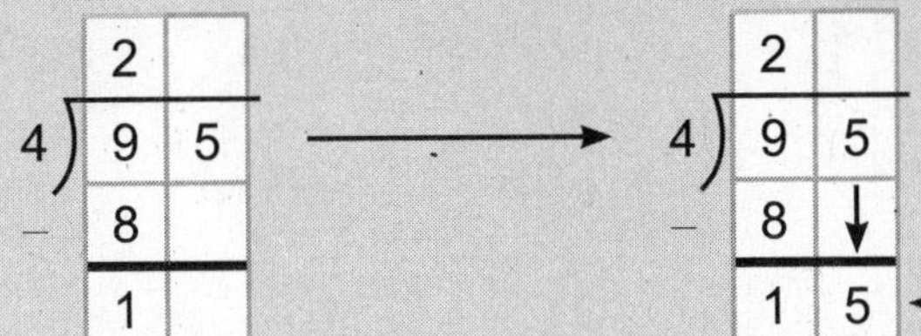

There are still 15 ones to place in 4 groups.

4. Carry out the first four steps of long division.

a) 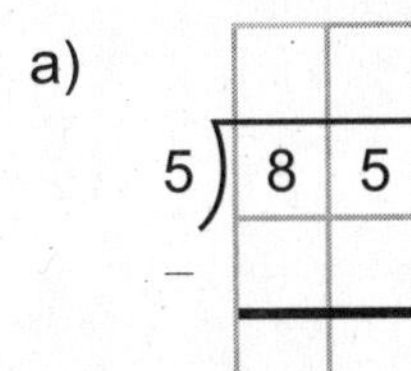
b) 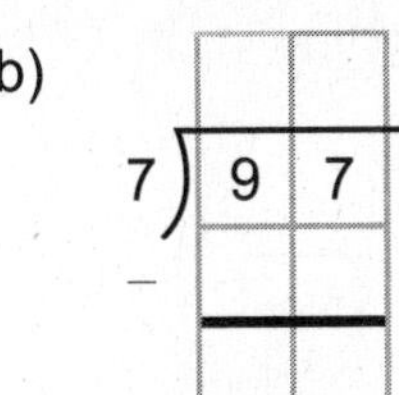
c) 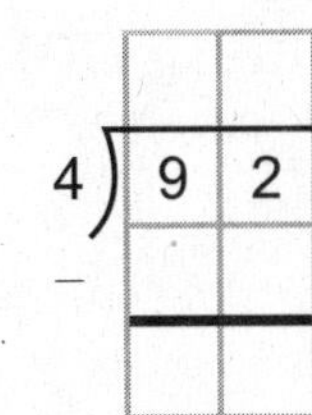
d) 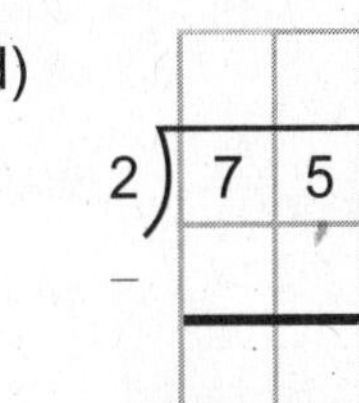
e) 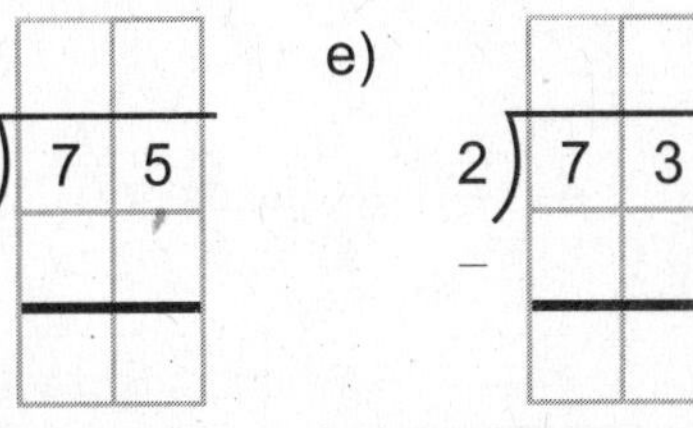

Step 5: How many ones can you put in each group?

Divide to find out:

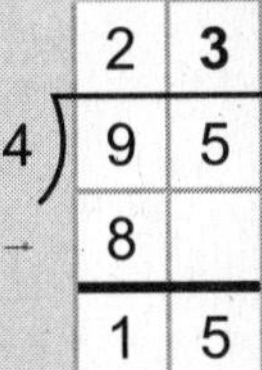

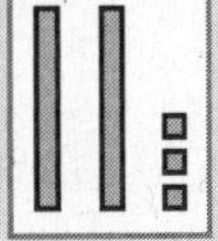
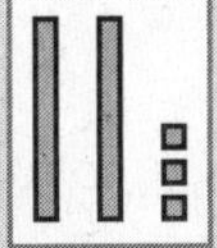
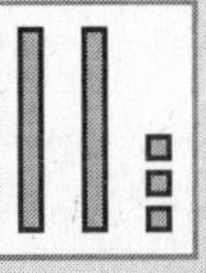

How many ones are left over?

5. Carry out the first five steps of long division.

a) 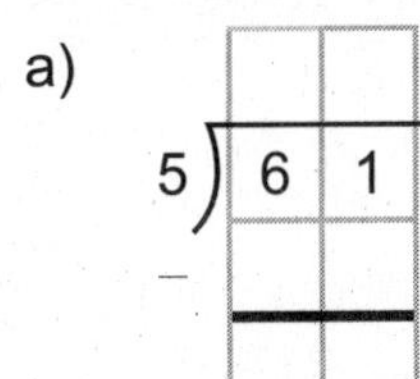
b) 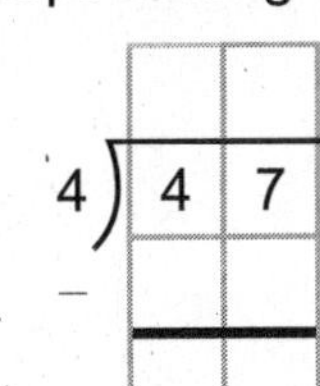
c) 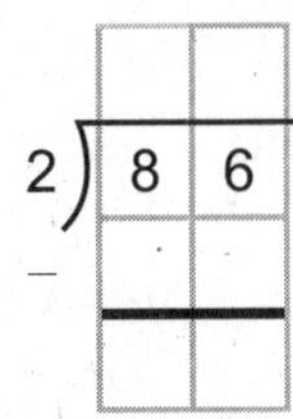
d) 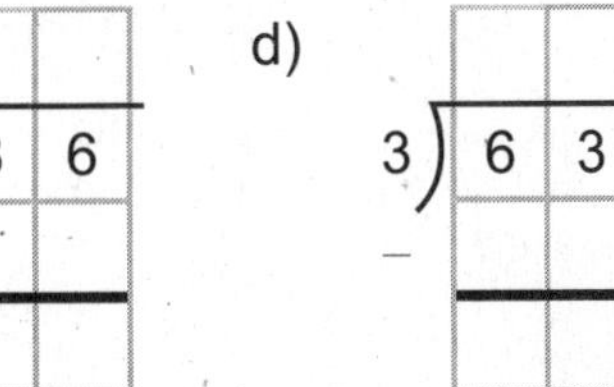
e) 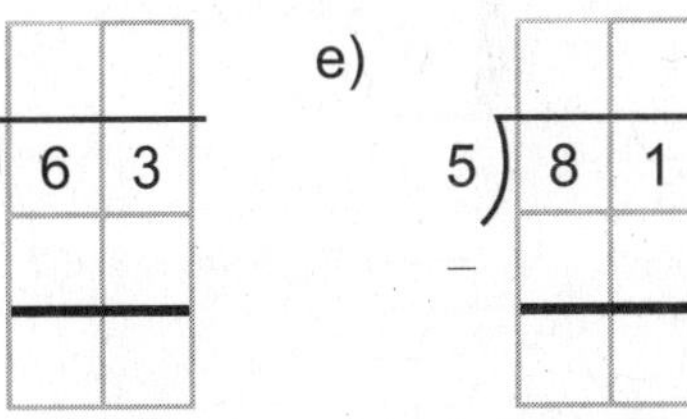

Steps 6 and 7: Find the number of ones left over.

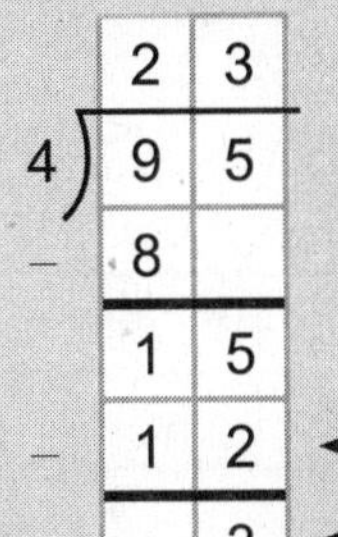

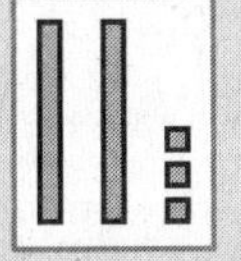

Long division and the model both show that **95 ÷ 4 = 23 with 3 left over**.

6. Carry out all the steps of long division on grid paper.

a) 6)81 b) 4)52 c) 3)95 d) 3)82 e) 4)64 f) 7)87

NS7-43 Long Division *(continued)*

The diagram shows how to divide 334 objects into 2 groups using a base ten model and long division.

Base ten model of 334:

Step 1: Divide the hundreds into 2 groups.

← remaining blocks

	1			← 1 hundreds block in each group
2)	3	3	4	
–	2			← 2 hundreds placed
	1			← 1 hundred left over

Step 2: Regroup the remaining hundreds as tens.

	1			
2)	3	3	4	
–	2			
	1	3		← 13 tens

Step 3: Divide the tens into 2 groups.

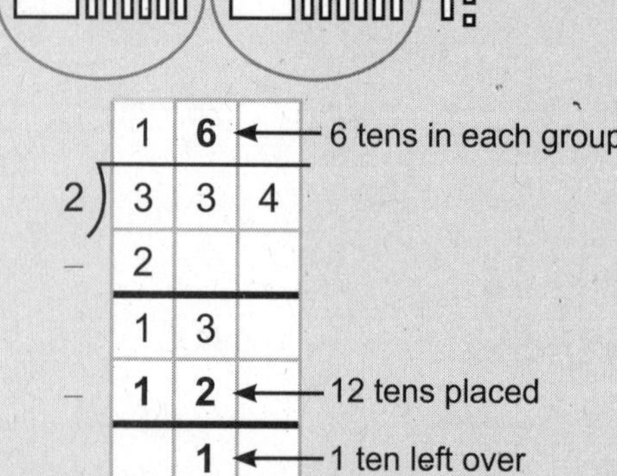

	1	6		← 6 tens in each group
2)	3	3	4	
–	2			
	1	3		
–	1	2		← 12 tens placed
		1		← 1 ten left over

Step 4: Regroup and divide the remaining ones.

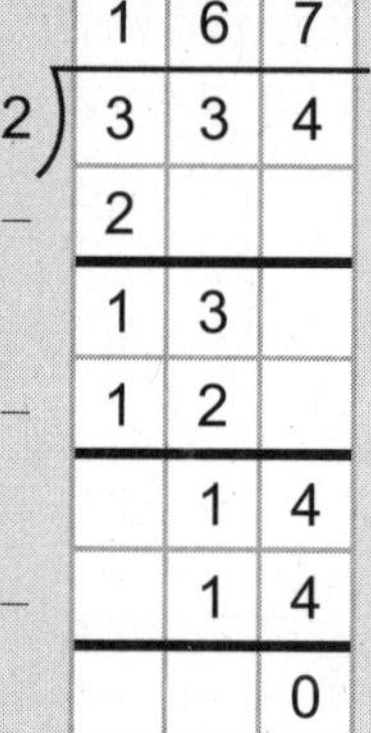

	1	6	7
2)	3	3	4
–	2		
	1	3	
–	1	2	
		1	4
–		1	4
			0

7. Divide.

a) $5\overline{)812}$

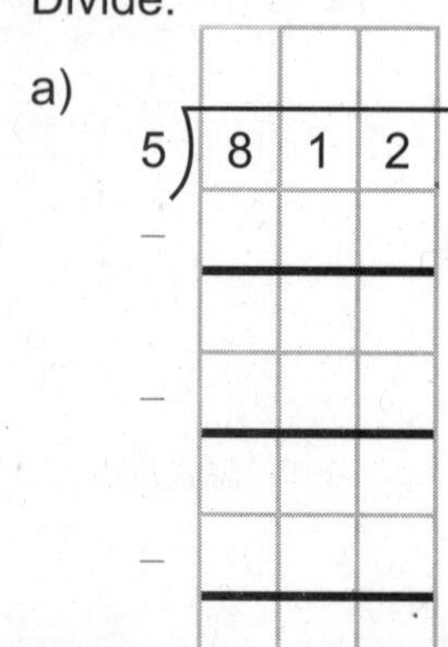

b) $3\overline{)327}$

c) $6\overline{)731}$

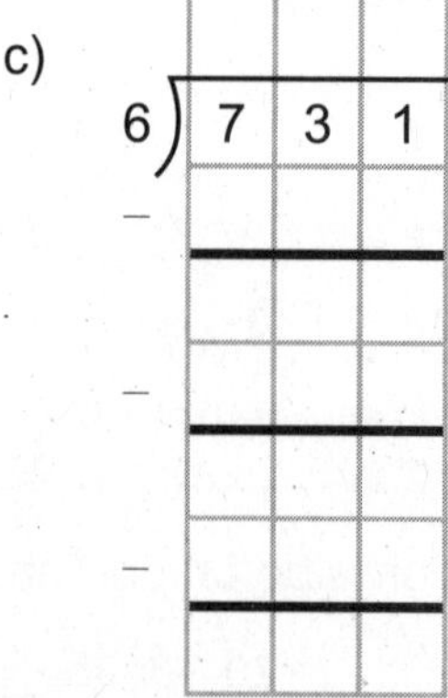

d) $8\overline{)989}$

NS7-43 Long Division *(continued)*

8. In each question below, there are fewer hundreds than the number of groups.

Write a zero in the hundreds position to show that no hundreds can be placed in equal groups. Then perform the division as if the hundreds had automatically been exchanged for tens.

a) 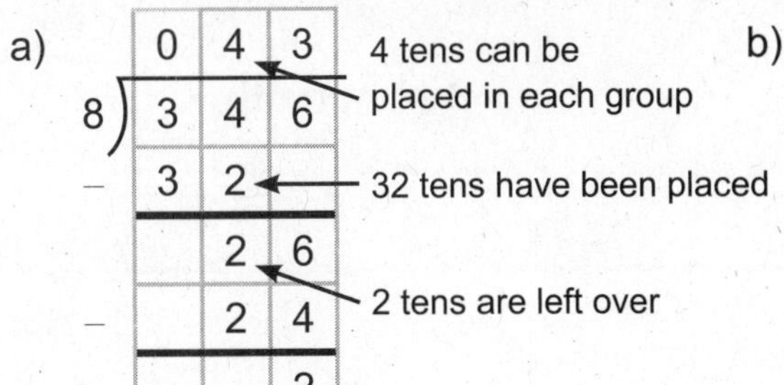

b) 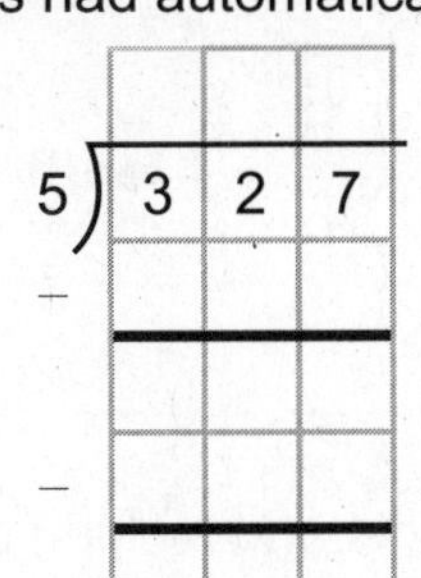

c) 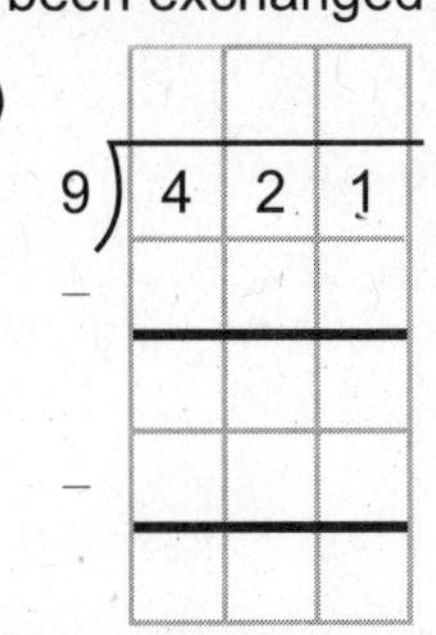

d) 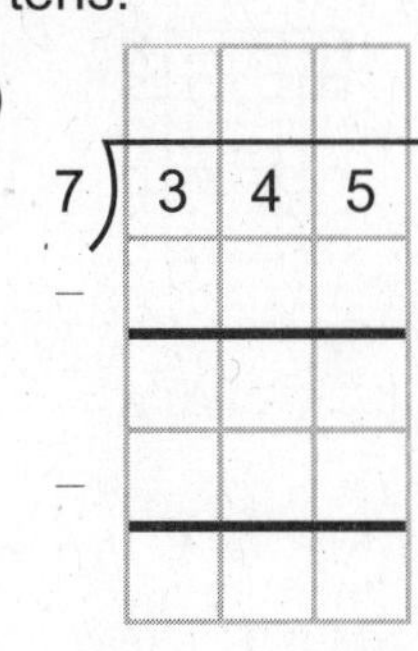

9. In each question below, say how many tens or hundreds can be placed in 5 groups. Underline the place values you will divide by 5.

a) $5\overline{)315}$ *31 tens*

b) $5\overline{)726}$ *7 hundreds*

c) $5\overline{)623}$ ______

d) $5\overline{)321}$ ______

e) $5\overline{)892}$ ______

f) $5\overline{)240}$ ______

g) $5\overline{)987}$ ______

h) $5\overline{)412}$ ______

10. Divide.

a) 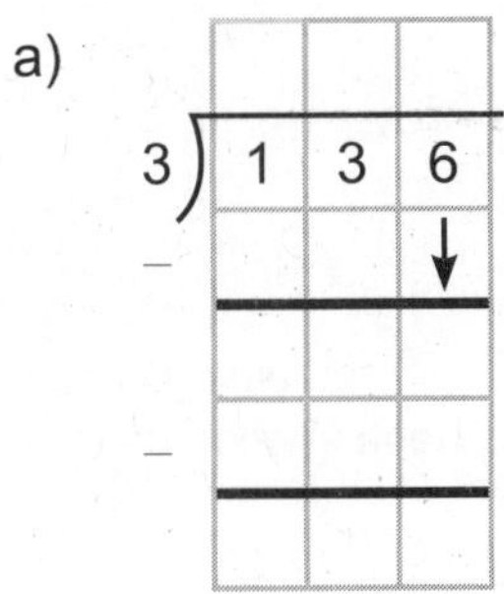

b) 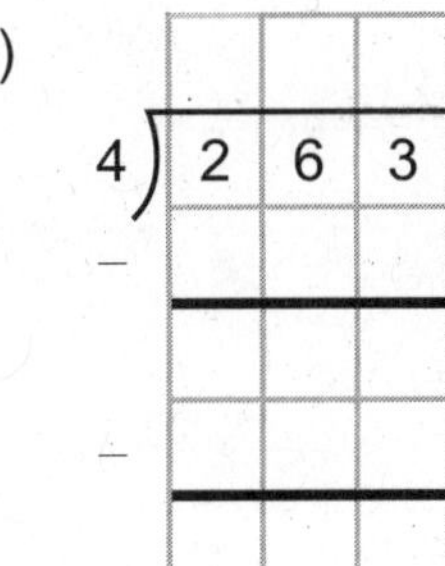

c) 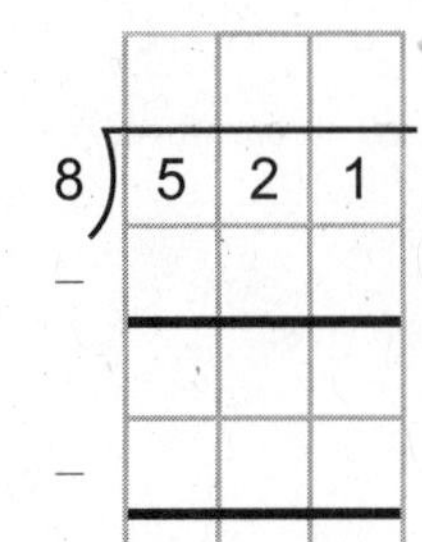

d) 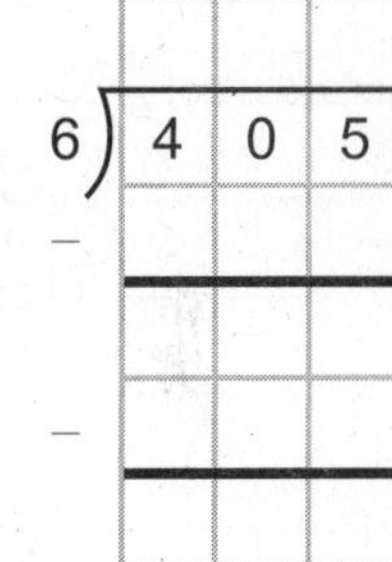

e) 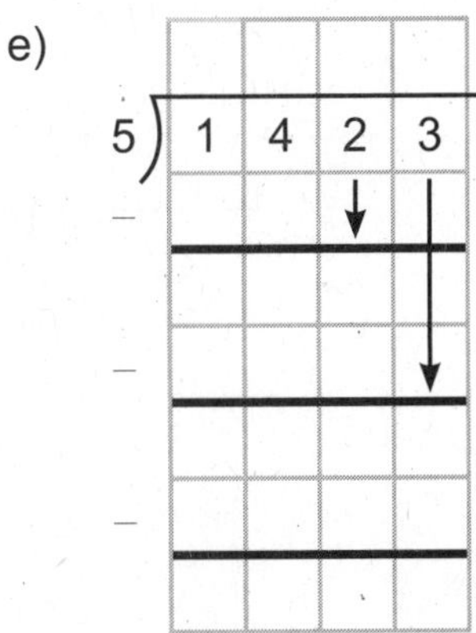

f) 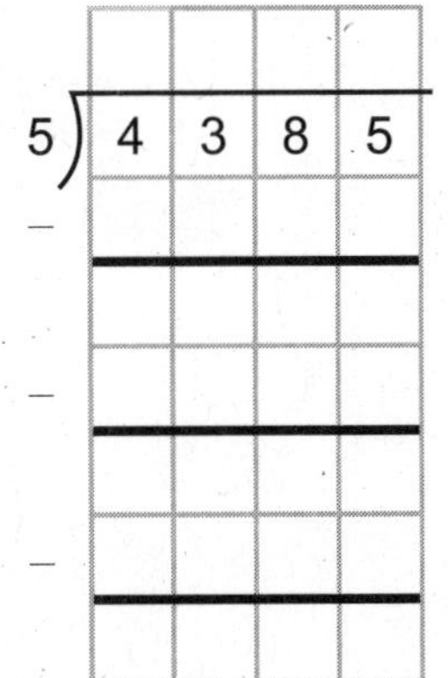

g) 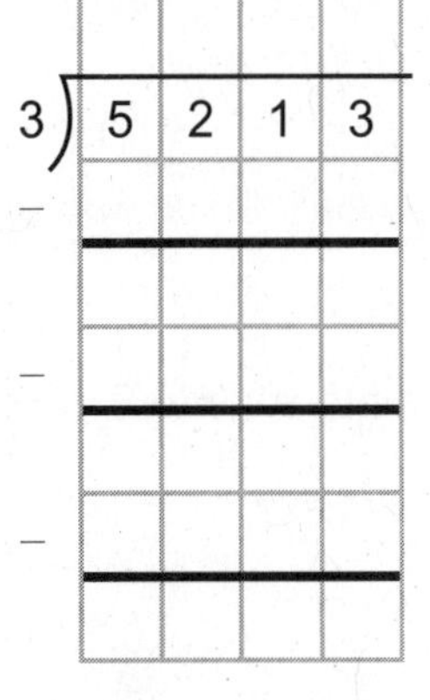

h) 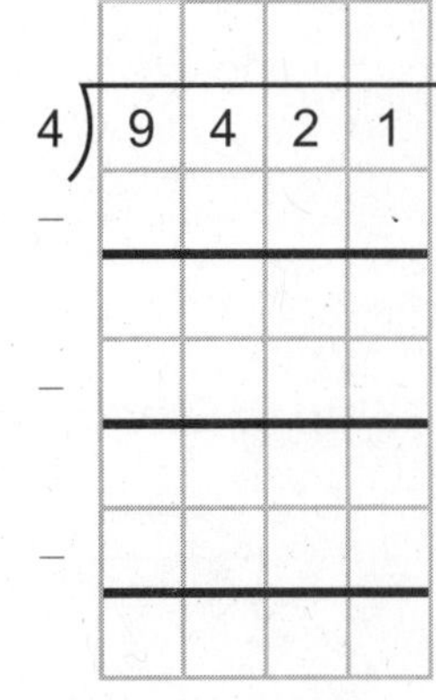

i) $9\overline{)684}$ j) $7\overline{)3\,512}$ k) $8\overline{)312}$ l) $6\overline{)4\,935}$ m) $2\overline{)7\,463}$

n) $3\overline{)7\,913}$ o) $5\overline{)1\,862}$ p) $5\overline{)2\,764}$ q) $4\overline{)9\,807}$ r) $4\overline{)1\,986}$

NS7-44 Dividing Decimals by Whole Numbers

You can divide a decimal by a whole number by making a base ten model. Here is what the blocks represent:

 = **1 one** or **unit** 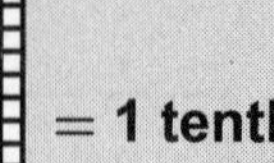 = **1 tenth** ▫ = **1 hundredth**

Keep track of your work using long division.

1. Find **5.12 ÷ 2** by making a base ten model and by long division.

Step 1: Draw a base ten model for 5.12.

Draw your model here.

Step 2: Divide the largest (unit) blocks into 2 equal groups.

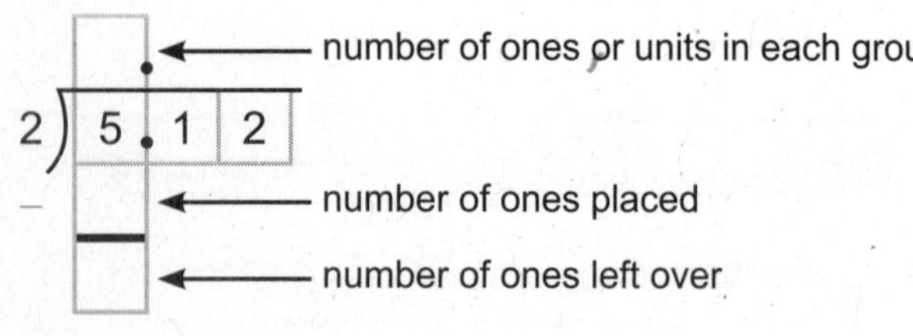

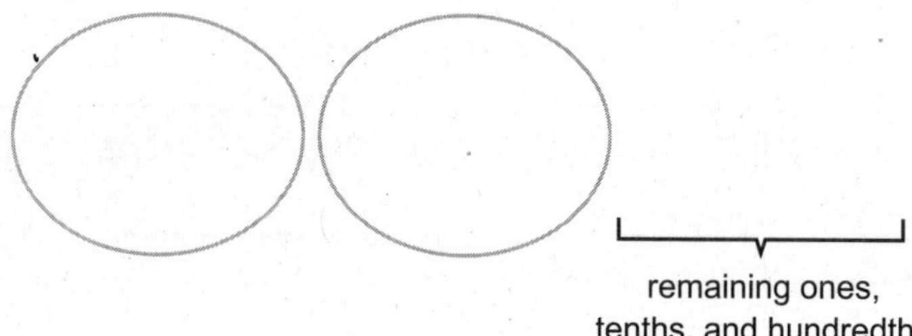

Step 3: Exchange the leftover unit blocks for 10 tenths.

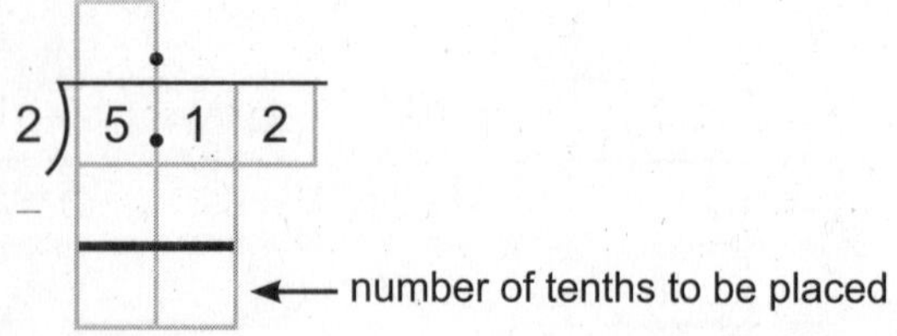

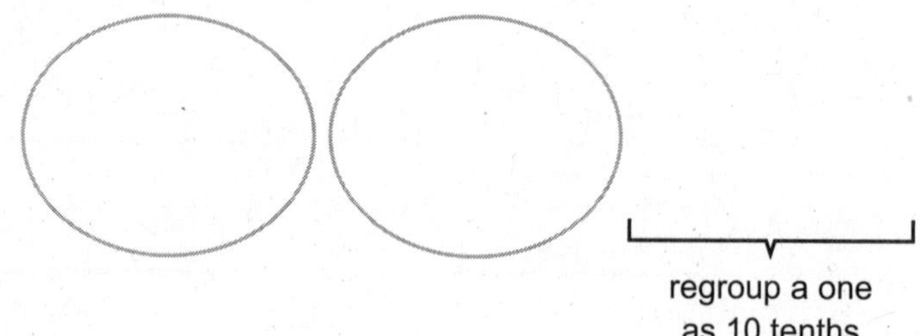

Step 4: Divide the tenths blocks into 2 equal groups.

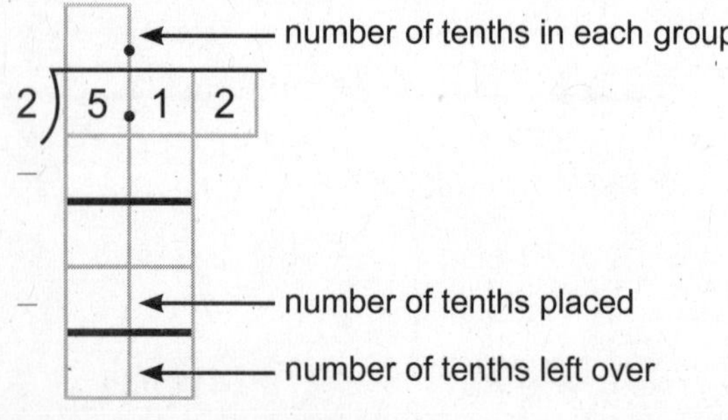

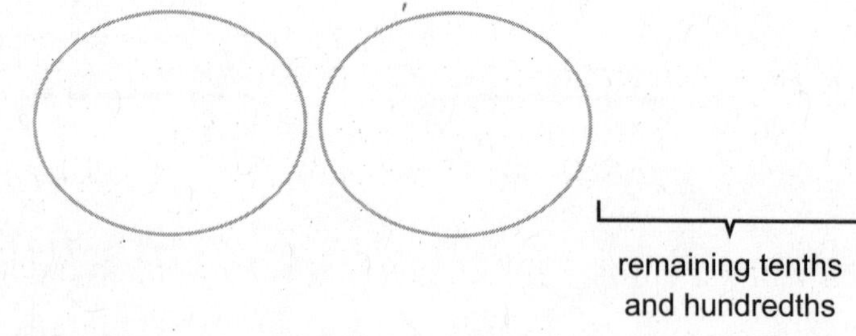

NS7-44 Dividing Decimals by Whole Numbers *(continued)*

Step 5: Exchange the leftover tenth block for 10 hundredths.

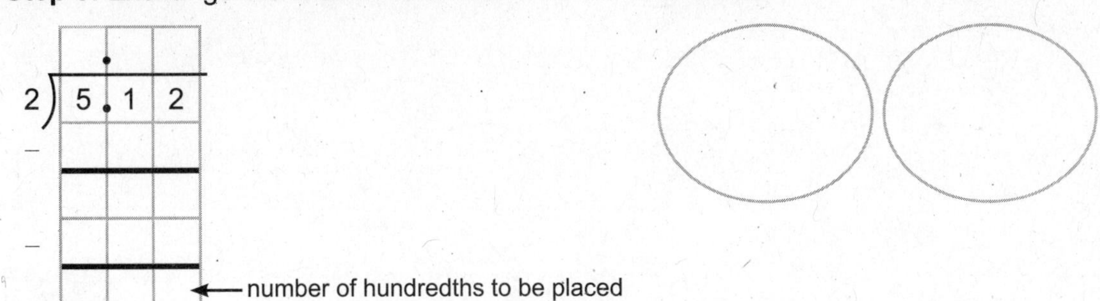

regroup a tenth as 10 hundredths

Steps 6 and 7: Divide the hundredths into 2 equal groups.

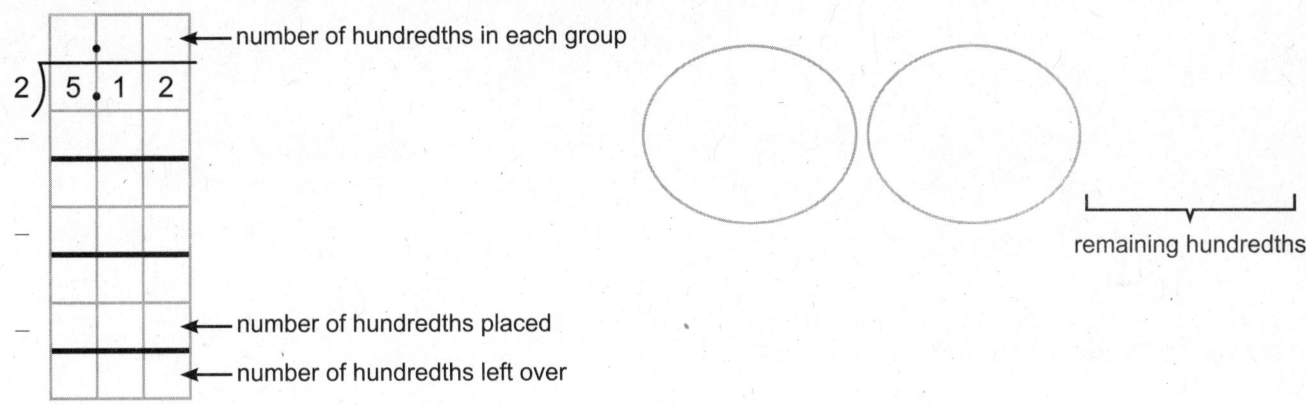

2. Divide.

a)
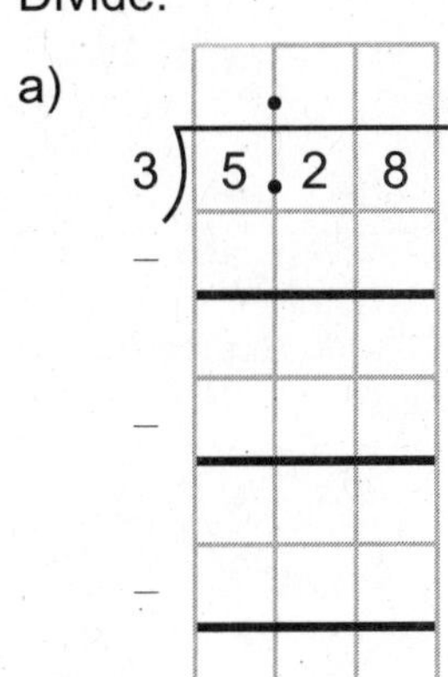

b) 4) 7.2 8

c)
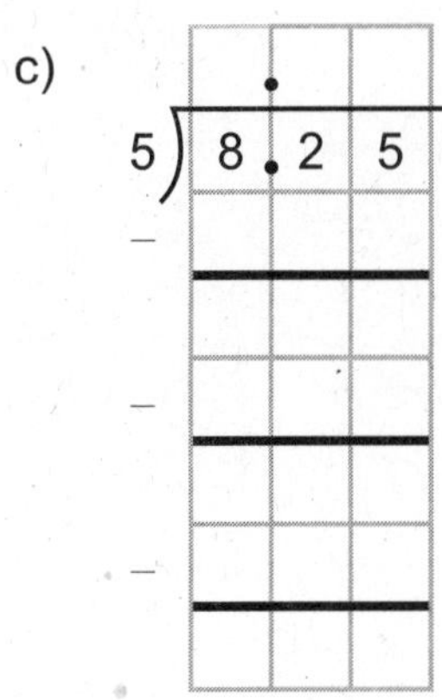

d)
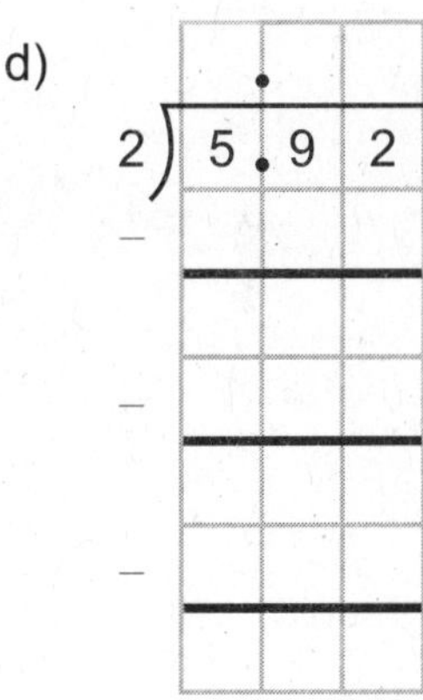

3. Divide.

a) $8\overline{)2.56}$ b) $7\overline{)5.6}$ c) $8\overline{)4.48}$ d) $9\overline{)6.21}$ e) $5\overline{)32.45}$

4. Five oranges cost $3.65. How much does each orange cost?

5. An equilateral triangle has a perimeter of 3.12 m. How long is each side?

6. Philip cycled 58.4 km in 4 hours. How many kilometres did he cycle in an hour?

7. Ahmed earned $97.36 in 8 hours. How much did he earn each hour?

8. Which is a better deal, 8 pens for $6.16 or 7 pens for $5.46?

UNIT 4

Measurement 1

ME7-1 Changing Units

1. Fill in the blanks.

a) $2.32 \times 1\,000 =$ _________ b) $254 \div 1\,000 =$ _________ c) $.36 \times 1\,000 =$ _________

d) $5.07 \div 1\,000 =$ _________ e) $.043 \times 1\,000 =$ _________ f) $.79 \div 1\,000 =$ _________

Kilometres (km) and millimetres (mm) are measures of **length**.

1 km = 1 000 m
1 m = 1 000 mm
1 mm = .001 m

Kilograms (kg) and milligrams (mg) are measures of **mass**.

1 kg = 1 000 g
1 g = 1 000 mg
1 mg = .001 g

Litres (L) and millilitres (mL) are measures of **capacity**.

1 L = 1 000 mL
1 mL = .001 L

The prefix **kilo** means "1 000 times larger." The prefix **milli** means "1 000 times smaller."

2. a) Change 275 mg to g.

i) The new units are *1 000* times *bigger*.

ii) So I need *1 000* times *fewer* units.

iii) I *divide* by *1 000*.

275 mg = *.275* g

b) Change 3 700 mm to m.

i) The new units are _______ times _______.

ii) So I need _______ times _______ units.

iii) I _______ by _______.

3 700 mm = _______ m

c) Change 2 700 g to kg.

i) The new units are _______ times _______.

ii) So I need _______ times _______ units.

iii) I _______ by _______.

2 700 g = _______ kg

d) Change .3456 L to mL.

i) The new units are _______ times _______.

ii) So I need _______ times _______ units.

iii) I _______ by _______.

.3456 L = _______ mL

3. Change the units by following the steps in Question 2 in your head.

a) 700 m = _______ km b) .93 m = _______ mm c) 37 mm = _______ m

d) 2 340 mL = _______ L e) 15.4 L = _______ mL f) 0.05 mL = _______ L

g) 7.43 kg = _______ g h) .93 g = _______ mg i) 37 mg = _______ g

j) 2.34 m = _______ km k) 22.6 g = _______ mg l) 0.08 m = _______ km

m) 3 569 km = _______ m n) 6 789 kg = _______ g o) 0.02 km = _______ m

BONUS▶

p) 0.569 km = _______ m
= _____________ mm

q) 67 890 mg = _______ g
= _____________ kg

r) 90 875 mm = _______ m
= _____________ km

ME7-1 Changing Units *(continued)*

4. How many metres, centimetres, and millimetres are in 1 km?

1 km = _______ m = _________ cm = ____________ mm

REMINDER▸ 1 m = 100 cm
1 cm = 10 mm

Units increase in size as you go up the stairs. Each step is **10 times larger**.

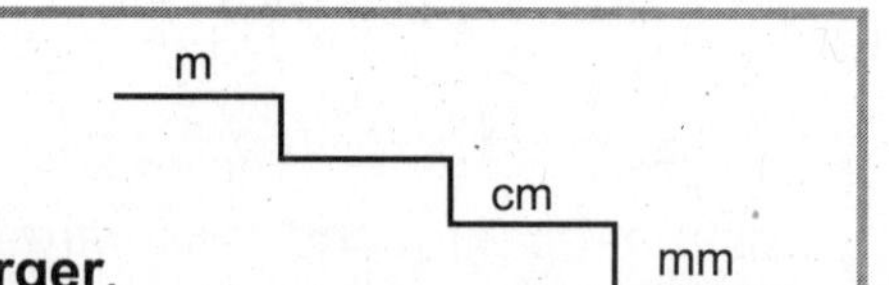

5. a) Change 35 cm to m.

The new units are *100* times *bigger*,

so I need *100* times *fewer* units.

I *divide* by *100* : 35 cm = *.35* m.

b) Change 35 cm to mm.

The new units are _______ times _______,

so I need _______ times _______ units.

I _______ by _______ : 35 cm = _______ mm.

c) Change 35 mm to m.

The new units are _______ times _______,

so I need _______ times _______ units.

I _______ by _______ : 35 mm = _______ m.

d) 46 m = _____ cm e) .3 m = _____ cm

f) .8 mm = _____ cm g) 2.6 cm = _____ m

h) .03 m = _____ mm i) .23 mm = _____ cm

BONUS▸ j) 76.6 mm = _______ km k) .7 km = _______ cm l) .8 cm = _______ km

6. Is 5 m 28 cm equal to 5.28 m or 5.28 cm? Explain.

7. $1.72 stands for 1 dollar 7 dimes 2 pennies. In the measurement 1.72 m, are cm like dimes or like pennies? Explain.

8. Is 362 mm longer or shorter than 20 cm? How do you know?

9. Which is taller, a 2 350 cm tree or a 24 m building? Explain.

10. A fence is made of four parts, each 32 cm long. Is the fence longer or shorter than a metre?

11. 1 cm of ribbon costs 3¢. How much will 1.2 m cost?

12. Jack cycled 10 km in 1 hour. Jane cycled 44 000 m in 4 hours. Who rode faster?

13. Here are the masses of some primates.

- Gorilla: 175 kg
- Baboon: 35 kg
- Squirrel Monkey: 500 g
- Pygmy Mouse Lemur: 30 g

a) How many grams does a gorilla weigh?
b) How many squirrel monkeys weigh 1 kg?
c) About how many times heavier than a mouse lemur is a baboon?

ME7-2 Changing Units to Divide Decimals

1. a) How many strings of length 2 mm fit into a string of length 14 mm? _______

   b) Convert the measurements to cm. 2 mm = _______ cm and 14 mm = _______ cm

   c) How many strings of length 0.2 cm fit into a string of length 1.4 cm? _______

   d) Explain why 14 ÷ 2 and 1.4 ÷ 0.2 have the same answer.

   e) Why is the quotient easier to find when the measurements are written in millimetres than in centimetres?

2. These decimal numbers represent the length of strings in centimetres. Convert the measurements to millimetres, then find the quotient.

   a) 1.8 ÷ 0.6

   1.8 cm = _____ mm and 0.6 cm = _____ mm

   So 1.8 ÷ 0.6 = _____ ÷ _____ = _____

   b) 4.2 ÷ 0.7

   4.2 cm = _____ mm and 0.7 cm = _____ mm

   So 4.2 ÷ 0.7 = _____ ÷ _____ = _____

   c) 7.2 ÷ 0.8 d) 8 ÷ 0.4 e) 8 ÷ 0.5 f) 6.4 ÷ 0.4 g) 9.1 ÷ 0.7

3. Multiply both terms by 10 to find the quotient.

   a) 8.1 ÷ 0.3 = _____ ÷ _____ = _____

   b) 72 ÷ 0.6 = _____ ÷ _____ = _____

   c) 35 ÷ 0.7 = _____ ÷ _____ = _____

4. These decimal numbers represent the length of strings in metres. Convert the measurements to centimetres, then find the quotient.

   a) 2.64 ÷ 0.02 = _____ ÷ _____ = _____

   b) 8.9 ÷ 0.05 = _____ ÷ _____ = _____

   c) 7.26 ÷ 0.03 = _____ ÷ _____ = _____

5. These decimal numbers represent the length of strings in metres. Convert the measurements to millimetres, then find the quotient.

   a) 1.096 ÷ 0.008 b) 1.778 ÷ 0.007 c) 3.6 ÷ 0.009 d) 5.16 ÷ 0.006

6. Multiply both the dividend and divisor by 10, 100, or 1 000 to change them to whole numbers. (Be sure to multiply both by the same number!) Then divide.

   a) 12 ÷ 0.4 = _____ ÷ _____ = _____

   b) 51 ÷ 0.03 = _____ ÷ _____ = _____

   c) 16 ÷ 0.2 d) 35 ÷ 0.07 e) 640 ÷ 0.4 f) 60 ÷ 0.005 g) 9 ÷ 0.003

   h) 2. 5 ÷ 0.5 i) 0.08 ÷ 0.4 j) 0.42 ÷ 0.2 k) 16.8 ÷ 0.2 l) 3.3 ÷ 1.1

ME7-3 Equivalent Ratios

We can write the same ratio in different ways. In each picture, there are 2 circles for every 1 square, so the ratio of circles to squares does not change.

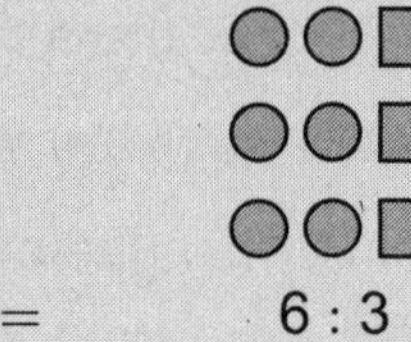
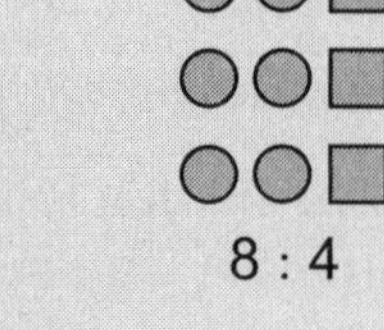

2 : 1 = 4 : 2 = 6 : 3 = 8 : 4

These ratios are called **equivalent ratios** because they represent the same ratio.

1. Write an equivalent ratio by multiplying each term by the same number.

a) 3 : 4 = 6 : 8 (× 2, × 2) b) 1 : 6 = ____ : ____ c) 2 : 7 = ____ : ____ d) 5 : 2 = ____ : ____

2. Write an equivalent ratio by dividing each term by the same number.

a) 20 : 15 = ____ : ____ b) 9 : 18 = ____ : ____ c) 12 : 15 = ____ : ____ d) 24 : 36 = ____ : ____

A ratio is in **lowest terms** when the numbers in the ratio are as small as they can be.

To write the ratio 30 : 36 in lowest terms:

Step 1: List the factors of 30 and 36:

30: 1, 2, 3, 5, **6**, 10, 15, 30

36: 1, 2, 3, 4, **6**, 9, 12, 18, 36

Step 2: Find the greatest common factor (GCF) of 30 and 36. The GCF is the greatest number that both lists have in common: 6.

Step 3: Divide each term in the ratio by the GCF.

30 : 36 = 5 : 6 (÷ 6, ÷ 6)

3. a) List the factors of each number. Do the rough work in your notebook.

i) 10: 1, 2, 5, 10 ii) 12: ________ iii) 30: ________ iv) 75: ________

b) Find the GCF of each pair.

i) 10 and 12 ii) 10 and 30 iii) 10 and 75 iv) 12 and 30 v) 12 and 75 vi) 30 and 75

c) Write each ratio in lowest terms by dividing both terms by their GCF.

i) 30 : 12 ii) 10 : 30 iii) 12 : 75 iv) 12 : 10 v) 75 : 10 vi) 30 : 75

4. Write each ratio in lowest terms.

a) 25 : 35 b) 21 : 6 c) 20 : 12 d) 14 : 21 e) 84 : 27 f) 90 : 75

ME7-4 Solving Proportions

A **proportion** is an equation that shows two equivalent ratios. Example: 1 : 4 = 2 : 8

To solve a proportion, you need to find the number you multiply (or divide) each term in one ratio by to get the other ratio. Example: Solve 10 : 3 = 50 : ☐

Proportions are easier to solve if you write the proportions using fraction notation: $\frac{10}{3} = \frac{50}{\square}$.

1. Solve the following proportions. Draw arrows to show what you multiply by.

a) $\frac{4}{5} \overset{\times 4}{\underset{\times 4}{=}} \frac{\ }{20}$ b) $\frac{1}{5} \underset{\times 5}{=} \frac{\ }{25}$ c) $\frac{2}{5} \overset{\times 4}{=} \frac{8}{\ }$ d) $\frac{6}{7} = \frac{\ }{35}$

e) $\frac{3}{4} = \frac{18}{\ }$ f) $\frac{2}{3} = \frac{\ }{12}$ g) $\frac{5}{9} = \frac{\ }{45}$ h) $\frac{15}{25} = \frac{60}{\ }$

Note: Sometimes, the arrow may point from right to left.

i) $\frac{15}{\ } \overset{\times 5}{\underset{\times 4}{=}} \frac{3}{4}$ j) $\frac{10}{\ } = \frac{2}{5}$ k) $\frac{9}{\ } = \frac{3}{7}$ l) $\frac{\ }{35} = \frac{4}{7}$

m) $\frac{10}{15} = \frac{\ }{3}$ n) $\frac{30}{48} = \frac{5}{\ }$ o) $\frac{18}{22} = \frac{9}{\ }$ p) $\frac{63}{72} = \frac{\ }{8}$

2. Decide which way the arrow points. Then solve the proportions.

a) $\frac{\ }{10} = \frac{12}{40}$ b) $\frac{35}{\ } = \frac{7}{10}$ c) $\frac{3}{11} = \frac{9}{\ }$ d) $\frac{12}{42} = \frac{\ }{7}$

3. Solve the proportions by first writing the ratios using fraction notation.

a) 6 : 24 = ☐ : 8 b) ☐ : 15 = 2 : 5 c) 72 : 18 = ☐ : 3

4. Solve the proportions. Begin by writing the ratio that is complete in lowest terms.

a) $\frac{8}{10} = \frac{4}{5} = \frac{\ }{15}$ b) $\frac{4}{6} = \frac{\ }{\ } = \frac{\ }{9}$ c) $\frac{60}{100} = \frac{\ }{\ } = \frac{\ }{45}$

d) $\frac{\ }{30} = \frac{\ }{\ } = \frac{40}{50}$ e) $\frac{70}{100} = \frac{\ }{\ } = \frac{\ }{30}$ f) $\frac{\ }{24} = \frac{\ }{\ } = \frac{50}{75}$

5. Solve the proportions by first writing the ratios using fraction notation.

a) 6 : 24 = ☐ : 16 b) 11 : 22 = 5 : ☐ c) 26 : 12 = ☐ : 30

d) 30 : 9 = 50 : ☐ e) ☐ : 25 = 4 : 10 f) ☐ : 7 = 6 : 3

ME7-5 Word Problems

PROBLEM ▶ In a pet shop, there are 3 cats for every 4 dogs. If there are 12 dogs in the shop, how many cats are there?

SOLUTION ▶ Write the names of the two things being compared. **cats dogs**
Write the quantities under the names, as a ratio. 3 : 4
Re-read the question to determine which quantity is given and which is unknown.
Write this information in a new row under the right names. ? : 12
Solve the proportion. 3 : 4 = ? : 12

? = 9, so there are 9 cats in the shop.

1. Mike can run 3 laps in 5 minutes. How many laps can he run in 20 minutes?

2. Jared can run 4 laps in 10 minutes. How long will it take Jared to run 6 laps?

3. The ratio of boys to girls in a class is 5 : 6. If there are 20 boys, how many girls are there?

4. If 9 bus tickets cost $19, how many bus tickets can you buy with $57?

5. Two out of every 5 students are wearing shorts. There are 300 students. How many are wearing shorts?

6. Four out of every 7 students like rap music. If 360 students like rap music, how many students are there altogether?

7. There are 2 rap songs for every 3 rock songs on Will's MP3 player. There are a total of 120 rock songs. How many rap songs are there?

8. Two out of every 12 students in a class say history is their favourite subject. There are 24 students in the class. How many students like history best?

9. The ratio of students in string band to students in brass band is 3 : 4. There are 36 students in the brass band. How many students are in the string band?

10. A basketball team won 2 out of every 3 games it played. The team played a total of 15 games. How many games did the team win?

11. There are 3 red fish for every 5 blue fish in an aquarium.

a) If there are 30 blue fish, how many red fish are there?
b) If there are 30 red fish, how many blue fish are there?

12. Sophia has 64 jazz CDs and 80 rock CDs. Is the ratio of jazz CDs to rock CDs 3 : 4 or 4 : 5?

ME7-6 Rates

A **rate** is a comparison of two quantities measured in different units. Rates are written with a slash or as a fraction.

Example: $1 / 2 min (we read this as "$1 **per** 2 minutes") or $\frac{\$1}{2\text{ min}}$

1. Find the equivalent rate by first drawing arrows.

a) $\frac{10\text{ km}}{2\text{ h}} \overset{\times 2}{=} \frac{5\text{ km}}{1\text{ h}}$ (×2)

b) $\frac{18\text{ km}}{3\text{ h}} = \frac{\quad\text{ km}}{1\text{ h}}$

c) $\frac{20\text{ m}}{8\text{ s}} = \frac{\quad\text{ m}}{2\text{ s}}$

d) $\frac{42\text{ km}}{3\text{ L}} = \frac{\quad\text{ km}}{1\text{ L}}$

e) $\frac{\$35}{7\text{ kg}} = \frac{\$5}{\quad\text{ kg}}$

f) $\frac{\$96}{6\text{ h}} = \frac{\$32}{\quad\text{ h}}$

g) $\frac{\$1.50}{10\text{ min}} = \frac{\$\quad}{2\text{ min}}$

h) $\frac{6\text{ m}^2}{0.5\text{ L}} = \frac{\quad\text{ m}^2}{1\text{ L}}$

In a **unit rate**, the second term is 1. The 1 is often left out. Example: 80 km / 1 h = 80 km/h

2. Find the unit rate by reducing the ratio to lowest terms. (Include the units.)

a) 20 km / 5 h = *4 km* / 1 h

b) $5 / 2 boxes = ______ / 1 box : 1 apple

c) $30 / 2 h = ______ / 1 h

d) 96 m / 12 s = ______ / 1 s

e) $68 / 4 kg = ______ / 1 kg

f) $80 / 16 jars = ______ / 1 jar

BONUS▶ $1 / 6 min = ______ / 1 h

3. Solve each problem by first changing the rate to a unit rate.

a) Dana rode 100 kilometres in 5 hours. How far could she ride in 8 hours?

b) Cindy can type 60 words in 3 minutes. How many words can she type in 5 minutes?

c) A runner's heart beats 30 times in 10 seconds. How many times would it beat in a minute?

4. Change both prices to a unit rate to find out which offer is a better buy.

a) $119 for 7 CDs or $64 for 4 CDs

b) $36.52 for 2 cans of paint or $46.20 for 3 cans

c) 6 golf balls for $10 or 12 golf balls for $24

5. Clare can cycle at a speed of 23 km/h. Erin can cycle at a speed of 17 km/h. How much farther can Clare cycle in 3 hours than Erin?

6. a) A truck travels 40 km in half an hour. What is its average speed in km/h?
b) A car travels 30 km in 15 minutes. What is its average speed in km/h?

Hint: Convert the time given to minutes and find the number of kilometres per 60 minutes.

7. Estimate to the nearest half hour how long would it take to drive each distance at 100 km/h.

a) 254 km

b) 723 km

c) 1 426 km

UNIT 5

Number Sense 3

NS7-45 Relating Fractions and Decimals (Review)

1. Match the fractions and decimals.

A $\frac{4}{10}$ B $\frac{4}{1000}$ C $\frac{44}{100}$ D $\frac{4}{100}$ E $\frac{44}{1000}$

0.04 ___ 0.4 ___ 0.004 ___ 0.44 ___ 0.044 ___

REMINDER ▶ A **decimal fraction** has a power of 10 (10, 100, 1000, ...) in the denominator.

2. Write the fraction as an equivalent decimal fraction and as a decimal.

a) $\frac{1}{2} = \frac{1 \times 5}{2 \times 5} = \frac{}{10} = 0.$___ b) $\frac{1}{5} =$ c) $\frac{1}{4} =$

d) $\frac{3}{4} =$ e) $\frac{6}{25} =$ f) $\frac{17}{50} =$

3. Write three different fractions that are equivalent to the decimal.

a) 0.5 b) 0.2 c) 0.25 d) 0.60

4. Write the decimal as a fraction in lowest terms.

a) $0.35 = \frac{}{100} = \frac{}{20}$ b) 0.25 = c) 0.6 = d) 0.40 = e) 0.48 =

5. a) Describe the patterns in the numerator and in the denominator of the equivalent fractions.

i) $\frac{1}{5} = \frac{2}{10} = \frac{3}{15} = \frac{4}{20} = \frac{5}{25} = \frac{6}{30}$ ii) $\frac{3}{4} = \frac{6}{8} = \frac{9}{12} = \frac{12}{16} = \frac{15}{20} = \frac{18}{24}$

b) What decimal do the equivalent fractions equal?

6. a) Circle the fractions in which the numerator and denominator have at least one common factor.

$\frac{3}{5}$ $\frac{2}{10}$ $\frac{3}{10}$ $\frac{5}{12}$ $\frac{12}{15}$ $\frac{8}{20}$ $\frac{13}{40}$ $\frac{2}{100}$ $\frac{7}{100}$ $\frac{15}{100}$ $\frac{17}{100}$ $\frac{125}{1000}$

b) Which fractions in part a) can be written in lower terms (e.g., $\frac{6}{8} = \frac{3}{4}$)? Explain.

c) Use your answer in part b). Circle the decimals that can be written as a fraction with a denominator smaller than 100.

Example: $0.16 = \frac{16}{100} = \frac{4}{25}$

0.12 0.33 0.24 0.07 0.13 0.06 0.29 0.55 0.99 0.01

7. Would you use a fraction or a decimal in each case? Explain.

a) $\frac{1}{4}$ h or 0.25 h b) 0.25 m or $\frac{1}{4}$ m c) $\frac{1}{8}$ kg or 0.125 kg d) $\frac{3}{4}$ cup or 0.75 cup

NS7-46 Fraction and Decimal Patterns

A **unit fraction** has 1 in the numerator. Examples: $\frac{1}{2}, \frac{1}{3}, \frac{1}{7}$

1. Write the fraction as a sum of unit fractions and as a product of a fraction and a whole number.

a) $\frac{3}{8} = \frac{1}{8} + \frac{1}{8} + \frac{1}{8} = \_\_\_ \times \frac{1}{8}$ b) $\frac{3}{4} =$ c) $\frac{4}{5} =$

2. Write the fraction as a sum of unit fractions. Then write the unit fractions as decimals and add.

a) $\frac{3}{5} = \frac{1}{5} + \frac{1}{5} + \frac{1}{5} = 0.2 + 0.2 + 0.2 = 0.6$ b) $\frac{4}{5} =$

c) $\frac{3}{4} =$ d) $\frac{3}{2} =$

3. Write the fraction as the product of a unit fraction and a whole number. Then write the unit fraction as a decimal and multiply.

a) $\frac{4}{5} = 4 \times \frac{1}{5} = 4 \times 0.2 = 0.8$ b) $\frac{3}{4} =$

c) $\frac{3}{5} =$ d) $\frac{5}{4} =$

4. a) What is the rule for the pattern 0.05, 0.10, 0.15, 0.20, … ?

b) $\frac{1}{20} = 0.05$, $\frac{2}{20} = 0.10$, $\frac{3}{20} = 0.15$, …Continue the pattern to write $\frac{11}{20}$ as a decimal.

c) If you know $\frac{1}{20} = 0.05$, how can you use multiplication to find $\frac{11}{20}$ as a decimal?

5. a) $\frac{1}{4} = 0.25$, so $\frac{7}{4} = \underline{7} \times \underline{0.25}$ $= \underline{1.75}$ b) $\frac{1}{5} = 0.\_\_\_$, so $\frac{21}{5} = \_\_\_ \times \_\_\_$ $= \_\_\_$ c) $\frac{1}{2} = 0.\_\_\_$, so $\frac{13}{2} = \_\_\_ \times \_\_\_$ $= \_\_\_$

6. Write the fractions as decimals. Add the decimals. Write the sum as a fraction in lowest terms. Check your answer by adding the fractions.

a) $\frac{1}{4} + \frac{2}{5} = 0.25 + 0.4 = 0.65 = \frac{65}{100} = \frac{13}{20}$ b) $\frac{1}{2} + \frac{1}{5}$

Check: $\frac{5 \times 1}{5 \times 4} + \frac{2 \times 4}{5 \times 4} = \frac{5}{20} + \frac{8}{20} = \frac{13}{20}$

c) $\frac{1}{2} + \frac{4}{5}$ d) $\frac{3}{2} + \frac{3}{4}$

NS7-47 Relating Fractions and Division

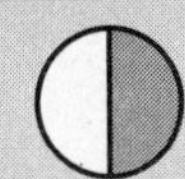 $\frac{1}{2}$ is one whole divided into 2 parts, so $\frac{1}{2} = 1 \div 2$.

1. a) $\frac{1}{4} = 1 \div$ ____ b) $\frac{1}{3} =$ ____ $\div$ ____ c) $\frac{1}{6} =$ ____ $\div$ ____

2. a) Explain why $24 \div 2$ is three times $8 \div 2$.
   b) Explain why $3 \div 8$ is three times $1 \div 8$.
   c) Explain why $3 \div 8$ is $3 \times \frac{1}{8}$.
   d) Explain why $3 \div 8 = \frac{3}{8}$.

3. Use $\frac{a}{b} = a \div b$ to write the fraction as a decimal. Keep dividing until the remainder is 0.

   a) 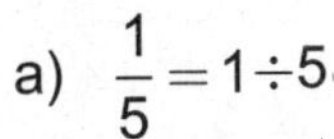 $\frac{1}{5} = 1 \div 5$
   b) $\frac{2}{5} =$ ____ $\div$ ____
   c) 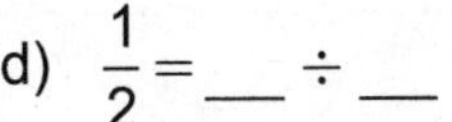 $\frac{3}{6} =$ ____ $\div$ ____
   d) $\frac{1}{2} =$ ____ $\div$ ____
   e) 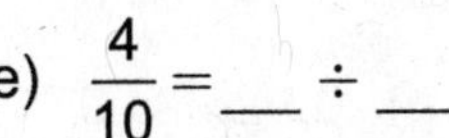 $\frac{4}{10} =$ ____ $\div$ ____

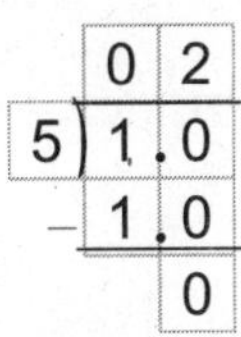

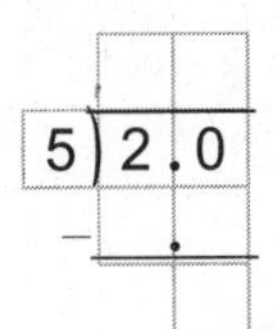

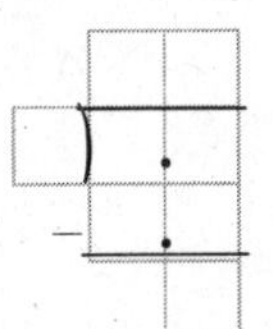
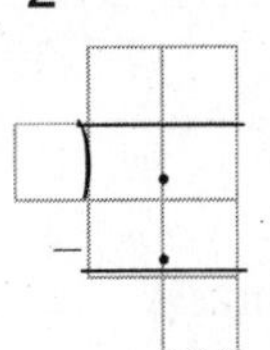
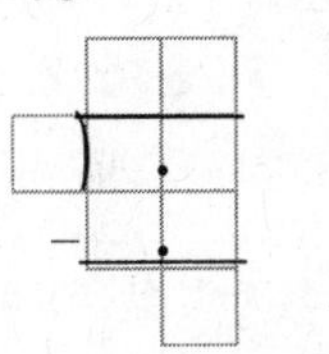

So, $\frac{1}{5} = 0.$____ So, $\frac{2}{5} = 0.$____ So, $\frac{3}{6} = 0.$____ So, $\frac{1}{2} = 0.$____ So, $\frac{4}{10} = 0.$____

   f) $\frac{7}{2}$ g) $\frac{9}{4}$ h) $\frac{7}{10}$ i) $\frac{3}{5}$ j) $\frac{12}{30}$

4. a) Change the fraction to a decimal using long division. Keep dividing until the remainder is 0.

   $\frac{1}{8} = 8\overline{)1.000} = ?$ $\frac{2}{8} = 8\overline{)2.000} = ?$ $\frac{3}{8} = 8\overline{)3.000} = ?$

   b) What is the pattern in the decimal equivalents in part a)?
   c) Extend the pattern from part a) to predict the decimals equivalent to $\frac{4}{8}, \frac{5}{8}, \frac{6}{8}, \frac{7}{8}$, and $\frac{8}{8}$.

5. Convert each fraction to a decimal fraction. Then change the fraction to a decimal. Check your answers using a calculator.

   a) $\frac{3}{40} = \frac{75}{1000} = 0.075$
   Check: $3 \div 40 = 0.075$

   b) $\frac{17}{20} = \frac{\quad}{100}$
   Check:

   c) $\frac{19}{125} = \frac{\quad}{1000}$
   Check:

   d) $\frac{13}{25}$ e) $\frac{3}{5}$ f) $\frac{351}{500}$ g) $\frac{39}{200}$ **BONUS ▶** $\frac{5}{16}$

NS7-48 Repeating Decimals

A **repeating decimal** is a decimal with a digit or group of digits that repeats forever.

The digit or sequence of digits that repeats can be shown by a bar. Example: $4.121212\ldots = 4.\overline{12}$.

A **terminating decimal** is a decimal that does not go on forever. Examples: 5.68, 0.444

Some decimals do not terminate or repeat. Example: $\pi = 3.14159\ldots$

1. Write each decimal to eight decimal places.

a) $0.\overline{3} \approx 0.$ *3* ___ ___ ___ ___ ___ ___ ___ ___

b) $0.0\overline{3} \approx 0.$ *0 3 3 3* ___ ___ ___ ___

c) $0.00\overline{3} \approx 0.$___ ___ ___ ___ ___ ___ ___ ___

d) $0.\overline{52} \approx 0.$___ ___ ___ ___ ___ ___ ___ ___

e) $0.\overline{817} \approx 0.$___ ___ ___ ___ ___ ___ ___ ___

f) $0.8\overline{17} \approx 0.$___ ___ ___ ___ ___ ___ ___ ___

g) $0.9\overline{26} \approx 0.$___ ___ ___ ___ ___ ___ ___ ___

h) $0.25\overline{37} \approx 0.$___ ___ ___ ___ ___ ___ ___ ___

i) $7.2\overline{3} \approx 7.$___ ___ ___ ___ ___ ___ ___ ___

j) $8.2\overline{539} \approx 8.$___ ___ ___ ___ ___ ___ ___ ___

2. Circle the repeating decimals.

0.123412312   0.77   0.222222222…   0.512512512…   0.123238…

3. Write each repeating decimal using bar notation.

a) 0.555555… = ______

b) 2.343434… = ______

c) 5.237237… = ______

d) 57.121212… = ______

e) 8.162626… = ______

f) 0.910591059105 = ______

4. Find the decimal value of each fraction to 3 decimal places. Then write the fraction as a repeating decimal.

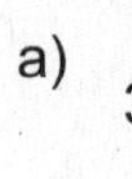

a) 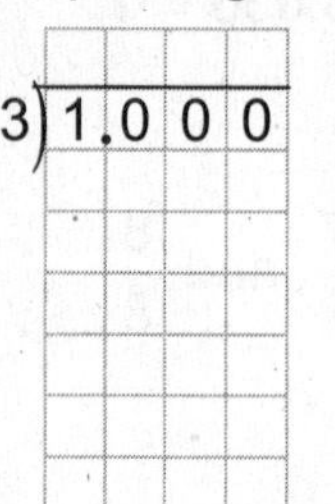 $\frac{1}{3} \approx$

b) 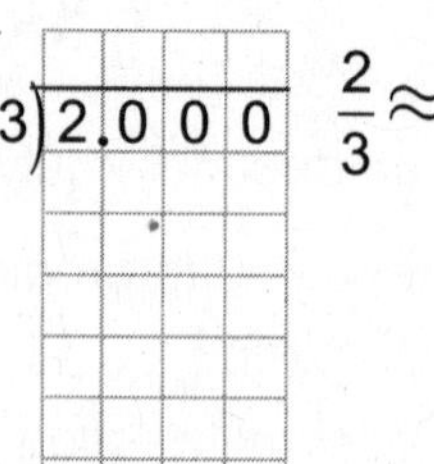 $\frac{2}{3} \approx$

5. Use long division to calculate the decimal equivalent of the fraction to 6 decimal places. Then write the decimal using bar notation.

a) $\frac{1}{6}$ b) $\frac{4}{9}$ c) $\frac{1}{11}$ d) $\frac{5}{12}$

NS7-48 Repeating Decimals *(continued)*

6. Match the fractions with their decimal equivalents. Use a calculator.

A $\frac{1}{3}$ B $\frac{55}{99}$ C $\frac{2}{3}$ D $\frac{2}{9}$ ___ $0.\overline{6}$ ___ $0.\overline{2}$ ___ $0.\overline{3}$ ___ $0.\overline{5}$

7. Round the repeating decimals to the nearest tenth, hundredth, and thousandth.

	nearest tenth	nearest hundredth	nearest thousandth
$\frac{2}{7} = 0.285714285714285714285714...$			
$\frac{5}{13} = 0.384615384615384615384615...$			

How to Compare Decimals

Step 1: Write out the first few digits of each decimal. (Add zeros at the end of terminating decimals.)

Step 2: Circle the first digits where the decimals differ.

Step 3: The decimal with the greater circled digit is greater.

Example: 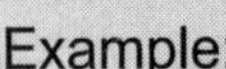

$.678$? $.\overline{67}$

.6 7 8 0 0 0

.6 7 6 7 6 7

$.678 > .\overline{67}$

8. Compare the decimals.

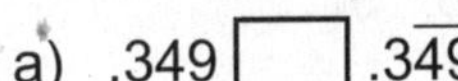

a) $.349$ ☐ $.3\overline{49}$ b) $.278$ ☐ $.\overline{27}$ c) $.\overline{613}$ ☐ $.61\overline{3}$

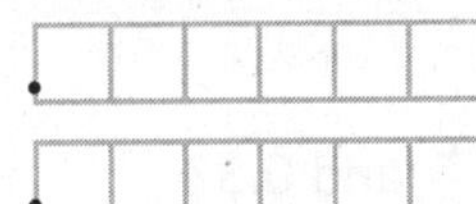

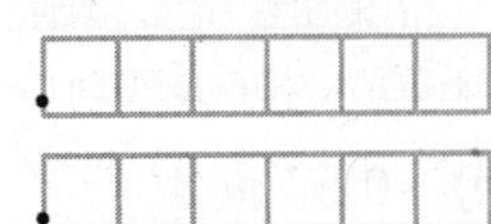

9. Write each group of numbers in order from least to greatest.

a) 0.4 $0.4\overline{2}$ $0.\overline{42}$ 0.42

b) 0.16 $0.\overline{1}$ $0.1\overline{6}$ $0.\overline{16}$

c) 0.387 $0.38\overline{7}$ $0.3\overline{87}$ $0.\overline{387}$

d) 0.546 $0.54\overline{6}$ $0.5\overline{46}$ $0.\overline{546}$

e) 0.383 $0.38\overline{3}$ $0.3\overline{83}$ $0.\overline{383}$

f) 0.786 $0.78\overline{6}$ $0.7\overline{86}$ $0.\overline{786}$

10. a) Use long division to write the fractions as repeating decimals. Copy your answers below.

$\frac{1}{9} =$ $\frac{2}{9} =$ $\frac{3}{9} =$ $\frac{4}{9} =$

b) Use the pattern you found in part a) to find...

$\frac{5}{9} =$ $\frac{6}{9} =$ $\frac{7}{9} =$ $\frac{8}{9} =$ $\frac{9}{9} =$

NS7-49 Using Decimals to Compare Fractions

1. Write each fraction as a decimal. Circle the decimal that is closest to the fraction.

a) $\frac{1}{4}$ = .25

$\frac{1}{4}$ is closest to: 0.2 0.4 0.6

b) $\frac{3}{4}$ = ______

$\frac{3}{4}$ is closest to: 0.5 0.7 0.9

c) $\frac{1}{5}$ = ______

$\frac{1}{5}$ is closest to: 0.14 0.25 0.36

d) $\frac{2}{5}$ = ______

$\frac{2}{5}$ is closest to: 0.25 0.42 0.52

2. Express each fraction as a decimal (round your answer to three decimal places). Circle the fraction that is closest to the decimal.

a) $\frac{4}{5}$ .800 $\frac{7}{10}$ ☐ $\frac{2}{3}$ ☐ 0.65 is closest to: $\frac{4}{5}$ $\frac{7}{10}$ $\frac{2}{3}$

b) $\frac{1}{7}$ ☐ $\frac{1}{8}$ ☐ $\frac{1}{9}$ ☐ 0.125 is closest to: $\frac{1}{7}$ $\frac{1}{8}$ $\frac{1}{9}$

c) $3\frac{1}{2}$ ☐ $\frac{10}{3}$ ☐ $\frac{8}{3}$ ☐ 3.28 is closest to: $3\frac{1}{2}$ $\frac{10}{3}$ $\frac{8}{3}$

3. Use decimal equivalents to order these fractions from greatest to least: $\frac{5}{6}, \frac{13}{17}, \frac{56}{73}, \frac{4}{5}$.

4. a) Compare each fraction and decimal by writing them as fractions with a common denominator.

i) 0.57 and $\frac{3}{5}$ ii) 0.83 and $\frac{4}{5}$ iii) $\frac{2}{3}$ and 0.37

b) Compare each fraction and decimal from part a) by writing the fraction as a decimal.

c) Do you prefer the method you used in part a) or part b)? Explain.

5. a) Which of $\frac{6}{11}, \frac{23}{45}$, and $\frac{11}{21}$ is closest to $\frac{1}{2}$? b) Which of 0.285, $0.\overline{286}$, and $0.28\overline{5}$ is closest to $\frac{2}{7}$?

6. 0.24 is close to 0.25, so a fraction close to 0.24 is $\frac{1}{4}$. Write a fraction that is close to...

a) 0.52 b) 0.32 c) 0.298 d) 0.38 e) 0.59 f) 0.12

7. a) Use a calculator to write each fraction as a decimal: $\frac{8}{13}, \frac{9}{11}, \frac{5}{36}, \frac{3}{17}, \frac{89}{121}$.

b) Order the fractions in part a) from least to greatest.

NS7-50 Is the Fraction a Terminating or Repeating Decimal?

INVESTIGATION ▶ How can you tell from the fraction whether the equivalent decimal repeats or terminates?

A. Write three different fractions, one with each denominator: 10, 100, and 1 000. Will the decimal representations of these fractions terminate? Explain.

B. Why can a terminating decimal always be written as a decimal fraction?
Examples: $0.3 = \frac{3}{10}$, $0.17 = \frac{17}{100}$

C. Divide using a calculator. Does the decimal equivalent of the fraction terminate or repeat?

a) $\frac{5}{8}$ b) $\frac{7}{12}$ c) $\frac{6}{13}$ d) $\frac{7}{15}$ e) $\frac{3}{17}$ f) $\frac{13}{2000}$

Write the fractions with equivalent terminating decimals as decimal fractions.

D. $10 = 2 \times 5$. Write 100 and 1 000 as a product of 2s and 5s.

E. Write a fraction with a denominator that is a product of 2s, 5s, or a combination of 2s and 5s. Use a calculator to divide the numerator by the denominator. Does the equivalent decimal terminate?

F. Write $\frac{1}{6}, \frac{2}{6}, \frac{3}{6}, \frac{4}{6}$, and $\frac{5}{6}$ in simplest form. Why is $\frac{3}{6}$ the only one of the sixths that terminates?

How to Decide If a Fraction Is Equivalent to a Terminating Decimal or a Repeating Decimal

Step 1: Write the fraction in **lowest terms**.

Step 2: Look at the **denominator**.
If it can be written as a product of only 2s and/or 5s, the decimal terminates.
If it cannot be written as a product of only 2s and/or 5s, the decimal repeats.

1. a) Calculate the first few powers of 3 ($3, 3 \times 3, 3 \times 3 \times 3, \ldots$).
b) Are the decimal equivalents for $\frac{1}{3}, \frac{1}{9}$, and $\frac{1}{27}$ repeating decimals? How can you tell without calculating the decimal?

2. a) Write out the twelfths from $\frac{1}{12}$ to $\frac{11}{12}$. Write them all in lowest terms.
b) Predict which of the twelfths will terminate. Explain.
c) Use a calculator to calculate the decimal equivalents for all the twelfths.
d) Which of the twelfths terminate? Was your prediction in part b) correct?

3. The denominators of $\frac{3}{6}, \frac{3}{12}, \frac{6}{12}, \frac{3}{15}, \frac{6}{15}, \frac{9}{15}$ and $\frac{12}{15}$, all have 3 as a factor. But they are all terminating decimals. Why?

NS7-51 Adding and Subtracting Repeating Decimals

1. Add or subtract the decimals by lining up the decimal places.

a) $.\overline{25}+.33=.58\overline{25}$

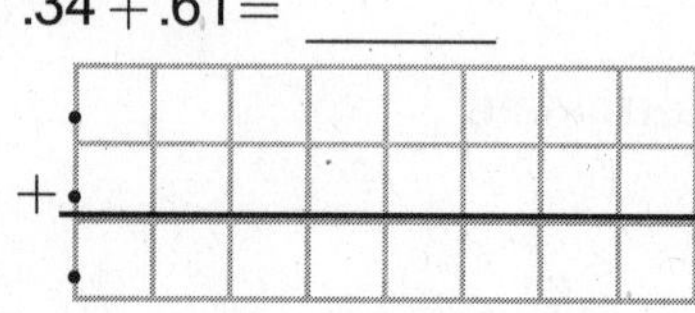

b) $.125+.\overline{2}=$

c) $.\overline{34}+.\overline{61}=$ ______

d) $.\overline{342}+.2\overline{51}=$ ______

e) $.\overline{52}-.\overline{22}=$ ______

f) $.\overline{345}-.\overline{123}=$ ______

2. $\frac{1}{9}=0.111...$, $\frac{2}{9}=0.222...$, $\frac{2}{9}=0.333...$, and so on.

a) Add the repeating decimals by lining up the decimal places.

i) $0.\overline{1}+0.\overline{2}=$ ______ ii) $0.\overline{2}+0.\overline{5}=$ ______ iii) $0.\overline{4}+0.\overline{4}=$ ______

b) Add the repeating decimals in part a) by changing them to fractions, adding the fractions, then writing the sum as a decimal.

c) Do you prefer the method you used in part a) or part b)? Explain.

3. a) Add by lining up the decimal places.

i) $0.3+0.7$ ii) $0.33+0.77$ iii) $0.333+0.777$ iv) $0.3333+0.7777$

b) Use the pattern in part a) to predict $0.\overline{3}+0.\overline{7}$.

c) Why is it not possible to add $0.\overline{3}+0.\overline{7}$ by lining up the decimal places?

d) Change the repeating decimals in part b) to fractions. (Hint: Use the pattern in Question 2.)

Add the fractions. Was your prediction in part b) correct?

4. Add or subtract by...

a) lining up the decimal places.

b) changing the decimals to fractions, adding or subtracting the fractions, then changing the fraction to a decimal by dividing.

i) $0.25+0.\overline{3}$ ii) $0.\overline{3}-0.25$ iii) $0.5+0.\overline{4}$ iv) $0.5-0.\overline{4}$

NS7-52 Writing Repeating Decimals as Fractions

1. a) Use long division to write $\frac{1}{11}, \frac{2}{11}, \frac{3}{11}$, and $\frac{4}{11}$ as decimals.

b) Extend the pattern to find $\frac{5}{11}, \frac{6}{11}, \frac{7}{11}, \frac{8}{11}, \frac{9}{11}, \frac{10}{11}$, and $\frac{11}{11}$.

c) Use $\frac{9}{9} = \frac{11}{11} = 0.\overline{9}$ to show that $0.\overline{9} = 1$.

d) Calculate the first three products, then predict the fourth.

0.09×5 0.0909×5 0.090909×5 $0.\overline{09} \times 5$

e) Calculate $0.\overline{09} \times 5$ by changing the decimal to a fraction. Then change your answer back to a decimal. Was your prediction correct?

2. a) Use long division to show that $\frac{1}{99} = 0.\overline{01}$.

b) Calculate the first three products, then predict the fourth.

0.01×17 0.0101×17 0.010101×17 $0.\overline{01} \times 17$

c) Write $\frac{17}{99}$ as a repeating decimal. Explain your answer.

3. Write the fraction as a repeating decimal.

a) $\frac{25}{99}$ b) $\frac{38}{99}$ c) $\frac{97}{99}$ d) $\frac{86}{99}$ e) $\frac{7}{99}$ f) $\frac{4}{99}$

4. Change the fraction to an equivalent fraction with denominator 9 or 99. Then write the repeating decimal.

a) $\frac{13}{33}$ b) $\frac{2}{3}$ c) $\frac{4}{11}$ d) $\frac{34}{66}$ e) $\frac{10}{18}$ f) $\frac{30}{55}$

5. Change each repeating decimal to a fraction. Write your answer in lowest terms.

a) $0.\overline{46}$ b) $0.\overline{07}$ c) $0.\overline{15}$ d) $0.\overline{98}$ e) $0.\overline{6}$ f) $0.\overline{48}$

6. a) We know that $\frac{1}{9} = 0.\overline{1}$ and $\frac{1}{99} = 0.\overline{01}$.   Predict: $\frac{1}{999} =$ ______

Check your answer by long division.

b) Use your answer in part a) to calculate the equivalent decimal for…

i) $\frac{34}{999}$ ii) $\frac{8}{999}$ iii) $\frac{734}{999}$ iv) $\frac{46}{999}$ v) $\frac{25}{333}$ vi) $\frac{47}{111}$

NS7-53 Writing Repeating Decimals as Fractions (Advanced)

1. Write the repeating decimal as a fraction.

a) $0.\overline{7} = \dfrac{}{9}$ b) $0.\overline{23} = \dfrac{}{99}$ c) $0.\overline{05} = \dfrac{}{99}$ d) $0.\overline{441} = \dfrac{}{999}$ e) $0.\overline{652} = \dfrac{}{999}$

f) $0.\overline{98} =$ g) $0.\overline{5} =$ h) $0.\overline{461} =$ i) $0.\overline{38} =$ j) $0.\overline{061} =$

2. Multiply or divide by moving the decimal point the correct number of places, left or right.

a) $25.44444\ldots \times 10$ b) $2.66666\ldots \times 100$ c) $24.919191\ldots \div 10$

d) $0.\overline{32} \times 100$ e) $0.3\overline{2} \div 100$ f) $54.\overline{361} \times 100$

g) $0.3\overline{41} \div 10$ h) $7.4\overline{32} \div 1000$ i) $36.\overline{432} \times 10$

3. a) $\dfrac{1}{9} =$ *0.111...* b) $\dfrac{4}{9} =$ ______ c) $\dfrac{2}{3} =$ ______

So $\dfrac{1}{90} =$ *0.0111...* So $\dfrac{4}{900} =$ ______ So $\dfrac{2}{3000} =$ ______

4. $\dfrac{137}{999} = 0.\overline{137}$. What is $\dfrac{137}{9990}$? ______

5. a) $13 \times 0.01 =$ ______ $13 \times 0.011 =$ ______ $13 \times 0.0111 =$ ______

b) Predict: $13 \times 0.0111\ldots =$ ______

c) Why should $\dfrac{13}{90}$ be equal to your answer to part b)? Check using a calculator.

d) Use $\dfrac{13}{9} = 1\dfrac{4}{9}$ to find $\dfrac{13}{90}$ in a different way.

6. Write each decimal as a fraction.

a) $0.\overline{1} =$ ____ $0.\overline{8} =$ ____ $0.\overline{80} =$ ____ b) $0.\overline{01} =$ ____ $0.\overline{27} =$ ____ $0.0\overline{27} =$ ____

$0.5\overline{8} = 0.5 + 0.0\overline{8} =$ ____ + ____ = ____ $0.4\overline{27} = 0.4 + 0.0\overline{27} =$ ____ + ____ = ____

c) $0.\overline{001} =$ ____ $0.\overline{253} =$ ____ $0.0\overline{253} =$ ____ d) $0.\overline{5} =$ ____ so $4.\overline{5} =$ ____

$5.\overline{6253} =$ ____ + ____ = ____ + ____ = ____ $0.0\overline{5} =$ ____ so $4.0\overline{5} =$ ____

e) $0.1\overline{5}$ f) $1.\overline{7}$ g) $2.\overline{35}$ h) $0.24\overline{361}$ i) $2.4\overline{361}$

NS7-54 Percents

The words "per cent" mean "out of 100." A **percent** is a ratio that compares a number or amount to 100.

The symbol for a percent is %. Example: $45\% = 45 : 100 = \frac{45}{100}$

1. a) 30 out of 100 squares are shaded. The ratio of shaded squares to all squares is ____ : 100.

So, ____% of the grid is shaded.

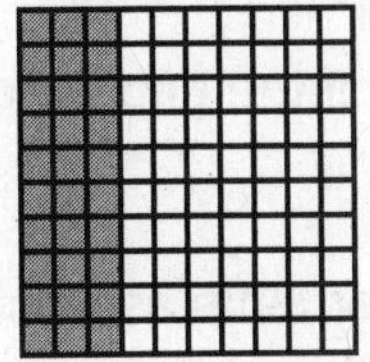

b) 47 out of 100 letters are Bs. The ratio of Bs to all letters in the set is ____ : 100.

So, ____% of the letters are Bs.

ABBBCCBBAABBCABBBCCB
AAABBBCCBBAABAAABBBC
CBCABBBCCBBBCCBBAAAB
BAAABBABCBBAABCCBBAB
BCCBAABBAAAABBCCABAA

2. Write the ratio as a percent.

a) 20 : 100 = ____% b) 63 : 100 = ____% c) 5 : 100 = ____% d) 55 : 100 = ____%

3. Write the percent as a ratio.

a) 30% = ____ : *100* b) 12% = ____ : ____ c) 25% = ____ : ____ d) 34% = ____ : ____

4. Write the ratio as a fraction and as a percent.

a) $50 : 100 = \frac{\quad}{100}$ = ____% b) $10 : 100 = \frac{\quad}{100}$ = ____%

5. Write the fraction as a percent.

a) $\frac{40}{100}$ = ____% b) $\frac{28}{100}$ = ____% c) $\frac{43}{100}$ = d) $\frac{1}{100}$ = e) $\frac{10}{100}$ =

6. Write the percent as a fraction.

a) $11\% = \frac{\quad}{100}$ b) $89\% = \frac{\quad}{100}$ c) 9% = d) 75% = e) 100% =

7. Complete the chart.

Drawing				
Fraction	$\frac{23}{100}$	$\frac{\quad}{100}$	$\frac{45}{100}$	$\frac{\quad}{100}$
Percent	23%	63%	____%	____%

NS7-55 Adding and Subtracting Percents

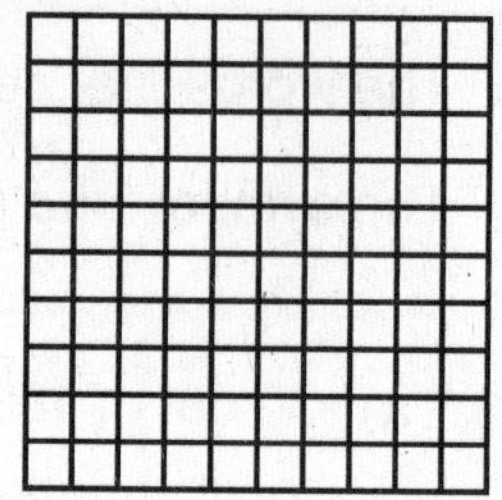

1. There are 100 squares on the grid.

   Colour 10 out of 100 squares red. The red area is ____% of the grid.

   Colour 40 out of 100 squares blue. The blue area is ____% of the grid.

   There are now 10 + 40 = ____ coloured squares on the grid.

   So, ____% of the grid is coloured.

2. Write the percents as fractions. Add or subtract. Then write the sum or difference as a percent.

   a) $30\% + 20\% = \frac{\quad}{100} + \frac{\quad}{100} = \frac{\quad}{100} =$ ____% b) $10\% + 50\% = \frac{\quad}{100} + \frac{\quad}{100} = \frac{\quad}{100} =$ ____%

   c) $50\% - 25\% = \frac{\quad}{100} - \frac{\quad}{100} = \frac{\quad}{100} =$ ____% d) $70\% - 30\% = \frac{\quad}{100} - \frac{\quad}{100} = \frac{\quad}{100} =$ ____%

3. Calculate.

   a) 12% + 20% = ____% b) 33% + 44% = ____% c) 56% − 23% + 8% = ____%

4. Determine the missing percent in the circle graph. The whole circle represents 100%.

   a) **Gases in Earth's Atmosphere**

   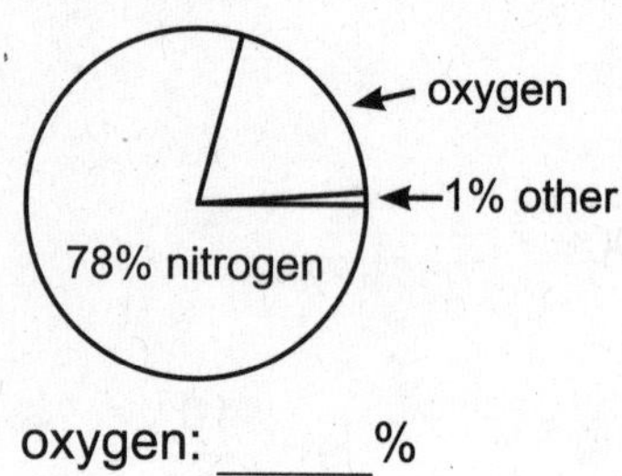

   oxygen: ______%

   b) **Composition of Earth's Water**

   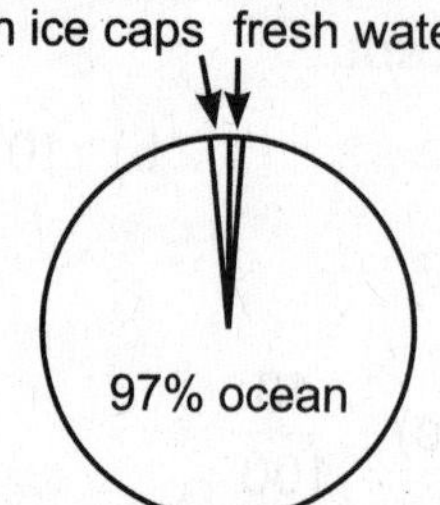

   unfrozen fresh water: ______%

   c) **Land Cover in North America**

   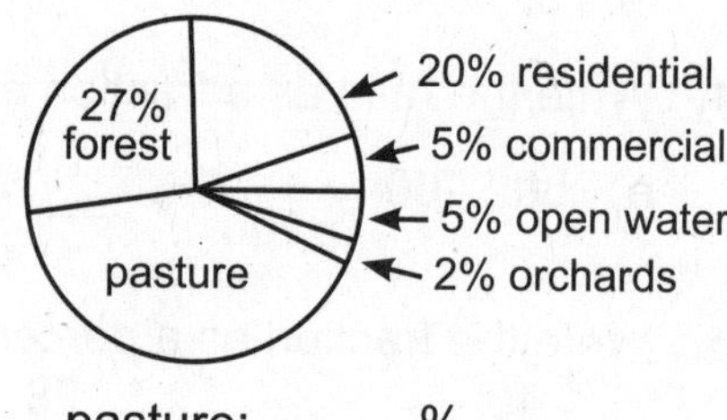

   pasture: ______%

5. a) The ratio of cents in a penny to cents in a dollar is 1 : 100, so a penny is ____% of a dollar.

   The ratio of cents in a dime to cents in a dollar is ____ : 100, so a dime is ____% of a dollar.

   A quarter is ____ cents out of 100, so a quarter is ____% of a dollar.

   b) What percent of a dollar is 35 cents? ____%

   What percent of a dollar is two pennies and two quarters? ____%

   c) You have a dollar and you spend 26¢. What percent of the dollar do you have left? ____%

NS7-56 Tenths, Decimals, and Percents

1. Shade the percent.

a) 50%

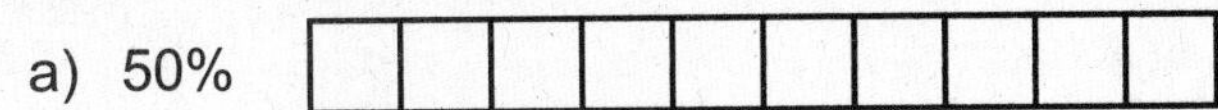

b) 30%

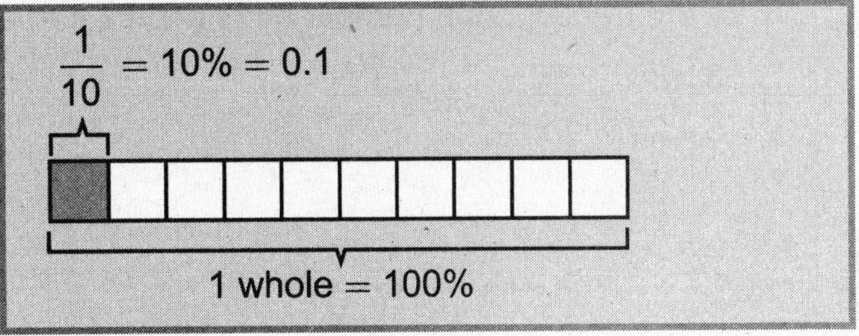

2. ____% of the 10 dots are white.

____% of the 10 dots are grey.

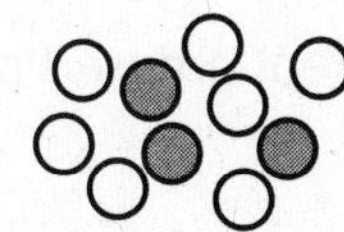

3. a) Shade 80% of the 10 dots.

b) What percent of the dots are not shaded? ____

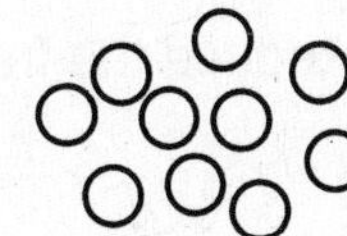

4. 10% of 100 marbles are blue. How many of the marbles are not blue? ____

5. Write the percent as a fraction and then as a decimal.

a) $90\% = \frac{}{100} = 0.$__ __ b) $35\% = \frac{}{100} = 0.$__ __ c) $22\% = \frac{}{100} = 0.$__ __ d) $6\% = \frac{}{100} = 0.$__ __

e) 52% = ____ = ____ f) 2% = ____ = ____ g) 60% = ____ = ____ h) 100% = ____ = ____

6. Write the percent as a decimal.

a) 25% = 0.__ __ b) 75% = 0.__ __ c) 13% = ____ d) 40% = ____

e) 7% = ____ f) 9% = ____ g) 70% = ____ h) 1% = ____

7. Write the decimal as a percent.

a) $0.2 = \frac{2}{10} = \frac{}{100} =$ ____% b) $0.3 = \frac{}{10} = \frac{}{100} =$ ____% c) 0.7 =

d) $0.23 = \frac{}{100} =$ ____% e) 0.57 = f) 0.08 =

8. Write the decimal as a percent by moving the decimal point two places to the right.

a) 0.4 = ____% b) 0.6 = ____% c) 0.3 = d) 0.1 = e) 0.8 =

f) 0.72 = ____% g) 0.20 = ____% h) 0.45 = i) 0.06 = j) 0.88 =

9. Approximately what percent does the decimal represent? Example: 0.1234 ≈ 0.12 = 12%.
Hint: Remember to round to two decimal places.

a) 0.382 ≈ ____% b) 0.925 ≈ ____% c) 0.3779 ≈ d) 0.1036 ≈

10. Kay bought 6 jazz CDs and 4 rock CDs. What fraction of the CDs are jazz?
What percent are rock?

NS7-57 Fractions and Percents

1. Write the fraction as a percent by changing it to a fraction over 100.

a) $\frac{3\times 20}{5\times 20}=\frac{60}{100}=60\%$

b) $\frac{4}{5}$

c) $\frac{3}{20}$

d) $\frac{8}{25}$

2. Two out of five friends, or $\frac{2}{5}$, ordered pizza. What percent ordered pizza? ____

3. Change the fraction to a percent. Reduce the fraction to lowest terms if necessary.

a) $\frac{9}{15}=\frac{3}{5}=\frac{60}{100}=60\%$

b) $\frac{3}{15}=$

c) $\frac{9}{18}=$

d) $\frac{6}{24}=$

e) $\frac{3}{4}$ f) $\frac{1}{2}$ g) $\frac{4}{10}$ h) $\frac{18}{25}$ i) $\frac{28}{40}$

4. Divide to change the fraction to a decimal. Then write the decimal as a percent.

a) $\frac{3}{4}=3\div 4=0.$____ ____ $=$ ____% b) $\frac{4}{5}$ c) $\frac{3}{15}$ d) $\frac{15}{25}$ e) $\frac{65}{500}$

5. Write the percent as a decimal, then as a fraction, then in lowest terms.

a) 40% b) 75% c) 65% d) 5% e) 80%

6. Is the fraction closest to 10%, 25%, 50%, 75%, or 100%?

a) $\frac{4}{5}$ b) $\frac{2}{10}$ c) $\frac{2}{5}$ d) $\frac{9}{10}$ e) $\frac{11}{20}$ f) $\frac{16}{20}$ g) $\frac{4}{25}$

7. Estimate what percent the fraction is. Say what fraction you used to make your estimate. Then divide to change the fraction to a decimal. Was your estimate close?

a) $\frac{11}{40}$ b) $\frac{23}{49}$ c) $\frac{60}{84}$ d) $\frac{14}{24}$ e) $\frac{4}{42}$ f) $\frac{21}{31}$

8. Write the fraction as a decimal. Round to two decimal places. Write the approximate percent.

a) $\frac{5}{12}=5\div 12=0.41\overline{6}\approx 0.42=$ ____% b) $\frac{1}{3}$ c) $\frac{2}{3}$ d) $\frac{2}{9}$ e) $\frac{5}{6}$ f) $\frac{1}{7}$

NS7-58 Visual Representations of Percents

1. What percent of the figure is shaded?

a) ____% b) ____% c) ____%

d) ____% e) ____% f) ____% g) ____%

2. Shade 50% of the rectangle.

a) b)

3. Write different expressions for the shaded area.

$\frac{\quad}{20} = \frac{\quad}{100} = 0.$____ = ____%

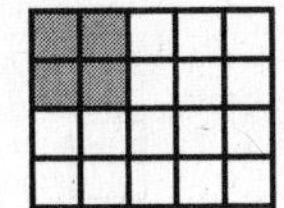

4. Write the percents that are equivalent to the fractions.

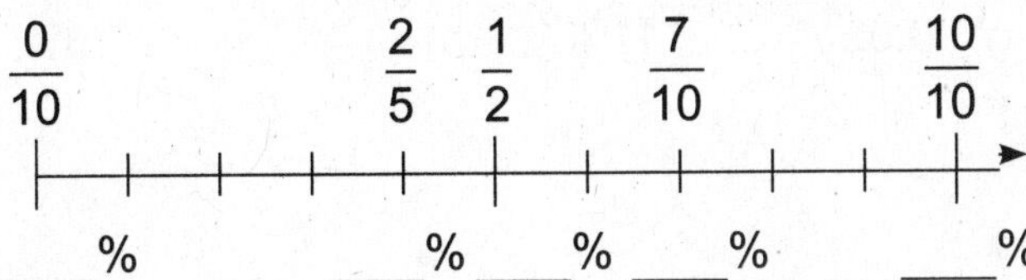

5. Measure the line segment. Extend the segment to show 100%.

a) 50% b) 20% c) 75%

6. Estimate the percent of the line segment to the left of the mark.

a) 0% 100%

about ____%

b)

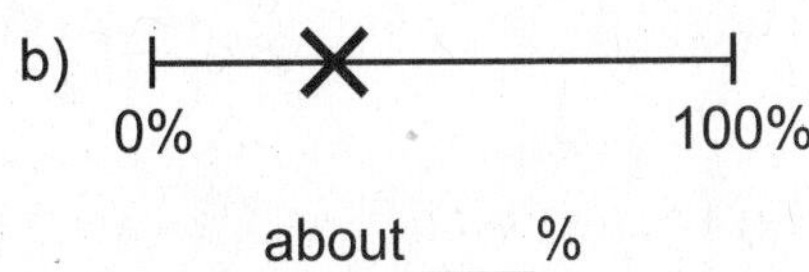

about ____%

7. 20 m² of a 50 m² field is used for growing potatoes. What fraction and percent of the field is this?

8. David has run 4 km of a 20 km cross-country race. What fraction and percent of the race has he completed? What percent of the race is left to run?

9. When would you use the measurement to describe the amount, and when would you use the percent (if ever)? Write a sentence using each expression.

a) 3 h of the school day or 50% of the school day b) 12 kg of berries or 40% of the berries

NS7-59 Comparing Fractions, Decimals, and Percents

1. Complete the chart.

Fraction	$\frac{1}{4}$		$\frac{3}{20}$			$\frac{6}{15}$	$\frac{23}{25}$		
Decimal		0.35			0.60				0.55
Percent				40%				75%	

2. Write < or > or = between each pair of numbers. First change the numbers to a pair of decimal fractions with the same denominator.

a) $\frac{1}{2}$ 47% b) $\frac{1}{2}$ 53% c) $\frac{1}{4}$ 23% d) $\frac{3}{4}$ 70%

$\frac{1 \times 50}{2 \times 50}$ $\frac{47}{100}$

$\frac{50}{100}$ [>] $\frac{47}{100}$ ☐   ☐   ☐

e) $\frac{2}{5}$ 32% f) 0.27 62% g) 0.02 11% h) $\frac{1}{10}$ 10%

☐   ☐   ☐   ☐

i) $\frac{19}{25}$ 93% j) $\frac{23}{50}$ 46% k) 0.9 10% l) $\frac{11}{20}$ 19%

☐   ☐   ☐   ☐

3. Change the numbers in each set to decimals. Then order the decimals from least to greatest.

a) $\frac{3}{5}$, 42%, 0.73 b) $\frac{1}{2}$, 0.73, 80% c) $\frac{1}{4}$, 0.09, 15%

4. a) In Abeed's school, $\frac{3}{5}$ of students like gym and 65% like drama. Which class is more popular?

b) In Rachel's class, 0.45 of the students like pepperoni pizza best, 35% like cheese, and $\frac{1}{5}$ like vegetarian. Which type of pizza do the most students like best?

NS7-60 Finding Percents

If you use a thousands cube to represent 1 whole, you can see that taking $\frac{1}{10}$ of a number is the same as dividing by 10 (the decimal shifts one place left):

$\frac{1}{10}$ of 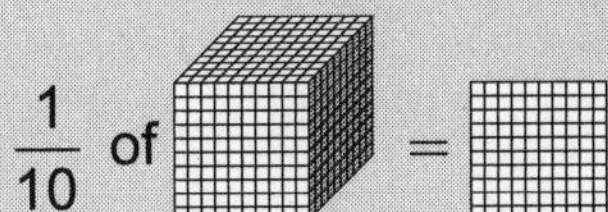 = [hundreds flat] $\frac{1}{10}$ of [hundreds flat] = [tens rod] $\frac{1}{10}$ of [tens rod] = [ones cube]

$\frac{1}{10}$ of $1 = 0.1$ $\frac{1}{10}$ of $0.1 = 0.01$ $\frac{1}{10}$ of $0.01 = 0.001$

1. Find $\frac{1}{10}$ of each number by shifting the decimal. Write your answers in the boxes provided.

a) 7 b) 10 c) 35 d) 210 e) 6.4 f) 50.6

2. 10% is short for $\frac{10}{100}$ or $\frac{1}{10}$. Find 10% of each number.

a) 1 b) 3.9 c) 4.05 d) 6.74 e) 0.09 f) 60.08

How to Find Percents That Are Multiples of 10

Step 1: Find 10% of the number.

Step 2: Multiply the result by the number of tens in the percent.

Example: Find 30% of 21.

10% of 21 = 2.1

There are 3 tens in 30 ($30 = 3 \times 10$).

$3 \times 2.1 = 6.3$

So 30% of 21 = 6.3.

3. Find the percent using the method above.

a) 30% of 15
10% of *15* = ☐
3 × ☐ = ___

b) 50% of 24
10% of ___ = ☐
___ × ☐ = ___

c) 20% of 7.8
10% of ___ = ☐
___ × ☐ = ___

d) 40% of 75
10% of ___ = ☐
___ × ☐ = ___

e) 90% of 86
10% of ___ = ☐
___ × ☐ = ___

f) 80% of 0.5
10% of ___ = ☐
___ × ☐ = ___

NS7-60 Finding Percents *(continued)*

4. If you know 10% of a number *n*, then 5% of *n* is 10% divided by 2. Complete the chart.

5%	3			
10%	6	20	42	1
100%	60			

Use these steps to find 1% of a number:

Step 1: Change the percent to a decimal and replace "of" with "×."

Step 2: Multiply by 0.01 by shifting the decimal two places left.

5. Fill in the blanks.

a) 1% of 300 = *0.01* × *300* = ___ b) 1% of 2000 = ___ × ___ = ___

c) 1% of 15 = ___ × ___ = ___ d) 1% of 60 = ___ × ___ = ___

6. Find 1% of 200 and use your answer to calculate each percent.

a) 2% of 200 = ______ b) 3% of 200 = ______ c) 12% of 200 = ______

7. Use the method of Question 6 to calculate…

a) 4% of 800 b) 2% of 50 c) 11% of 60 d) 2% of 4 e) 7% of 45

8. Fill in the missing numbers. (Hint: 8% = 4% + 4%.)

2%	**4%**	**8%**	**10%**	**20%**	**50%**	**25%**	**100%**
	20						
	30						
					60		
			50				

9. a) If 45% is 9, what is 90%? b) If 3% is 12, what is 1%?
c) If 40% is 64, what is 100%? d) If 20% is 13, what is 100%?

10. Arti wants to leave a 15% tip on a meal that cost $60. How much tip should she leave? (Hint: 15% = 10% + 5%.)

11. a) A shirt that usually costs $40 is on sale for 25% off. What is 25% of $40? What is $40 – (25% of $40)? What is the sale price of the shirt?

b) How would you estimate the price if a shirt that usually costs $32.99 is on sale for 25% off?

NS7-61 Further Percents

35% is short for $\frac{35}{100}$. To find 35% of 27, Sadie finds $\frac{35}{100}$ of 27.

Step 1: She multiplies 27 by 35.

$$\begin{array}{r} {}^{2\,3} \\ 27 \\ \times\ 35 \\ \hline 135 \\ 810 \\ \hline 945 \end{array}$$

Step 2: She divides the result by 100.

$945 \times 100 = 9.45$

So 35% of 27 is 9.45.

1. Find the percent using Sadie's method.

a) 25% of 44

Step 1:

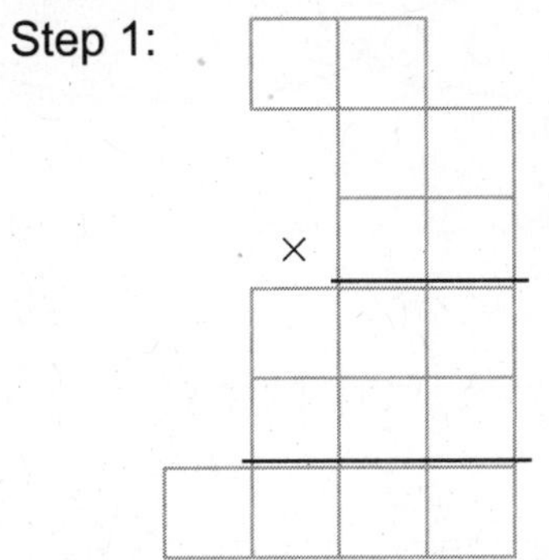
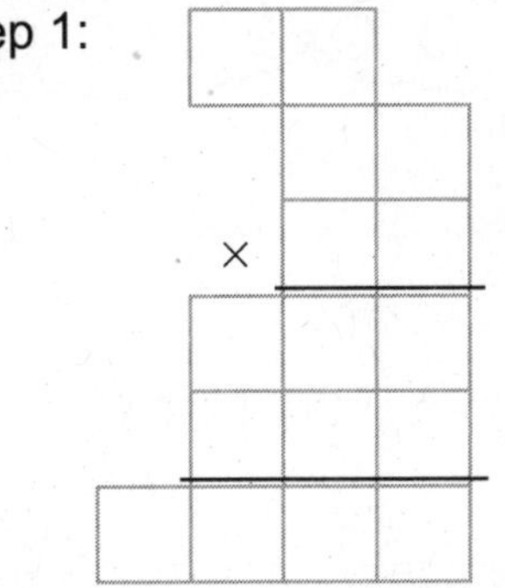

Step 2: ________ × 100 = ________

So ________ of ________ is ________.

b) 18% of 92

Step 1:

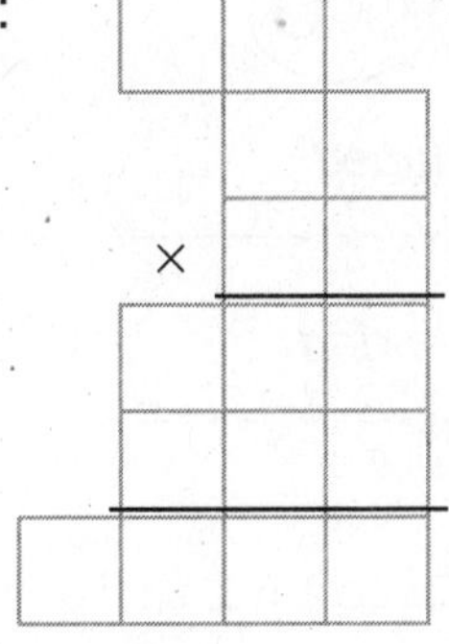

Step 2: ________ × 100 = ________

So ________ of ________ is ________.

2. Find the percent using Sadie's method.

a) 23% of 23 b) 15% of 26 c) 26% of 15 d) 64% of 58

e) 58% of 64 f) 50% of 81 g) 81% of 50 h) 92% of 11

3. a) Find 35% of 40 in two ways. Do you get the same answer both ways?

i) Use Sadie's method.

ii) Use 35% = 25% + 10%.

b) 35% is less than 50% = $\frac{1}{2}$. Is your answer to part a) less than half of 40?

c) Is 35% closer to 0 or $\frac{1}{2}$? ________

Was your answer to part a) closer to 0 or to half of 40? ________

Is your answer to part a) reasonable? Explain.

4. Find 30% of 50 and 50% of 30. What do you notice? Why is this the case?

NS7-62 Writing Equivalent Statements for Proportions

These are equivalent statements:

$\frac{6}{9}$ of the circles are shaded.

$\frac{2}{3}$ of the circles are shaded.

6 is $\frac{2}{3}$ of 9.

6 : 9 = 2 : 3

part ↗ ↖ whole

1. Write four equivalent statements for each picture.

a) 

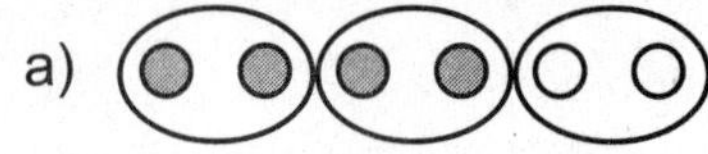

$\frac{4}{6}$ are shaded

$\frac{2}{3}$ are shaded

4 is $\frac{2}{3}$ of 6

4 : 6 = 2 : 3

b) 

______

______

______

______

c) 

______

______

______

______

d)

______

______

______

______

2. For each picture, write a pair of equivalent ratios.

a) 4 is $\frac{1}{2}$ of 8

4 : *8* = *1* : *2*

part whole

b) 6 is $\frac{3}{5}$ of 10

___ : ___ = ___ : ___

part whole

c) 2 is $\frac{1}{4}$ of 8

___ : ___ = ___ : ___

part whole

3. For each statement, write a pair of equivalent ratios and equivalent fractions.

a) 15 is $\frac{3}{4}$ of 20   ___ : ___ = ___ : ___ (part : whole) $\frac{\text{part}}{\text{whole}}$ ___ = ___

b) 18 is $\frac{9}{10}$ of 20   ___ : ___ = ___ : ___ (part : whole) $\frac{\text{part}}{\text{whole}}$ ___ = ___

NS7-62 Writing Equivalent Statements for Proportions *(continued)*

4. Write a question mark where you are missing a piece of information.

a) 12 is $\frac{4}{5}$ of what number? $\frac{12}{\text{part}} : \frac{?}{\text{whole}} = \underline{4} : \underline{5}$ $\frac{\text{part}}{\text{whole}}$ $\frac{12}{?} = \frac{4}{5}$

b) 6 is how many quarters of 8? $\frac{6}{\text{part}} : \frac{8}{\text{whole}} = \underline{?} : \underline{4}$ $\frac{\text{part}}{\text{whole}}$ ___ = ___

c) What is $\frac{3}{4}$ of 16? $\frac{\quad}{\text{part}} : \frac{\quad}{\text{whole}} =$ ___ : ___ $\frac{\text{part}}{\text{whole}}$ ___ = ___

d) 20 is how many thirds of 30? $\frac{\quad}{\text{part}} : \frac{\quad}{\text{whole}} =$ ___ : ___ $\frac{\text{part}}{\text{whole}}$ ___ = ___

5. For each statement, write a pair of equivalent ratios and a pair of equivalent fractions.

a) 15 is what percent of 20? $\frac{15}{\text{part}} : \frac{20}{\text{whole}} = \underline{?} : \underline{100}$ $\frac{\text{part}}{\text{whole}}$ $\frac{15}{20} = \frac{?}{100}$

b) What is 25% of 80? $\frac{\quad}{\text{part}} : \frac{\quad}{\text{whole}} =$ ___ : ___ $\frac{\text{part}}{\text{whole}}$ ___ = ___

c) 9 is what percent of 12? $\frac{\quad}{\text{part}} : \frac{\quad}{\text{whole}} =$ ___ : ___ $\frac{\text{part}}{\text{whole}}$ ___ = ___

d) 18 is 3% of what number? $\frac{\quad}{\text{part}} : \frac{\quad}{\text{whole}} =$ ___ : ___ $\frac{\text{part}}{\text{whole}}$ ___ = ___

6. Write the two pieces of information you are given and what you need to find (?). Then write an equation for the problem.

a) What percent of 30 is 5? part _5_ whole _30_ percent _?_ $\frac{5}{30} = \frac{?}{100}$

b) If 7 is 20%, what is 100%? part ___ whole _?_ percent ___ $\frac{\quad}{?} = \frac{\quad}{100}$

c) What is 6% of 24? part _?_ whole ___ percent ___ $\frac{?}{\quad} = \frac{\quad}{100}$

d) If 3 is 12%, what is 100%? part ___ whole ___ percent ___ $\frac{\quad}{\quad} = \frac{\quad}{100}$

e) What percent of 90 is 4? part ___ whole ___ percent ___ $\frac{\quad}{\quad} = \frac{\quad}{100}$

f) What is 52% of 18? part ___ whole ___ percent ___ $\frac{\quad}{\quad} = \frac{\quad}{100}$

g) 7 is what percent of 25? part ___ whole ___ percent ___ $\frac{\quad}{\quad} = \frac{\quad}{100}$

NS7-63 Using Proportions to Solve Percent Problems

If 5 subway tickets cost $4, how much do 20 tickets cost? Write the ratio of tickets to dollars as a fraction, then find an equivalent fraction by multiplying.

Step 1: $\frac{4}{5} = \frac{?}{20}$	Step 2: $\frac{4}{5} \overset{\times 4}{\underset{\times 4}{=}} \frac{\quad}{20}$	Step 3: $\frac{4}{5} \overset{\times 4}{\underset{\times 4}{=}} \frac{16}{20}$

1. Solve the ratio. Draw arrows and show what you multiply by.

a) $\frac{3}{4} = \frac{\quad}{20}$ b) $\frac{1}{5} = \frac{\quad}{15}$ c) $\frac{3}{5} = \frac{\quad}{35}$ d) $\frac{4}{7} = \frac{\quad}{49}$

e) $\frac{3}{8} = \frac{\quad}{24}$ f) $\frac{2}{3} = \frac{\quad}{18}$ g) $\frac{13}{20} = \frac{\quad}{100}$ h) $\frac{5}{9} = \frac{\quad}{72}$

2. Solve the ratio as you did in Question 1. Note: The arrows will point from right to left.

a) $\frac{15}{\quad} = \frac{3}{4}$ b) $\frac{12}{\quad} = \frac{2}{5}$ c) $\frac{15}{\quad} = \frac{3}{7}$ d) $\frac{12}{18} = \frac{\quad}{3}$

3. For each question, you will have to reduce the fraction given before you can find the equivalent fraction. The first one has been started for you.

a) $\frac{8}{10} = \frac{4}{5} = \frac{\quad}{15}$ b) $\frac{4}{6} = \frac{\quad}{\quad} = \frac{\quad}{15}$ c) $\frac{40}{100} = \frac{\quad}{\quad} = \frac{\quad}{45}$

d) $\frac{15}{18} = \frac{\quad}{\quad} = \frac{\quad}{30}$ e) $\frac{70}{100} = \frac{\quad}{\quad} = \frac{\quad}{90}$ f) $\frac{50}{75} = \frac{\quad}{\quad} = \frac{\quad}{36}$

4. Write a proportion to represent the percent problem. Solve the proportion.

a) What percent of 20 is 4? part ____ whole ____ percent ____ $\frac{\quad}{\quad} = \frac{\quad}{100}$

b) If 6 is 25%, what is 100%? part ____ whole ____ percent ____ $\frac{\quad}{\quad} = \frac{\quad}{100}$

c) What is 17% of 10? part ____ whole ____ percent ____ $\frac{\quad}{\quad} = \frac{\quad}{100}$

d) What is 17% of 50? part ____ whole ____ percent ____ $\frac{\quad}{\quad} = \frac{\quad}{100}$

e) 4 is what percent of 5?

f) 6 is 25% of what number?

g) 24 is 80% of what number?

NS7-63 Using Proportions to Solve Percent Problems *(continued)*

5. Explain why the proportion $\frac{3}{25} = \frac{x}{100}$ will be easy to solve.

6. Write a proportion $\frac{a}{b} = \frac{x}{100}$ to represent each problem. Solve by first writing $\frac{a}{b}$ in lowest terms.

a) What percent of 15 is 3?

b) What percent of 24 is 6?

c) What percent of 30 is 12?

7. Write a proportion to represent the percent problem. Find an equivalent ratio to rewrite the proportion. Solve the new proportion.

a) If 6 is 40%, what is 100%? part *6* whole *?* percent *40* $\frac{6}{?} = \frac{40}{100}$ $\frac{6}{?} = \frac{2}{5}$

Hint: Start by writing $\frac{40}{100}$ as an equivalent ratio with numerator 2.

b) What is 75% of 48? part ____ whole ____ percent ____ $\frac{\ }{\ } = \frac{\ }{100}$ $\frac{\ }{\ } = \frac{\ }{\ }$

Hint: Start by writing 75% as an equivalent ratio with denominator 4.

c) What percent of 60 is 45? part ____ whole ____ percent ____ $\frac{\ }{\ } = \frac{\ }{100}$ $\frac{\ }{\ } = \frac{\ }{\ }$

Hint: Start by writing $\frac{45}{60}$ as an equivalent ratio with denominator 20.

d) What is 64% of 15? part ____ whole ____ percent ____ $\frac{\ }{\ } = \frac{\ }{100}$ $\frac{\ }{\ } = \frac{\ }{\ }$

Hint: Start by writing $\frac{64}{100}$ as an equivalent ratio with denominator 5.

8. Explain why the proportions in Question 7 were more challenging to solve than those in Question 4.

9. Solve.

a) 9 is 60% of what number?

b) What is 75% of 24?

c) 16 is 80% of what number?

d) What percent of 360 is 72?

10. If 5 of 20 cars are red, what percent of the cars are red? What percent are not red?

11. If 35% of 120 students use an MP3 player, how many of the students use an MP3 player?

12. Ten students in a class (40% of the class) bike to school. How many students are in the class?

NS7-64 Percent Problems

1. Calculate.

a) 90% − 75% + 34% = ______ b) 39% + ______ = 100% c) 86% − ______ = 14%

2. What is the sales tax where you live? ____________

Calculate the amount of tax you would pay on each price.

a) $20 ________ b) $35 ________ c) $82.75 ________ d) $93.24 ________

3. In the school elections, $\frac{3}{5}$ of the students voted for Laura and 12% voted for Zamir. The rest voted for Shaw-Han. What percent voted for Shaw-Han?

4. A painter spent $500.00 on art supplies. Complete the chart.

Item	Money spent		
	Fraction	**Percent**	**$ Amount**
Brushes			$125.00
Paint	$\frac{3}{10}$		
Canvas		45%	

5. A student hopes to raise $200 for his favourite charity. He has already raised $60 by having a garage sale. What percent of the $200 does he still need to raise?

6. Complete the chart.

Item	Regular Price	Discount (percent)	Discount ($ amount)	Sale Price
Sweater	$52.00	10%	$5.20	$52.00 − $5.20 = $46.80
Boots	$38.96	25%		
Book	$9.80	30%		

7. Simone bought a bass guitar at a 20% discount. She paid $600. How many dollars did she save by buying the guitar at a discount?

8. Stephen spent $670 on furniture. He spent 25% on a chair, $234.50 on a table, and the rest on a sofa. What fraction and what percent of the $670 did he spend on each item?

9. A lake has about 1 200 fish, 12% of them sturgeon. As part of a conservation program, 200 more sturgeon are released into the lake. How many sturgeon are now in the lake? What percent and what fraction of the fish in the lake are sturgeon?

NS7-65 Relating Fractions, Ratios, and Percents

1. Write the number of boys (**b**), girls (**g**), and children (**c**) in each class.

a) There are 8 boys and 5 girls in a class. **b** ______ **g** ______ **c** ______

b) There are 4 boys and 7 girls in a class. **b** ______ **g** ______ **c** ______

c) There are 12 boys and 15 girls in a class. **b** ______ **g** ______ **c** ______

d) There are 9 girls in a class of 20 children. **b** ______ **g** ______ **c** ______

2. Write the number of boys, girls, and children in each class. Then write the fraction of children who are boys and the fraction who are girls in the boxes provided.

a) There are 5 boys and 6 girls in a class. **b** ___ [—] **g** ___ [—] **c** ___

b) There are 15 children in the class and 8 are boys. **b** ___ [—] **g** ___ [—] **c** ___

3. Fill in the missing numbers for each classroom.

	Ratio of boys to girls	Fraction of boys	Fraction of girls	Percentage of boys	Percentage of girls
a)	3 : 2	$\frac{3}{5}$	$\frac{2}{5}$	$\frac{3}{5} = \frac{60}{100} = 60\%$	40%
b)	1 : 4				
c)		$\frac{3}{4}$			
d)				20%	
e)		$\frac{27}{50}$			
f)	9 : 16				
g)			$\frac{11}{20}$		
h)					35%
i)				44%	

NS7-65 Relating Fractions, Ratios, and Percents *(continued)*

4. Fill in the missing numbers for each classroom.

	Number of students	Fraction of boys	Fraction of girls	Number of boys	Number of girls
a)	20	$\frac{4}{5}$	$\frac{1}{5}$	$\frac{4}{5} \times 20 = 16$	4
b)	30	$\frac{1}{3}$			
c)	28		$\frac{3}{4}$		
d)	26	$\frac{7}{13}$			

5. Determine the number of girls and boys in each class.

a) There are 20 children and $\frac{2}{5}$ are boys.

b) There are 42 children and $\frac{3}{7}$ are girls.

c) There are 15 children.
The ratio of girls to boys is 3 : 2.

d) There are 24 children.
The ratio of girls to boys is 3 : 5.

e) There are 25 children and 60% are girls.

f) There are 28 children and 25% are boys.

6. For each question, say which classroom has more girls.

a) In classroom A, there are 40 children and 60% are girls.
In classroom B, there are 36 children. The ratio of boys to girls is 5 : 4.

b) In classroom A, there are 28 children. The ratio of boys to girls is 5 : 2.
In classroom B, there are 30 children and $\frac{3}{5}$ of the children are boys. How many girls

7. Ron and Ella shared $35 in the ratio 4 : 3. What fraction of the money did each person receive? What amount of money did each person receive?

8. Indra spent 1 hour doing homework. The chart shows the time she spent on each subject. Complete the chart. How did you find the amount of time Indra spent on math?

Subject	Time			
	Fraction of an hour	Percent	Decimal (hours)	Minutes
English	$\frac{1}{4}$		.25	15
Science		5%		
Math				
French			.20	

NS7-66 Using Linear Models to Solve Problems

1. Fill in the blank.

a) 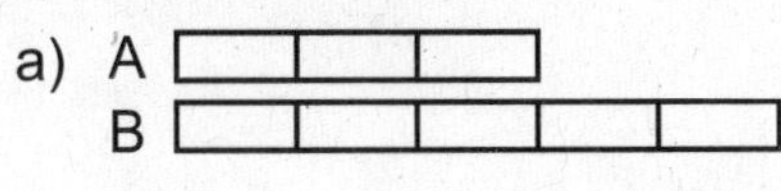

Bar A is $\frac{3}{5}$ the length of B.

b) 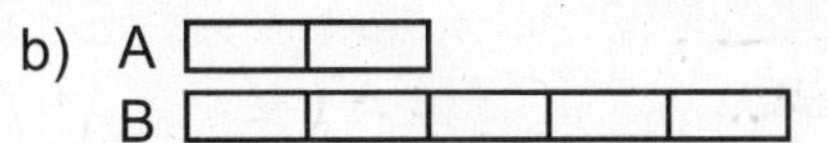

Bar A is ____ the length of B.

c) 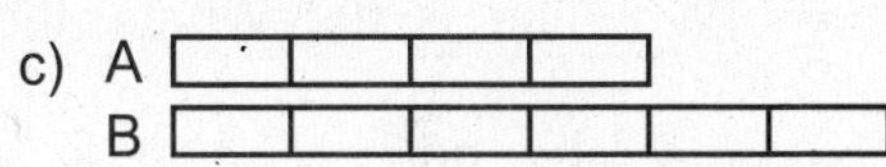

Bar A is ____ the length of B.

Problem: Seventy-five students are on a bus. There are $\frac{2}{3}$ as many boys as girls. How many boys are there?

Solution: The 5 units in the diagram represent the 75 students. So 1 unit represents $75 \div 5 = 15$ students. The bar representing boys is 2 units long. So there are $2 \times 15 = 30$ boys.

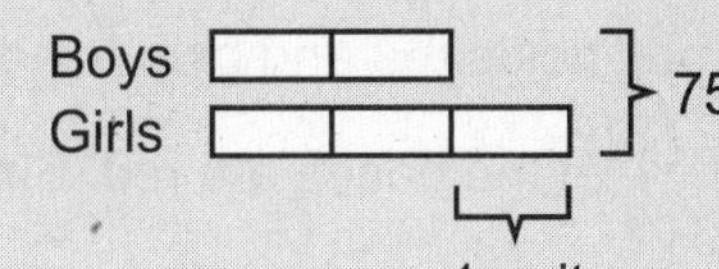

2. Find the number of boys by drawing a linear model, as in the example above.

a) There are 40 students on a bus. There are $\frac{3}{5}$ as many girls as boys.

b) There are 27 students on a bus. There are $\frac{2}{7}$ as many boys as girls.

3. The bars below represent the number of red (r) and green (g) beads in a box. Fill in the blanks.

a) 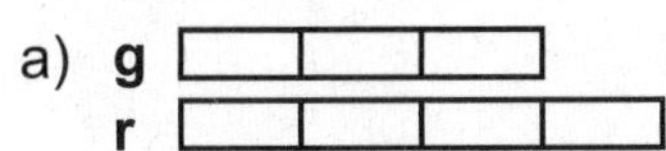

10 more red than green

1 unit = ______ beads

______ beads altogether

b) **g** / **r**

8 more red than green

1 unit = ______ beads

______ beads altogether

c) 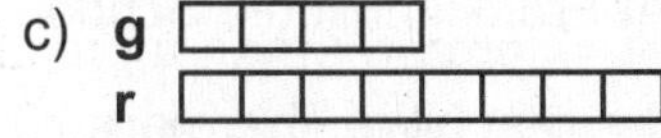

40 more red than green

1 unit = ______ beads

______ beads altogether

4. Draw a model to find the number of red and green beads in each problem.

a) $\frac{2}{3}$ as many green beads as red beads

10 more red beads than green beads

b) red beads : green beads = 3 : 5

6 more green beads than red beads

5. Solve the following problem using the diagram as a model.

One quarter of the fish in a tank are red. The rest are blue and green. There are 6 more green fish than red fish. There are 24 blue fish.

How many fish are in the tank?

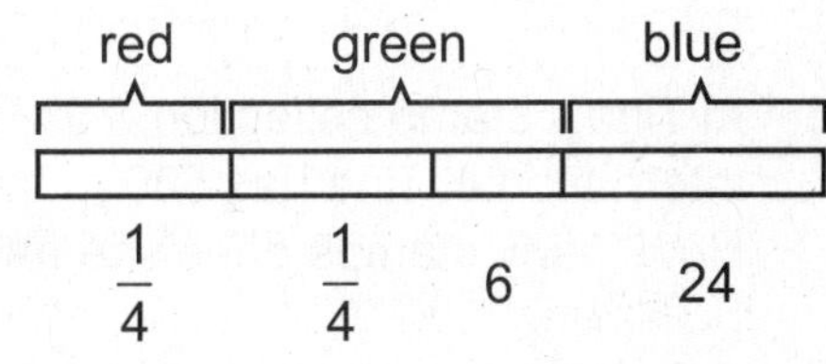

6. Draw a model to solve this problem: One third of the fish in a tank are orange. The rest are yellow and blue. There are 9 more yellow fish than orange fish. There are 10 blue fish. How many fish are in the tank?

NS7-67 Finding the Whole from the Part

$\frac{2}{3}$ of a number is 100. What is the number?

$\frac{2}{3} = \frac{100}{?}$ part / whole $\quad \frac{2}{3} \xrightarrow{\times 50} \frac{100}{?}$ (× 50) $\quad \frac{2}{3} = \frac{100}{150}$ The number is 150.

1. Find the number.

a) $\frac{2}{5}$ of a number is 4. b) $\frac{3}{7}$ of a number is 9. c) $\frac{5}{11}$ of a number is 25.

2. A box holds red and blue beads. Find the total number of beads in the box.

a) $\frac{3}{4}$ of the beads are red. Six beads are red.

b) $\frac{3}{5}$ of the beads are blue. Twelve beads are blue.

c) 60% of the beads are red. Fifteen beads are red.

d) The ratio of red to blue beads is 4 : 5. There are 20 red beads.

3. Ron and Lisa share a sum of money. Ron receives $\frac{2}{5}$ of the money. Lisa receives $24.

a) What fraction of the sum does Lisa receive? b) How much money do Ron and Lisa share?

4. At Franklin Middle School, $\frac{3}{8}$ of the students take a bus to school, $\frac{3}{5}$ walk, and the rest bike. There are 20 students who bike to school. How many students are in the school?

5. In a fish tank, $\frac{2}{3}$ of the fish are red, $\frac{1}{4}$ are yellow, and the rest are green. There are 42 more red fish than green fish.

a) What fraction of the fish are green?

b) What fraction of the total number of fish does 42 represent? Hint: 42 is the difference between the number of red and green fish.

c) How many fish are in the tank?

6. In Tina's stamp collection, 70% of the stamps are Canadian and the rest are international. Tina has 500 more Canadian stamps than international stamps. How many stamps does she have?

7. On a neon sign, $\frac{1}{5}$ of the lights are yellow and the rest are blue and red. There are twice as many blue lights as yellow lights, and there are 200 red lights on the sign. How many lights of all colours are on the sign?

NS7-68 Multiplying Fractions by Whole Numbers

REMINDER ▶ Multiplication is a short form for addition.

$3 \times 4 = 4 + 4 + 4$ $\quad$ $5 \times 7 = 7 + 7 + 7 + 7 + 7$ $\quad$ $2 \times 9 = 9 + 9$

1. Write each product as a sum.

a) $3 \times \frac{1}{4} = \frac{1}{4} + \frac{1}{4} + \frac{1}{4}$ $\quad$ b) $2 \times \frac{3}{7} =$ $\quad$ c) $4 \times \frac{5}{11} =$

2. Write each sum as a product.

a) $\frac{1}{2} + \frac{1}{2} + \frac{1}{2} =$ $\quad$ b) $\frac{5}{9} + \frac{5}{9} =$ $\quad$ c) $\frac{3}{4} + \frac{3}{4} + \frac{3}{4} + \frac{3}{4} + \frac{3}{4} =$

REMINDER ▶ To add fractions with the same denominator, add the numerators.

3. Find each product by first writing it as a sum.

a) $4 \times \frac{3}{5} = \frac{3}{5} + \frac{3}{5} + \frac{3}{5} + \frac{3}{5}$

$= \frac{12}{5} = 2\frac{2}{5}$

b) $2 \times \frac{3}{4} =$ $\quad$ c) $2 \times \frac{4}{7} =$

d) $5 \times \frac{4}{11} =$ $\quad$ e) $6 \times \frac{3}{7} =$

To multiply a fraction with a whole number, multiply the numerator by the whole number and leave the denominator the same.

Example: $\frac{2}{9} + \frac{2}{9} + \frac{2}{9} = \frac{2+2+2}{9}$ so $3 \times \frac{2}{9} = \frac{3 \times 2}{9}$

4. Multiply the fraction with the whole number. Write your answer as a mixed number.

a) $4 \times \frac{3}{7} = \frac{4 \times 3}{7} = \frac{12}{7} = 1\frac{5}{7}$ $\quad$ b) $5 \times \frac{2}{3} = \frac{\quad}{3} = \frac{\quad}{3} = \frac{\quad}{3}$

c) $3 \times \frac{4}{5} = \frac{\quad}{5} = \frac{\quad}{5} = \frac{\quad}{5}$

5. Find the product. Simplify your answer. (Show your work in your notebook.)

a) $3 \times \frac{4}{6} = \frac{12}{6} = 2$ $\quad$ b) $8 \times \frac{3}{4} =$ $\quad$ c) $5 \times \frac{4}{10} =$ $\quad$ d) $3 \times \frac{6}{9} =$ $\quad$ e) $12 \times \frac{2}{8} =$

6. Find the product.

a) $4 \times \frac{5}{4} = \frac{20}{4} = 5$ $\quad$ b) $3 \times \frac{2}{3} =$ $\quad$ c) $7 \times \frac{9}{7} =$ $\quad$ d) $8 \times \frac{5}{8} =$ $\quad$ e) $a \times \frac{b}{a} =$

NS7-68 Multiplying Fractions by Whole Numbers *(continued)*

In mathematics, the word "of" can mean multiply.

Examples: "2 groups of 3" means 2×3

"6 groups of $\frac{1}{2}$" means $6 \times \frac{1}{2} = \frac{1}{2} + \frac{1}{2} + \frac{1}{2} + \frac{1}{2} + \frac{1}{2} + \frac{1}{2}$

"$\frac{1}{2}$ of 6" means $\frac{1}{2} \times 6$ Reminder: $\frac{a}{b}$ of c is $a \times c \div b$

7. Calculate each product by finding the fraction of the whole number.

a) $\frac{1}{3}$ of 6 = ________ so $\frac{1}{3} \times 6 =$ ________

b) $\frac{3}{5}$ of 10 = ________ so $\frac{3}{5} \times 10 =$ ________

c) $\frac{2}{3}$ of 6 = ________ so $\frac{2}{3} \times 6 =$ ________

d) $\frac{3}{4}$ of 20 = ________ so $\frac{3}{4} \times 20 =$ ________

When multiplying whole numbers, the order we multiply in does not affect the answer.

Examples: $2 \times 3 = 3 \times 2 = 6$ $4 \times 5 = 5 \times 4 = 20$

INVESTIGATION 1 ▶ When multiplying a fraction and a whole number, does the order we multiply in affect the answer?

A. Calculate the product in both orders.

i) $8 \times \frac{1}{4} = \frac{1}{4} + \frac{1}{4} + \frac{1}{4} + \frac{1}{4} + \frac{1}{4} + \frac{1}{4} + \frac{1}{4} + \frac{1}{4} =$ ______

$\frac{1}{4} \times 8 = \frac{1}{4}$ of 8 = ______

ii) $6 \times \frac{2}{3} = \frac{2}{3} + \frac{2}{3} + \frac{2}{3} + \frac{2}{3} + \frac{2}{3} + \frac{2}{3} =$ ______

$\frac{2}{3} \times 6 = \frac{2}{3}$ of 6 = ______

iii) $10 \times \frac{3}{5}$ and $\frac{3}{5} \times 10$

iv) $12 \times \frac{5}{6}$ and $\frac{5}{6} \times 12$

B. Does changing the order we multiply in affect the answer? ________

INVESTIGATION 2 ▶ The fractions $\frac{1}{3}$ and $\frac{2}{6}$ are equivalent. Does multiplying by $\frac{2}{6}$ result in the same answer as multiplying by $\frac{1}{3}$?

A. Multiply these numbers by both $\frac{1}{3}$ and $\frac{2}{6}$. Reduce your answer to lowest terms.

i) $4 \times \frac{1}{3} =$ ______ $4 \times \frac{2}{6} =$ ______ = ______

ii) $11 \times \frac{1}{3} =$ ______ $11 \times \frac{2}{6} =$ ______ = ______

B. Does multiplying by $\frac{2}{6}$ result in the same answer as multiplying by $\frac{1}{3}$? ________

NS7-69 Multiplying Fractions by Fractions

Here is $\frac{1}{3}$ of a rectangle.	Here is $\frac{1}{4}$ of $\frac{1}{3}$ of the rectangle.	How much is $\frac{1}{4}$ of $\frac{1}{3}$? Extend the lines to find out.
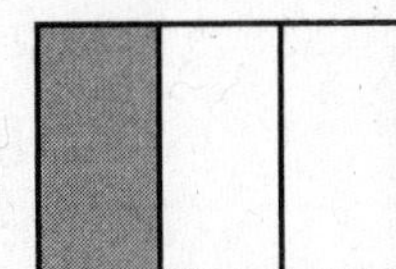	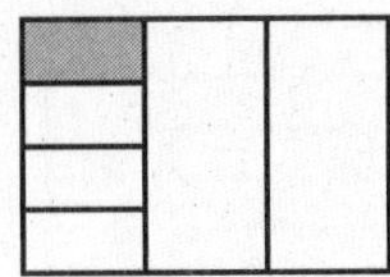	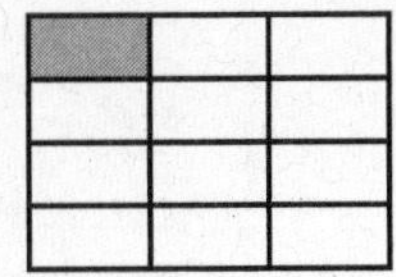 $\frac{1}{4}$ of $\frac{1}{3} = \frac{1}{12}$

1. Extend the horizontal lines in each picture, then write a fraction statement for each figure using the word "of."

a) 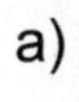 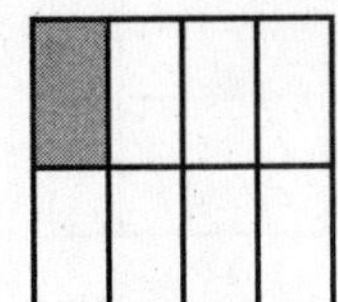

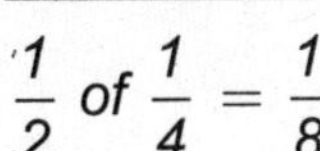

$\frac{1}{2}$ of $\frac{1}{4} = \frac{1}{8}$

b) 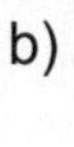 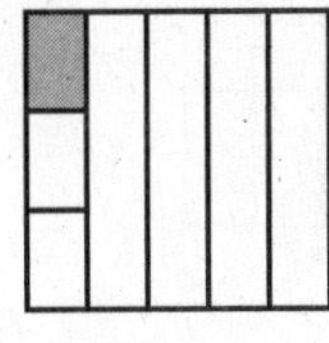

$\frac{1}{3}$ of $\frac{1}{5} =$

c) 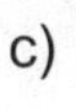 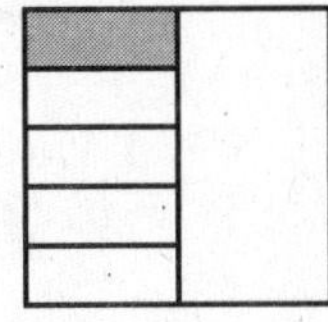

$\frac{1}{5}$ of $\frac{1}{2} =$

d) 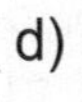 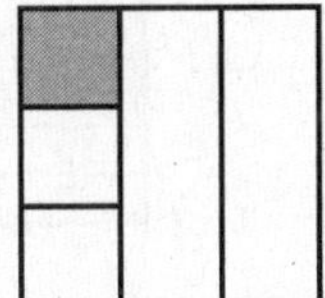

e)  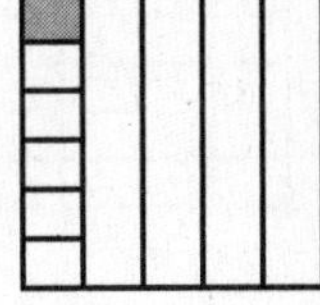

2. Rewrite the fraction statements from Question 1 using the multiplication sign instead of the word "of."

a) $\frac{1}{2} \times \frac{1}{4} = \frac{1}{8}$ b) c) d) e)

3. Write a multiplication statement for each figure.

a)  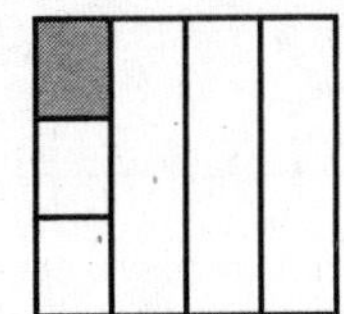

$\frac{1}{3} \times \frac{1}{4} = \frac{1}{12}$

b) 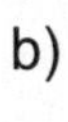 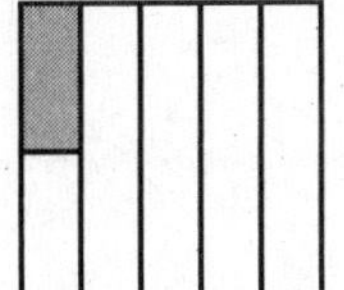 ____________

c) 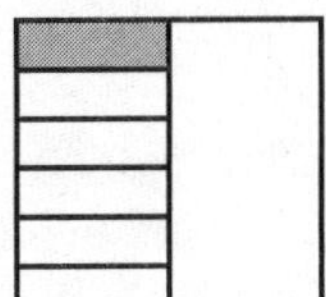 ____________

d) 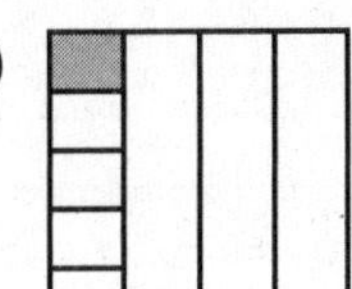 ____________

e) 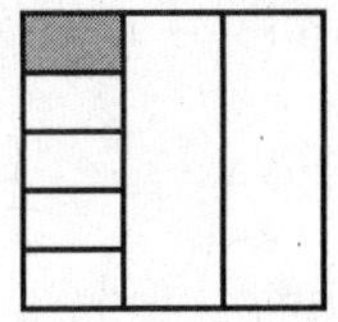 ____________

4. Write a formula for multiplying fractions that both have numerator 1.

$\frac{1}{a} \times \frac{1}{b} =$ ____________

5. Multiply.

a) $\frac{1}{2} \times \frac{1}{5} =$ b) $\frac{1}{2} \times \frac{1}{7} =$ c) $\frac{1}{3} \times \frac{1}{6} =$ d) $\frac{1}{5} \times \frac{1}{7} =$

e) $\frac{1}{5} \times \frac{1}{2} =$ f) $\frac{1}{7} \times \frac{1}{2} =$ g) $\frac{1}{6} \times \frac{1}{3} =$ h) $\frac{1}{7} \times \frac{1}{5} =$

6. Look at your answers to Question 5. Does the order you multiply in affect the answer? ____________

NS7-69 Multiplying Fractions by Fractions *(continued)*

Here is $\frac{2}{3}$ of a rectangle.

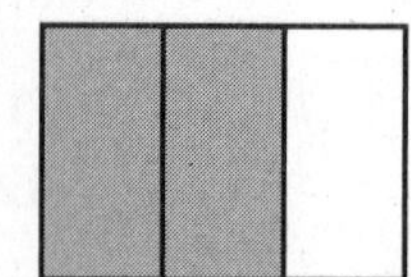

Here is $\frac{4}{5}$ of $\frac{2}{3}$.

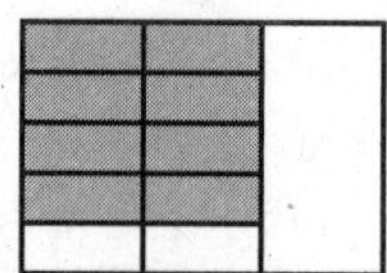

How much is $\frac{4}{5}$ of $\frac{2}{3}$?
Extend the lines to find out.

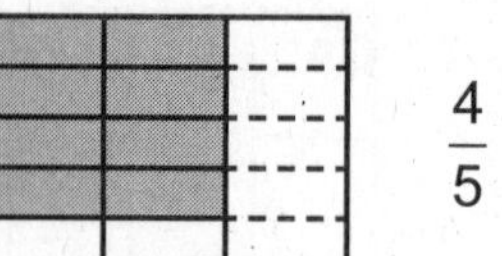

$\frac{4}{5}$ of $\frac{2}{3} = \frac{8}{15}$

Notice:

$\frac{4}{5}$ of $\frac{2}{3} = \frac{4 \times 2}{5 \times 3}$

$= \frac{8}{15}$

7. Write a fraction statement for each figure. Use multiplication instead of the word "of."

a) 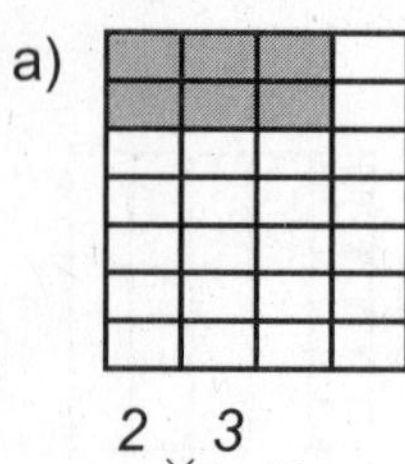

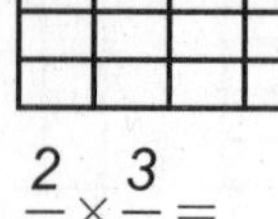

$\frac{2}{7} \times \frac{3}{4} =$

b) 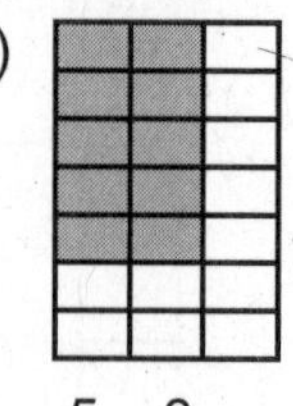

$\frac{5}{7} \times \frac{2}{3} =$

c) 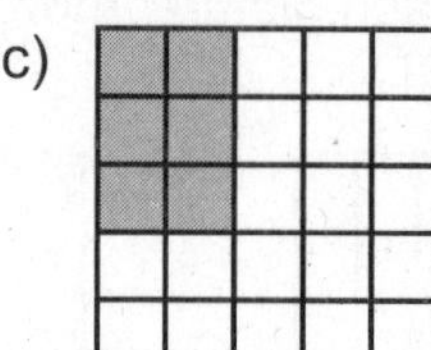

d) 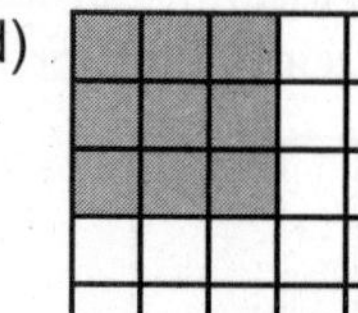

8. Find each amount by multiplying the numerators and denominators of the fractions.

a) $\frac{2}{3} \times \frac{4}{7} = \frac{8}{21}$ b) $\frac{1}{2} \times \frac{3}{5} =$ c) $\frac{3}{4} \times \frac{5}{7} =$ d) $\frac{2}{5} \times \frac{3}{8} =$

9. Write a formula for multiplying fractions by fractions.

$\frac{a}{b} \times \frac{c}{d} =$ ____________________

10. Multiply the fractions. (Reduce your answer to lowest terms.)

a) $\frac{2}{3} \times \frac{3}{5} =$ b) $\frac{3}{4} \times \frac{5}{7} =$ c) $\frac{1}{3} \times \frac{4}{5} =$ d) $\frac{4}{6} \times \frac{8}{7} =$ e) $\frac{3}{7} \times \frac{8}{9} =$

11. Multiply the fractions. (Reduce your answer to lowest terms.) What do you notice?

a) $\frac{3}{5} \times \frac{5}{3}$ b) $\frac{2}{7} \times \frac{7}{2}$ c) $\frac{3}{2} \times \frac{2}{3}$ d) $\frac{4}{5} \times \frac{5}{4}$ e) $\frac{7}{9} \times \frac{9}{7}$

12. a) Circle the fractions that are more than $\frac{2}{3}$.

$\frac{5}{7}$ $\frac{5}{8}$ $\frac{3}{5}$ $\frac{7}{10}$

b) Without calculating the products, circle the products that are greater than 1 $(= \frac{2}{3} \times \frac{3}{2})$.

$\frac{5}{7} \times \frac{3}{2}$ $\frac{5}{8} \times \frac{3}{2}$ $\frac{3}{5} \times \frac{3}{2}$ $\frac{7}{10} \times \frac{3}{2}$

c) Verify your answers to part b) by calculating the products.

NS7-70 Dividing Whole Numbers by Fractions

Lina divides a string 6 m long into pieces 2 m long:

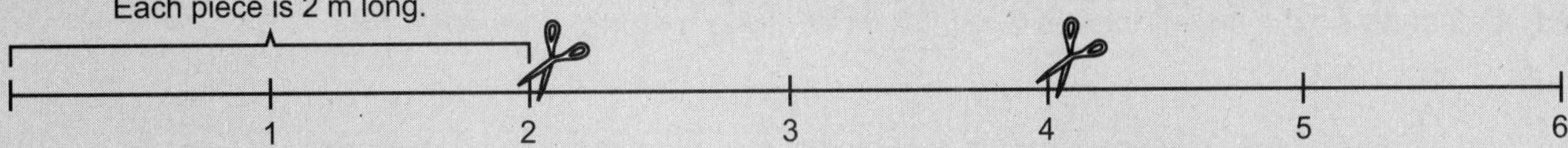

3 pieces of length 2 fit into 6, so $\mathbf{6 \div 2 = 3}$

James divides a string 3 m long into pieces $\frac{1}{2}$ m long:

2 pieces of length $\frac{1}{2}$ fit into 1 metre, so 6 pieces fit into 3 metres ($3 \times 2 = 6$) and $\mathbf{3 \div \frac{1}{2} = 6}$

1. Answer the questions and complete the division statements.

a) How many pieces of length $\frac{1}{3}$ fit into 1? ___3___ $1 \div \frac{1}{3} =$ ___3___

How many pieces of length $\frac{1}{3}$ fit into 2? ___$2 \times 3 = 6$___ $2 \div \frac{1}{3} =$ ___6___

How many pieces of length $\frac{1}{3}$ fit into 5? ______ $5 \div \frac{1}{3} =$ ______

b) How many pieces of length $\frac{1}{4}$ fit into 1? ______ $1 \div \frac{1}{4} =$ ______

How many pieces of length $\frac{1}{4}$ fit into 3? ______ $3 \div \frac{1}{4} =$ ______

How many pieces of length $\frac{1}{4}$ fit into 7? ______ $7 \div \frac{1}{4} =$ ______

c) How many pieces of length $\frac{1}{a}$ fit into 1? ______ $1 \div \frac{1}{a} =$ ______

How many pieces of length $\frac{1}{a}$ fit into 3? ______ $3 \div \frac{1}{a} =$ ______

How many pieces of length $\frac{1}{a}$ fit into b? ______ $b \div \frac{1}{a} =$ ______

2. Find each quotient.

a) $9 \div \frac{1}{5} =$ ___ × ___ = ___ b) $8 \div \frac{1}{4} =$ ___ × ___ = ___ c) $7 \div \frac{1}{6} =$ ___ × ___ = ___

d) $8 \div \frac{1}{3} =$ ___ e) $6 \div \frac{1}{6} =$ ___ f) $5 \div \frac{1}{7} =$ ___

g) $7 \div \frac{1}{7} =$ ___ h) $8 \div \frac{1}{9} =$ ___

NS7-70 Dividing Whole Numbers by Fractions *(continued)*

How many strings of length $\frac{2}{5}$ m fit along a string of length 4 m?

Step 1: Calculate how many strings of length $\frac{1}{5}$ m fit along a string of length 4 m.

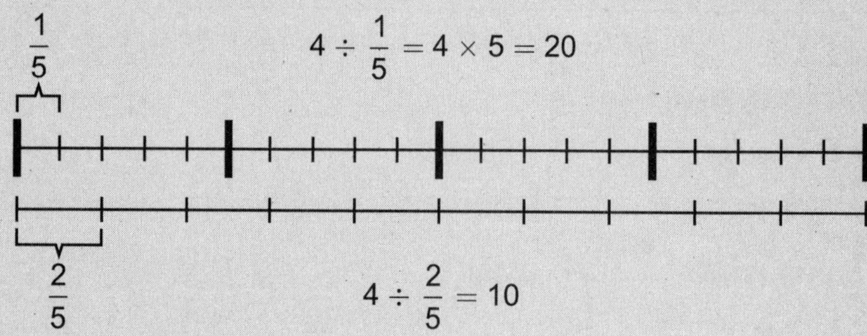

Step 2: Since $\frac{2}{5}$ is twice as long as $\frac{1}{5}$, only half as many will fit.

So divide the answer from Step 1 by 2: $20 \div 2 = 10$

3. Determine how many pieces will fit.

a) How many pieces of length $\frac{2}{3}$ fit into 4?

__*12*__ pieces of length $\frac{1}{3}$ fit into 4 so __*12*__ ÷ __*2*__ = __*6*__ pieces of length $\frac{2}{3}$ fit into 4.

b) How many pieces of length $\frac{2}{5}$ fit into 4?

______ pieces of length $\frac{1}{5}$ fit into 4 so ______ ÷ ______ = ______ pieces of length $\frac{2}{5}$ fit into 4.

c) How many pieces of length $\frac{3}{5}$ fit into 6?

______ pieces of length $\frac{1}{5}$ fit into 6 so ______ ÷ ______ = ______ pieces of length $\frac{3}{5}$ fit into 6.

d) How many pieces of length $\frac{a}{b}$ fit into c?

______ pieces of length $\frac{1}{b}$ fit into c so ______ ÷ ______ = ______ pieces of length $\frac{a}{b}$ fit into c.

4. Write each answer from Question 3 as a division statement.

a) $4 \div \frac{2}{3} = 6$ b) c) d)

5. Find each quotient.

a) $9 \div \frac{3}{4} =$ ______ × ______ ÷ ______ = ______ b) $8 \div \frac{4}{5} =$ ______ × ______ ÷ ______ = ______

c) $8 \div \frac{2}{7} =$ ______ d) $6 \div \frac{3}{4} =$ ______ e) $10 \div \frac{5}{6} =$ ______ f) $12 \div \frac{4}{5} =$ ______ g) $12 \div \frac{2}{5} =$ ______

NS7-71 Word Problems

1. To make 1 pie, a recipe calls for $\frac{3}{4}$ of a cup of blueberries. How many cups of blueberries are needed for 3 pies?

2. Kira's exercise routine takes $\frac{2}{3}$ of an hour. She exercises 4 days a week. How many hours a week does she exercise?

3. How many people will 9 pizzas feed if each person eats $\frac{3}{4}$ of a pizza?

4. Paul cuts a rope into pieces. Each piece is $\frac{3}{5}$ of a metre long. The rope was 60 m long. How many pieces has Paul made?

5. It takes $\frac{3}{4}$ of an hour to pick the peaches on one tree. How long will it take to pick the peaches on 12 trees?

6. Anne took $\frac{1}{5}$ of a pie. She gave $\frac{2}{3}$ of her piece to Ron. What fraction of a pie did Ron get?

7. a) What fraction of a year is a month?

b) What fraction of a decade is a year?

c) What fraction of a decade is a month?

8. Philip gave away 35% of his hockey cards.

a) What fraction of his cards did Philip keep?

b) Philip put his remaining cards in a scrapbook. Each page holds 18 cards and he filled $46\frac{2}{9}$ pages. How many cards did he put in the scrapbook?

c) How many cards did Philip have before he gave part of his collection away?

9. Two-thirds of Helen's age is half of Dale's age. Dale is 10 years older than Helen. How old is Helen?

10. Ron's age is two-thirds of Mark's age. Mark's age is three-fifths of Sara's age. Sara is 9 years older than Ron. How old is Mark?

NS7-72 Gains and Losses

1. Write a plus sign (+) if the net result is a gain. Write a minus sign (–) if the net result is a loss.

a) a gain of \$4 ___+___
b) a loss of \$2 ______
c) a gain of \$3 ______
d) a gain of \$1 and a loss of \$4 ___–___
e) a gain of \$4 and a loss of \$2 ______
f) a loss of \$2 and a gain of \$3 ______
g) a loss of \$5 and a gain of \$1 ______

2. Write each sequence of gains and losses using numbers and signs (+ and –).

a) a gain of \$3 and a loss of \$5 ___+3 – 5___
b) a loss of \$3 and a gain of \$7 ___– 3 + 7___
c) a loss of \$5 and a gain of \$4 ______
d) a gain of \$7 and a loss of \$6 ______
e) a loss of \$6, a gain of \$9, a loss of \$3, then a gain of \$2 ___– 6 + 9 – 3 + 2___
f) a gain of \$2, a gain of \$4, a loss of \$5, then a gain of \$1 ______
g) a loss of \$4, a loss of \$7, a gain of \$9, then a gain of \$4 ______
h) a gain of \$3, a loss of \$2, a loss of \$1, then a gain of \$4 ______

3. Decide whether each sequence of gains and losses is a net gain (+) or a net loss (–).

a) + 5 – 3 ___+___
b) + 3 – 5 ______
c) – 4 + 3 ______
d) – 6 + 1 ______
e) + 9 – 8 ______
f) + 6 – 9 ______
g) – 3 + 6 ______
h) – 1 + 34 ______
i) – 8 + 35 ______

4. How much was gained or lost overall? Use + for a gain, – for a loss, and 0 for no gain or loss.

a) + 6 – 5 = ___+ 1___
b) – 4 + 3 = ______
c) + 5 – 5 = ______
d) – 6 + 6 = ______
e) – 3 + 5 = ______
f) + 7 – 11 = ______
g) + 4 + 2 = ______
h) – 3 – 1 = ______
i) – 6 – 2 = ______
j) – 6 + 2 = ______
k) + 6 – 2 = ______
l) + 6 + 2 = ______
m) + 3 – 8 = ______
n) – 5 + 2 = ______
o) + 9 – 4 = ______
p) – 5 + 7 = ______
q) – 3 + 3 = ______
r) + 8 – 87 = ______

5. Group the gains (+'s) together and the losses (–'s) together. Then write the total gain and the total loss.

a) + 4 – 3 + 2 = ___+ 4 + 2 – 3___
= ___+ 6 – 3___

b) – 3 + 4 – 2 = ______
= ______

c) – 6 + 8 – 4 = ______
= ______

d) + 9 – 6 + 2 = ______
= ______

BONUS ▶ – 3 + 4 + 2 – 1 – 5 + 4 + 1 + 2 – 3 = ______
= ______

NS7-72 Gains and Losses *(continued)*

6. Circle all the gains first. Then group the gains (+'s) and losses (–'s). Then say how much was gained or lost overall.

a) $+7-6+2=$ ______
$=$ ______
$=$ ______

b) $+5-7+4=$ ______
$=$ ______
$=$ ______

c) $-5-1+3-2+4+6-4=$ *+3 + 4 + 6 – 5 – 1 – 2 – 4*
$=$ *+13 – 12*
$=$ *+1*

d) $+6+3-4-5-8+2-1=$ ______
$=$ ______
$=$ ______

e) $-4+5+6-3-2+8-5+1-4=$ ______
$=$ ______
$=$ ______

> When the same number is gained and lost, the two numbers add 0 to the expression, so we can cancel them.

7. Cancel the numbers that make 0. Then write the total gain or loss.

a) $-\cancel{3}+7+\cancel{3}=$ *+7*

b) $-5-2+5=$ ______

c) $+3+4-3=$ ______

d) $-6-4+6=$ ______

e) $-8+7+8=$ ______

f) $-4+4+2=$ ______

g) $+3+5-5=$ ______

h) $-8-6+6=$ ______

i) $-7-8+7=$ ______

j) $+8-3+4+3-4=$ ______

k) $-3+4+2+3-2=$ ______

l) $-8+8-6+7-7=$ ______

m) $-4-3+2+3-2=$ ______

n) $-5-4+4-3+5=$ ______

o) $+6-5-6-2+5=$ ______

p) $-\cancel{3}+\cancel{2}+4-5-\cancel{2}+\cancel{6}+\cancel{3}-\cancel{6}=$ *+4 – 5*
these cancel
$=$ *–1*

q) $-5+2+6-2+3+4+5-3=$ ______
$=$ ______

r) $+8-10-4+7-2+10-7-4=$ ______
$=$ ______

s) $-4-3+2-7+4+2+3=$ ______
$=$ ______

8. Find the mistake in the cancelling. Circle the two numbers that should not have been cancelled.

$-\cancel{3}+\cancel{4}+\cancel{2}+6-\cancel{2}+\cancel{3}+\cancel{4}-\cancel{7}+\cancel{7}=+6$

NS7-73 Integers

An **integer** is any one of these numbers: ..., –4, –3, –2, –1, 0, 1, 2, 3, 4, ...

Sometimes the numbers 1, 2, 3, 4, ... are written +1, +2, +3, +4, ...

An integer is **less than** another integer if it is **farther left** on the number line.

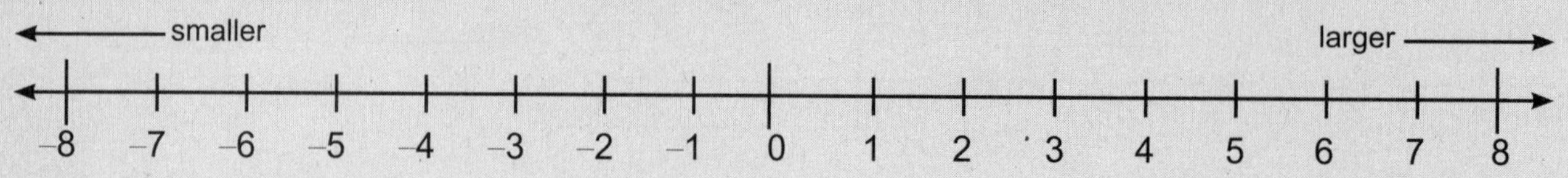

1. Write three integers that are less than zero. ______ ______ ______

Integers that are **greater than 0** are called **positive**. Integers that are **less than 0** are called **negative**.

2. Circle the integers that are positive. +5 8 –2 10 +3 +9 –4 –12

3. Circle the least integer in each pair.

a) –4 or +6 b) –7 or –4 c) 9 or 7 d) –2 or –4
e) 9 or –4 f) +7 or +2 g) –3 or –4 h) –7 or –5

4. Write $<$ (less than) or $>$ (greater than) in each box.

a) +2 ☐ +7 b) –6 ☐ +5 c) 5 ☐ –3 d) –2 ☐ –4 e) –4 ☐ –10

5. Write two integers that are between –8 and –3. ______ and ______

6. Mark each integer on the number line with an X and label it with the correct letter.

A +4 **B** –2 **C** +6 **D** –3 **E** –5

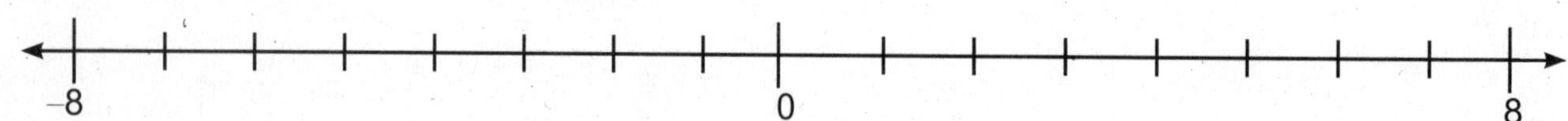

7. Put the integers into the boxes in **increasing** order.

+6 –1 +10 –8 –3

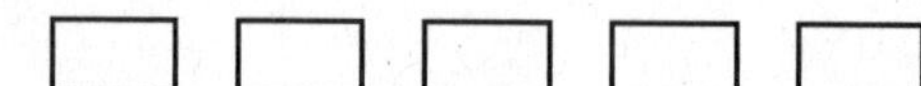

8. Put the temperatures into the boxes in order from hottest to coldest.

14°C –16°C 27°C –15°C –41°C

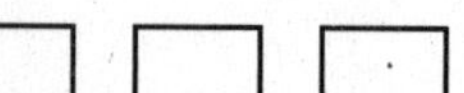

9. a) If $0 < a < b$, mark possible places for a and b on the number line.

b) Mark $-a$ and $-b$ on the same number line.

c) Write the correct symbol ($<$ or $>$) in each box.

If $0 < a < b$, then 0 ☐ $-a$ ☐ $-b$.

0

NS7-74 Adding Integers

A negative integer can represent a loss and a positive integer can represent a gain.

1. Write the gain or loss represented by the integer.

a) –6 *loss of 6* ______ b) +4 ______ c) –1 ______ d) +9 ______

Any sequence of gains and losses can be written as a sum of integers.

Example: $-3 + 4 - 5 = (-3) + (+4) + (-5)$
$= (-3) + 4 + (-5)$.

2. Write each sequence of gains and losses as a sum of integers.

a) $+4 - 3 - 5$ *4 + (–3) + (–5)*
b) $-2 + 6 - 3$ ______
c) $+4 + 2 - 6$ ______
d) $+7 - 5 - 4$ ______
e) $-3 + 2 + 4$ ______
f) $-3 + 5 - 4$ ______

3. Write each sum of integers as a sequence of gains and losses.

a) $(+2) + (-7) =$ *+ 2 – 7*
b) $(+2) + (+7) =$ ______
c) $(-2) + (+7) =$ ______
d) $(-2) + (-7) =$ ______
e) $(+a) + (-b) =$ ______
f) $(+a) + (+b) =$ ______
g) $(-a) + (+b) =$ ______
h) $(-a) + (-b) =$ ______

4. Add the integers by first writing the sum as a sequence of gains and losses.

a) $(+5) + (-2) =$ *+ 5 – 2*
= *+3*

b) $(-3) + (+4) =$ ______
= ______

c) $(-5) + (-4) =$ ______
= ______

d) $(+3) + (+4) =$ ______
= ______

e) $(-3) + (-8) =$ ______
= ______

f) $(-7) + (+9) =$ ______
= ______

g) $(+5) + (-2) + (+3) =$ *+ 5 – 2 + 3*
= + *8* – *2* = *+6*

h) $(-6) + (+3) + (+5) =$ ______
= + ___ – ___ = ___

i) $3 + (-5) + (-2) + 6$
j) $(-2) + (-5) + 4 + 3$
k) $4 + 0 + (-5) + (-3)$
l) $3 + 5 + (-5) + (-3)$

Integers that add to 0 are called **opposite integers**.

Example: +3 and –3 are opposite integers because $(+3) + (-3) = +3 - 3 = 0$.

5. Write the opposite of each integer.

a) The opposite of +2 is ______.
b) The opposite of –5 is ______.
c) The opposite of 3 is ______.
d) The opposite of –142 is ______.

BONUS ▶ The opposite of 0 is ______.

NS7-74 Adding Integers *(continued)*

6. Add the integers by cancelling the opposite integers.

a) $(+5) + (-5) + (+3) =$ *+3*
b) $(-5) + 7 + (-7) =$ ______
c) $(+5) + (-4) + (+4) =$ ______
d) $(-4) + (+6) + (-6) =$ ______
e) $(+4) + (-1) + (+1) =$ ______
f) $(+8) + (-8) + (+2) =$ ______
g) $(-6) + 6 + (-3) =$ ______
h) $(+9) + (-9) + (+4) =$ ______

All integers can be written as sums of +1s or −1s.

Examples: $3 = (+1) + (+1) + (+1) = 1 + 1 + 1$ $\quad -3 = (-1) + (-1) + (-1) = -1 - 1 - 1$

7. Write each number as a sum of +1s and −1s. Then find the sum by cancelling pairs of +1s and −1s.

a) $(+4) + (-2) =$ *+2*
$+1 + 1 + 1 + 1 - 1 - 1$
b) $(-2) + (-1) =$ ______
c) $(+6) + (-7) =$ ______
d) $(+5) + (-3) =$ ______
e) $(+4) + (+5) =$ ______
f) $(-1) + (-2) =$ ______
g) $(-3) + (-2) =$ ______
h) $(-2) + (+2) =$ ______

Remember: Two losses add to a bigger loss. Example: $-7 - 2 = -9$

A gain and a loss cancel each other. Example: $-8 + 6 = -2$

8. Add the integers mentally. Hint: Start by writing + or − to show whether you have a net gain or a net loss.

a) $(+5) + (-6)$
$= -1$
b) $(+2) + (-6)$
$=$
c) $(+2) + (+4)$
$=$
d) $(-3) + (-5)$
$=$
e) $(-7) + (+10)$
$=$
f) $(-3) + (+3)$
$=$
g) $(-2) + (-8)$
$=$
h) $(-3) + (-4)$
$=$
i) $(-4) + (-8)$
$=$
j) $(-5) + (+3)$
$=$
k) $(-2) + (-3)$
$=$
l) $(-15) + (+20)$
$=$

9. Decide whether each statement is true or false. If you circle false, give a counter-example.

a) The sum of two negative integers is negative. **T F**

b) If you add a negative integer to a positive integer, the result is negative. **T F**

NS7-75 Adding Integers on a Number Line

To add a negative integer, **move left**.

Example: **(+3)** + **(–4)** = + 3 – 4, so subtract 4 from +3. Start at +3 and move left 4 places.

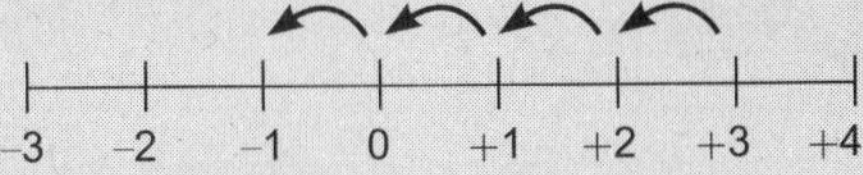

(+3) + (–4) = (–1) or 3 – 4 = –1

To add a positive integer, **move right**.

Example: **(–2)** + **(+4)** = – 2 + 4, so add 4 to –2. Start at –2 and move right 4 places.

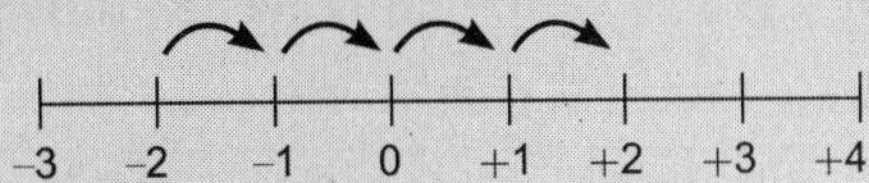

(–2) + (+4) = (+2) or –2 + 4 = 2

1. Use a number line to add the integers.

a) (+3) + (–5) = _______

–3 –2 –1 0 +1 +2 +3 +4

b) (–4) + (–1) = _______

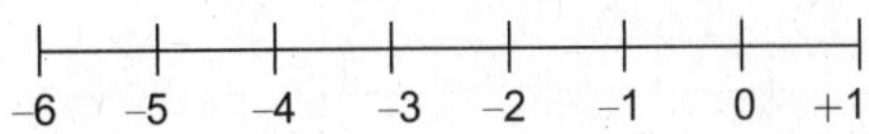

c) (+1) + (+3) = _______

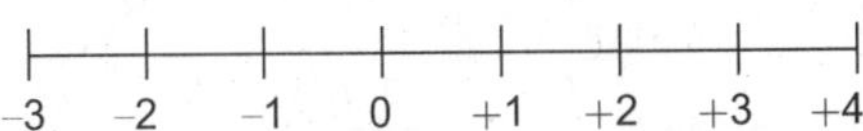

d) (–3) + (+2) = _______

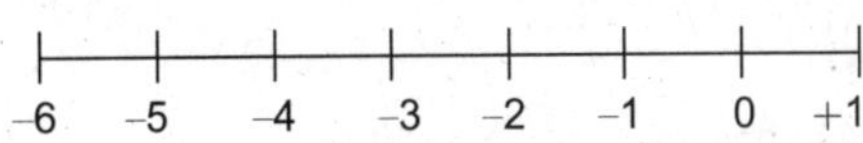

e) (+2) + (–2) = _______

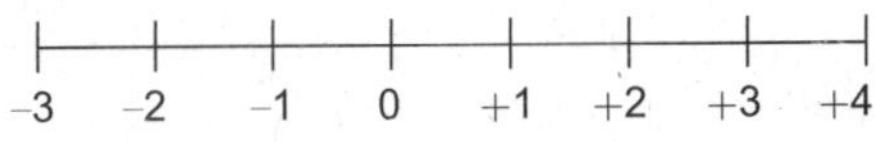

f) (–3) + (+3) = _______

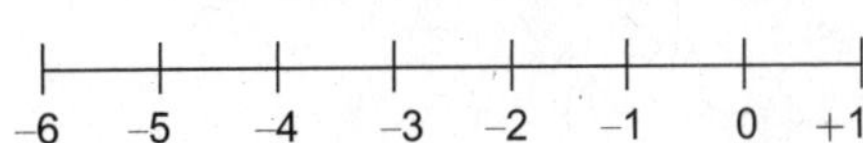

2. Write each addition from Question 1 as a sequence of gains and losses to check your answers.

INVESTIGATION ▶ Does adding integers in a different order affect the answer?

A. Draw a number line to add the integers in a different order.

a) (–3) + (–5) and (–5) + (–3)

b) (+8) + (–2) and (–2) + (+8)

c) (–3) + (–7) and (–7) + (–3)

d) (–6) + (+2) and (+2) + (–6)

e) (+3) + (–4) + (+2) + (–5) + (+1) and (+3) + (+2) + (+1) + (–4) + (–5)

B. Look at your answers in part A. Does adding integers in a different order affect the answer?

---

3. Use a number line to continue the pattern.

a) +11, +8, +5, +2, _______, _______, _______

b) –10, –8, –6, –4, _______, _______, _______

NS7-76 Subtracting Integers on a Number Line

Subtraction undoes addition, so to subtract an integer, do the opposite of what you would do to add the integer.

Example: (–5) – (–2) To add (–2), move 2 units to the left.

To subtract (–2), move 2 units to the right.

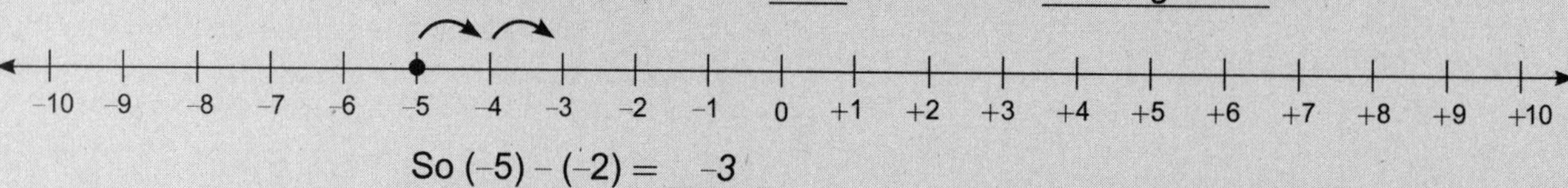

So (–5) – (–2) = –3

1. Use a number line to subtract.

a) (+6) – (–3)

To add (–3), move _____ units _________.
To subtract (–3), move _____ units _________.

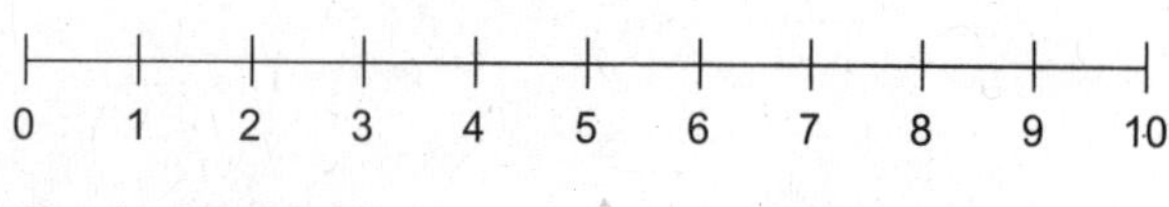

So (+6) – (–3) = _____

b) (+5) – (+2)

To add (+2), move _____ units _________.
To subtract (+2), move _____ units _________.

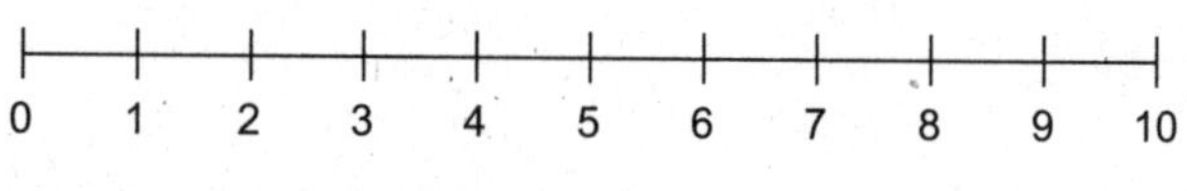

So (+5) – (+2) = _____

c) (–5) – (+4)

To add (+4), move _____ units _________.
To subtract (+4), move _____ units _________.

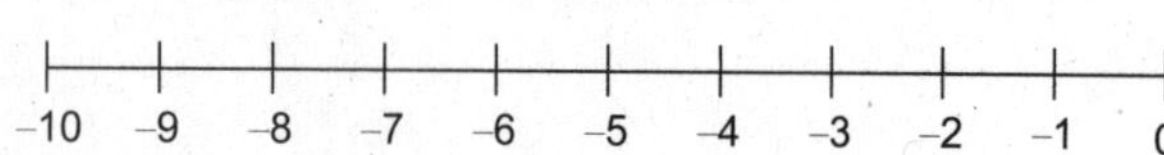

So (–5) – (+4) = _____

d) (–5) – (–3)

To add (–3), move _____ units _________.
To subtract (–3), move _____ units _________.

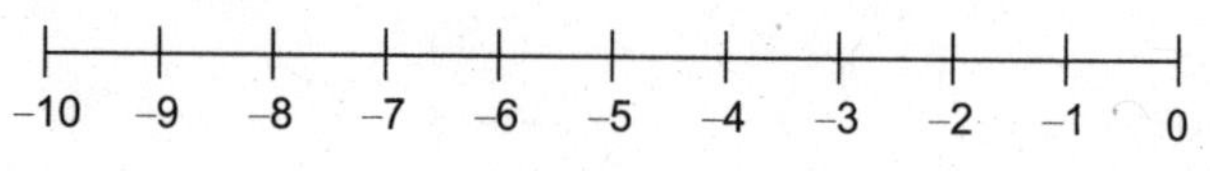

So (–5) – (–3) = _____

e) (+3) – (+5)

To add (+5), move _____ units _________.
To subtract (+5), move _____ units _________.

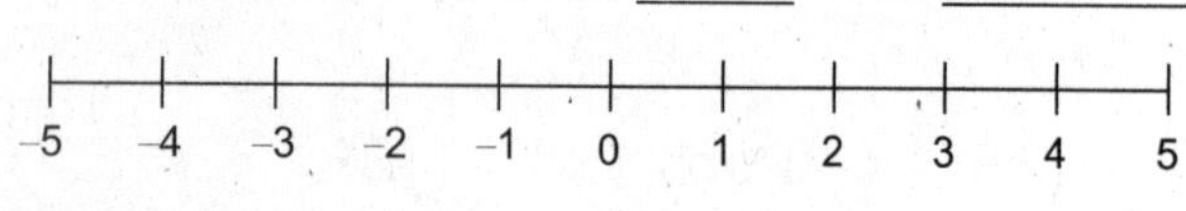

So (+3) – (+5) = _____

f) (+2) – (–1)

To add (–1), move _____ units _________.
To subtract (–1), move _____ units _________.

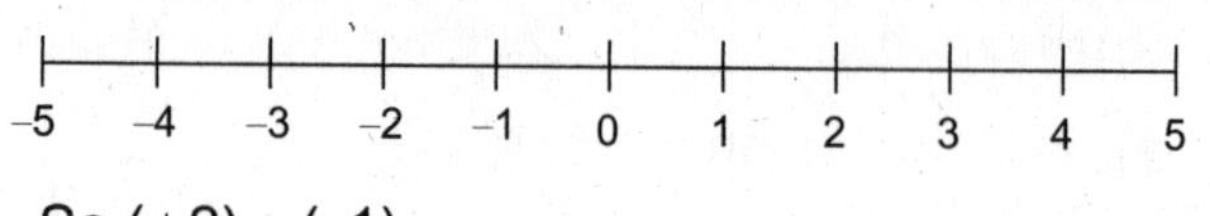

So (+2) – (–1) = _____

g) (–1) – (–3)

To add (–3), move _____ units _________.
To subtract (–3), move _____ units _________.

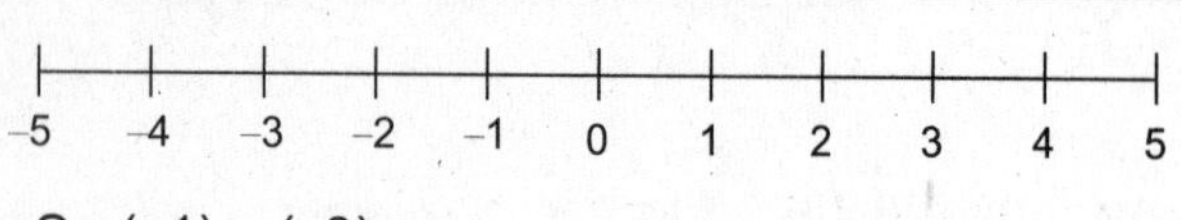

So (–1) – (–3) = _____

h) (–2) – (+3)

To add (+3), move _____ units _________.
To subtract (+3), move _____ units _________.

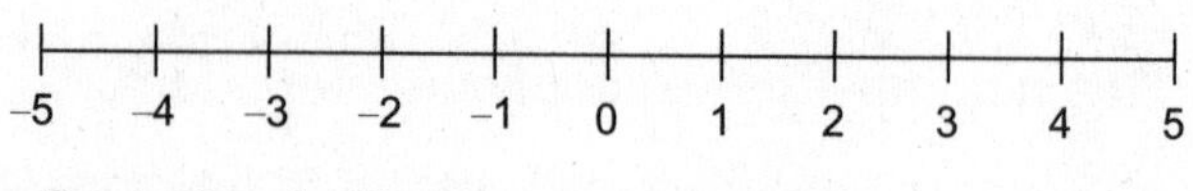

So (–2) – (+3) = _____

NS7-76 Subtracting Integers on a Number Line *(continued)*

2. a) Would you move **left** or **right** on a number line?

To add +5, move ____________ 5 units.

To add −5, move ____________ 5 units.

To subtract +5, move ____________ 5 units.

To subtract −5, move ____________ 5 units.

b) Look at your answers in part a).

Subtracting +5 gives the same result as adding ______ so ■ − (+5) = ■ + ______.

Subtracting −5 gives the same result as adding ______ so ■ − (−5) = ■ + ______.

3. Write each difference as a sum and then calculate the answer.

a) (−3) − (−5) = (−3) + 5
= ______

b) (+2) − (+5) = (+2) + ______
= ______

c) (+4) − (−7) = (+4) + ______
= ______

d) (−3) − (+6) = (−3) + ______
= ______

e) (−1) − (+6) = (−1) + ______
= ______

f) (+3) − (−8) = (+3) + ______
= ______

4. Write the correct integer in the blank.

a) $x - (-3) = x +$ ______

b) $x - (+7) = x +$ ______

c) $x - (-25) = x +$ ______

5. Subtract by continuing the pattern.

a)	b)	c)
9 − 4 = ______	5 − 4 = ______	12 − 4 = ______
9 − 3 = ______	5 − 3 = ______	12 − 3 = ______
9 − 2 = ______	5 − 2 = ______	12 − 2 = ______
9 − 1 = ______	5 − 1 = ______	12 − 1 = ______
9 − 0 = ______	5 − 0 = ______	12 − 0 = ______
9 − (−1) = ______	5 − (−1) = ______	12 − (−1) = ______
9 − (−2) = ______	5 − (−2) = ______	12 − (−2) = ______
9 − (−3) = ______	5 − (−3) = ______	12 − (−3) = ______
9 − (−4) = ______	5 − (−4) = ______	12 − (−4) = ______
9 − (−36) = ______	5 − (−36) = ______	12 − (−36) = ______

6. Look at the patterns in Question 5. As the number being subtracted decreases by 1, what happens to the difference? How does 17 − (−15) compare to 17 − 0?

NS7-77 Subtraction Using a Thermometer

What does 2 – 5 mean on a thermometer?

Look at 5 – 2. If the temperature is 5° and drops 2°, the temperature becomes **5 – 2 = 3°**.

Now switch the 2 and the 5. If the temperature is 2° and drops 5°, the temperature becomes **2 – 5 = –3°**.

5°C
4°C
3°C
2°C
1°C
0°C
–1°C
–2°C
–3°C

1. Use the thermometer model to calculate each expression.

a) If the temperature is 4° and the temperature drops 3°, the temperature becomes 4° – 3° = ______°.

If the temperature is 3° and the temperature drops 4°, the temperature becomes 3° – 4° = ______°.

b) If the temperature is 5° and the temperature drops 1°, the temperature becomes 5° – 1° = ______°.

If the temperature is 1° and the temperature drops 5°, the temperature becomes 1° – 5° = ______°.

c) 6 – 4 = ______ and 4 – 6 = ______

d) 5 – 4 = ______ and 4 – 5 = ______

e) 4 – 1 = ______ and 1 – 4 = ______

f) 6 – 3 = ______ and 3 – 6 = ______

g) 6 – 2 = ______ and 2 – 6 = ______

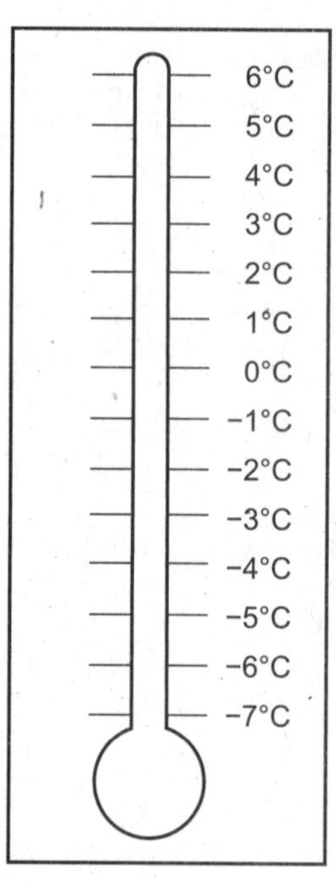

2. a) Look at your answers in Question 1. In general, how does $a - b$ compare to $b - a$?

____

b) Use your answer to part a) to predict 98 – 101: ______

c) Check your prediction on a calculator. Were you correct? ______

3. Use the thermometer model to subtract.

a) (–2) – 3 = ______ and (–3) – 2 = ______   b) (–1) – 5 = ______ and (–5) – 1 = ______

c) (–4) – 2 = ______ and (–2) – 4 = ______   d) (–4) – 3 = ______ and (–3) – 4 = ______

4. Look at your answers in Question 3.

How does $(-a) - b$ compare to $(-b) - a$? ______________________

How do both of these compare to $a + b$? ______________________

NS7-77 Subtraction Using a Thermometer *(continued)*

5. Use the thermometer model to find the negative integer minus the positive integer. Then change the sign (as you did in Question 2) to find the positive integer minus the negative integer.

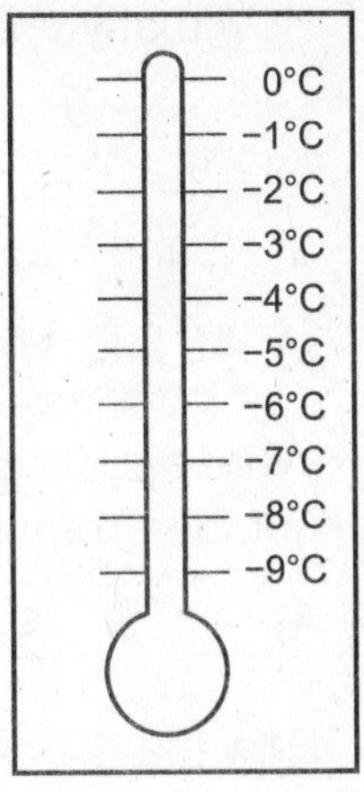

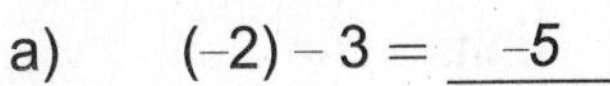

a) (−2) − 3 = −5
so 3 − (−2) = +5

b) (−1) − 4 = ______
so 4 − (−1) = ______

c) (−5) − 3 = ______
so 3 − (−5) = ______

d) (−5) − 4 = ______
so 4 − (−5) = ______

e) (−4) − 5 = ______
so 5 − (−4) = ______

f) (−6) − 3 = ______
so 3 − (−6) = ______

6. Copy each answer from Question 5. How can you get the same answer by adding instead of subtracting? Write the correct positive integer in the blank.

a) 3 − (−2) = +5
so 3 − (−2) = 3 + (+2)

b) 4 − (−1) = ______
so 4 − (−1) = 4 + ______

c) 3 − (−5) = ______
so 3 − (−5) = 3 + ______

d) 4 − (−5) = ______
so 4 − (−5) = 4 + ______

e) 5 − (−4) = ______
so 5 − (−4) = 5 + ______

f) 3 − (−6) = ______
so 3 − (−6) = 3 + ______

7. In general, $a - (-b)$ gives the same result as $a +$ ______.

8. Change the subtraction of a negative integer to the addition of a positive integer.

a) 4 − (−2) = 4 + 2
= 6

b) 7 − (−7) = 7 + ______
= ______

c) 8 − (−3) = 8 + ______
= ______

d) (−5) − (−1) = (−5) + ______
= ______

e) (−3) − (−4) = −3 + ______
= ______

f) (−2) − (−5) = −2 + ______
= ______

> To subtract a positive integer, imagine moving down the thermometer.
>
> To subtract a negative integer, add its opposite or move up the thermometer.

9. a) (−4) − 6 = ______
b) (−4) − (−6) = ______
c) (−2) − (−4) = ______
d) 6 − 7 = ______
e) (−9) − 4 = ______
f) 6 − (−7) = ______
g) 2 − 7 = ______
h) 2 − (−7) = ______
i) −2 − (−7) = ______
j) (−2) − 7 = ______
k) (−7) − 2 = ______
l) 7 − (−2) = ______

NS7-78 Subtraction Using Distance Apart

1. How many units apart are the two whole numbers?

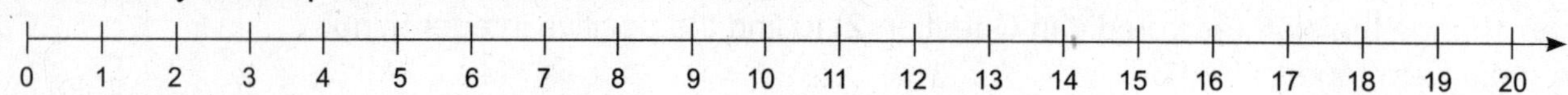

a) 2 and 5 are _______ units apart.   b) 9 and 14 are _______ units apart.

c) 15 and 17 are _______ units apart.   d) 7 and 13 are _______ units apart.

2. Write each statement in Question 1 as a subtraction sentence. Subtract the smaller number from the larger number.

a) *5 − 2 = 3*   b) ____________   c) ____________   d) ____________

3. How many units apart are the two integers?

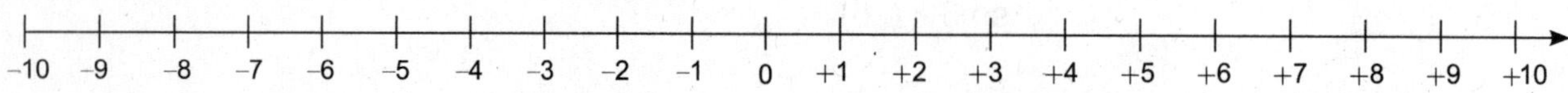

a) −5 and 2 are _______ units apart.   b) −3 and 3 are _______ units apart.

c) −8 and −4 are _______ units apart.   d) −6 and 2 are _______ units apart.

4. Write each statement in Question 3 as a subtraction sentence. Subtract the smaller number from the larger number.

a) *2 − (−5) =* ______   b) ____________   c) ____________   d) ____________

> $a - b$ and $b - a$ are opposite integers because $a - b + b - a = 0$. So to get $a - b$ from $b - a$, just change the sign (from + to − or from − to +).

5. Subtract the smaller integer from the larger integer by using the distance apart. Then subtract the larger integer from the smaller integer by changing the sign.

a) 4 − (−3) = _______
so (−3) − 4 = _______

b) (−2) − (−9) = _______
so (−9) − (−2) = _______

c) 7 − 3 = _______
so 3 − 7 = _______

d) 6 − (−2) = _______
so (−2) − 6 = _______

e) (−7) − (−10) = _______
so (−10) − (−7) = _______

f) 204 − 198 = _______
so 198 − 204 = _______

6. Write **positive** or **negative**.

a) Circle the answers from Question 5 where a smaller integer is subtracted from a larger integer. When you subtract a smaller integer from a larger integer, the answer is ____________________.

b) Underline the answers from Question 5 where a larger integer is subtracted from a smaller integer. When you subtract a larger integer from a smaller integer, the answer is ____________________.

7. Decide which integer is larger and then whether the answer is positive or negative. Then subtract by writing the correct sign in the circle and the distance apart in the blank.

a) (−5) − (−3) = (−) 2   b) 9 − (−3) = ◯___   c) 5 − 8 = ◯___

d) (−6) − (−11) = ◯___   e) (−4) − 5 = ◯___   f) 12 − 8 = ◯___

NS7-79 Subtraction Using Gains and Losses

Remember: **Sums of integers** can be written as sequences of gains and losses.

$+5+(+3)=+5+3$ $\quad$ $+2+(-5)=+2-5$ $\quad$ $-3+(-2)=-3-2$

Differences of integers may also be written as sequences of gains and losses.

$+3-(-5)=+3+5$ $\quad$ $+2-(+5)=+2-5$

Taking away a loss gives a gain

Taking away a gain gives a loss

+ (+ → +
+ (− → −
− (+ → −
− (− → +

1. Rewrite each expression as a sequence of gains and losses.

a) $+3+(-5)$
$=+3-5$

b) $-4-(+2)$
$=$

c) $-5-(-6)$
$=$

d) $8-(+5)$
$=$

e) $+3-(-5)+(-4)+(+2)-(+6)$
$=$

f) $(-6)+(-7)-(+3)-(-5)+(+4)-(+8)-(-7)$
$=$

2. a) Rewrite each algebraic expression as a sequence of gains and losses.

$a+(+b)=$ $\quad$ $a+(-b)=$ $\quad$ $a-(-b)=$ $\quad$ $a-(+b)=$

b) Which two expressions are equal to $a+b$? ____________ and ____________

c) Which two expressions are equal to $a-b$? ____________ and ____________

3. Simplify each expression and then add to find the result.

a) $-5+(-3)$
$=-5-3$
$=-8$

b) $+3+(+2)$
$=$
$=$

c) $+2-(+3)$
$=$
$=$

d) $-4-(-6)$
$=$
$=$

e) $-11-(-6)$ $\quad$ f) $+14+(-8)$ $\quad$ g) $-3+(+7)$ $\quad$ h) $-25-(-5)$

i) $-2+(-3)+(+4)$ $\quad$ j) $+3+(-5)+4$ $\quad$ k) $-9-(+8)-(-12)$ $\quad$ l) $-4+5-(-6)+(-3)$

4. Do you need a gain or a loss to get to +3? How much of a gain or loss do you need?

a) -2 <u>$+5$</u> $=+3$ $\quad$ b) $+8$ _____ $=+3$ $\quad$ c) $+1$ _____ $=+3$ $\quad$ d) -12 _____ $=+3$

5. Fill in the missing integer that will make the statement true.

a) $(-3)+$ <u>2</u> $=-1$ $\quad$ b) $+7-$ _____ $=+10$ $\quad$ c) $(-1)-$ _____ $=+3$ $\quad$ d) $(-6)+$ _____ $=-10$

e) _____ $-(-4)=+3$ $\quad$ f) _____ $+(-2)=-6$ $\quad$ g) _____ $-(+5)=-3$ $\quad$ h) _____ $+(+4)=-7$

6. In Question 5, how can you use your answer to part c) to check your answer to part e)? Explain.

Glossary

algebraic expression a combination of one or more variables that may include numbers and operation signs

array an arrangement of things (for example, objects, symbols, or numbers) in rows and columns

billion 1 000 000 000

cancel to eliminate parts of an expression when their sum is equal to zero

centimetre (cm) a unit of measurement used to describe length, height, or thickness

circumference the distance around a circle

coefficient a number that is multiplied by a variable in an expression

common multiple a multiple of two or more numbers

composite number a number that has more than two factors

consecutive numbers numbers that occur one after the other on a number line

constant term a number that is not multiplied by a variable in an expression

decimal fraction a fraction in which the denominator is a power of ten

decimal place one place value to the right of the decimal point

decimetre (dm) a unit of measurement used to describe length, height, or thickness; equal to 10 cm

decreasing sequence a sequence where each number is less than the one before it

denominator the number in the bottom portion of a fraction

diagonal things (for example, objects, symbols, or numbers) that are in a line from one corner to another corner

diameter the distance across a circle, measured through its centre

dividend in a division problem, the number that is being divided or shared

divisible by containing a number a specific number of times without having a remainder (for example, 15 is divisible by 5 and 3)

divisor in a division problem, the number that is divided into another number

equation a mathematical statement that two expressions are equal

equivalent fractions fractions that represent the same amount but have different denominators (for example, $\frac{2}{3} = \frac{4}{6}$)

equivalent ratios two ratios that represent the same ratio

factor rainbow a diagram that shows the pairs of factors of a number

factors whole numbers that are multiplied to give a product

factor tree a diagram that uses branches (lines) to show prime factorization

Fibonacci sequence the sequence 1, 1, 2, 3, 5, 8, . . ., where each term is the sum of the previous two terms

greatest common factor (GCF) the greatest number that is a factor of two or more given numbers

hexagon a polygon with six sides

improper fraction a fraction that has a numerator that is larger than the denominator; this represents more than a whole

increasing sequence a sequence where each number is greater than the one before it

integer a whole number that is either positive, negative, or zero

kilometre (km) a unit of measurement for length; equal to 1 000 cm

litre (L) a unit of measurement to describe capacity; equal to 1 000 mL

lowest common multiple (LCM) the least nonzero number that is a multiple of two or more given numbers

lowest terms terms that have a GCF of 1

metre (m) a unit of measurement used to describe length, height, or thickness; equal to 100 cm

millilitre (mL) a unit of measurement used to describe capacity

millimetre (mm) a unit of measurement used to describe length, height, or thickness; equal to 0.1 cm

mixed fraction or number a mixture of a whole number and a fraction

model a physical representation (for example, using base-10 materials to represent a number)

multiple of a number that is the result of multiplying one number by another specific number (for example, the multiples of 5 are 0, 5, 10, 15, and so on)

numerator the number in the top portion of a fraction

numeric expression a combination of numbers, operation signs, and sometimes brackets, that represents a quantity

part-to-part ratio a ratio of one part to another part of a whole

part-to-whole ratio a ratio of one part to the whole

pentagon a polygon with five sides

percent a ratio that compares a number to 100

perfect square the product of a positive whole number with itself

perimeter the distance around the outside of a shape

place values the values of ones, tens, hundreds, and so on, that are represented by the placement of digits in a number

polygon a figure containing three or more vertices joined by line segments

prime factorization a number written as a product of prime numbers

prime number a number that has only two factors: itself and 1

proportion an equation between two equivalent ratios

quadrilateral a polygon with four sides

radius the distance from any point on a circle to its centre

rate a comparison of two quantities measured in different units

ratio a comparison indicating the relative size of two or more numbers, e.g., 2 : 3 or "2 to 3"

remainder the number left over after dividing or subtracting (for example, 10 ÷ 3 = 3 R1)

repeating decimal a decimal with a group of one or more digits that repeats forever

rhombus a parallelogram with all four sides equal

sequence an ordered set of terms: 1st term, 2nd term, 3rd term, . . .

set a group of like objects

solve for a variable to find the value(s) of a variable for which an equation is true

square centimetre (cm^2) a unit of measurement used to describe area

square root a number that may be multiplied by itself to produce a given number

substitute to replace a variable in an expression with a number

term a number in a sequence

term number the position of a term in a sequence

terminating decimal a decimal that does not repeat forever

unit fraction a fraction with numerator 1

unit rate a comparison of two quantities where one quantity is equal to 1

variable a letter or symbol that represents a number

About the Authors

JOHN MIGHTON is a mathematician, author, and playwright. He completed a Ph.D. in mathematics at the University of Toronto and is currently a fellow of the Fields Institute for Mathematical Research. The founder of JUMP Math (www.jumpmath.org), Mighton also gives lectures to student teachers at York University and the Ontario Institute for Studies in Education, and invited talks and training sessions for parents and educators. He is the author of the *JUMP at Home* workbooks and the national bestsellers *The Myth of Ability* and *The End of Ignorance*. He has won the Governor General's Literary Award and the Siminovitch Prize for his plays.

DR. ANNA KLEBANOV received her B.Sc., M.Sc., Ph.D., and teaching certificate from the Technion – Israel Institute of Technology. She is the recipient of three teaching awards for excellence. She began her career at JUMP Math as a curriculum writer in 2007, working with Dr. John Mighton and Dr. Sindi Sabourin on JUMP Math's broad range of publications.

DR. SINDI SABOURIN received her Ph.D. in mathematics from Queen's University, specializing in commutative algebra. She is the recipient of the Governor General's Gold Medal Award from Queen's University and a National Sciences and Research Council Postdoctoral Fellowship. Her career with JUMP Math began in 2003 as a volunteer doing in-class tutoring and one-on-one tutoring, as well as working on answer keys. In 2006, she became a curriculum writer working on JUMP Math's broad range of publications.